Teaching and Learning in Jewish Day Schools

The Mandel-Brandeis Series in Jewish Education

SHARON FEIMAN-NEMSER, JONATHAN KRASNER, *and* JON A. LEVISOHN, *Editors*

The Mandel-Brandeis Series in Jewish Education, established by the Jack, Joseph and Morton Mandel Center for Studies in Jewish Education, publishes scholarly monographs and edited volumes of compelling research on Jewish educational settings and processes. The series is made possible through the Mandel Foundation.

For a complete list of books that are available in the series, visit https://brandeisuniversitypress.com/series/jewish-education/.

JONATHAN B. KRASNER, JON A. LEVISOHN, and SHARON AVNI, eds.
Teaching and Learning in Jewish Day Schools

SIVAN ZAKAI and MATT REINGOLD, eds.
Teaching Israel: Studies of Pedagogy from the Field

ZIVA R. HASSENFELD
The Second Conversation: Interpretive Authority in the Bible Classroom

JOSEPH REIMER
Making Shabbat: Celebrating and Learning at American Jewish Summer Camps

ALEX POMSON and JACK WERTHEIMER
Inside Jewish Day Schools: Leadership, Learning, and Community

Teaching and Learning in Jewish Day Schools

Edited by

JONATHAN B. KRASNER

JON A. LEVISOHN

and

SHARON AVNI

BRANDEIS UNIVERSITY PRESS

Waltham, Massachusetts

Brandeis University Press

Manufactured in the United States of America
Composed in Meno types

LIBRARY OF CONGRESS CATALOGING-IN-PUBLISHING DATA
Names: Krasner, Jonathan B., editor. | Levisohn, Jon A., editor. | Avni, Sharon, 1970– editor.
Title: Teaching & learning in Jewish day schools / edited by Jonathan B. Krasner, Jon A. Levisohn and Sharon Avni.
Other titles: Teaching and learning in Jewish day schools
Description: Waltham, Massachusetts : Brandeis University Press, [2025] | Series: The Mandel-Brandeis series in Jewish education | Includes index. | Summary: "This volume seeks to better understand how day schools are educating diverse Jewish youth in a variety of content areas. The authors question some bedrock principles of Jewish education, address how day schools intersect with broader societal issues like race and gender, and reveal potential future directions"—Provided by publisher.
Identifiers: LCCN 2025000477 (print) | LCCN 2025000478 (ebook) | ISBN 9781684582709 (cloth) | ISBN 9781684582594 (paperback) | ISBN 9781684582761 (ebook)
Subjects: LCSH: Jewish religious education. | Jewish day schools.
Classification: LCC LC715 .T43 2025 (print) | LCC LC715 (ebook) | DDC 371.076—dc23/eng/20250120
LC record available at https://lccn.loc.gov/2025000477
LC ebook record available at https://lccn.loc.gov/2025000478

5 4 3 2 1

Contents

Editors' Note

The authors of the chapters in this volume gathered their data and conducted their analyses before October 7, 2023, and did not revise their chapters afterward, with the exception of Sivan Zakai, whose chapter deals directly with teaching Israel and the conflict, and who made minor revisions to chapter 1. Therefore, while we do briefly address the educational implications of October 7 in the Conclusion, the impact of the Middle East war on Israel education and day school education more generally is not addressed by the authors. Nevertheless, we believe that the book chapters stand on their own and continue to hold relevance to discussions of teaching and learning in Jewish day schools.

Introduction

JONATHAN B. KRASNER

It is difficult to overestimate the role of schools in Western society as a locus of cultural transmission and socialization. In the Jewish context, historian David Ellenson observed that,

> By creating schools, and providing a model of Judaism that is not identical to, but interacts with, the larger world of values and culture of which we are a part, Judaism may make its greatest contribution to individual Jews and our larger society. (Ellenson, 2008)

With formal learning still at the center of Jewish educational efforts, Jewish educators navigate two overlapping perennial concerns: defining and prioritizing which content constitutes Jewish education and wading through a sea of prescriptive literature on how to approach this subject matter. This effort has been particularly evident in day schools, institutions that have been prioritized by many communal leaders, foundations, and segments of the public with an interest in Jewish literacy and Jewish intellectual and cultural transmission.

While the Consortium for Applied Studies in Jewish Education maintains on its website[1] that "the field of Jewish education lacks a robust evidence base of useable and shareable knowledge that can inform and advance Jewish educational practice as well as investment of financial resources," this claim should be evaluated in relative terms. As a matter of fact, increased investment in and professionalization of day school education since the 1990s has promoted a veritable explosion in research, albeit of varying quality. When the landmark report on Jewish education, *A Time to Act*, was published in 1990, the sponsors were compelled to commission most of the studies upon which it relied. Indeed, the report singled out the scant research base as one of the key challenges confronting the field.

Thirty-five years later, academic research on Jewish education is routinely published in the *Journal of Jewish Education* and other academic journals and scholarly works, while philanthropic foundations, university research centers, and organizations periodically publish reports. Frustratingly, much of the data from privately commissioned impact studies remains inaccessible, and the quality of the published studies and dissertations is uneven. Nevertheless, we know considerably more about the state of American Jewish education, including the actual teaching and learning processes in Jewish day schools, than in the past.

Even so, day schools face an ever-changing litany of new variables as a result of broader sociocultural and demographic changes among American Jews. They are likewise contending with changing educational trends in secular schooling regarding pedagogical approaches and philosophical positions about the purpose and goals of teaching and learning, not to mention challenges and opportunities presented by the rise of digital learning. We can think about this as a kind of paradox that demands closer investigation: As Jewish day schools strive to educate Jewish youth about Jewish traditions, texts, heritage, and history, they must also remain attentive to present-day concerns and orient themselves to the challenges and opportunities of a changing Jewish community. By and large, Jewish educators, researchers, communal leaders, and funders still have much to learn about how day schools are addressing this paradox, along with myriad other curricular and pedagogic challenges.

Jewish schools are hardly unique in this regard. Those on the periphery of the educational process have access to inputs (e.g., financial and human resources, etc.) and outputs (test scores, credentialed graduates, etc.), but the transformation process remains obscure. Even parents must rely on the fragmentary and often egocentric reports of their children as well as selective communications from school administrators who are concerned with public relations. Recent influential studies (Pomson & Wertheimer, 2022; Zakai, 2022) have revealed important directions scholarship is addressing, as have older works, such as Daniel Pekarsky's *Vision at Work: The Theory and Practice of Beit Rabban* (2006).[2] Nonetheless, there is still a lot to explore about the culture of schools, about the students, about the teachers, about the families, and about the curriculum and pedagogy.

This volume contributes to the literature with an especial focus on teaching and learning, both within and outside of the classroom. It seeks to better understand how day schools are educating diverse Jewish youth in a variety of content areas. The urgency for a holistic and critical look at day school educational practices cannot be overstated. The lack of data on the classroom and the day school as an educating institution is highly problematic. From a societal perspective, a dearth of empirical data contributes to a devaluing of teachers and the educational process. Absent a clear understanding of and appreciation for complexity of classroom processes, the public is liable to default to what Paulo Freire dubbed the "banking concept of education," where learners are reduced to passive receptacles into which teachers deposit information (Freire, 2014). This model is particularly inappropriate and irrelevant for Jewish education.

Scholars and practitioners have consistently rejected the idea that it is enough to fill up a student's mind with facts, beliefs, a set of experiences—what Stuart Charmé calls the "drink-your-milk" model in Jewish education—particularly in a world in which people are yearning to make knowledge personally meaningful (Charmé et al., 2008). Alternatively, falling back on the notions that teaching about Torah, Jewish history, culture, and ideas is a calling rather than a profession, that teaching is an innate ability, and that learning is entirely an outgrowth of inspiration also obscures the important work happening in the everyday classroom practices and policies. Of course, Jewish tradition is replete with rabbinic and modern voices valorizing the role of the teacher[3] But leading scholars in the field of pedagogy have argued that teaching is a complex practice that draws on teachers' own prior learning experiences and develops over time as novice educators interact with effective mentors and develop through teaching induction programs and classroom experiences (Feiman-Nemser, 2003). In both cases, whether the discourse defaults to a "banking model" or whether it embraces the role of the charismatic pied piper who inspires Jewish kids to follow in their footsteps, teaching and learning are oversimplified and trivialized.

More fundamentally, the historical record underscores how a lack of attention to the processes of education contributes to the failure of reform efforts. Educationalists and policymakers mistakenly draw a straight line between inputs and outputs without an appreciation for how teachers teach and how learners learn. Nor do they sufficiently factor in the social, economic, developmental, and environmental influences that shape these processes. In a 2019 issue of Prizmah's journal *HaYidion*, Jewish education researcher Jeffrey Kress warns readers to "beware [of] the aisle of abandoned innovations." Contending that "Rapidly Cycling Innovation Syndrome is at epidemic levels," Kress worries that teachers, administrators, and students alike come to take the failure of reform efforts as an inevitability and that educational innovations frequently lack staying power because they do not respond to the perceived needs of teachers and staff, particularly around growing expertise (Kress, 2019). In short, Kress underscores a common refrain in educational circles: educators are reluctant to change their practices when innovations seem foreign and consequently disempowering. Larry Cuban and David Tyack go even further, reminding us that teachers and other school officials are invested in "the familiar institutional practices of the school" (Tyack & Cuban, 1997, p. 9). They are socialized to take for granted traditional models of education as opposed to viewing them as historically contingent. And then there are the pragmatics of educational reform efforts. Change also frequently involves additional work without commensurate compensation and can lead to confusion in the implementation of policies and policy churn. Jewish day schools, unsurprisingly, are not immune to the vicissitudes of schooling.

In light of the difficulties initiating, evaluating, and sustaining educational innovation as well as understanding classroom practices more generally, this volume takes stock of what is happening in contemporary Jewish day school classrooms and among Jewish day school students and teachers. As the Ellenson quote at the start of this chapter suggests, day schools were created with the lofty goals of making a dramatic impact on the American Jewish community by offering a dual curriculum of secular and Jewish content in a full-day school model. This volume offers a portrait of how this objective has been playing out in the twenty-first century. The authors of this volume directly confront and question some bedrock principles of Jewish education and some address how day schools intersect with broader societal issues, including race and gender. They point to themes and topics that scholars and practitioners are grappling with and reveal potential future directions worthy of attention.

With our own lofty goals of generating discussion about contemporary day schools with this edited volume, we strove to include as many voices as possible in the conversation. This book grew out of a conference entitled "Inside Jewish Day Schools," sponsored by the Mandel Center for Studies in Jewish Education at Brandeis University in the spring of 2018. The book does not, however, consist of conference proceedings or papers. While many of the chapters are the result of direct participation in this conference, other chapters were written by a broad range of scholars and practitioners who responded to a call for papers, drawing on data mostly collected over the last dozen years. In total, about half of the chapters in the volume emerged from the conference while the other half came from scholars who responded to a CFP. This volume was conceived prior to the Covid upheaval, October 7, and the 2024 presidential election; thus, there are no chapters that address how day schools have emerged in the post-pandemic educational and religious landscape, or responded to new political realities in Israel and North America.

Readers will search in vain for a unifying theme or a common methodology that cuts across the chapters, aside from their interest in the teaching and learning process—broadly construed—in Jewish day schools. We understand "teaching and learning" in an expansive sense to include not just studies of particular classrooms (although a few of the chapters do exactly that) but also inquiries into the various stakeholders and how they think about and experience the teaching and learning of particular subject areas. Unlike the contemporary discourse on public education, which tends to be dominated by a few central topics and theoretical constructs and frameworks, the academic literature on Jewish day schools is more diffuse. This diffusion is born out of the decentralized nature of day schools, as well as the varying populations day schools are serving in a range of Jewish communities across the United States. There is no quintessential day school teaching and learning experience. Nor is there common consensus around which issues are most critical for scholars to address. With this in mind, we see the eclectic nature of the chapters reflecting a scholarly field that is in the process of maturity and telegraphing the diversity and breadth of the field with all of its richness and challenges.

The authors come from a range of social science disciplines and backgrounds and offer a variety of conceptual perspectives. Stylistically, the chapters are written for a mixed audience of scholars and practitioners of

Jewish education. Most chapters are framed as empirical investigations of some aspect of contemporary Jewish day schools; even the most conceptual and exploratory chapters are based on data from groups of teachers, parents, students, or classrooms. Finally, in most cases (although not all), the scholars have taken a deep dive into particular institutions or particular groups of students or teachers. While this kind of rich qualitative inquiry cannot be generalized to the broader population, it does what good empirical data does best: open up new insights and raising new questions that can shape the field.

In particular, the chapters reflect on one or more of the following questions:

- What do we know and what can we learn about what students are learning in Jewish day schools? What do we know about the alignment, or lack of alignment, between desired and actual student learning outcomes?
- What do we know about teaching and learning in specific core subject areas (e.g., Bible, rabbinics, Hebrew, etc.) in day school education? What do we know about developmental (i.e., "whole child") outcomes beyond, outside, or across the content of subject areas?
- How do broader social and environmental factors in the Jewish day school contribute to learning?
- How do social categories such as race, ethnicity, class, and gender shape student learning and school culture?

The book begins with a pair of topical chapters that explore the content that day school students are learning. Specifically, these two chapters examine how day school students make sense of Zionism and their relationship with the state of Israel. In "Learning the Language of Zionism," Sivan Zakai asks what Jewish day school students actually know about Zionism and how they conceive of and relate to Zionist history and ideology. Drawing on data from a longitudinal study of day school students, Zakai examines their evolving conceptions of Zionism over the course of elementary school and demonstrates that while the term *Zionism* is generally unfamiliar to day school students until the late years of elementary school, as early as kindergarten, day school students begin to understand the language of Zionism—its core beliefs, principles, and attitudes. Finally, she makes a case for the ways that students ought to be taught to participate in the Zionist discourse. Jonah Hassenfeld's chapter, "Knowledge and Connection as Outcomes of Israel Education," draws on interview data from a diverse group of tenth graders and offers a portrait of how Jewish day school students articulate their thoughts and feelings about Israel. Their answers suggest new ways of thinking about what it means to *connect* to Israel and to *know* about Israel. Based on the analysis of his data, he argues that Jewish educational institutions should abandon a focus on fostering positive emotions and instead offer students opportunities for substantive engagement with Israel's history, politics, and culture.

Aside from their focus on Israel education, Zakai and Jonah Hassenfeld's chapters share an interest in exploring the dynamics of student learning. Similarly, Ziva Hassenfeld's "Intercomprehending in Action: Text-Based Discussion in a Seventh-Grade Bible Classroom" analyzes classroom talk from her own seventh-grade Tanakh (Hebrew Bible) classroom. Hassenfeld shows that class discussion is an opportunity for students to not only share their well-developed interpretations but also co-construct interpretations and knowledge. Recognizing that students' interpretations are constructed through talking has major implications for the place of classroom discussion in curricula.

The next two chapters shed light on the learners themselves. Based on her re-analysis of data from 3,703 middle and high school students in ninety-six Jewish day schools in North America (from the "Hearts and Mind" study; Pomson & Wertheimer, 2014), Ilana Horwitz presents "Connected but Not Confident: The Gender Confidence Gap Regarding Israeli Politics and History," which documents a gender confidence gap that is unique to Jewish day schools: girls are significantly less confident than boys when discussing Israeli history and politics. She explores the implications of this finding for our understanding of gender in the Jewish day school classroom more generally. Using data from the same study as Horwitz, Janet Krasner Aronson and Raquel Magidin de Kramer's "Understanding Attitudes of Jewish Day School Students" develops a typology of engagement among Jewish day school students that reflects the multidimensional nature of Jewish engagement and identity. The dual purpose of this typology is to (1) identify the characteristics of individual students and of schools that are associated with various patterns of Jewish engagement and (2) understand the patterns of interests and attitudes among students in order to enable educators to better tailor educational activities for them.

In the following chapters, the focus turns our attention to the teachers. In "'Responsive Classroom' Meets the Rabbis: The Impact of DeLeT on Teachers' Classroom Community-Building Practice," Sharon Feiman-Nemser and Shira Horowitz present research on the DeLeT (Day School Leadership Through Teaching) program at Brandeis University, which Feiman-Nemser developed and oversaw for almost two decades. The authors describe how DeLeT provided a Jewish context for teacher preparation, how that preparation shaped the identity and practice of program graduates, and what students learned about building a (Jewish) classroom community. They then explore the continuing influence of that preparation on the professional identity and teaching practices of two students after graduating from the DeLeT program.

The next chapter, Sharon Avni's, "What Do Parents Want from Hebrew Studies in Jewish Day School Education?" throws parental desires and expectations into the mix when considering the role of the Hebrew language teacher. Presenting a case study of two fifth-grade Hebrew classes taught by a highly regarded teacher at a non-Orthodox Jewish day school, Avni probes how parents define successful Hebrew learning and what parents perceive as an effective Hebrew teacher. The findings point to a degree of ambivalence about how parents think about success and highlights the tensions that emerge between what students feel about the teacher, the subject of Hebrew language, and their learning achievements.

At this point, the book brackets two chapters that focus on the contested landscape of rabbinics education—a content topic that more than many others encapsulates the core of the Jewish studies curriculum of day school learning. Joshua Ladon's "Three Conceptions of Rabbinics: Understanding Teachers' Thinking" emerges from his analysis of ten interviews with day school rabbinics teachers. Ladon uncovers a lack of consensus about how to define rabbinics as a classroom subject. He distills three distinct conceptions of rabbinics and argues that these differing understandings in turn influence teachers' conceptions of what constitutes expertise in rabbinics. In a similar vein, Yaakov Jaffe's "Four Approaches to the Instruction of Halakha" examines how a Jewish day school's stated vision or approach to halakha (Jewish legal) instruction influences or aligns with the curricular, school structure, or classroom decisions related to halakha. Jaffe offers a case study of a Modern Orthodox high school and situates the school's choices within a matrix of different approaches to teaching halakha.

The volume then considers the day school as a site of socialization and enculturation, inviting the reader to think about the school as an ecosystem. Moshe Krakowski's "Signature Pedagogy and Constituent Authenticity: A New Model of Authentic Activity in Jewish Day School Classrooms" focuses on the classroom as a microcosm of community. Specifically, Krakowski argues that American yeshivish haredi (ultra-Orthodox) elementary schools' pedagogical practices function very similarly to what Lee Shulman called "signature pedagogies." Drawing on an ethnographic study of a first-grade boys' Bible class in a haredi school, he maps Shulman's notion of signature pedagogy to a form of authenticity that he calls "constituent authenticity," generating broader questions about how Jewish studies classrooms prepare for or draw upon broader Jewish cultural practices. In "Orienting Students to Engage with Pluralism: A Cultural Approach," Susan Shevitz examines how pluralism is conceptualized and enacted within an intentionally pluralistic Jewish high school. Focusing on the experiences of first-year students, Shevitz describes and analyzes the ways in which the school's freshman orientation inducted students into a pluralistic Jewish setting. Shira Hammerman's "Designing Schools Around Five Dimensions of Community" probes the familiar notion that Jewish day schools should be designed as communities by asking what schools might think about when integrating staff members into a school community. Her analysis yields five distinct dimensions that provide entry points into a school community.

Finally, Erik Ludwig's "Sometimes Seen: The Experience of Latine Students in Jewish Day Schools" represents the burgeoning interest in race and ethnicity in Jewish education. Informed by the general literature on equity and inclusion, Jewish educational researchers are beginning to explore and interrogate the apparent and hidden diversity within Jewish educational institutions. Ludwig's chapter offers a modest but significant contribution to our knowledge about the Jewish educational experiences of American Jews of Latin American descent by exploring how they speak about their experiences as students at one Jewish day school. Among his initial findings, Ludwig posits that examining their narratives helps locate characteristics of culturally responsive pedagogies that the students perceived made for effective teaching. Ludwig's analysis also sheds light on how Latine Jewish day school students in California (many of whom are part of the Mexican Jewish population) experience the activation or dismissal of their racial or ethnic identities by their teachers. Ludwig's study underscores that the topic of intra-Jewish ethnic and racial difference is ripe for further exploration, as the American Jewish community continues to recognize and embrace its cultural, religious, linguistic, and political diversity as part of larger American sociological trends and directions.

Taken together, the chapters in this volume demonstrate that day schools are sites of educational challenges and opportunities, as they grapple with addressing the particulars of Jewish education, as well as broader concerns about pedagogy and learning facing secular schooling today. What is so striking about all of these chapters, indeed, is that while they are firmly rooted in the context of Jewish learning, they draw from and extend conceptual and theoretical frameworks in the fields of pedagogy, literacy, and learning sciences. No doubt, over the years to come, Jewish day schools will continue to evolve to meet the needs of its families and the wider Jewish community. In this regard, this volume is not a final picture of the American Jewish day school. Rather, it offers a glimpse into these diverse institutions in the early twenty-first century, and it demonstrates the need for more in-depth empirical research that can inform the various stakeholders committed to this form of Jewish education.

In closing, Ellenson's quote that opens this introduction highlights the critical role that Jewish education plays in the American Jewish community. But equally salient in his proposition is that Jewish education is also part of the "larger world of values and culture of which we are a part" (Ellenson, 2008) and has the potential to shape Jewish life, as well as the larger society. This volume is a step in better understanding these dynamics and pointing us in the direction of future research in the Jewish day school context.

NOTES

1. www.casje.org/about#Mission. Accessed February 19, 2024.

2. This list is not meant to be exhaustive.

3. To cite but two examples, in *Avot* 4:12, Rabbi Elazar ben Shammua teaches that "the reverence for your teacher [should match your] reverence for Heaven," while Abraham Joshua Heschel asserts that "Judaism is teacher-centered. We do not celebrate kings and heroes—we celebrate teachers—Moses and Rabbi Akiva. The teacher is the central pillar of Jewish living, past, present, and future" (Heschel, 1953, p. 9).

REFERENCES

Charmé, S., Horowitz, B., Hyman, T., & Kress, J. S. (2008). Jewish identities in action: An exploration of models, metaphors, and methods. *Journal of Jewish Education*, *74*(2), 115–143.

Ellenson, D. (2008). An ideology for the liberal Jewish day school: A philosophical-sociological investigation. *Journal of Jewish Education*, *74*. https://doi.org/10.1080/15244110802418328.

Feiman-Nemser, S. (2003). What new teachers need to learn. *Educational Leadership*, *60*(8), 25–29.

Freire, P. (2014). *Pedagogy of the oppressed, 30th Anniversary Edition*. Translated by Myra Berman Ramos. Bloomsbury Publishing.

Heschel, A. J. (1953). The spirit of Jewish education. *Journal of Jewish Education*, *24* (Fall), 9–19.

Kress, J. (2019). Beware the aisle of abandoned innovations. *HaYidion*. www.prizmah.org/hayidion/educational-innovation/beware-aisle-abandoned-innovations/.

Limonic, L. (2019). *Kugel and frijoles: Latino Jews in the United States*. Wayne State University Press.

Pekarsky, D. (2006). *Vision and theory at work: The theory and practice of Beit Rabban*. JTS Press.

Pomson, A., & Wertheimer, J. (2022). *Inside Jewish day schools*. Brandeis University Press.

Pomson, A., Wertheimer, J., & Hacohen-Wolf, H. (2014). *Hearts and minds: Israel in North American Jewish day schools*. Avi Chai Foundation.

Schuster, D. T. (2018). *Portraits of Jewish learning*. Wipf & Stock.

Tyack, D., & Cuban, L. (1997). *Tinkering toward utopia: A century of public school reform*. Harvard University Press.

Zakai, S. (2022). *My second favorite country: How American Jewish children think about Israel*. New York University Press.

Teaching and Learning in Jewish Day Schools

1

Learning the Language of Zionism[1]

SIVAN ZAKAI

Israel and Zionism in the Elementary Jewish Day School

At one American Jewish elementary school, each new week begins with a school-wide assembly, and each assembly begins with the students singing "Hatikvah," the Israeli national anthem. Across town, students at a second Jewish elementary school belt out the same words as part of their daily morning circle. And at a third Jewish school nearby, the children also know this anthem; they sing it every Friday as part of their weekly prayer service.

In each of these schools, the rhythm of children's lives is interlaced with symbolic engagement with the Jewish state (Kopelowitz, 2005; Pomson et al., 2014). But what do the children actually *know* about Israel and Zionism?

For many adults in the Jewish community, the answer to this question has high stakes. Expressing anxiety that the next generation of American Jews may not be as connected to Israel as their parents and grandparents have been, scholars and Jewish communal leaders have exerted great efforts to measure and bolster attachment to Israel (e.g., Cohen & Kelman, 2007; Saxe et al., 2009). In this context, Israel education is often viewed as a bulwark against the rising tides of detachment and ambivalence (e.g., Bryfman & Cohen, 2015), and thus it has become an increasingly integral part of the enterprise of American Jewish education (Horowitz, 2012; Grant & Kopelowitz, 2012). Yet even as Israel has played more of a central role in Jewish education, it has also played a more contested one, highlighting profound disagreements about both the nature of education and the nature of present day Israel (Davis & Alexander, 2023; Zakai, 2023).

Jewish educational institutions—and Jewish day schools in particular—have come to bear an increasing burden of responsibility for helping young

Jews make sense of Israel (Pomson, 2010; Pomson et al., 2011). Day school students are, by definition, actively engaged in organized Jewish life, and it is often assumed that they will "play a leading role in Jewish life when they come of age" (Pomson et al., 2014, p. 35). Thus, day schools shoulder both the hopes of an older generation of American Jews seeking to connect its progeny to the Jewish state and the frustrations of a younger generation of American Jews who are increasingly divided in their beliefs about Israel and the role it ought to play in Jewish education (Harpaz, 2023).

Day school Israel education has long been marked by a confusion of goals and purposes (Zakai, 2011; Pomson et al., 2009). On the one hand, it is clear that "Israel remains a central feature of Jewish educational programming in North America, perhaps nowhere more ubiquitously and intensively than in Jewish day schools" (Pomson et al., 2014, p. 5). On the other hand, the place of Israel in the day school curriculum is often unclear (Gerber & Mazor, 2003), and "schools' efforts are undermined by poorly coordinated and fragmented practices" (Pomson et al., 2009, p. 7). The very goals of day school Israel education are also contested. Some day school educators and parents believe that day schools are responsible for cultivating attachment to Israel among young Jews (Pomson, 2010), while others express deep skepticism of attachment as a worthy educational goal (Hassenfeld, 2023).

If Israel education is fraught with tension, then learning about Zionism may be even more so. The twenty-first century has ushered in a new era of "Israel education" focused on the "emergence of an effort to more deeply and explicitly weave present-day Israel into the enterprise of American Jewish education" (Horowitz, 2012, p. 2). Under this broad umbrella, which is a departure from earlier Jewish educational focus on "teaching about Israel" (Horowitz, 2012) and "Zionist education" (Krasner, 2006), the place of Zionism remains unclear. Israel education may embrace a Zionist philosophy, but it needn't necessarily, as there is a "clear distinction that need[s to] be made between teaching about Israel and Zionism, and Zionist education itself" (Breakstone, 1994, p. 6). Some Jewish educational institutions have an explicitly Zionist mission (Pomson & Deitcher, 2010), while others have no particular Zionist commitments even as they work to teach students about the land and state of Israel (Isaacs, 2011).

Given the unclear role of Zionism in contemporary Israel education, what do children who have grown up in the Jewish day school system actually know about Zionism? How do Jewish day school students conceive of and relate to Zionist history and ideology? This chapter will address these questions by examining day school students' evolving conceptions of Zionism over the course of elementary school. It will demonstrate that while the *term* Zionism is generally unfamiliar to day school students until the late years of elementary school, as early as kindergarten, day school students begin to understand the *language* of Zionism—its core beliefs, principles, and commitments. In so doing, this chapter will elucidate the ways that young day school students currently understand Zionism and will make a case for the ways that they ought to be taught to participate in the *discourse* about Zionism, an ongoing and highly contested conversation about the national aspirations of the Jewish people.

Windows into Children's Thinking about Israel and Zionism

To make this case, this chapter draws upon data from the Children's Learning About Israel Project, a longitudinal study of Jewish day school students.[2] By tracking a group of thirty-five children throughout the course of elementary school, the project aims to understand how these children think and feel about Israel, and how their thoughts and feelings about Israel develop or change over time.

The children were recruited from the kindergarten classes of three Jewish day schools during the 2012–2013 school year. The day schools that these children attend were selected because they cater to different segments of the American Jewish community, making it possible to enlist participants who varied in their Jewish practices and affiliations, as well as their experiences and relationships to Israel. Thus, the schools represent different religious denominations within American Judaism: one is Reform, one Conservative, and one a nondenominational community school. The ethnic background of the schools' typical families also varies; one has a large Persian-Jewish population, one has predominantly children of Ashkenazi descent, and one serves many Israeli expatriate families.

By design, the children exhibit varying exposure to and experiences with Israel (see table 1.1). Some of the children have never been to Israel, while others have visited for extended periods of time. Some have Israeli parents and/or relatives living in Israel; others do not. Although all of the children have been taught about Israel in some form during their day school education, their schools' approaches to Israel education—including both the formal curriculum and Israel's role in the school environment (Chazan, 1979)—differ widely.

To understand what the children know about Israel, we sought "windows into children's thinking" (Wright et al., 2008; McGee, 1996): glimpses into the ways that the children themselves viewed Israel and made sense of its relationship to their own lives. Over the six years of this study, we peeked into the children's minds through three "windows"—interviews,

TABLE 1.1. Participant Demographic Information

Participant	Gender	Affiliation	Parents' Birthplace(s)	Visited Israel	Relatives in Israel
Ari	M	Reform	United States, Israel	Yes	Father, Grandmother
Avigail	F	Chabad	Israel	Yes	Cousins
Bella	F	Reform	Iran	No	None
Brent	M	Reform	Iran, United States	No	None
Caleb	M	Reform	Iran, United States	No	None
Carly	F	Conservative	United States, Iran	Yes	None
David	M	Reform	United States	Yes	None
Dina	F	Chabad	Israel, Swaziland	Yes	Aunt, Uncle, Cousins
Elliott	M	Reform	Iran	Yes	None
Esther	F	Reform	Iran	No	None
Gabe	M	Reform	United States, Iran	Yes	None
Gia	F	Reform	United States	Yes	None
Hannah	F	Reform	United States	No	None
Hayim	M	Reform	Iran	Yes	Cousins
Isaac	M	Reform	Iran	Yes	None
Isabelle	F	Unaffiliated	Israel	Yes	Grandmother
Jacob	M	Conservative	Israel	Yes	Grandmother, Aunt. Uncle, Cousins

continued→

elicitation exercises, and storytelling exercises—each of which was specifically designed for capturing the ways that children understand the worlds around and inside of them.

1. *Semi-structured interviews*. Interviews solicit demographic information about the participants and offer them a chance to reflect upon the ways that they understand, think, and feel about Israel. The interviews are semi-structured, based on a prewritten script but allowing for fluid conversation and follow-up probes (Miles & Huberman, 1994; Gillham, 2005). The semi-structured nature of these interviews

Participant	Gender	Affiliation	Parents' Birthplace(s)	Visited Israel	Relatives in Israel
Julia	F	Conservative	United States	Yes	Grandmother
Keren	F	Conservative	Israel, Canada	No	None
Kevin	M	Conservative	United States	No	Cousins
Lailah	F	Unaffiliated	Israel	No	Grandparents, Uncle, Cousins
Lior	M	Unknown	Israel	Yes	Deceased Great Grandparents
Maya	F	Unaffiliated	Israel, Czech Republic	Yes	Grandparents
Micah	M	Unknown	United States, Israel	Yes	Great Grandmother
Naomi	F	Conservative	United States	No	Grandfather
Noah	M	Unaffiliated	United States	No	None
Olivia	F	Conservative	Israel, Peru	No	None
Owen	M	Unknown	United States	Yes	Grandparents
Pearl	F	Chabad	United States, Israel	Yes	None
Peretz	M	Unknown	United States, Israel	Yes	Unknown
Rina	F	Conservative	United States	No	None
Ryan	M	Conservative	United States	No	None
Samantha	F	Reform	United States	No	None
Seth	M	Reform	Israel, Argentina	Yes	Cousins
Tzvi	M	Unaffiliated	United States	Yes	None

allows both focus and flexibility, each of which is useful when interviewing children (Drever, 1995). The questions we ask children vary from formal (e.g., "What is Zionism?") to playful (e.g., "If you were visited by someone from another planet, someone who spoke English and understood everything you were saying, but really didn't know anything about life on Earth, how would you explain to them what it means to be Israeli?").

2. *Photo and music elicitation exercises*. Children are asked to examine and discuss a variety of visual and audio prompts (Harper, 2002; Allett, 2010) that highlight different aspects of Israeli political, religious, and cultural life. Visual and audio prompts elicit both what participants see or hear and also what is brought up for them internally when they interact with the prompt (Banks, 2001). When combined with interviews, photo and music elicitation exercises evoke responses from children that are more detailed and comprehensive than those provided by interviews alone (Collier, 1987; Epstein et al., 2008). We show the children a map of the Middle East, Israeli and Palestinian flags, paintings of people praying at the Kotel and eating at a Tel Aviv cafe, an audio clip of the Israeli national anthem, and dozens of other visual and auditory stimuli as a way of eliciting what the children know and how they feel about different aspects of Israeli culture and society.
3. *Storytelling exercises*. Children are asked to tell stories about life in Israel, revealing how they view and explain the world. Storytelling is a "fundamental structure of human experience" (Connelly & Clandinin, 1990, p. 2), one familiar to adults and children alike. For children in particular, telling stories can be a way of making sense of the world, serving as "a child's way of exploring, inquiring, probing, and… playing her way into deeper understanding" (Lindfors, 2004, p. 149). We ask children to "*tell us a story about how Israel became Israel*" as a window into how they view Israeli history, and we ask them to "*tell us a story about what's been happening in Israel recently*" as a window into how they understand current events.

Together, these "windows" offer myriad glimpses into children's thoughts and feelings about Israel and how Israel factors into their own self-understanding as Jews. Data are coded in the spirit of grounded theory (Glaser & Strauss, 1967; Charmaz, 2014), based on the children's own categories and ways of speaking. The goal is to understand how the children themselves conceive of and relate to Israel.

The study has tracked these children over time, examining the ways that their thoughts and feelings about Israel have changed as the children have grown. This chapter will focus on the children's perceptions of Zionism between kindergarten (2012–2013 school year) and fifth grade (2017–2018 school year), highlighting particular moments in time that are crucial for understanding the children's evolving conceptions of what Zionism is and the role it plays in American Jewish life.

Understanding the Term Zionism

What is Zionism? This seemingly simple question has a multitude of answers, as Zionism has been used as an "umbrella term for many ideologies" encompassing the cultural, political, spiritual, and national aspirations of the Jewish people (Rechnitzer, 2018, p. 26). Historically, Zionism was a "movement calling for the establishment and support of an independent state for the Jewish people in its ancient homeland" (Stanislawski, 2016, p. 1). Yet, as historian Anita Shapira (2012) asks, what was the nature of that movement? Was it "a renaissance movement directed towards reshaping the Jews, Jewish society, Jewish culture? A colonization movement aiming to establish a Jewish territorial entity that would grant Jews what other people had: a homeland where they could find refuge? A spiritual or political movement?" (p. 3) Pre-state Zionists vehemently disagreed about both the aims and the tactics of Zionism.

Today, the existence of a Jewish state is a reality, not an aspiration. What, then, is the meaning of Zionism in light of the existence of such a state? Some see Zionism as having ended in 1948 with the establishment of the state of Israel (e.g., Pfeffer, 2108). Yet contemporary Zionists have shifted the definition of Zionism from an attempt to establish a Jewish nation-state to a movement dedicated to shaping the character of that state. In this view, contemporary Zionism is an ideological commitment to "strengthening Israel as a Jewish . . . and democratic state" (Engel, 2009/2013, p. 1). Many see an inherent tension between Israel's Jewish and democratic attributes.

Some liberal Zionists embrace the "inescapable complexity [of these] multiple and sometimes conflicting commitments" (Beit-Halachmi, 2018, p. 37). Others, many of whom identify as post-Zionist, argue that Israel must choose between being a Zionist "ethnocracy and a post-Zionist liberal democracy" (Nimni, 2003, p. 3). Thus, at the heart of contemporary discussions of Zionism lie questions about what the state of Israel should—and should not—do to reflect Jewish and/or liberal democratic values.

Many contemporary American Jews—especially young Jews—have voiced skepticism about Zionism. Some Jews are uncomfortable with Zionism as a politicized term even as they continue to embrace Israel as a locus for personal Jewish meaning (Pomson & Held, 2012). Others self-identify as Zionists even as they raise concerns that the realities of the Jewish state do not live up to their ideals for the exercise of Jewish power (Beinart, 2012). Others still reject Zionism altogether, either seeking to reframe contemporary Jewish life in non-Zionist theological terms rather than Zionist nationalist ones (Omer, 2019) or taking an explicitly anti-Zionist stance against ethnonationalism (Kroll-Zeldin, 2024).

Regardless of how Jews have defined and thought about it, Zionism has long been understood as a "crucial issue" of Jewish life in the modern world (Hertzberg, 1984/1997). Thus, by any standard of cultural literacy, young Jews living in the United States should have at least a basic understanding of what Zionism is.[3] Even if they cannot explain how multiple iterations of Zionism have developed over time (Brenner, 2011); even if they are entirely unaware of the existence of Christian Zionism (Spector, 2009); even if they cannot articulate the ways that Israeli and Palestinian claims function as competing nationalisms (Peters & Newman, 2013); and even if they know nothing of the debate about whether Zionism has constituted a radical break from or a continuation of the Jewish past (Biale, 1986); they ought at the very least know that Zionism—historical and contemporary—is an ideological position that highlights the Jewish people's connection to the land and state of Israel. Zionism at its most basic definition "reflects the fact that Jews and Judaism are tightly bound up with the Land of Israel" (Holo, 2018, p. 18), though what that bond ought to look like has long been a matter of disagreement.

Can Jewish day school students in elementary school define Zionism at this very basic level? The answer, quite simply, is no. The vast majority of day school students in the Children's Learning About Israel Project were entirely stumped by the question *What is Zionism?* Whether they were in kindergarten, fifth grade, or in the intervening years, students struggled to answer the question *What is Zionism?*, not because they understood that the question itself has often been mired in disputes among its proponents (Shapira, 2012) and detractors alike (Engel, 2009/2013), but because many were unable to recognize the word itself.

A look at third graders' answers to the question *What is Zionism?* is instructive, as it shows how, at the midpoint of their elementary school learning, the children attempted to define Zionism. (See table 1.2 for a complete record of students' answers in third and fourth grade.) Four of the thirty-five children in the study readily admitted that they had no familiarity with the very term. "I don't know," replied Isaac, "because I've never heard of the word Zionism." Similarly, Jacob explained, "I don't know that word," and Tzvi insisted, "I don't know! I've never heard that word before." It is important to note here that Isaac, Jacob, and Tzvi attend three different day schools. Their lack of familiarity with the term, which may appear jarring given their schools' explicit commitment to Israel and Israel education, cannot be attributed to a single school's inattention to Zionism in curriculum or programming.

The vast majority of these children's classmates were unable to offer any definitions at all. They gave answers like Bella's "I'm not sure," Isabelle's "I don't know," and Pearl's "I have no clue." Once again, these children attend three different day schools, and yet their responses are remarkably similar. Across the board, the third graders in this study were unable to define Zionism, with only two children explicitly linking the term to anything Israel related. Dina, as a "random guess," hypothesized that Zionism "has something to do with Israel . . . maybe believe in their people." Hannah, who readily admitted, "I don't know," continued, "I think it might mean that different people from the world come to Israel." Even these children, whose answers explicitly connected the term Zionism to Israel, admitted that they were guessing because of the larger context of an interview about Israel.

Yet it is not that the very term Zionism is an anathema to the elementary school context. Myriad curricular resources, including the Center for Israel Education's *Israel: A Curriculum for Grades 2–7* (Center for Israel Education,

2015) and Torah Aura's *Artzeinu: An Israel Encounter* (Grishaver et al., 2008), craft elementary school–friendly definitions of Zionism. The third graders in this study, however, could neither define nor explain Zionism despite attending day schools that care deeply about Israel and Israel education.

The children fared slightly better with their answers by the time they reached fourth grade. In that year, many of the children continued to insist that they were completely unaware of the term Zionism, such as Bella's "I don't think I've ever heard that before" or Olivia's "I've never heard of Zionism." Many others didn't even hazard a guess as to what it means, such as Avigail's "I'm not sure what Zionism is" or Dina's "I actually don't really know." But beginning in fourth grade, a sizable minority of students (eight of thirty-five), including children from each of the day schools in this study, began to offer rudimentary definitions that explicitly linked Zionism to the Jewish people's connection to the land or state of Israel.

Consider, for example, the definitions of Keren and Tzvi, who attend different schools. While in third grade Tzvi insisted that he had never heard of the word Zionism, in fourth grade he was able to explain, "The root word Zion was the name of Israel before it actually became Israel. Well, it was Palestine . . . There was this guy who started this Zionist thing . . . He made something called the Zionist group, and lots of people wanted to do that because they wanted a Jewish state, somewhere they could settle instead of having to move from place to place and stuff. So what happened was, they had to, they became Zionist and ended up creating a Jewish state in 1948."

Keren, when in third grade, said that she did not know what Zionism was, but in fourth grade she spoke with great confidence, saying, "Zionism are people who want to help Israel . . . They fight against people who want to take over . . . [A Zionist] is a person who wants to help Israel be a better place." In Tzvi's definition are signs of a rudimentary understanding of the historical roots of Zionism, and in Keren's definition are echoes of contemporary definitions that characterize Zionists as supporters and defenders of the nation-state.

Even so, these children remained a minority; most of their classmates offered only guesses about what Zionism is, and their hypotheses were often wildly off the mark. For example, Isabelle confused Zionism with monotheism, and Hayim, Micah, Hannah, and Lailah all assumed it to

TABLE 1.2. What Is Zionism?

Participant	What Is Zionism? (third-grade answer)	What Is Zionism? (fourth-grade answer)
Ari	I don't know.	I don't know.
Avigail	I don't even know what it is.	I'm not sure what Zionism is.
Bella	I'm not sure.	I don't think I've ever heard that before, so I don't really know.
Brent	*No answer*	*No answer*
Caleb	*No answer*	*No answer*
Carly	Um...I don't really know.	Something about like how Israel like maybe like fights and gets their rights, maybe. I don't know.*
David	Uh...This is hard...um...Maybe it could mean like...like...it could be like a religion?	*No answer*
Dina	As a random guess, it has something to do with Israel... maybe believe in their people?*	I actually don't really know.
Elliott	I don't know what that is. They believe in God, uh, one God?	I don't know what that is.
Esther	I don't know.	*No answer*
Gabe	I don't know.	I don't know. I've never heard that word.
Gia	Studying Zion, except I don't know what Zion is.	I have no idea. Maybe the study of rabbis?
Hannah	I don't know. I think it might mean that different people from, um, the world come to Israel.*	I don't know. Sounds to me like a religion or something.
Hayim	I don't know.	I don't know. Uh, a religion?
Isaac	I don't know because I've never heard of the word *Zionism*.	I've never heard of Zionism.
Isabelle	I don't know.	Zionism? Belief? In God.

continued→

NOTE: *No answer* was recorded for some children who declined to answer the specific question, were not available for the particular interview from which this data was drawn, or were unable to complete the entire interview due to issues of focus or school scheduling constraints. An asterisk (*) in the chart indicates an answer that could be generously interpreted as a rudimentary definition of the word Zionism.

Participant	What Is Zionism? (third-grade answer)	What Is Zionism? (fourth-grade answer)
Jacob	I don't know that word.	I don't know.
Julia	*No answer*	*No answer*
Keren	I don't know.	Zionism are people who want to help Israel . . . They fight against people who want to take over . . . [A Zionist] is a person who wants to help Israel be a better place.*
Kevin	*No answer*	*No answer*
Lailah	Zionism? Freedom.	Um, maybe it's a religion? I don't know.
Lior	Zionism? I don't know what that is.	I don't know.
Maya	Zionism is like a good place to live in, not a perfect, but a good place.*	I don't know. Probably an important place, like somewhere that lots of people care about.*
Micah	I have no clue.	No clue. Maybe a religion or something?
Naomi	I don't know. Maybe it's another religion? But I'm not sure what it is.	Zion, the Zionists were a group of Jews who lived not in Israel, trying to go back in Israel; but it was under Palestinian rule. But eventually they had the war. Then they got Israel back.*
Noah	*No answer*	*No answer*
Olivia	I have no idea.	I've never heard of Zionism.
Owen	*No answer*	*No answer*
Pearl	I have no clue.	I don't really know. Like the Zionist people? We're starting to learn about them [but . . .] we didn't really get into everything yet.
Peretz	*No answer*	No answer
Rina	I don't know. Zionism is . . . a Greek god, something?	Zionism, well I heard that Israel once was called Zion. And how it was a very important name and how like it was like the name that Theodor Herzl came with . . . came up with.*

continued→

Participant	What Is Zionism? (third-grade answer)	What Is Zionism? (fourth-grade answer)
Ryan	I don't know, but Zion is a place in Utah.	Zion is somewhere in Israel, but Zion's also a place in Utah with that big rock. Zion National Park. A Zionist, we talked about this in class. It was a person who wants to live in Israel, who has to go for a little while but always wants to go back to Israel.*
Samantha	I'm not sure.	Zion was another name for Israel before it was named Israel. I think it had, like, seven or eight different names and Zion was one of them. I don't know what Zionism means but I know Zion.*
Seth	I don't know what is that.	I guess, I don't know. Isn't it like kind of baptism, but like, Israeli baptism?
Tzvi	I don't know! I've never heard that word before.	The root word *Zion* was the name of Israel before it actually became Israel. Well, it was Palestine... There was this guy who started this Zionist thing... He made something called the Zionist group, and lots of people wanted to do that because they wanted a Jewish state, somewhere they could settle instead of having to move from place to place and stuff. So what happened was, they had to, they became Zionist and ended up creating a Jewish state in 1948.*

be some kind of religion, likely hypothesizing based on the word ending "ism" as in "Judaism."

Thus, by even the most generous measures, the fourth graders as a collective appear to have very little understanding of the terms Zionism and Zionist. The same was true in fifth grade, when only a few more of the children were able to link the terms to any conception of Jewish aspirations for, or Jewish presence in, a Jewish state. By the end of elementary school, only about a quarter of the children, all of whom have received a Jewish day school education from schools whose missions explicitly mention Israel, can offer a rudimentary definition of Zionism. On a test of basic Israel literacy, these students would appear to come up short.

Understanding the Language of Zionism

Yet a basic literacy approach is not the only way to understand students' knowledge of Zionism. As philosopher of Jewish education Jon Levisohn (2016) asks, "Rather than devising an instrument that tells us the facts that students do not know, how might the landscape look different once we understood what students do know?" (p. 13). In other words, if elementary day school students do not understand the term Zionism, what *do* these students know about Zionist beliefs and ideologies? It turns out that while even many fifth graders can't define the *word* Zionism, as early as kindergarten these same children begin to understand the *language* of Zionism—explaining its core beliefs, principles, and commitments in rudimentary form. Like children from other ethnic backgrounds who cannot define nationalism but nonetheless have some understanding of the concepts related to it (e.g., Zembylas, 2010), these children are working to understand Zionist ideas even when they cannot explain the term Zionism.

In order to understand the children's beliefs about Zionism in elementary school, it is necessary to understand two things: one about children's developmental capacities for understanding nationalism and one about the nature of Zionism itself. There is a substantive body of research devoted to uncovering the ways that children think and feel about nationality and nationalism that demonstrates that children's understanding of these concepts is a result of both external influences (e.g., family and culture) and internal factors (e.g., cognitive readiness and motivation) (Barrett, 2004). Although there is some variation depending on the particular cultural context and the specific child (Barrett, 2007), starting at age five or six, children generally understand that the world is divided into countries (Jahoda, 1963a, 1964). At this young age children begin to recognize national symbols (e.g., Barrett et al., 1997; Jahoda, 1963b) and can characterize themselves as members of their own national groups (e.g., Karakozov & Kadirova, 2001; Kipiani, 2001). Even in their first years of elementary school, children are beginning to construct initial theories about what constitutes national identity (Penny et al., 2001), and they believe that national identity is important (Barrett, 2001). As children grow, so too does their understanding of nations as historical and cultural communities, along with an awareness of the political nature of nationalism (Barrett, 2007).

Thus, while children's understanding of national identity and of the unique features of nation-states develops over time, even children in early elementary school are developmentally capable of thinking about some of the core ideas related to nationalism.

To understand day school students' understanding of Zionism as a particular form of Jewish nationalism, it is also necessary to recognize that contemporary discourse about Zionism and Zionist history frames Zionism not as one unified ideology, but rather as "many Zionisms" (Brenner, 2011, p. 99) with different "meanings and performances" (Penslar, 2023, p. 11). In fact, in a present-day reframe of Arthur Hertzberg's (1984/1997) classic *The Zionist Idea*, historian Gil Troy (2018) has highlighted the plurality of Zionisms in *The Zionist Ideas*. Troy's iteration classifies six different Zionist schools of thought, including Political, Labor, Revisionist, Religious, Cultural, and Diaspora Zionisms.

The pages that follow explore data from spring of children's kindergarten year, when the children had not yet completed even a single year of day school education (though some had previously attended Jewish preschools). The same children who could not define Zionism toward the end of elementary school had begun to develop basic mental schema for understanding core ideas about Zionism even at ages five and six. Concepts central to Political, Labor, Revisionist, Religious, Cultural, and Diaspora Zionisms were evident in the children's ways of speaking about Israel both as they responded to open-ended questions and as they reflected on specific visual and audio prompts. With only one exception, each child in the study was able to articulate a germinal understanding of at least one of these forms of Zionist ideology, and over half of the children (twenty of thirty-five) were able to articulate rudimentary conceptions of three or more of these forms of Zionist thought in the spring of kindergarten. Just as five- and six-year-olds are beginning to understand the building block ideas of nationalism, so too are they developing an emerging understanding of multiple iterations of Jewish nationalism.

At the center of Political Zionism lie the twin concepts of peoplehood and statehood. As Peretz Smolenskin, a Russian Jewish novelist of the late nineteenth century, explained, "we are a people"; Jews share not only religious ties but also national ones (Smolenskin, 1875–1877, in Troy, 2018, p. 3). Because of these national ties, father of Political Zionism Theodor Herzl insisted, Jews—like other nations of the world—deserve "sovereignty... over a portion of the globe large enough to satisfy the rightful requirements of a nation" (Herzl, 1896, in Troy, 2018, p. 15).

In speaking about Israel, the kindergarteners frequently used the language of both peoplehood and statehood. When asked *What does Israel make you think about?*, children replied with answers like "the Jewish people" (Brent) or "all the Jewish people" (Gia). When asked *What is Israel?*, they responded with answers like "a Jewish state" (Hayim), "a small state for the Jewish people" (Lior), or "a Jewish home" (Gia). For many of these children, the concepts of peoplehood and statehood were inexorably linked. With echoes of the myopic early Zionist phrase "for a people without a land, a land without a people,"[4] children like Owen explained that Israel is "a place for the Jews. It's because that the Jews needed a place, needed their own country, but they didn't have one." There is much, of course, about Political Zionism and its contested history that the children do not understand, but a basic schema for it exists in their minds even at age five and six.

One of the tenets of Cultural Zionism is the idea that Hebrew is and should be "the simple, natural language of everyday life" in Israel (Ben-Yehuda, 1880, in Troy, 2018, p. 106). Transforming Hebrew from the language of sacred texts to the Jewish vernacular was not only a technical challenge for Ben-Yehuda and his followers, but it was also an explicit ideological commitment of their Zionism (Sachar, 2007).

Many of the children reflected this commitment in their own words. While the children generally understood that Hebrew "is their language they speak in Israel" (Rina), some were able to articulate an ideological position that wove Hebrew into the very fabric of Israeli society. As Avigail explained, it isn't only that people in Israel "always only speak Hebrew" but also that "Israel is meant for Hebrew." Echoing the directive "*Ivri daber Ivrit*" (a Hebrew speaks Hebrew),[5] these children viewed Israel as a place where "Hebrew and Hebrew people live" (Hannah). For, as Ryan explained,

Jews around the world might speak many languages, as he spoke English, but only Hebrew was the true language of the Israeli people. While none of the children were familiar with the phrase Cultural Zionism at any point in their elementary school years, even at age five and six many had begun to incorporate into their own stories about Israel the Cultural Zionist belief that Israel is and should be "made of Hebrew" (Avigail).

Among the principles of Revisionist Zionism is a belief in the importance of a "Jewish majority in *Eretz Yisrael*" (Jabotinsky, 1934, in Troy, 2018, p. 69). In its origins, this idea was aspirational, but contemporary iterations of Revisionist Zionist ideology view the successes of the modern state in light of an "Israel built around a cohesive and overwhelming Jewish majority" (Hazony, 2014, in Troy, 2018, p. 394).

Many of the kindergarteners understood the concept of a Jewish majority, both as a demographic reality and as an ideological commitment of the Jewish state. These children understood three interrelated ideas about Israel's majority Jewish population. First, the children knew that Israel is "full of Jewish people" (Dina). Second, many (but not all) of the children understood that, as Bella explained, Israel is "a place where Jewish people live," and yet it is possible to live in Israel if you're not a Jewish person, or outside of Israel (as she does) if you are Jewish. Third, the children recognized that Israel's very character, in Brent's words "why Israel is special," is precisely because "there's lots of Jewish people there." For, as Caleb explained, "Israel is a safe place for Jews because there's a lot of Jewish people [there]." While these children were familiar with neither the phrase Revisionist Zionism nor any of its historical or contemporary advocates, they had internalized the Revisionist Zionist idea that Israel's existence is contingent on a "Jewish majority in *Eretz Yisrael*."

Religious Zionism hinges on the assumption that Israel's "land, language, history, and customs are vessels of the spirit of the Lord" (Kook, 1910–1930, in Troy, 2018, p. 96) and should therefore be governed "on the basis of our heritage of Torah" (Bar Ilan, 1922, in Troy, 2018, p. 101). For Religious Zionists, commitments to the land and state of Israel are theological, rooted in a belief that Jerusalem sits at the spiritual center of the world.

Echoing a Religious Zionist ideology, many of the children described Israel as a place with a direct connection to God. Olivia called Israel "a country made by God," Jacob labeled it "God's favorite state," and according to Caleb, "God made Israel, and then He made it safe." Naomi described God as intervening on Israel's behalf in wars, when "God is surrounding it with a big bubble." Yet the children also understood that this connection to God, which made Israel "a very holy place" (Samantha), was enacted in its laws and customs. The children knew that the holidays celebrated in Israel include Jewish holidays (like Shabbat and Passover), and not only Israeli holidays (like Yom HaZikaron and Yom HaAtzmaut), and many could explain the ways that Jewish symbols are tied to Israeli ones (e.g., the Israeli flag's relationship to a *tallit*). For these children, Israel's character was a religious Jewish one, a place where "they study Torah" (Pearl) and where "there's no shrimp, they don't catch shark, they don't catch squid, they don't catch crab, they don't catch lobster, no pig" (Hayim). The children did not have the metacognitive awareness to identify their own beliefs as Religious Zionist even at the end of elementary school, but as early as kindergarten many embraced a Religious Zionist ideology that connected the state of Israel, the rituals of Judaism, and the intercession of the Divine.

Diaspora Zionism, at its core, revolves around the fact that it is possible to be both a passionate Zionist and a Jew living outside of the state of Israel. Although many Israelis, from David Ben-Gurion to A. B. Yehoshua, consider the concept of Diaspora Zionism to be an oxymoron, many Jews in North America believe that Jews outside of the state play an important role in shaping and responding to the development of Jewish statehood (Troy, 2018). As Alan Dershowitz (1997, in Troy, 2018) explains, "I am a committed Zionist. I believe passionately in the Jewish state... But I am an American, and I love America and believe in its future" (p. 480).

This sentiment was shared by several of the kindergarteners. In the words of Micah, America is "my state" and Israel is a place "I love." Kevin described Israel as "our second country" and Rina, flipping the order, called Israel "my first favorite country... [and] here is my second favorite country, in America." Ryan described the two countries as different teams, and when asked what team he was on, responded without hesitation: "both." This idea was mirrored by Samantha's insistence that "both sides are special in their own way." Samantha imagined having formed a special connection to Israel in utero, "when I was in my mom's tummy." The other children could not describe when or where they formed this belief, but they knew, in Gia's words, that "I'm in America... and Israel is a Jewish home." Although these children had neither the language nor the conceptual sophistication of adults, they nonetheless embraced the dual commitments of Diaspora Zionism.

A few children even exhibited an inchoate conception of contemporary Labor Zionism. In its initial conception, Labor Zionism was intended to be a synthesis of Zionist and socialist commitments, emphasizing the importance of Jewish labor in the soil of *Eretz Yisrael* (Sachar, 2007). Yet, as Troy (2018) explains, "even as communism's collapse discredited socialism and Israel's culture of abundance led most kibbutzim to privatize, the desire to make the Zionist state epitomize liberal ideas with a Jewish twist persisted." Thus, the contemporary iteration of Labor Zionism frames Zionism as a "permanent revolution" constantly striving for economic and social justice (Avineri, 2017, p. 227). In this view, Zionism is "a call to recognize that in a world in which Jewish fortunes have radically changed, the best way to memorialize the history of Jewish suffering is through the ethical use of Jewish power" (Beinart, 2010, in Troy, 2018, p. 382).

For the children who embraced this ideology, in nascent form, their entire conception of Israel revolved around "helping people" (Ryan) and "helping Israel to make it a better country" (Avigail). As Avigail explained at age six, "Israel is counting on all the Jewish people. You have to make [Israel] a better place... and [work hard]." She and many of the other children envisioned their own labor—picking up trash on the street, visiting the hungry, feeding the sick, and building a more peaceful place—as contributions to the "ongoing project of nation building within the Jewish state" (Grant, 2010, p. 21). For, as Lior explained, the *making* of Israel was only the beginning; even now "we're never going to give up. We're going to build *Yisrael*." The children could not have identified the Labor Zionist roots in their words and imagined deeds, nor did they situate this work in the belief that "Israel must be (and can be) a democracy that upholds human rights, including freedom of religion and conscience, along with the right to equality, while fulfilling the Jewish people's right to self-determination" (Gavison, 2003, in Troy, 2018, p. 369). Nonetheless, they clearly understood the idea that Israel is both built and incomplete, established and constantly striving, and they imagined contributing their own labor to a project of continual betterment for Israeli society.

When viewed as a whole, these children do not appear to be developmentally ready to define Zionism, or even recognize the word, before fourth or fifth grade at the earliest—even when they have had repeated exposure to Zionist ideas. Yet well before they can define Zionism or explicitly discuss its meanings, most children are developing an ability to "understand the language" of Zionism, which starts as early as kindergarten. All of the children know "Hatikvah" (even if they cannot identify it by name), and several can belt out the lyrics of other nationalist Israeli songs, including "*Eretz Yisrael sheli yafah v'gam porachat*" (my land of Israel is beautiful and also blooming) and "*Kachol v'lavan*" (blue and white). A few can speak unprompted about major figures in Israeli history and society, like Israel's first prime minister, David Ben-Gurion, or its prime minister for the majority of their own lives, Benjamin Netanyahu. The children weave this knowledge into their own ways of speaking and talking about Israel.

More important than the details that they use to populate their accounts is the fact that, when young American Jewish day school students craft their own narratives about Israel, their stories exhibit evidence of some of the central ideas of historical and contemporary Zionisms. This is crucial because, as Jon Levisohn (2016) explains, "We operate with what psychologists call 'schemata,' larger frameworks into which we organize information; we learn (and retain) facts only when we contextualize them in some schema, narrative, or conceptual framework. That is where we ought to focus our pedagogic attention" (p. 13).

By this measure, day school students are, from a very early age, capable of developing the building blocks for understanding what Zionism is and how it functions in Jewish life. Even when they are unaware that they are doing so, they clearly tell stories about the Jewish past and present that indicate an awareness of multiple ways of thinking about Judaism and its relationship to nationalism and the state.

Increasing Fluency with Zionism

Even as they near the end of their elementary school studies, many day school students cannot define Zionism even at the most basic level. Yet this inability to define the term Zionism should not be mistaken for an inability to "understand the language" of Zionism. Day school students begin to make sense of that language as early as kindergarten, demonstrating that they actually understand a great deal about the Jewish people's historic and contemporary connection to the land and state of Israel. Many day school students at the elementary level also believe that Israel plays a meaningful role in their own lives, even though they do not label that connection as Zionist.

Given this reality, many day schools will view it as their mission to increase children's fluency with the language of Zionism, helping students speak in increasingly sophisticated ways about Zionist symbols, figures, and ideas as children grow. This is certainly an attainable goal. If the day school students of the Children's Learning About Israel Project are any indication, children ought to be able to increase their literacy about Zionism throughout elementary school. As kindergarteners, these children indicated familiarity with multiple tenets of Zionist thought. Each year thereafter, the children were able to add additional language and ideas to their discussions about Israel and Zionism.

By first or second grade, most children could identify and explain Zionist symbols. While even in kindergarten many children could identify the Israeli flag or national anthem as connected to Israel, as first or second graders the children could speak about the *meanings* of these symbols. For example, first-grader Rina spoke about how the colors of the Israeli flag were reminders of the *tallit* and the Jewish people's prayers for Israel across time. Second graders could identify, in the words of Avigail, "Hatikvah" as "the national song of Israel." As second-grader Dina explained, singing "Hatikvah" was an expression of Jewish connection to Israel, so that when she and her classmates sing it "we all feel like we're surrounded by Israel."

By third grade, most of the children understood that the yearning for the land of Israel and Jerusalem has been expressed not only by Jews, but also by other people(s). Hayim, for example, explained the special connection that both Jews and Christians have for the land, saying, "For Jews, that's their homeland and its where all their ancestors were. And, for Christians, that was the birthplace and the place Jesus died and that's their God." Similarly, Keren explained that Israel has been special for both "the Jews and the Arabs: the Jews because they know that God promised them the land, and the Arabs thought it was theirs and they got a share, too." As third graders, the children began to think about ways that non-Jews, like Jews, have laid claim to the land.

By fourth grade, many of the children were able to speak about a wide range of figures from Zionist history. As they told stories about Israel's past, they began to populate those stories with figures like Theodor Herzl, David Ben-Gurion, Golda Meir, Chaim Weizmann, Hayim Nahman Bialik, and Hannah Szenes—even without a specific prompt asking them to do so. These figures from Zionist history had become part of their storytelling about Israel.

By fifth grade, many of the children were able to tell a basic narrative about the origins of Political Zionism. As Maya explained, "Theodor Herzl thought of the idea that Jewish people should be in their own place." In Rina's words, "Theodor Herzl. That guy was a visionary. He had so many ideas of what Israel should be like. A homeland for the Jewish people." While most fifth graders were able to tell a basic story about Herzl and the rise of Zionism in Europe, some were also able to speak, in broad brush-strokes, about British Mandate Palestine, the U.N. vote on the partition of Palestine, and/or the 1948 War of Independence.

Day schools that take seriously the task of Israel education should not mistake children's struggles to define the *word* Zionism with an inability to understand basic *ideas* about Zionism. Even in early elementary school, students are capable of understanding the basic tenets of multiple iterations of Zionism, and they can populate their conceptions with greater detail as they grow. For, as renowned education reformer Deborah Meier (1995/2002) explains, "little kids, lo and behold, are capable of some very fancy abstractions" (p. 47).

Participating in the Discourse about Zionism

Yet while increasing fluency with the language of Zionism may be a necessary step in a day school students' early educational trajectory, it should not be the goal of a robust program of Israel education. In order to be able to participate in the ongoing life of the Jewish people—both within Israel and outside of it—day school students must be ready not only to understand the *language* of Zionism, but also to participate in the ongoing *discourse* about Zionism. In other words, it's not enough for day school students to know about the key ideas and figures of Political, Labor, Revisionist, Religious, Cultural, and Diaspora Zionisms. Day school students must also be able to engage in thoughtful and informed conversations about what Zionism is and what it ought to be in two distinct contexts. The first is "an internal debate" among Jews about the relationship between Judaism and Zionism and the form(s) it ought to take in the present moment, and the second is a debate about Zionism that "comes largely from without, from Zionism's critics" (Penslar, 2023, p. 11).

In recent years, the idea that day school students ought to be able to participate in the discourse about Zionism has typically been equated with preparing high school students for politically divisive conversations about Zionism on college campuses. Responding to fears that contemporary college campuses may be increasingly hostile to Zionist Jewish students (Marcus, 2007; Saxe, et al., 2016), some day schools have begun to focus on equipping students to counter anti-Zionist sentiments on campus (Fish, 2016). A push for a greater emphasis on Israel education at the high school level (e.g., Borenstein & Fish, 2018; Bryfman & Cohen, 2015) has often meant asking day school students to "defend the state of Israel" and asking day school educators to "inoculate our students so that they have heard the narratives on the other side before they arrive on campus" (Harcsztark, 2021).

This approach to preparing students to participate in the discourse about Zionism is overly narrow for three reasons. First, it equates the work of Israel education with that of political advocacy (e.g., Horowitz, 2012; Grant & Kopelowitz, 2012), glossing over crucial concepts that students ought to learn about the history, culture, and diverse communities of Israel. Second, and perhaps even more troubling, it relegates conversations about Zionism to the upper grades, ignoring the important ways that even the youngest day school students can and do think about Zionist ideas. Third, and most shortsighted of all, it privileges the external debates about Zionism and its critics over the internal debates about Zionism and its contested meanings in contemporary Jewish life.

Yet there is another way that day school students can learn to participate in the discourse about Zionism: by practicing—in a low-stakes, supportive environment—reflecting on, and deliberating about key unresolved questions regarding contemporary Zionism: What should twenty-first-century Jewish religious and national aspirations look like, and should they even be called Zionism? How should Judaism be practiced given the realities of the Jewish state, and how (if at all) should Judaism influence political, diplomatic, and military decision-making? What responsibility ought the Jewish state take for Jews outside its borders and non-Jews under its rule and military reach? How should Jews living outside of Israel shape, support, and/or challenge the policies of its government and voting citizens? How should Diaspora Jewish communities account for young Jews who are skeptical of or hostile toward Jewish nationalism? These questions are normative, asking students not only to learn what currently is but also to imagine and help create the world that they would like to see. They are all examples of what scholars of civic education Diana Hess and Paula McAvoy (2014) call "open policy questions," or questions that require political deliberation because they highlight multiple, competing viewpoints. And each of these questions, in different moments and with shifting language, is appropriate even for elementary school Israel education.

This approach to participating in the discourse about Zionism asks students—primary and secondary alike—not to face outward, but rather to face one another, participating in the ongoing conversations of the collective Jewish people. It frames education about Israel and Zionism as a part of an ongoing quest to shape the Jewish present and future in ways that require students to navigate Jewish and universal commitments and values. It calls upon Jewish students to recreate, reshape, or reimagine Zionist and/or other viable Jewish ideologies for the twenty-first century. And it is a form of education that is "practiced in such [a] manner as to respect the student's intellectual integrity and capacity for independent judgment" (Scheffler, 1965, p. 131), not assuming that adopting a particular set of Zionist beliefs is a foregone conclusion for all committed young Jews.

In this view, successful day school Israel education is not about the basic literacy goal of helping students define the term Zionism. It is not even about the higher order comprehension goal of helping students understand the language of Zionism—its core beliefs, principles, and commitments—or about helping students increase their fluency with Zionist terminology as they grow. Each of these may be useful, but ultimately each is insufficient if students cannot develop an Israel "stance" (Hassenfeld, 2017; Golden & Kadden, 2024), a term used to connote the ability to take an informed position on matters of ideology and/or policy. Hassenfeld

(2017) explains, in the context of high school education, "When students know about Israel and connect to Israel, they will be able to take stances (provisional though they may be). That is, they will be able to articulate a vision for the future of Israel and take action to bring their vision about." Developing a stance on key issues of contemporary Zionism is different from the Zionist education goal of inculcating students into a particular Zionist ideology; it allows students themselves not only to learn about but also to shape the meanings of Zionism in present-day Jewish life.

Practice developing a provisional stance on any of the open policy questions facing contemporary Jews ought to be central to the education of day school students of all ages and grade levels. This is an essential skill that students need in order to participate in the ongoing life of the Jewish people, and one that requires practice and careful deliberation. Given what kindergarteners know and understand about the multiple iterations of Zionist ideas, it is clear that even the youngest day school learners can engage in conversations not only about what the Jewish state *does* look like, but also about what it *ought* to look like and the role it *should* (and should not) play in Jewish life in North America.

As fifth-grader Tzvi explained, "Herzl's famous quote was, 'If you will it, it is not a dream.' Zionism comes from the hopes and dreams of all the Jewish people, and that includes me. It makes me feel part of a community and part of Israel." As this elementary school student understands, Zionism today—like Zionism since the time of Herzl—reflects the collective, sometimes clashing, hopes and dreams of the Jewish people's national aspirations. Day school students must not only understand but also participate in ongoing conversations about the present and future of the Jewish people. For this to happen, day school students and their educators must recognize that learning to understand the language of Zionism is only the first step in their ongoing role of contributing to the larger communal discourse about contemporary Zionism and its contested role in Jewish life.

NOTES

1. Editors' Note: The research for this chapter was conducted before the October 7, 2023, Hamas attacks on Israel and the ensuing war and its effects. Therefore, readers should be mindful of the very different circumstances in which this material was developed, while considering the ways that the findings in this chapter may remain relevant today.

2. The Children's Learning About Israel Project is a project of the Jack, Joseph and Morton Mandel Center for Studies in Jewish Education at Brandeis University.

3. An educational approach that values cultural literacy, rooted in the tradition of education reformers like E. D. Hirsch Jr. (1988), assumes that there is a body of knowledge that educated Jews must know about Israel (e.g., Troen & Fish, 2017). Experts in Israel studies determine what constitutes that body of knowledge, and today's American Jewish youth are often viewed as having an "information deficit" when measured against that body of knowledge (Koren et al., 2015, p. 20).

4. For a discussion of the historical origins and development of this idea, both within and outside of early Zionist circles, see Garfinkle (1991).

5. The phrase "!עברי דבר עברית" (*Ivri daber Ivrit*) originated in 1930s Palestine, as part of the Militia for the Protection of the Language's campaign to encourage the use of Hebrew as the spoken language of the Yishuv (Shohamy, 2008; Halperin, 2014).

REFERENCES

Allett, N. (2010). *Sounding out: Using music elicitation in qualitative research* (National Center for Research Methods Working Paper No. 14). University of Manchester, Morgan Centre.

Avineri, S. (2017). The *making of modern Zionism: The intellectual origins of the Jewish state*. Basic Books.

Banks, M. (2001). *Visual method in social research*. Sage.

Barrett, M. (2001). The development of national identity: A conceptual analysis and some data from Western European studies. In M. Barrett, T. Riazanova, & M. Volovikova (eds.), *Development of national, ethnolinguistic and religious identities in children and adolescents* (pp. 16–58). Institute of Psychology, Russian Academy of Sciences (IPRAS).

Barrett, M. (2004). Children's understanding of, and feelings about, countries and national groups. In M. Barrett & E. Buchanan-Barrow (eds.), *Children's understanding of society* (pp. 251–285). Psychology Press.

Barrett, M. (2007). *Children's knowledge, beliefs, and feelings about nations and national groups*. Psychology Press.

Barrett, M., Lyons, E., Bennett, M., Vila, I., Giménez, A., Arcuri, L., & de Rosa, A. S. (1997). *Children's beliefs and feelings about their own and other national groups in Europe*. Final Report to the Commission of the European Communities, Directorate-General XII for 25 Science, Research and Development, Human Capital and Mobility (HCM) Programme, Research Network No. CHRX-CT94-0687.

Beinart, P. (2012). *The crisis of Zionism*. Macmillan.

Beit-Halachmi, R. S. (2018). An evolving covenant: Renewing the liberal commitment to a Jewish democratic state. In S. M. Davids & L. A. Englander (eds.), *The fragile dialogue: New voices of liberal Zionism* (pp. 37–46). CCAR Press.

Biale, D. (1986). *Power & powerlessness in Jewish history*. Schocken.

Borenstein, M., & Fish, R. (2018, March 13). The case for rigorous Israel education for high school students. *eJewishPhilanthropy.* https://ejewishphilanthropy.com/the-case-for-rigorous-israel-education-for-high-school-students/.

Breakstone, D. (1994). Zionist education in the Diaspora: Overview and prognosis. *Journal of Jewish Education, 61*(2), 3–9.

Brenner, M. (2011). *Zionism: A brief history expanded edition.* Markus Wiener.

Bryfman, D., & Cohen, S. M. (2015, June). *A case for more teen Israel trips.* www.thejewishweek.com/editorial-opinion/opinion/case-more-teen-israel-trips/.

Center for Israel Education. (2015). *Israel: A curriculum for grades 2–7.* Center for Israel Education.

Charmaz, K. (2014). *Constructing grounded theory.* (2nd ed.). Sage.

Chazan, B. (1979). Israel in American Jewish schools revisited. *Journal of Jewish Education, 47*(2), 7–17.

Cohen, S. M., & Kelman, A. (2007). *Beyond distancing: Young adult American Jews and their alienation from Israel.* Andrea and Charles Bronfman Philanthropies.

Collier, J. (1987). Visual anthropology's contributions to the field of anthropology. *Visual Anthropology, 1,* 37–46.

Connelly, F. M., & Clandinin, D. J. (1990). Stories of experience and narrative inquiry. *Educational Researcher, 19*(5), 2–14.

Davis, B., & Alexander, H. (2023). Israel education: A philosophical analysis. *Journal of Jewish Education, 89*(1), 6–33.

Drever, E. (1995). *Using semi-structured interviews in small-scale research. A teacher's guide.* Scottish Council for Research in Education.

Engel, D. (2009/2013). *Zionism.* Routledge.

Epstein, I., Stevens, B., McKeever, P., & Baruchel, S. (2008). Photo elicitation interview (PEI): Using photos to elicit children's perspectives. *International Journal of Qualitative Methods, 5*(3), 1–11.

Fish, R. (2016, August 3). From anti-Zionism to anti-Semitism: An educators conference. *eJewishPhilanthropy.* https://ejewishphilanthropy.com/from-anti-zionism-to-anti-semitism-an-educators-conference/.

Garfinkle, A. M. (1991). On the origin, meaning, use and abuse of a phrase. *Middle Eastern Studies, 27*(4), 539–550.

Gerber, K. A., & Mazor, A. (2003). *Mapping Israel education: An overview of trends and issues in North America.* Gilo Family Foundation.

Gillham, B. (2005). *Research Interviewing: The range of techniques: A practical guide.* McGraw-Hill Education.

Glaser, B. G., & Strauss, A. L. (1999/1967). *The discovery of grounded theory: Strategies for qualitative research.* AdlineTransaction.

Golden, J., & Kadden, Y. (2024). Knowledge, connection, and stance: Toward a more enduring Israel engagement. In S. Zakai & M. Reingold (eds.), *Teaching Israel: Studies of pedagogy from the field* (pp. 151–176). Brandeis University Press.

Grant, L. (2010). When the Jewish people and Israel conflict. *The peoplehood papers 5: Jewish peoplehood and Zionism* (pp. 21–23). Center for Jewish Peoplehood Education. www.hjpa.org/content/upload/bjpa/peop/Peoplehood%20Papers%205-Lisa%20Grant.pdf/.

Grant, L., & Kopelowitz, E. (2012). *Israel education matters: A 21st century paradigm for Jewish education.* Center for Jewish Peoplehood Education.

Grishaver, J., Barkin, J., & Blair, E. (2008). *Artzeinu: An Israel encounter.* Torah Aura.

Halperin, L. (2014). *Babel in Zion: Jews, nationalism, and language diversity in Palestine, 1920–1948*. Yale University Press.

Harcsztark, T. (2021, June 11). Teaching American Zionism through civics education. *Machon Siach.* https://machonsiach.org/teaching-american-zionism-through-civics-education-2/.

Harpaz, B. (2023, December 19). Controversy over letter from Jewish day school alumni saying they were fed "false narratives" about Israel. *Forward.* https://forward.com/news/574053/charles-smith-jewish-day-school-israel-alumni-debate/.

Harper, D. (2002). Talking about pictures: A case for photo elicitation. *Visual Studies, 17*(1), 13–26.

Hassenfeld, J. (2017, October 16). Israel education for knowledge, connection, and stance. *eJewishPhilanthropy*. https://ejewishphilanthropy.com/israel-education-for-knowledge-connection-and-stance/.

Hassenfeld, J. (2023). What's love got to do with it: Reevaluating attachment as the goal of Israel education. *Journal of Jewish Education, 89*(1), 75–81.

Hertzberg, A. (1984/1997). *The Zionist idea: A historical analysis and reader*. Jewish Publication Society.

Hess, D. E., & McAvoy, P. (2014). *The political classroom: Evidence and ethics in democratic education*. Routledge.

Hirsch Jr., E. D. (1988). *Cultural literacy: What every American needs to know*. Vintage.

Holo, J. (2018). Peering into the nationalist mirror. In S. M. Davids & L. A. Englander (eds.), *The fragile dialogue: New voices of liberal Zionism* (pp. 11–24). CCAR Press.

Horowitz, B. (2012). *Defining Israel education.* The iCenter.

Isaacs, A. (2011). The purposes and practices of Israel education. In H. Miller, L. Grant, & A. Pomson (eds.), *The international handbook of Jewish education* (pp. 479–496). Springer.

Jahoda, G. (1963a). The development of children's ideas about country and nationality, Part I: The conceptual framework. *British Journal of Educational Psychology, 33*, 47–60.

Jahoda, G. (1963b). The development of children's ideas about country and nationality, Part II: National symbols and themes. *British Journal of Educational Psychology, 33*, 143–153.

Jahoda, G. (1964). Children's concepts of nationality: A critical study of Piaget's stages. *Child Development, 35*, 1081–1092.

Karakozov, R., & Kadirova, R. (2001). Socio-cultural and cognitive factors in Azeri children and adolescents' identity formation. In M. Barrett, T. Riazanova, & M. Volovikova (eds.), *Development of national, ethnolinguistic and religious identities in children and adolescents* (pp. 59–83). Institute of Psychology, Russian Academy of Sciences (IPRAS).

Kipiani, G. (2001). Ethnic identification in the structure of personal identifications and sociocultural conditions of development. In M. Barrett, T. Riazanova, & M. Volovikova (eds.), *Development of national, ethnolinguistic and religious identities in children and adolescents* (pp. 84–104). Institute of Psychology, Russian Academy of Sciences (IPRAS).

Kopelowitz, E. (2005). *Towards what ideal do we strive? A portrait of social and symbolic engagement with Israel in Jewish community day schools*. Survey commissioned by RAVSAK and The Jewish Agency for Israel. www.researchsuccess.com/images/public/articles/RavsakReport.pdf/.

Koren, A., Fishman, S., Aronson, J. K., & Saxe, L. (2015). *The Israel literacy measurement project: 2015 report.* Cohen Center for Modern Jewish Studies.

Krasner, J. (2006). Jewish education and American Jewish education, Part III. *Journal of Jewish Education*, *72*(1), 29–76.

Kroll-Zeldin, O. (2024). *Unsettled: American Jews and the movement for justice in Palestine.* New York University Press.

Levisohn, J. (2016, Spring). Redeeming Jewish literacy. *HaYidion: The RAVSAK Journal*, 12–13.

Lindfors, J. W. (2004). A written conversation with Vivian Gussin Paley, outstanding educator in the language arts. *Language Arts*, *82*(2), 148–153.

Marcus, K. L. (2007). The resurgence of anti-Semitism on American college campuses. *Current Psychology*, *26*(3–4), 206–212.

McGee, L. (1996). Response-centered talk: Windows on children's thinking. In L. B. Gambrell & J. F. Almasi (eds.), *Lively discussions! Fostering engaged reading.* International Reading Association.

Meier, D. (1995/2002). *The power of their ideas: Lessons for America from a small school in Harlem*. Beacon Press.

Miles, M. B., & Huberman, A. M. (1994). *Qualitative data analysis: An expanded sourcebook*. Sage.

Nimni, E. (2003). *The challenges of post-Zionism: Alternatives to fundamentalist politics in Israel*. Zed Books.

Omer, A. (2019). *Days of awe: Reimagining Jewishness in solidarity with Palestinians*. University of Chicago Press.

Penny, R., Barrett, M., & Lyons, E. (2001). *Children's naïve theories of nationality: A study of Scottish and English children's national inclusion criteria*. Poster presented at the 10th European Conference on Developmental Psychology, Uppsala University, Uppsala, Sweden, August 2001.

Penslar, D. (2023). *Zionism: An emotional state.* Rutgers University Press.

Peters, J., & Newman, D. (2013). *The Routledge handbook on the Israeli-Palestinian conflict*. Routledge.

Pfeffer, A. (2018, January 11). Why I'm not a Zionist and why you're not either. *Haaretz*. www.haaretz.com/opinion/.premium-why-i-m-not-a-zionist-and-why-you-re-not-either-1.5730410/.

Pomson, A. (2010). A sense of distance through the classroom window. *Contemporary Jewry*, *30*(2), 263–267.

Pomson, A., & Deitcher, H. (2010). Day school Israel education in the age of Birthright. *Journal of Jewish Education*, *76*(1), 52–73.

Pomson, A., Deitcher, H., & Held, D. (2011). *How do Jewish day school students think and feel about Israel?* Melton Centre for Jewish Education.

Pomson, A., Deitcher, H., & Rose, D. (2009). *Israel curriculum in North American Jewish day schools: A study of untapped transformative potential*. Melton Centre for Jewish Education.

Pomson, A., & Held, D. (2012). "Why Israel?": Re-viewing Israel education through the lenses of civic and political engagement. *Journal of Jewish Education*, *78*(2), 97–113.

Pomson, A., Wertheimer, J., & Hacohen-Wolf, H. (2014). *Hearts and minds: Israel in North American Jewish day schools*. AVI CHAI Foundation.

Rechnitzer, H. O. (2018). To be a post-nationalist Zionist: A theo-political reflection. In S. M. Davids & L. A. Englander (eds.), *The fragile dialogue: New voices of liberal Zionism.* CCAR Press.

Sachar, H. M. (2007). *A history of Israel: From the rise of Zionism to our time* (3rd ed.). Alfred A. Knopf.

Saxe, L., Phillips, B., Sasson, T., Hecht, S., Shain, M., Wright, G., & Kadushin, C. (2009). *Generation Birthright Israel: The impact of an Israel experience on Jewish identity and choices*. Maurice and Marilyn Cohen Center for Modern Jewish Studies.

Saxe, L., Wright, G., Hecht, S., Shain, M., Sasson, T., & Chertok, F. (2016). *Hotspots of Antisemitism and anti-Israel sentiment on US campuses*. Cohen Center for Modern Jewish Studies.

Scheffler, I. (1965). Philosophical models of teaching. *Harvard Educational Review, 35*(2), 131–143.

Shapira, A. (2012). *Israel: A history*. Brandeis University Press.

Shohamy, E. (2008). At what cost? Methods of language revival and protection: Examples from Hebrew. In K. A. King (ed.), *Sustaining linguistic diversity: Endangered and minority languages and language varieties* (pp. 205–218). Georgetown University Press.

Spector, S. (2009). *Evangelicals and Israel: The story of American Christian Zionism*. Oxford University Press.

Stanislawski, M. (2016). *Zionism: A very short introduction*. Oxford University Press.

Troen, S. I., & Fish, R. (2017). *Essential Israel: Essays for the 21st century.* Indiana University Press.

Troy, G. (ed). (2018). *The Zionist ideas: Visions for the Jewish homeland—then, now, tomorrow*. University of Nebraska Press.

Wright, C., Bacigalupa, C., Black, T., & Burton, M. (2008). Windows into children's thinking: A guide to storytelling and dramatization. *Early Childhood Education Journal, 35*(4), 363–369.

Zakai, S. (2011). Values in tension: Israel education at a U.S. Jewish day school. *Journal of Jewish Education, 77*(3), 239–265.

Zakai, S. (2023). The philosophies of Israel education. *Journal of Jewish Education, 89*(1), 1–5.

Zembylas, M. (2010). Children's construction and experience of racism and nationalism in Greek-Cypriot primary schools. *Childhood, 17*(3), 312–328.

2

Knowledge and Connection as Outcomes of Israel Education[1]

JONAH HASSENFELD

Imagine a teacher saying, "I hope my students will learn to read, but the most important thing is that they love reading." This teacher wouldn't last long. But as recent research has found, most Israel educators focus more on how students feel about Israel than what they know about Israel (Pomson et al., 2014).

This wasn't always true. For most of the twentieth century, learning about Israel meant studying several different subjects. Students might learn Hebrew, Jewish history, and Israeli geography as well as participate in cultural rituals such as Israeli Independence celebrations (Zakai, 2014). In that period, educators didn't seek to shape students' feelings in part because they took American Jews' attachment to Israel for granted. And they were right to. During the 1960s and 1970s, American Jews felt so attached to Israel that sociologists struggled to ask questions that could distinguish levels of attachment (Cohen, 1983). Everyone scored near the upper end of the scale.

But during the 1980s, things began to change. Debates in Israel over the status of non-Orthodox conversions, the 1982 invasion of Lebanon, the Sabra and Shatila Massacre, and the internationally televised footage of the Intifada gave many American Jews their first glimpse inside the day-to-day realities of Israeli politics and undermined belief in the superior morality of the Israeli Defense Force. The idealized image of Israel began to fray. American Jews' relationships with Israel became more complicated (Elazar, 1995; Sasson, 2014).

In the 1990s, Jewish educators recognized that they couldn't assume that their students felt attached to Israel. If they wanted their students to love Israel, they would have to teach them to love Israel. This idea led to the question that has dominated discussion of Israel education for the last three decades: How do you make sure your students feel good about Israel? As American Jews became more ambivalent about Israel, a cottage industry of thought pieces appeared to reconcile love of Israel with criticism of Israel's actions (Sinclair et al., 2013). Writers encouraged American Jews to love "the real Israel" (Eisen & Rosenak, 2007; Sinclair, 2013), love Israel "warts and all" (Eizenstat, 1990), and practice "hugging and wrestling" (Gringras, 2004). In attempting to take criticism of Israel into account, these approaches pushed back against pure advocacy approaches (e.g., Hasbara) that sought to minimize Israel's misdeeds. Nonetheless, the idea of "hugging and wrestling" relied on an unstated assumption: American Jewish ambivalence about Israel is a problem in need of a solution. Israel educators became responsible for solving the problem. They became responsible for teaching students to love Israel.

These trends intensified during the early 2000s. In the aftermath of the Second Intifada, educators, fueled by Jewish philanthropists, sought to conceptualize "Israel education" as a field in its own right (Horowitz, 2012; Kopelowitz & Grant, 2012). Many American Jewish educators saw Israel as under threat physically and politically. The field of Israel education would help young American Jews navigate the challenging issues Israel posed and, ultimately, produce knowledgeable adults deeply committed to the state of Israel and its defense.

This paper reports on a set of interviews with a group of tenth-grade students about their thoughts and feelings in connection to Israel. It explores two questions that lie at the intersection of theory and practice: (1) What do young American Jews know and feel about Israel today? and (2) How can understanding students' knowledge and feelings help Israel educators clarify their desired outcomes? Ultimately, the interviews offer an intimate portal into how a diverse group of American Jewish day school students articulate their thoughts and feelings about Israel. Their answers suggest new ways of thinking about what it means to *connect* to Israel and to *know* about Israel. This chapter challenges the premise that Israel education can only be successful if students feel good about Israel and argues that a deep connection to Israel must go hand in hand with deep knowledge. Its findings suggest that Jewish educational institutions should abandon a focus on fostering positive emotions and instead offer students opportunities for substantive engagement with Israel's history, politics, and culture. Ultimately, students will connect to Israel through their study of it.

Measuring Outcomes in Israel Education

Israel education researchers obsess over how young people feel about Israel. Study after study, article after article explores this issue (see e.g., Pomson & Deitcher, 2010; Pew Research Center, 2013; Saxe & Chazan, 2008; Saxe, 2012; Rosov Consulting, 2018). Do Jews feel connected? Disconnected? Do they love Israel? Do they feel alienated? Are American Jews distancing themselves from Israel (Cohen & Kelman, 2010; Sasson et al., 2010)? This research agenda aligns with an educational agenda designed to produce certain feelings: love, connection, commitment, care, relationship (Pomson et al., 2014). This unwavering focus on American Jews' feelings about Israel has eclipsed knowledge as an outcome. Many researchers ask how students feel (Pomson & Deitcher, 2010; Pew Research Center, 2013; Saxe & Chazan, 2008; Saxe, 2012); few ask what they know (for the few studies of student knowledge, see Hassenfeld, 2016; Koren et al., 2015; Zakai, 2015).

Sinclair (2009) articulated the most popular model for talking about Israel education outcomes. He proposed a two-dimensional matrix of knowledge and connection. He argued that a successful student will have high-resolution knowledge, meaning highly detailed knowledge and feel strongly connected. Sinclair's model reveals one of the central challenges of measuring outcomes in Israel education: What does it mean to be "knowledgeable" and "connected"?[2]

Those studies that do evaluate student knowledge tend to measure knowledge either by asking multiple-choice questions (see e.g., Koren et al., 2015) or by asking participants to self report their confidence in talking about certain aspects of Israel (see e.g., Saxe, 2012). This conception of knowledge has long been criticized (Freire, 2018) and has come to be seen as fundamentally flawed (Hassenfeld, 2011). Decades of educational research have shown that tests of arbitrary factoids seem predetermined to find that students' don't know much about the topic in question. For that reason, they are of limited utility in evaluating students' knowledge (Bransford et al., 2000). In recent years, other studies have adopted what Zakai (2019) calls an "inventory" model.

Instead of looking for what's missing, by testing whether students possess the items of knowledge deemed essential, the inventory model asks students open-ended questions to give them the chance to show what they know. Hassenfeld (2016), for example, asked day school students to "tell the history of Israel in as much or as little detail as you want."

Evaluations of students' feelings about Israel also lack clarity in what exactly they are measuring. A decade of reports on Taglit-Birthright trips (see e.g., Saxe, 2012), for example, ask participants, "To what extent do you feel a connection to Israel?" Participants answer on a five-point scale. These types of questions reveal a limitation of surveys. Surveys work best when they are getting at clearly defined concepts.

But it's hard to know what "connection to Israel" is. When respondents report that they feel "connected" to Israel, what are they reporting? What exactly is the feeling of "connection" to Israel? Even those studies that adopt qualitative methods often assume that we know what feeling "connected" looks like. In the piece where Sinclair (2009) proposed the two-dimensional matrix of knowledge and connection, he relied on ethnographic observations of Camp Ramah during the summer of 2006. One incident in particular stuck out to him:

> Over dinner, the feeling is Israel, not America ... O. from the mishlachat gets up with his guitar and Y. does the vocals. They sing a few Israeli songs from recent and not so recent times. The moment that bowls me over is when they sing "*Lo kalah hi lo kalah darkeinu*." All the campers join in and the roof is raised. I look at one table of girls and they're standing on their benches singing madly just like at a pop concert, hands swaying in the air, eyes shut, at the top of their voices. I find this amazing. These kids are quite literally in some kind of ecstatic state over Israeli music ... If this isn't Israel alive at camp, nothing is.

Over the course of the next few paragraphs, Sinclair expressed his amazement at these young people's deep connection to Israel. They are certainly feeling something powerful, but is it necessarily a connection to Israel? They might be excited to sing together. It might be a testament to how they feel at camp or how close they feel to their friends. How might we tell the difference?

In sum, there is broad consensus that educators want students to "know" about Israel and to feel "connected" to Israel. There is little agreement on what those terms mean. For the most part, knowledge has been conceived of as comprehending particular facts and connection has been conceived of as positive emotion. This study reports a set of open-ended interviews with a diverse sample of Jewish day school students designed to shed light on what it means to "know about" and be "connected" to Israel.

Methods

Tikvah is one of a growing number of Jewish parochial schools that do not affiliate with a particular denomination (i.e., Orthodox, Conservative, Reform, etc.). Like other Jewish day schools, Tikvah offers a dual curriculum of both Judaic and secular studies. But as a nondenominational school, Tikvah attracts a more diverse student population, including many students who don't see their Jewishness as a religious identity.

Participants

I interviewed a small but diverse group of tenth graders. I believed that in a carefully chosen set of tenth graders, we would be likely to find examples of a wide range of possible Israel education outcomes. To make sure that our interviewees embodied the diversity of Tikvah students, I sampled for range (Small, 2009). I identified ten students who represented the extremes of Tikvah's student population with respect to denominational background, interest in Jewish life, previous travel to Israel, and academic achievement.

I designed an interview protocol and conducted the first round of interviews in December 2016. The interview comprised a number of open-ended prompts designed to elicit students' knowledge and feelings about Israel. I offered them several opportunities to share about Israel without building assumptions into the questions.

At the time of the study, I was a teacher at Tikvah and a member of the faculty team overseeing the school's approach to Israel education. My simultaneous roles as researcher, teacher, and member of the oversight team presented some challenges. I was no disinterested outside observer. I had a professional stake in the success of our Israel education mission and several of the students I interviewed were students that I taught in my class. I hewed carefully, therefore, to the best practices in qualitative research outlined in the literature (Corbin & Strauss, 2008; Patton, 2002; Small, 2009). At the same time, my role as an "insider" offered benefits as well. I had immediate rapport with many of the students who shared far more readily than other high school students I have interviewed.

The goal of these interviews was not to assess the outcomes of Israel education across the school or even for these individual students. Neither was it to establish a causal relationship between our approach to teaching Israel and student outcomes. No doubt the same students, if interviewed on a different day, might give different answers. We hoped the diverse set of students would capture extremes of knowledge and feelings about Israel, and thereby, shed light on the possible outcomes of high school Israel education.

Connection

To understand what students mean when they say they feel connected (or disconnected) from Israel, I asked them, "Tell me about your relationship to Israel." This open-ended question allowed them as much flexibility as possible to talk about how they felt about Israel.

Their answers revealed different avenues of connection. They mentioned many themes. They talked about trips they had taken (seven out of ten), family in Israel (five out of ten), or Israel as a Jewish place (four out of ten). Two mentioned learning about Israel either in school or on their own and their connection to the history of the land, and two denied any connection to Israel whatsoever.

But the most notable difference among the students was the intensity with which they talked about their relationship to Israel. Three students seemed almost indifferent when talking about Israel. These students peppered their responses with expressions of ambivalence, such as "sort of" and "whatever." When I asked Jeff to describe his relationship to Israel, he told me that he has wanted to travel there for a long time. I asked him why.

"I don't know. Maybe being Jewish? It's just sort of the Jewish homeland and just sort of something I'm interested in."

Clara and Rachel stated their lack of connection explicitly. "I like Israel," Clara told me. "It's cool. I like the food. I don't really see [Israel] as my homeland or anything." Rachel told me, "I don't really have much of a relationship to Israel." She went on: "[The rabbi at my synagogue] gives sermons at the end of each service and a lot of the time if there were things happening in Israel he would talk about it and I would just zone out because I didn't feel connected to it and I was just like, 'Oh, okay, politics, whatever.'" These students didn't have much to say about Israel. They were ambivalent about the idea of Israel as a homeland. And although they may have been interested in traveling to Israel, they saw Israel as an interesting or fun destination, but nothing more.

Five students described their relationship to Israel in opposite terms. They could barely contain their excitement. It was almost as if they had been waiting for a chance to share the depth of their feelings for Israel. They spoke for much longer and described the intensity of their feeling in many different ways as if no words could quite capture the way they felt.

Over the course of a minute, Michelle told me she loved Israel six different ways: "I have this love for Israel. It means the world to me. I have such a strong connection." Michelle described Israel as a special place: A "land of milk and honey," and "where God intended us to be." She pulled out the pendant of the necklace she was wearing. It was a tiny map of Israel. "See?" she asked. "I'm literally wearing this." She looked at me and concluded, "I love Israel."

Isaac tried to express the centrality of Israel in his life. me. He said, "I feel a strong connection to Israel. I view it as central to who I am. It is the key part of my Judaism. I take immense interest in it. It's very important to me." Like Michelle, Isaac filled his answer with several different expressions of the intensity of his connection to Israel.

But intense feelings didn't always go hand and hand with positive feelings. Ellie told me that her strong Jewish identity, her family in Israel, and the several trips she has taken "created my relationship, a very deep relationship. My family likes to be informed, and we talk about Israel a lot. I've always cared about what's going on in Israel." While Ellie made clear that she felt deeply connected to Israel, she was also deeply critical.

Unlike Michelle and Isaac, who focused on describing their relationship to Israel as it is, Ellie quickly looked toward the future. Ellie told me that "I want [Israel] to continue and be as close to all my Jewish and ethical values as possible. My connection to Israel stems from Jewish peoplehood and Israel is a place where Jews are. My constant desire to be related to it has to do with my desire for it to be the best it can be." Later in the interview, Ellie made explicit what she left implicit here: the current state of Israel failed to live up to her values and this bothers her. For Ellie, Israel was still in the process of becoming. She felt most close to Israel when she imagines it in the future. She imagines it becoming a place that lives up to its stated ideals.

The comparison of the two groups of students sheds light on what it means to be connected to Israel (see figure 2.1). For these students, connection didn't necessarily mean positive feelings about Israel. Instead, the distinguishing characteristic in the way they spoke about Israel rested in the intensity of those emotions. Their connection to Israel could find expression in strong emotions whether positive or negative. Some students felt vaguely curious or interested, but Israel didn't take up much space in their daily life. It was a place at a distance. It might be fun to visit, but it didn't hold any special significance for them. Other students thought about Israel all the time. They struggled to find the words to capture their feelings. They followed current events in Israel or wore a necklace to symbolize their relationship. They sometimes spoke about "loving Israel," but they also expressed intense curiosity, disappointment, and sometimes, sadness.

Knowledge

Evaluating students' knowledge of Israel poses challenges similar to connection. I wanted to avoid the trap of defining an authoritative, yet arbitrary body of facts that define "knowledge of Israel." These types of lists set students up for failure by determining in advance what it means to know. I wanted to see their knowledge in action. Instead of factual questions, I asked open-ended questions that would allow them to apply what they knew. I asked them to tell me the history of Israel, share the people and places in Israel they might want to visit, and identify the most important issues facing Israel today. These prompts allowed them to talk about whatever aspects of Israel they wanted. Some students, for example, used the history question to share their knowledge of the Bible; others began in the twentieth century. Some students talked about wanting to meet politicians; others talked about musicians and athletes.

It quickly became clear that students fell into two groups. Some students struggled to say anything at all specific about Israel. Other students spoke about Israel fluently. They drew on a wealth of names and places. They could talk through the pros and cons of various contemporary issues in Israeli life. Their knowledge, however, didn't always overlap. While one student focused on the ins and outs of the conflict, another talked about economic inequality in Israel. A third expressed her disappointment in the Israeli rabbinate's treatment of non-Orthodox Jews. What set these students apart from the others was not that they knew particular facts. Rather, it was that they could speak in detail about some aspect of Israeli life.

Michelle and Clara spoke about Israel in the abstract even when I prompted them to fill in more detail. When I asked Michelle, who repeatedly emphasized the intensity of her connection to Israel, where she would like to go if she were to visit Israel, she told me that she would like "to go to [Israeli] parliament and see who's there, meet the people in the government because I'm very into politics and stuff like that." But when I asked her what she would talk to them about, she demurred, "I don't know, that's a hard question. I would have to sit on that one, do more research about policy and stuff. I would want to ask about policies and other things too."

FIGURE 2.1. Connection to Israel by Intensity and Valence.

Throughout the interview, Michelle rarely mentioned specific people or places. Her knowledge of Israel was general.

Clara, too, stayed general. When I asked her who she might like to meet in Israel, she said, "If I could meet anyone, I'd probably want to go meet with some politicians." I probed for her to tell me more, asking, "How do you imagine that going?" Clara answered, "I don't know, I just think it would be kind of cool. I'm not sure I would have a discussion with them, but it would be cool to meet people." I asked her whether there are any particular politicians she would want to meet. "Not really," she answered, "I'd just like to visit ... I forget what it's called. Oh my God, it's the place where all the politicians work." Clara is no political novice. She is the leader of a political club at school and debates American politics passionately and in detail. However, her interest and knowledge of politics didn't extend to Israel.

In contrast, Isaac and Ellie filled their responses with specific names, places, and events. They spoke fluently on any number of issues in Israel and Israeli society. Isaac's response to the question "Where would you like to visit in Israel?" though long, quickly reveals what knowledge of Israel looks like. Isaac spoke at length on a variety of topics.

> I think it would be important to try to touch on each of Israel's core geographies. The Hula Valley deserves its own day trip from the north. Maybe even the Golan Heights and make sure to cover the Negev, Eilat has extraordinarily rare geographic phenomena for example, how the reef's there, and Mitzpe Ramon, not that far away, is incredible, also trying to touch on both Tel Aviv and Jerusalem.
>
> Also even, obviously this can get controversial, except I would probably visit the West Bank, though maybe stay away from some of the more controversial areas. Certainly East Jerusalem, the Old City is worth visiting. And I would try to connect with different aspects of each of those geographic regions. Maybe one night in a more touristy hotel. And at the same time, highlighting the lives of Bedouins and, if possible, trying to meet some.
>
> Or some of the first real Bedouin towns are emerging, and seeing those can be historic in the sense of they'll likely be much larger in really only a decade. And going to the north, Jewish farmers, the Druze

> communities. Just as we think of Israel as the core safe place for Jews, for the Druze, that is Israel as well. There's no other country with a major Druze population which is safe for them, where for Jews we often have America.

In about a minute, with only minimal prompting, Isaac demonstrated his familiarity with Israel's geography. Not only could he name particular sites, but he also had a sense of where they are and roughly organized his trip from north to south. He was aware that certain areas are "controversial," could name and describe several of the major non-Jewish groups in Israel, such as Arab Christians, Druze, and Bedouin, and he discussed Israel's ancient history, mentioning Philistines, Canaanite kingdoms, and Judeans.

In describing her ideal trip to Israel, Ellie highlighted what she called "the aspect of multiculturalism." She spoke about the refugee crisis in South Tel Aviv, Arab-Jewish relations in Haifa, and her desire to visit Rawabi, a Palestinian city in the West Bank. She told me, "I'd want to go there and talk to them because I want to hear Palestinian perspectives... [Rawabi] has been in the news a lot because the state of Israel was not giving it water, but then a year or a year and half ago, they were given water."

The preceding quotations reveal the knowledge differences among the participants. Isaac and Ellie's knowledge is highly textured. They have specific details at their fingertips. For them, Israel is a complicated and diverse place. Clara and Michelle's knowledge is relatively shallow. They can name a few big headings, but are light on details. These examples offer a clear portrait of what Sinclair (2009) called hi-resolution knowledge.

But the ability to produce details captures only part of what it means to "know." The clearest differences in knowledge emerged when I asked students to think through a pressing issue facing Israeli society. This line of questioning tried to move beyond their recall of names and places. I wanted to see whether they could use their knowledge to articulate a position on an important issue. Because understanding an issue is also about being able to articulate several different perspectives, I asked them to play devil's advocate as well to see how they could articulate the perspective of someone with whom they might disagree.

Michelle, for example, told me that one pressing issue that Israel faces is opposition to settlements in the West Bank. When I asked about her position, she told me, "I think that it's absurd. It's a Jewish state. There should be allowed to be settlements." Our conversation continued:

> Interviewer: Can you imagine someone disagreeing with you?
> Michelle: Of course. I know people disagree with me.
> Interviewer: What do you think they would respond to you?
> Michelle: They'll probably give their argument and give their evidence and their knowledge.
> Interviewer: Do you have any idea what they would say specifically?
> Michelle: I really don't care. I'm going to be honest. I don't care.

Clara identified the same issue. "I don't know a ton about Israeli politics," she told me, "but potentially settlements in the West Bank because that really ties into a possible two-state solution." I asked her how she thought Israel should address that issue. "I don't know a ton about it. I think it's kind of difficult to take out Israelis who have already settled there. So I think the first place to start would be just to stop any more settlements being made." I asked her to play devil's advocate:

> Interviewer: Can you imagine somebody disagreeing with your perspective?
> Clara: Certainly, I've met a lot of people who have.
> Interviewer: What do you think they would respond to what you've said?
> Clara: About settlements? I'm not really sure. I've met a ton of people who don't support a two-state solution, but I kind of forget . . . I'm not really sure why.

Michelle and Clara disagreed on the issue of settlements. Michelle spoke with tremendous confidence. She found it absurd that anyone could question the legitimacy of Jewish settlements in the West Bank. Clara expressed more ambivalence, but she clearly saw settlements as an obstacle to peace.

Although these two students expressed opposed political positions, their answers shared a great deal. Neither referenced any specific names or places. Both stayed at a high level of abstraction. Most notably, neither articulated the perspective of the other. Michelle admitted that she didn't really care what other people thought, while Clara couldn't remember the opposing viewpoint.

Isaac and Ellie took a different approach. Although at other points in the interview, each demonstrated their familiarity with debates over the future status of the West Bank, neither listed this issue as the most pressing one facing Israel.

Isaac told me, "The number one issue is a more equitable economy. Not in the sense of economic inequality, but in equitable participation. [The lack of ultra-Orthodox Jews' participation] is one of the most alarming trends right now. Well, there were some optimistic signs among ultra-Orthodox women in the most recent reports, but ultra-Orthodox Jews and Arabs, which are half of all kindergarteners, are the least participatory demographics."

When I asked Isaac what he thought Israel should do to develop more equitable economic participation, he told me, "First off, Yair Lapid and Naftali Bennet should get a backbone and try to do what they did in 2012 and get the draft applied to ultra-Orthodox Jews."

Although Isaac clearly knew a great deal about many different topics in Israel, the clearest distinguishing factor between him and many of the other students was the ease with which he drew on his knowledge, synthesizing it into a coherent perspective. While the other students clearly knew a great deal, their knowledge came across as less finely grained, and they seemed to have more difficulty drawing it out.

Also, in contrast to Michelle and Clara, Isaac had no trouble playing devil's advocate. I asked him, "Can you imagine someone disagreeing with you? What do you think they would respond to you?" Isaac responded, "They'd probably say that [draft exemptions] weren't creating some unreasonable exemption. The intellectual and religious practices of the Jewish people were often held in the custodianship of so few. It's because of the context... There were very, very, very few yeshiva educated Jews after the Holocaust. And still, the spiritual and moral development of the Jewish people is understanding what we do. It's driven a lot by yeshivas and yeshiva education. These exemptions, which are primarily for yeshiva education, are important for continuing a twenty-first-century legacy of Jewish understanding.

Ellie talked about the Israeli rabbinate as the most pressing issue. She began with a caveat, "As a non-Israeli, I don't know if I'm qualified to answer this question at all, but I think the issue is the *rabanut* being in charge of everything. Whether it's not allowing Conservative rabbis, or in terms of conversion or marriages or how they have a monopoly on everything. I think that needs to be changed." It was clear to me that she had strong feelings about the issue but was somewhat reluctant to share them. I reminded her that the interviews were confidential and that she should speak freely.

As Ellie elaborated, she demonstrated her knowledge of the Israeli rabbinate and its functioning:

> I think that conversions, if they're done by Conservative or Reform rabbis, should be considered conversions and people should not have to convert twice or be told that they're not Jewish or deemed less. I just feel that it's disrespectful and not okay.
>
> Separation between church and state, that's what [it] comes down to. It's really hard to have a Jewish nation because there are so many different denominations and how can you have a government? How can you have different sects in Judaism and at the same time say, "Oh no, only what this one believes is what we're going to do"? It's insulting to people and it's not the Jewish way. Conservative and Reform rabbis should be able to officiate at weddings without having an Orthodox rabbi sign off on it. I think that should just be done, but obviously I'm very biased, but that's okay.

In a paragraph, she displays her knowledge of several different controversies, such as recognition of non-Orthodox conversions and marriages, but she also frames her response in philosophical terms. She identifies the fundamental issue of separation of church and state and also reflects on the challenge of constituting a Jewish state made up of a diverse Jewish population. Ellie goes beyond listing facts. She can organize what she knows into a coherent and compelling perspective.

Like Isaac, Ellie felt strongly about the issue she was discussing. As a committed Conservative Jew, Ellie was highly conscious of the rabbinate's attitudes toward non-Orthodox Jews. She saw these attitudes as disrespectful of her as a person.

Nonetheless, she was able to play devil's advocate and argue on behalf of the policies she found discriminatory. I asked her, "Can you imagine someone disagreeing with you? What do you think they would say?" She responded, "They would say that it's not a conversion. You need a Beit Din [a Jewish legal court]. You need to follow halakha and in some cases [of non-Orthodox practices] not all the halakha is met." Ellie gave examples of some of the differences between Orthodox and Conservative conversion procedures.

It's worth emphasizing the care with which Isaac and Ellie played devil's advocate. Even though they each had a clear stance on the issue they discussed, they had no trouble speaking with the voice of someone who disagreed with them. Each articulated a strong counterpoint. Indeed, their capacity to explain both sides of the issue makes the depth of their knowledge clear.

The comparison between the two groups of students suggests that "knowledge" of Israel doesn't depend on knowing any particular facts. Instead, students who "know" about Israel can speak with a high degree of detail about several areas of Israeli life. Even more, they can use those details. They can organize what they know in order to articulate a range of positions on an issue. They can explain what they think and why, but strikingly, they can also play devil's advocate. They present opposing viewpoints not as straw men to be knocked down, but as positions worth engaging.

Discussion

For the most part, Israel educators want their students to feel connected to Israel and to know about Israel. Despite these two goals, the field has spent the last several decades focused more on students' feelings than on their knowledge. As American Jews learned more about Israel, particularly since the 1980s, they have discovered that, like any country, Israel is not always easy to love. This fact sparked thirty years of articles designed to show that loving Israel is fully compatible with learning about the darker parts of Israel's past and present. In other words, educators and researchers have assumed that knowledge is an obstacle, albeit a surmountable one, to feeling connected to Israel.

This study reported the efforts of one group of day school teachers to articulate new educational goals for school-wide Israel education. We agreed that our students should be knowledgeable and connected, but quickly realized that we, like the rest of the field, did not agree about what "knowledge" and "connection" meant. To shed light on our goals, we began descriptively. We interviewed a diverse set of ten high school students to produce some empirical portraits of what our students knew and felt about Israel.

Their answers suggested new ways of conceptualizing knowledge and feeling as goals of Israel education. It found that the intensity of students' relationships to Israel may reveal more about their connection than whether they feel "good" or "bad" about Israel. Clara, for example, had generally positive feelings about Israel. She described it as an interesting place with good food. She saw it as a fun tourist destination. Ellie, on the other hand, seemed much more ambivalent. She expressed disappointment in Israel for failing to live up to her values. She talked about the way that Israel's government devalued her as a Conservative Jew. Her comments revealed serious engagement with the challenges facing Israeli society. Clara feels good about Israel; Ellie's feelings are mixed. But could it make sense to describe Clara as more "connected" to Israel than Ellie?

This example is, perhaps, a subtle one. But it's easy to imagine extending it further. These interviews were conducted when these students were in tenth grade several months before they traveled to Israel as a class. Imagine that Clara comes back with photos of herself standing by the Dead Sea and describes how beautiful Israel is and talks about the incredible experiences she had. Imagine that Ellie comes back from Israel convinced that states should not have official religions. What if her disappointment in the Israeli rabbinate transforms into doubts about the necessity of a Jewish nation-state at all? Even in this case, it doesn't seem helpful to describe Clara as more connected than Ellie. For Clara, Israel is a fun travel destination; for Ellie, figuring out her relationship to Israel is central to who she is as a person. Of course, we could limit "connection" to positive feelings, but that choice would necessarily valorize Clara's more shallow relationship and delegitimize Ellie's deep investment.

Students' answers also suggested that educators must expand their conception of what counts as "knowing about Israel." Some students know little about Israel politics, but read Israeli novels and watch Israeli movies and television. We may still want to consider those students knowledgeable. Offering students more ways to know about Israel begins to spell out what it would mean to move from a deficit model of Israel knowledge to an inventory model.

But knowledge of Israel goes beyond detailed knowledge of a particular domain. In the interviews, there were clear differences in the ways students used what they knew to form positions and articulate disagreements. Some students struggled to organize their knowledge into a position. Their knowledge remained "in pieces" (DiSessa, 1993). Others could articulate a position, but they couldn't put that position in relationship with other possible positions. They struggled to imagine what a devil's advocate might say. Finally, some students could articulate multiple conflicting answers to the same question, act out a debate between them, and then articular their reasons for choosing a single perspective. These students' answers point toward a new way to conceptualize knowledge of Israel: detailed knowledge combined with the ability to use that knowledge. This study suggests that knowing about Israel includes being able to use one's knowledge to take a stance on a question or issue.

Above all, this study suggests that it may not be as easy to separate knowledge and feeling as many Israel educators have thought. A person, it has been assumed, can be deeply connected to Israel without knowing much about it; a person can know about Israel without being connected to it. Indeed, Sinclair (2009) suggests that many American Jewish leaders are connected to Israel but are not particularly knowledgeable. He contrasts them with an imagined CNN Middle East correspondent who may know a lot without being connected to Israel.

But I wonder about these two examples: the ignorant but highly connected American Jew and the knowledgeable but disconnected journalist. Can we really imagine a Middle East correspondent living in Jerusalem, spending her days covering Israeli politics, and living as a member of Israeli society without becoming invested in Israel? How invested does she have to be before she is "connected"? Indeed, while some of the students in this study expressed deep love of Israel without deep knowledge, all of the students with deep knowledge also expressed a deep connection to Israel. It's hard to imagine a person like Ellie, who knows about the Israeli rabbinate and has a strong position about its appropriate role, seeing the conversation as a purely academic one. Whatever her opinions may be, it's hard to believe that it would make sense to describe her as "disconnected."

By the same token, what could it mean to care deeply about something but know little about it? If we include adamant statements of devotion as connection, then we can surely find many examples of people who know little but love deeply. But my conversations with students during this project made me wonder whether connection without knowledge can be called connection at all. Students' responses suggested that knowledge and feeling may only develop in conversation with each other.

These findings suggest that Israel educators must reevaluate their priorities. The "hugging and wrestling" approach, which emerged in the 1990s, opened up avenues for students to explore problematic episodes in Israel's history. Nonetheless, practitioners still enshrined positive feelings toward Israel as a necessary outcome of Israel education. This commitment to a particular affective outcome constrains Israel curricula to too great an extent. Teachers articulate versions of a developmental approach in which students may encounter problematic episodes in Israel's history but only after they have built a foundation of love.

The students in this study raise the possibility that students develop deep connections to Israel not in parallel to their study of Israel but as part and parcel of that study. Students can develop a deep and lasting connection to Israel by studying the relationship between religion and government in Israel, by learning about Israel's economic growth and growing economic inequality, and yes, even by studying the Palestinian Israeli conflict. These topics offer pathways toward deep understanding of Israel. A student's deep understanding can itself foster deep connection.

Educators and funders, therefore, must abandon developmental language in Israel education—the idea that students must first learn love and only later add knowledge. Activities and rituals aimed at cultivating feeling have their place, but they are in no way the primary avenue for developing connection to Israel. Instead, educators, curriculum developers, and funders must focus on developing high-quality educational materials that offer students as many avenues as possible for deep inquiry into Israel's history, politics, and culture.

NOTES

1. Editors' Note: The research for this chapter was conducted before the October 7, 2023, Hamas attacks on Israel and the ensuing war and its effects. Therefore, readers should be mindful of the very different circumstances in which this material was developed, while considering the ways that the findings in this chapter may remain relevant today.

2. Sinclair credits Robbie Gringrass and Esti Moskowitz Kalman for conceiving of the matrix.

REFERENCES

Bransford, J. D., Brown, A. L., & Cocking, R. R. (2000). *How people learn* (Vol. 11). National Academy Press.

Cohen, S. M. (1983). The 1981–1982 national survey of American Jews. *American Jewish Year Book*, *83*, 89–110.

Cohen, S. M., & Kelman, A. Y. (2010). Thinking about distancing from Israel. *Contemporary Jewry*, *30*(2–3), 287–296.

Corbin, J., & Strauss, A. (2008). *Basics of qualitative research*. Sage Publications.

DiSessa, A. A. (1993). Toward an epistemology of physics. *Cognition and Instruction*, *10*(2–3), 105–225.

Eisen, A., & Rosenak, M. (1997). *Israel in our lives*. Joint Authority for Jewish Zionist Education.

Eizenstat, S. E. (1990). Loving Israel. Warts and all. *Foreign Policy*, 81, 87–105.

Elazar, D. J. (1995). *Community and polity: The organizational dynamics of American Jewry*. Jewish Publication Society.

Freire, P. (2018). *Pedagogy of the oppressed*. Bloomsbury Publishing.

Gringras, R. (2004, May 13). Hugging and wrestling. http://makomisrael.org/blog/hugging-and-wrestling-2/.

Hassenfeld, J. (2014). *The limits of students' love for Israel*. www.tabletmag.com/scroll/175504/the-limits-of-students-love-for-israel/.

Hassenfeld, J. (2016). Negotiating critical analysis and collective belonging: Jewish American students write the history of Israel. *Contemporary Jewry*, *36*(1), 55–84.

Horowitz, B. (2012). *Defining Israel education*. iCenter.

Kopelowitz, E., & Grant, L. (2012). *Israel education matters*. Center for Jewish Peoplehood Education.

Koren, A., Fishman, S., Krasner Aronson, J., & Saxe, L. (2015). *The Israel literacy measurement project: 2015 report*. Cohen Center for Modern Jewish Studies.

Patton, M. Q. (2002). *Qualitative research and evaluation methods*. Sage.

Pew Research Center. (2013) *A portrait of Jewish Americans*. www.pewforum.org/files/2013/10/jewish-american-full-report-for-web.pdf/.

Pomson, A., & Deitcher, H. (2010). Day school Israel education in the age of Birthright. *Journal of Jewish Education*, *76*(1), 52–73.

Pomson, A., Wertheimer, J., & Hacohen Wolf, H. (2014). *Hearts and minds*. AVI CHAI Foundation.

Rosov Consulting. (2018). *Devoted, disengaged, disillusioned: The forces that shape a relationship with Israel.*

Sasson, T. (2014). *The new American Zionism*. New York University Press.

Sasson, T., Kadushin, C., & Saxe, L. (2010). Trends in American Jewish attachment to Israel: An assessment of the "distancing" hypothesis. *Contemporary Jewry, 30*(2–3), 297–319.

Saxe, L. (2012). *The impact of Taglit-Birthright Israel: 2012 update.* Cohen Center for Modern Jewish Studies.

Saxe, L., & Chazan, B. I. (2008). *Ten days of Birthright Israel*. Brandeis University Press.

Sinclair, A. (2009). A new heuristic device for the analysis of Israel education: Observations from a Jewish summer camp. *Journal of Jewish Education, 75*(1), 79–106.

Sinclair, A. (2013). *Loving the real Israel: An educational agenda for liberal Zionism*. Ben Yehuda Press.

Sinclair, A., Solmsen, B., & Goldwater, C. (2013, May 13). The Israel educator. Casje.com. http://casje.com/wp-content/uploads/2013/06/The-Israel-Educator.pdf/.

Small, M. L. (2009). How many cases do I need? On science and the logic of case selection in field-based research. *Ethnography, 10*(1), 5–38.

Zakai, S. (2014). "My heart is in the East and I am in the West": Enduring questions of Israel education in North America. *Journal of Jewish Education, 80*(3), 287–318.

Zakai, S. (2015). "Israel is meant for me": Kindergarteners' conceptions of Israel. *Journal of Jewish Education, 81*(1), 4–34.

Zakai, S. (2019). From the mouths of children: Widening the scope and shifting the focus of understanding the relationships between American Jews and Israel. *Contemporary Jewry*, 17–29.

3

Intercomprehending in Action

Text-Based Discussion in a Seventh-Grade Bible Classroom

ZIVA R. HASSENFELD

Introduction

It was midyear in Mr. Suffon's second-grade Jewish studies class and the students were studying Genesis 39, the story of Potiphar putting Joseph in charge of everything in his house. Everything except for the "food [literally: bread] that he ate" (Genesis 39:6). The students were taken by the word *lehem* (bread) and why this was withheld from Joseph's charge. One student, Adin, commented, "Speaking of bread, I think it connects to the [Joseph's] brothers. They sit to eat bread after they throw him in the pit. It could be that Potiphar knows his brothers or something." Another student, Rachel, excitedly jumped in: "Potiphar may have been the guy in the grass." A third student, Gil, seemingly aware of what Rachel and Adin were talking about, built on their connections: "That's why he [Potiphar] came so quickly to the place. Potiphar could have come all the way from there knowing Joseph was thrown into the pit. So he probably was the man." And finally, a fourth student, Amy, jumped in to summarize the incredible interpretive realization of the class: "He was the guy that the Ishmaelites sold Joseph to! So it might mean something bad for Joseph. His brothers ate bread after throwing him in the pit, so maybe Potiphar saving the bread means something bad will happen to Joseph!"

In the course of four talk turns, these seven-year-old students pulled together disparate characters, plotlines, and motivations. They decided, collectively, that the withholding of "bread" by Potiphar was a foreshadowing symbol that appeared throughout the Joseph saga. The appearance of bread signaled that something bad was about to happen to Joseph. Shifting the conventional understanding of symbols as a literary device employed by the author to a tangible prop knowingly employed by the characters themselves, the students decided together that the reemergence of bread in the Potiphar scene means Potiphar must have known Joseph's brothers who ate bread after throwing him in the pit (Genesis 37:25). Who, then, could Potiphar be? Someone involved in the initial sale of Joseph from the pit to Ishmaelites going to Egypt.

Putting aside the question of whether this interpretation is compelling, there is another, more pedagogically pressing question to consider: Who does this interpretation belong to? The interpretation does not belong to any single student. It emerged collaboratively. Adin contributed Joseph's brothers, Rachel contributed the man in the grass, Gil connected him to Potiphar, and Amy resolved the significance of bread. Together they decided that Potiphar was present at the assault and sale of Joseph by his brothers and that his presence at the scene adds resonance to the evolving symbol of bread in the text as an omen of bad things to come for Joseph. Bread was eaten at the scene of the assault, and at this point in the story, with Potiphar and Joseph, bread has come to symbolize bad things to come. Whatever the merit of the interpretation, it certainly was a group effort.

This chapter will argue several connected points. First, I will make the case for student-directed text discussion as an essential component of any text-based classroom. Second, I will outline the contours of a pedagogy that facilitates student-directed text discussion called dialogic instruction. Third, I will suggest that the very important comprehension work that such discussion facilitates among students is collaborative. When done well, the fiber of a student-directed text discussion is not an exchange of interpretations (where discussion is an opportunity for students to use their classmates as a sounding board to clarify, sharpen, and challenge *their own* independent interpretations). Rather, it is *a space where interpretations are co-constructed*. Classroom text discussion can facilitate a process of textual interpretation that goes beyond an individual project to become a collective project. Ideas about text can come into being through talk, contingent on the dialogue that unfolds, and collectively constructed and reconstructed in the course of discussion (Aukerman & Schuldt, 2015).

This chapter draws on data from my seventh-grade Tanakh classroom in a community day school, collected in the course of a two-year teacher research project (Hassenfeld, 2024). This chapter examines a phenomenon coined in literacy education as intercomprehending, which is defined as "the emergent, responsive work that readers undertake to make sense of a text while engaged in dialogue that builds, and builds on, a collaborative ideational repertoire" (Aukerman et al., 2017, p. 489). Close analysis of classroom talk from my seventh-grade Tanakh classroom shows how class discussion became the canvas upon which interpretations were co-constructed and ultimately built collectively among my students. For some, the difference between *exchanging* interpretations and *constructing* them may seem like a distinction without a difference. But, as I will argue at the end of this chapter, recognizing the fact that students' interpretations are constructed *through* talk has significant implications for the place of classroom discussion in curricula.

The Role of Discussion in Comprehension

Research in education continues to show that classroom text discussions are important for student learning. Several studies document gains in students' skills and knowledge following time in classrooms that prioritize text discussions. These include improved reasoning in new contexts, deeper conceptual understanding, increased inferential comprehension of text, and enhanced quality of argumentative writing (Asterhan & Schwartz, 2007; Reznitskaya et al., 2009). Nystrand and Gamoran (1991) conducted the largest correlational study to date of the relationship between class text discussion and students' comprehension. They observed the instructional practices in fifty-eight eighth-grade and fifty-four ninth-grade language arts and English classes in eight Midwestern communities in the United States. Their results indicated that classroom text discussion positively correlated with students' reading comprehension, as measured by recall and depth of understanding, as well as response to aesthetic aspects of literature. Similar results have been reported in other, smaller, more recent correlational studies (Langer, 2001; Wells, 1999; Saunders & Goldenberg, 1999).

The importance of talking to learn is now better understood among educators and researchers (Juzwik et al., 2013). Exploratory and expressive talk (and writing), times in instruction where "demands of correctness

[are] relaxed and teacher judgments [are] suspended" in service of creating space for students to develop their thinking, is now considered best practice (Nystrand, foreword in Juzwik et al., 2013, p. ix) by many educators, coaches, and scholars. Classroom discourse, we understand now, facilitates learning of all subjects better than recitation and lecture (Cazden, 2001). Juzwik et al. (2013, pp. 4–6) explain:

> Educational research consistently shows that dialogic teaching supports not only students' literacy learning but also their engagement in that learning... Research robustly correlates dialogic instructional practices with literacy achievement gains in reading comprehension, literary analysis and argumentative writing... research is clear on the learning benefits associated with dialogic teaching.

Classroom dialogue and discourse, in this view, serves as a step toward comprehension. Thinking out loud with others around text helps students recognize the thinking inherent in writing. This in turn allows them to understand the text better and to understand their own thinking better (Plaut, 2009).

The preceding argument suggests that text discussion in classroom dialogue and discourse is important because it *aids* in comprehension. It reflects most prominent theories of text discussion that understand interpretation as a process of individual meaning-making. Grounded mainly in cognitive models of learning, the idea is that discussions allow individuals to clarify, maybe even discover, their *own* ideas. Aukerman et al. (2017, p. 485) explain:

> A number of seminal theoretical works on meaning-making emphasize the individual reader, with limited attention to anything beyond the reader and the text. This is true of many traditional cognitive models of reading, such as schema theory (Rumelhart, 1981), which posits individuals as constructing meaning out of available schemas that help them establish a meaning for a text. It is equally true of many reader response models of reading, such as Rosenblatt's (1978) vision of the reading of literature as an aesthetic, personal transaction between the reader and the text.

But is this how reading works? An alternative theory that I will explore in this chapter argues that there is no comprehension without discussion. That is, text discussion is not a *tool* for achieving comprehension, but rather it *is* comprehension. Elizabeth Long (1982) writes about the iconographic history of portraying the reader and writer as alone and solitary and how this has contributed to "the theoretical location of reading in the private sphere or, more extremely, in the heads of isolated individuals" (p. 190). In our popular image, reading is a solitary act, done in private on one's own. We ignore all the ways that reading is fundamentally social. Long reminds us not only of how we have failed to recognize reading as social but also how we have worked hard as a society to imagine it as the opposite, as private and personal.

This alternative theory in which discussion is paramount to comprehension is rooted in the work of literary theorist Mikhail Bakhtin. It holds that dialogue shapes language and thought. Through dialogue, we respond to previous utterances and anticipate future responses. The tension that emerges between conversants, between self and other, as one voice "refracts" the second voice, is the critical sociocognitive event where a person's comprehension emerges (Nystrand, foreword in Juzwik et al., 2013, pp. ix–xi).

What does it mean for students to actively construct knowledge? It means allowing students to pursue inquiry. Jean-Jacques Rousseau's *Emile* (1905), John Dewey's *Democracy and Education* (2015), and Paulo Freire's *Pedagogy of the Oppressed* (1971) all start from the principle that the best education is rooted in a process of inquiry. It means starting with "real" questions that are generated by students' firsthand engagement with topics and problems that they are genuinely interested in. In classrooms where texts are studied, this is often as simple as allowing students to follow their own interpretive interests when they discuss the texts.

What happens during student inquiry–driven text discussion when done well? I believe this sort of instruction, and the pedagogies that support it, are not just valuable but essential to the reading process (Hassenfeld, 2019b; Hassenfeld et al., 2022; Hassenfeld, 2024). Intercomprehending refers to those moments when students' meaning-making is collaborative with the interconnected play of ideas among students. Students' ideas, however firmly and defiantly presented, reveal themselves as emergent, unfolding, and contingent on ideas already raised by classmates. Intercomprehending shines a light on a yet under-theorized phenomenon that happens during text discussion. This phenomenon is where students articulate proto-interpretations that then, through the process of talk and only with talk, evolve into fully developed interpretations, in conversation with, and co-constructed by, their classmates.

My Teaching Context

The Jewish day school at which I taught is part of a universe of Jewish day schools in North America. The growth of these schools was called "one of the most remarkable social facts of North American Jewish life" (Pomson, 2008, p. 306). Enrollment in American Jewish day schools reached 292,172 students by 2019, a 58.5 percent increase between the 1998–1999 and 2018–2019 school years (Besser, 2020). As in most Jewish day schools, Shalom Academy (pseudonym), the K–8 Jewish day school at which I taught, split the school day between Jewish studies and Hebrew language, on the one hand, and secular classes in language arts, mathematics, science, social studies, technology, the arts, and physical education, on the other.

Shalom Academy describes itself as "pluralistic." It accepts all Jewish students regardless of their beliefs or denominational affiliations. In its mission, it seeks to provide intentional opportunities for students to talk with each other about their different beliefs and relationships to Jewish culture. In this manner, Shalom Academy is distinct from the more common "community" Jewish day school, where diversity of Jewish practice is a reality of the demographics (all Jews are accepted into these schools regardless of practice) but not a celebrated feature of the schools. Shalom Academy, as a "pluralistic" school, sees the diversity in its school as a central asset of the curriculum and culture of the school. Shalom Academy does not have a strong commitment to any particular approach to Hebrew Bible instruction, though it does prioritize Hebrew language skills in both modern Hebrew and biblical Hebrew.

The biblical texts I taught were short excerpts that contained a compelling narrative arc, including character development, rich language, and conflict among characters. They ranged in length from eight to sixteen verses. To understand the interpretive work my students did in the class, it's important to understand that every biblical text discussed was presented to the students in the original biblical Hebrew, which required significant translation work. While students' comments and discussions were always in English, they were asked to read and respond to the biblical text in its biblical Hebrew. Reading the biblical text in the original biblical Hebrew required significant instructional scaffolding.

Because biblical Hebrew is such a complex language (Hassenfeld, 2019a; Hassenfeld, 2020; Hassenfeld et al., 2022; Walker & Goldberg, 2017) and my students were at very different levels with their biblical Hebrew comprehension, the study of the biblical texts in their original Hebrew required the following:

1. Creating different versions of the text with different levels of biblical Hebrew and English to differentiate for students' varying skill levels.
2. Choosing excerpts of biblical texts that weren't too long so that the biblical Hebrew was not overwhelming.
3. Spending time before each new text reviewing key biblical Hebrew vocabulary and grammatical constructs (and even syntactic structures unique to the Bible) that were going to show up in the next text the students were going to study.

I created my own translations for every text I taught. I consulted other translations I valued (e.g., Alter, 2019; Fox, 1995) as well as dictionaries and lexicons (*The Brown, Driver, Briggs Hebrew and English Lexicon*, 2007; Gesenius's *Hebrew Grammar*, 2006). I moved among them and put together a translation that balanced fidelity to the flow and form of the biblical Hebrew (a syntactic translation), easy comprehension (a semantic translation), and use of dictionary definitions as they appeared in the dictionary my students were using, the *Brown, Driver, Briggs Hebrew and English Lexicon* (a pragmatic translation). The goal was to make sure all the students arrived at the same translation for key phrases and words, whether they were translating on their own or using my translation. Besides any designated key phrases and words, my curriculum included twelve units with twelve texts.

Unit 1: God Commands Abraham to Leave, Genesis 11:30–12:7
Unit 2: A Famine in the New Land, Genesis 12:10–12:20

Unit 3: God Promises Descendants, Genesis 15:1–15:8
Unit 4: Sarah, Abraham, and Hagar, Genesis 16:1–16:10
Unit 5: God Promises Abraham and Sarah a Child, Genesis 18:1–18:15
Unit 6: Sodom and Gomorrah, Genesis 19:1–19:13
Unit 7: The Birth of Isaac, Genesis 21:1–21:8
Unit 8: The Akeda (Binding of Isaac), Genesis 22:1–22:13
Unit 9: Creation of Humans, Genesis 2:7–2:10, 2:15–2:25
Unit 10: Garden of Eden, Genesis 3:1–3:13
Unit 11: Cain and Abel, Genesis 4:1–4:16
Unit 12: The Aftermath of the Flood, Genesis 9:1–9:15

Each unit's cycle of classes moved students through the following activities, all designed to help the students understand the texts in the original biblical Hebrew:

1. Exposure to necessary background information
2. Preview of relevant vocabulary and grammatical constructs
3. Reading aloud
4. Translating the text in pairs (*hevruta*)
5. Generating questions
6. Reading *parshanut* (classical Jewish commentaries)
7. Reader's theater
8. Whole-class discussion

This was the structure of the class for every unit. The focus of this article is activity 8, but the class couldn't get to the whole-class culminating text discussions without all the work that came before.

When I began teaching my seventh-grade class, I wanted to prioritize student inquiry–driven text discussions. To do so, I committed myself to practicing dialogic instruction (Nystrand et al., 1997). Dialogic instruction is a pedagogy that grows out of the theoretical and empirical research on talking to learn and collaborative learning discussed previously. It focuses on shifting interpretive authority from the teacher to the students, distributing both interpretation and talk turns more evenly across the classroom (Aukerman & Schuldt, 2015; Juzwik et al., 2013). In dialogic instruction, students propose ideas, ask questions, debate, and work together to make meaning of what they read. Crucially, in dialogic instruction, the teacher refrains from evaluating a student's comment. The teacher plays the role of facilitator, ensuring the free flow of ideas without imposing direction or evaluation of the conversation.

One way to conceptualize the difference between dialogic instruction and more traditional pedagogies is through the distinction between inauthentic and authentic questions (Cazden, 2001). A teacher's question is inauthentic if the teacher has a particular answer in mind. When teachers structure their lessons as a series of inauthentic questions, they may give the appearance of encouraging student participation, but what they are encouraging is student passivity in the face of teachers' transmission of their authoritative interpretations emerging through a series of answers to inauthentic questions. What, then, makes an "authentic" question? One can't always tell whether a question is authentic merely because it is open-ended. A teacher might ask students, "What do you notice in this poem?" This question is only authentic if the teacher genuinely intends for students to share what they notice. If the question is posed because the teacher wants them to notice the rhyme scheme, then the question isn't authentic, but simply a vehicle for the teacher to elicit what she wants her students to say.

This is not to say anything goes. In my classroom, I used my teacher authority not to push particular interpretations on students but to enforce certain text-based interpretive rules as guideposts for their conversation (Hassenfeld, 2024). I asked that text discussion stay focused on the words in the text and not stray into other background knowledge of biblical texts. I asked that my students consider the words as intentional and full of potential meaning and not write odd phrases off as mistakes or errors in the text. And I asked my students not to consider authorial intent because we didn't necessarily have a shared understanding of authorship for biblical texts. As long as my students were following these rules, the interpretive conversation was theirs.

Intercomprehending in My Classroom: Sarah, Hagar, Abraham, and God

From the perspective of character development and character motivation, Genesis 16 is one of the most puzzling texts in Tanakh. This is the story of

Sarah instructing Abraham to use Sarah's maidservant Hagar as a surrogate to have a child and the disharmony that ensues. The quick plot development that takes place in the short chapter, the raw emotion expressed by each of the characters (Sarah, for example, yelling at her husband that God must judge between them and Abraham's cold dismissive response), combined with the haunting ellipses and lack of details, leaves the discerning reader grasping for answers.

The interpretive potential of the text was not lost on my students. After two weeks of preparing the text, translating the Hebrew, brainstorming questions, and studying commentators, the class was ready for the culminating activity of each unit in my class: whole-class text discussion (Hassenfeld, 2019a). The students were excited and eager. At the top of their agenda was procuring a judgment on Sarah.

In the class there seemed to be a unanimous negative evaluation of Sarah until one student, Greg, raised his hand and offered an alternative understanding of Sarah. Greg said:

> I feel like everyone is taking a critical stance toward Sarai, like she should have seen this coming. But when we see that the text says "listened to the voice of Sarai" (16:2) couldn't that be, we've heard commentaries, like it could be that she didn't think it through, but couldn't that also be God's voice? We looked a bit at that. So could Sarai not even mean it and could this be coming not from Sarai, but directly from God? And then her actions, therefore, are God's and not hers and that's partially why she's so outraged after.

Greg posited to the class that perhaps Sarah can't be held responsible for the poor decision to use Hagar as a surrogate because perhaps it wasn't her idea at all, but God's idea.

I will now present an abbreviated version of the discussion that ensued. The excerpt zooms in on the intercomprehending that took place among three students, Greg, Jessica, and Sam. Jessica immediately responded to Greg: "I disagree with Greg because why would God set up a plan that failed?" According to Jessica, Sarah acted consciously and autonomously in choosing Hagar to be a surrogate. It could not have been God's plan because the plan failed. Why Jessica believed that the surrogacy plan failed, especially given that a child was born to Hagar, was not clear. Before anyone could probe her interpretation, another classmate, Sam, offered his interpretation:

> I see a connection between "voice of Sarai" (16:2) and "hand of Sarai" (16:9), but I don't think it's necessarily God. Like Greg said, it's all part of His [God's] plan, but when it says "hand of Sarai" (16:9) I don't think that's God, I think there's a distinction right there. Now she's [Sarai's] back to being herself. First, it was God doing this, and then basically Sarai wakes up and is like, "Oh, my gosh, how did this happen? Okay, I need this to stop happening."

Sam was interested in a different question in the text, one Greg alluded to but did not focus on—Sarah's sudden change of heart in the story. Sam saw in Greg's interpretation an opportunity to answer his question. Sam suggested in his comment that Sarah's change of heart was due to the fact that at first she was under God's influence, as Greg suggested, but then she wasn't. To support this interpretation, Sam borrowed Greg's evidence of "voice of Sarai" (16:2) and added to it "hand of Sarai" [literally, "her hand"] (16:9). The parallelism, Sam argued, was a textual indication of when God's influence was controlling Sarah and when it wasn't. In other words, the contrast of "voice" and "hand" is a textual hint that Sarah's autonomy, suppressed by God's control at the beginning of the story, returned to Sarah later in the story.

Soon Jessica, following Sam's lead of examining Greg's textual support, offered another reason why Greg's interpretation was wrong:

> It says, "he listened to the voice of Sarai" (16:2). I think that's making it explicitly clear that this is the voice of Sarai and not of God because otherwise it would have said something else.

A few minutes later, Jessica found herself compelled to change her position on Sarah's initial autonomy. She offered her revised position:

> Before I thought it was Sarai's choice, but Sarai gets super mad afterward like she has no idea what she was doing. And I'm thinking, you

> literally just told him to do this. So it has to be, it wasn't even her. It was God speaking and then she woke up.

Jessica, vis-à-vis Sam and Sam's questions, came around to Greg's position. But Greg found himself no longer convinced:

> If everyone thinks she snapped out of it, that's the current theory, well, if it uses "voice of Sarai" (16:2) and there you guys are saying that was God, and then it says, "the hand of Sarai" (16:9), like if there is a parallel, how can you say one is God and one isn't? In the first God is possessing her but in the second she snaps out of it?! I think it's an all-or-nothing situation.

Greg, considering Sam's textual evidence, which was built off of Greg's initial textual evidence (Greg introduced "voice of Sarai" and Sam added "hand of Sarai"), decided that it has to be either Sarai was under the influence of God during the entire scene or during none of the scene. At the heart of this exchange was an effort to understand Sarah and her perplexing and eventually contradictory actions. Implicated in this exploration were God's motives and Abraham's actions. The exploration began with a general disapproval of Sarah's search for a surrogate and a potential way to excuse her request, relying on a rabbinic midrashic tradition students read in their preparation of the text. Then a new question was introduced by Sam: Why did Sarah get upset about the realization of her own plan? Uninterested in the *peshat*, or literal answer, that Hagar began to look down on Sarah (16:5), the three students pursued textual parallelism and symbolism. That is, they were willing to read the text together with the interpretive rule that words in the texts could have symbolic meanings and offer allusion beyond their literal meaning.

Greg started from an interpretation that Sarah's initial decision to offer Hagar as a surrogate was God's idea put into her head, and ended with the position that either it was or it was not. The textual parallelism introduced by Sam required one to hold that either she was under the influence of God the entire time or none of the time. Jessica started from the position that there was no way that "voice of Sarah" could indicate God's control over Sarah, and then evolved to the position that because of the change of heart/contradiction on Sarah's part, Sarah's initial request had to be God's idea put into her head. Sam took Greg's textual evidence and built on it to resolve Sarah's seemingly contradictory behavior.

By the end of the discussion, neither Sarah nor Greg's interpretations were their own. They were developed in response to one another (and other classmates) and evolved to incorporate different aspects of Sam's interpretation. This is intercomprehending in action. The students' meaning-making was collaborative. It was a tightly interconnected play of ideas that involved vehement disagreement and agreement. The students' ideas, though firmly and defiantly presented, revealed themselves to be emergent and cumulative, unfolding and contingent on ideas already raised.

Discussion

The theory of intercomprehending posits that something special happens when texts are discussed in groups. It offers teachers a new pedagogical perspective with which to go into whole-class, student-directed text discussions: curiosity about what children will do with each other's textual ideas, how they might bring to the shared sandbox of comprehension a not-yet fully formed interpretation, and how the class might, together, finish forming the interpretation. The theory of intercomprehending shines a light on the dynamics of text discussion. It is not a game of Ping-Pong or an interpretive "dog show" where every student parades around their interpretation. Rather, whole-class text discussion can be a unique and special space where students have the opportunity to build their interpretations together.

Maren Aukerman, who first coined the term intercomprehending, offers this insight: "Collaborative meaning-making amplifies [students'] resources when they are given opportunities to interpret text together in agentive and student-driven ways" (Aukerman et al., 2017, p. 504). Writing about her own findings among English language learners who were allowed to engage in dialogic whole-class discussion, Aukerman et al. (2017, p. 504) have this to say:

> Our findings provide empirical evidence that treating reading comprehension as constituted primarily in a stable binary reader-text

> relationship, as some scholars have proposed (e.g., Rumelhart, 1980), needs to be rethought . . . We theorize that the intercomprehending documented here occurred via interanimation of the reader, the text, and multiple other reader-interlocutors. We use the term interanimation to signal the ways in which these are not only interdependent but also breathe life into one another as readers make sense of text in the context of discussion. Where there is intercomprehending, student textual understandings evolve through dialogue with peers, as that dialogue occasions dynamic, contingent responsiveness.

Aukerman is careful to remind teachers that there is no reason to think that all students, in all contexts, engage in intercomprehending work similarly. She suggests that additional studies are needed in order to better understand what kinds of pedagogical parameters might need to be in place for intercomprehending to become visible in classroom dialogue. More work is needed to understand how intercomprehending might change or look different as children get older, as language proficiency changes, or even if the text genre is different. But the theory of intercomprehending "provides a meaningful contribution to the development of a robust theory" in making sense of "children's meaning-making as a social practice" (Aukerman et al., 2017, p. 505).

Recognizing the fact that students' interpretations are constructed *through* talk has significant implications for the place of classroom discussion in curricula. I once served on a dissertation committee for a doctoral thesis in which the doctoral student, a director of teaching and learning in a Jewish day school, conducted an intervention study in two elementary Jewish studies classrooms. As director of teaching and learning, she helped the teachers implement a "student-centered, student-autonomy-directed" Hebrew Bible unit. In the intervention, she pushed these two teachers, whose standard lesson plan involved choral reading, translation, and a teacher-led explanation of the moral of the text, to design a unit in which after the moral of the text was established, the students were then allowed to do a creative project that expressed the moral of the text.

In the dissertation defense, I asked her, "Is allowing these teachers to continue to teach the text in a didactic fashion but calling it student-centered because the kids get to make a poster at the end, not reifying the problem in Jewish education, that there is a serious absence of student voices in the textual meaning-making process?" To this, she responded, "Ziva, the idea that student questions and ideas about the text have value is so far from how these teachers understand their roles as religious educators, that such a goalpost is simply too far away in my school." This very honest and reflective response shook me. Let us contend seriously with what it means to prioritize student inquiry through discussion in a classroom. It is a fundamental shift not simply in final assignments but in the entire structure of a classroom. This sort of profound change requires profound appreciation of its purpose and importance. I hope the theory of intercomprehending helps articulate just that.

REFERENCES

Alter, R. (2019). *The Hebrew Bible: A translation with commentary* (1st ed.). W.W. Norton & Company.

Asterhan, C. S. C., & Schwarz, B. B. (2007). The effects of monological and dialogical argumentation on concept learning in evolutionary theory. *Journal of Educational Psychology*, *99*(3), 626–639. https://doi.org/10.1037/0022-0663.99.3.626/.

Aukerman, M., & Schuldt, L. C. (2015). Children's perceptions of their reading ability and epistemic roles in monologically and dialogically organized bilingual classrooms. *Journal of Literacy Research*, *47*(1), 115–145. https://doi.org/10.1177/1086296X15586959/.

Aukerman, M., Schuldt, L. C., Aiello, L., & Martin, P. C. (2017). What meaning-making means among us: The intercomprehending of emergent bilinguals in small-group text discussions. *Harvard Educational Review*, *87*(4), 482–511. https://doi.org/10.17763/1943-5045-87.4.482/.

Besser, M. (2020). *A census of Jewish day schools 2018–2019*. AVI CHAI Foundation. https://avichai.org/knowledge_base/a-census-of-jewish-day-schools-2018-2019-2020/.

Brown, F., Driver, S. R., Briggs, C. A., Robinson, E., Strong, J., & Gesenius, W. (2010). *The Brown, Driver, Briggs Hebrew and English lexicon: With an appendix containing the biblical Aramaic: Coded with the numbering system from Strong's Exhaustive Concordance of the Bible*. Hendrickson Publishers.

Cazden, C. B. (2001). *Classroom discourse: The language of teaching and learning* (2nd ed.). Heinemann.

Dewey, J. (2015). *Democracy and education*. Sheba Blake Publishing.

Fox, E. (1995). *The five books of Moses: Genesis, Exodus, Leviticus, Numbers, Deuteronomy*. Schocken.

Freire, P. (1971). *Pedagogy of the oppressed*. Herder and Herder.

Gesenius. (2006). *Hebrew grammar* (E. Kautzsch, ed.; A. E. Crowley, trans.). Dover.

Hassenfeld, Z. R. (2019a). Pursuing fluency: A curricular intervention in Tanakh education. *Journal of Jewish Education*, *85*(3), 293–311.

Hassenfeld, Z. R. (2019b). Studying sacred texts as a pathway to positive youth development: Middle school students read Hebrew Bible. *Religions, 10*(6), 397.

Hassenfeld, Z. R. (2020). A sacred language or the language of the Bible: A curricular study of Jewish Hebrew Bible instruction. *Religious Education, 115*(2), 158–170.

Hassenfeld, Z. (2022). A pedagogical approach to teaching biblical Hebrew in American day schools. *Journal of Jewish Education, 88*(4), 286–300.

Hassenfeld, Z. R. (2024). *The second conversation: Interpretive authority in the Bible classroom*. Brandeis University Press.

Hassenfeld, Z. R., Bogard, G., Fenwick, N., Stanhill, H., & Troper-Hochstein, G. (2022). First and second conversations: Remote learning and interpretive boundaries. *The Reading Teacher, 76*(3), 269–276.

Juzwik, M. M. (2014). American evangelical biblicism as literate practice: A critical review. *Reading Research Quarterly, 49*(3), 335–349.

Juzwik, M. M., Borsheim-Black, C., Caughlan, S. B., & Heintz, A. E. (2013). *Inspiring dialogue: Talking to learn in the English classroom. Language and Literacy Series*. Teachers College Press.

Kuhn, D., & Udell, W. (2003). The development of argument skills. *Child Development, 74*(5), 1245–1260. https://doi.org/10.1111/1467-8624.00605/.

Langer, J. A. (2001). Beating the odds: Teaching middle and high school students to read and write well. *American Educational Research Journal, 38*(4), 837–880. https://doi.org/10.3102/00028312038004837/.

Long, E. (1982). Textual interpretation as collective action. In J. Boyarin (ed.), *The ethnography of reading* (pp. 180–211). University of California Press.

Mercer, N., & Littleton, K. (2007). *Dialogue and the development of children's thinking: A sociocultural approach* (1st ed.). Routledge. https://doi.org/10.4324/9780203946657/.

Murphy, P. K., Wilkinson, I. A. G., Soter, A. O., Hennessey, M. N., & Alexander, J. F. (2009). Examining the effects of classroom discussion on students' comprehension of text: A meta-analysis. *Journal of Educational Psychology, 101*(3), 740–764. https://doi.org/10.1037/a0015576/.

Nystrand, M. (1997). *Opening dialogue: Understanding the dynamics of language and learning in the English classroom*. Teachers College Press.

Nystrand, M. (2013). Foreword. In Juzwik, M. M., Borsheim-Black, C., Caughlan, S. B., & Heintz, A. E. (eds.), *Inspiring dialogue: Talking to learn in the English classroom* (pp. ix–xi). Teachers College Press.

Nystrand, M., & Gamoran, A. (1991). Instructional discourse, student engagement, and literature achievement. *Research in the Teaching of English, 25*(3), 261–290.

Plaut, S. (ed.). (2009). *The right to literacy in secondary schools: Creating a culture of thinking*. Teachers College Press.

Pomson, A. (2008). "Dorks with yarmulkes": An ethnographic inquiry into the surprised embrace of parochial day schools by liberal American Jews. In Z. Bekerman & E. Kopelowitz (eds.), *Cultural education-cultural sustainability: Minority, diaspora, indigenous and ethno-religious groups in multicultural societies* (pp. 305–322). Routledge.

Reznitskaya, A., Kuo, L.-J., Clark, A.-M., Miller, B., Jadallah, M., Anderson, R. C., & Nguyen-Jahiel, K. (2009). Collaborative reasoning: A dialogic approach to group discussions. *Cambridge Journal of Education, 39*(1), 29–48. https://doi.org/10.1080/03057640802701952/.

Rousseau, J.-J. (1905). *Emile, or treatise on education* (W. H. Payne, ed.). D. Appleton and Company.

Saunders, W. M., & Goldenberg, C. (1999). Effects of instructional conversations and literature logs on limited- and fluent-English-proficient students' story comprehension and thematic understanding. *The Elementary School Journal*, 99(4), 277–301. https://doi.org/10.1086/461927/.

Walker, C., & Goldberg, S. (2017). *Learning Hebrew as a second or foreign language: Issues of directionality, orthography, and metalinguistic awareness* (Hebrew Language Education Literature Reviews). Consortium for Applied Studies in Jewish Education. www.casje.org/sites/default/files/docs/casje_hebrew_language_education_literature_review_-_chad_walker_-_20171129.pdf/.

Wells, C. G. (1999). *Dialogic.* Cambridge University Press.

4

Connected but Not Confident

The Gender Confidence Gap Regarding Israeli Politics and History[1]

ILANA M. HORWITZ

When Israel educators in Jewish day schools create curricula and lesson plans, they tend to focus on affective goals. They might ask themselves: How will my students feel about Israel at the end of this unit? As Pomson, Wertheimer, and Wolf found in their seminal study on Israel education in Jewish day schools, teachers' goals are "directed towards the cultivation of emotional states: identification, allegiance and attachment [toward Israel]" (2014, p. 10). Israel education, according to this study, is largely the work of the heart.

But is Israel education a success if students feel highly connected to Israel but don't feel confident talking about it? Confidence is a belief in our ability to succeed. Confidence is formed through self-efficacy beliefs, which are beliefs we hold about our capabilities and about the outcomes of our efforts (Bandura 1977). And it turns out that boys and girls have significantly different assessments about their abilities. Boys tend to overestimate their ability while girls tend to underestimate their ability—even when their abilities are the same (Ehrlinger & Dunning, 2003). The gender confidence gap exists in various domains and has long lasting effects (Pajares, 2005).

Gender confidence gaps are developed through stereotypes of gender roles. Math, science, and tech are viewed as male domains, which means that women have to contend with stereotypes that men are more competent in certain subjects (Gallagher & Kaufman, 2004). As girls progress through adolescence, their ideas about gender roles and achievement-related beliefs intensify (Hill & Lynch, 1983; Widgefield & Eccles, 2000). Based on studies of mathematics, boys and girls report similar confidence in their math ability during elementary years, but differences emerge in middle/junior high (Midgley et al., 1989; Usher & Pajares, 2008). Consequently, girls are less likely to major in math-related fields and pursue math-related careers. Various efforts are underway in public schools to close these gender confidence gaps, especially in math and science (Halpern et al., 2007).

Based on my analysis of surveys from 3,703 middle and high school students nested in 96 Jewish day schools in the United States and Canada, I describe a gender confidence gap[2] that is unique to Jewish day schools: girls are significantly less confident than boys discussing Israeli history and politics. This gender confidence gap exists in about four of every five Jewish day schools.[3] It is evident regardless of school denomination and grade level. This gender confidence gap is already in place among seventh/eighth graders and persists throughout high school. Let me put this in perspective: girls at the cusp of graduating high school (eleventh/twelfth graders) are about as confident (and in some cases less confident) discussing Israeli politics and history as boys who recently became bar mitzvah (seventh/eighth graders).

The Hearts and Minds Study

The findings I present about the gender confidence gap are based on data from the Hearts and Minds: Israel in North American Jewish Day Schools study, which was a multipronged effort to learn about Israel education in Jewish day schools (Pomson et al., 2014). During the 2012–2013 school year, 4,030 middle and upper school students in 96 Jewish day schools completed a survey designed to capture how they think about Israel, how confident they feel in talking about it, which aspects of Israel resonate the most and the least with them, and how Israel fits into their larger worldview.

The Hearts and Mindy study was an unprecedented study in terms of its research design. It was the first systematic attempt to gather data about Jewish day schools from school administrators, teachers, and students. One of the most unique elements of this study was that students were nested within schools. This dataset is also unique because the sample of schools and students is large enough to make inferences. The nested structure of these data, along with the large sample sizes, allows for more sophisticated analyses that might yield important new insights about Jewish day schools. Given the usefulness of this data, it is worthwhile to conduct further analyses that didn't fall into the scope of the original Hearts and Minds report. (See chapter 5, where Aronson and de Kramer present secondary analyses of these data.)

One particular finding from the Hearts and Minds study warrants further attention: Pomson et al. found that girls were less confident than boys in their ability to discuss the history of Zionism and Israel (2014, p. 39). In a footnote, Pomson and his colleagues say that this finding is consistent with extensive research showing that girls are less confident than boys, even when they have equal ability. The authors do not provide further analysis beyond this point. In this chapter, I expand upon their original finding by describing this gender confidence gap in greater detail. I show how students' confidence varies by grade level and by school denomination. I also explore potential reasons for the confidence gap. My goal is to provide a descriptive analysis that can help uncover why the gender confidence gap exists so that it can eventually be eradicated.

How Was the Sample of Day Schools and Students Constructed?

The research team constructed their sample of schools and students in the following way. First, they looked at the then most recent census of US Jewish day schools (Schick, 2009) to see how schools broke down by affiliation and region. The research team also included approximately 60 Canadian day schools. Although about 62 percent of all day school students in the United States are enrolled in haredi (ultra-Orthodox) or Chasidic schools, the research team did not ask these schools to participate in the survey because "the schools in this sector do not engage in the kinds of educational practices conventionally recognized as Israel education" (2014, p. 57).

Next, the research team surveyed administrators at approximately 286 non-haredi schools to provide an inventory of school characteristics. The inventory yielded responses from 154 schools. From this list, the research team identified a purposive sample of 100 schools to participate in the study. They employed a stratified purposive sampling strategy by dividing schools into "strata" based on religious denomination. Then, they selected a variety of "cases" within each stratum to represent the additional relevant variables (grade level, geographic location, and size). They developed a list of ranked invitees within each stratum that best matched their intention to construct a diverse sample. If a more highly desired school declined to participate, they moved down the list, endeavoring to preserve a balance of variables that reflected the broader composition of the day school sector.

Ultimately, 96 schools participated in the study. These include Centrist Orthodox, Modern Orthodox, Conservative, Reform, and community day schools. These sectors enroll approximately 38 percent of day school students. As the research team noted, "These schools do not constitute a random sample of the universe of North American Jewish day schools: Those that opted in are probably predisposed to learn more about Israel education. It is not unreasonable to assume that schools in our sample have a greater commitment to Israel education than those that chose not to participate" (2014, p. 7).

Participating schools were asked to field an online survey to all students in the relevant grades. By way of incentive, schools were offered an Amazon gift voucher worth the equivalent of $10 for each completed student survey. The target population for the student survey was young people in eighth and twelfth grades because these are the capstone years of middle and high school. The research team did not include institutions that had fewer than 15 students in a grade. They also did not include schools in which the relevant cohort of students had returned from an Israel experience within the previous three months because they "were concerned that a recent class trip to Israel would result in a halo effect of especially warm feelings toward Israel" (2014, p. 58). Because of some concerns about sample size, the research team also surveyed a small number of seventh- and eleventh-grade students who had not yet gone on a recent class trip to Israel. Ultimately, 4,030 students provided usable survey data. This includes 195 seventh graders; 2,340 eighth graders; 361 eleventh graders; and 1,139 twelfth graders.[4]

Who Is in My Analytic Sample?

When I conducted my analysis, I dropped 5 percent of respondents who didn't indicate their gender (n=189), and 3 percent of respondents who didn't respond to items related to their confidence levels (n=138). This yielded a sample of 3,703 from schools in the United States and Canada, and 2,995 students who were in the US-only sample (I differentiate between the two samples because in parts of the analysis, I examine only US students). Since there were so few seventh- and eleventh-grade students, I pooled seventh/eighth-grade students, and eleventh/twelfth-grade students, respectively. About 60 percent of the sample are seventh/eighth-grade students, while 40 percent are eleventh/twelfth-grade students (see table 4.1). About half of the sample (52 percent) identify as female. Approximately 36 percent of respondents from the full sample attend Orthodox schools, 14 percent attend Conservative schools, 47 percent attend community schools, and 3 percent attend Reform schools. In column 3, I compare the data from my sample to data from the US census of Jewish day schools (Schick, 2009). The main takeaway is that Orthodox schools are underrepresented in my sample, while community schools are overrepresented.

TABLE 4.1. Characteristics of Analytic Sample

	Full Sample (n=3,703 in 96 schools)	U.S. Sample (n=2,995 in 86 schools)	Universe of U.S. Day Schools (n=255,000 in 861 schools)
Grade Level			
7/8th grade	59%	60%	
11/12th grade	41%	40%	
Female	52%	52%	48%
School Denomination			
Orthodox	36%	41%	55%
Conservative	14%	15%	15%
Community	47%	41%	24%
Reform	3%	2%	5%

Measuring Confidence, Knowledge, and Connection

In this section, I refer to three variables: confidence, knowledge, and connection. Following, I describe how I measure each variable.

Confidence

Students were told to imagine that they were standing with a group of friends who were having a conversation about various topics. Students were then asked to assess how confident they are in their knowledge to talk about these topics. The survey responses were on a scale that includes the following: 1 (not at all confident), 2 (only a little confident), 3 (somewhat confident), 4 (confident), 5 (very confident), and 6 (completely confident). Six of the survey items fall into a domain that I broadly call "Israeli politics and history." The six items in this domain include the Arab-Israel conflict, the geography of the land of Israel, reasons for the emergence of Zionism, current events in Israel, the history of Jewish people in the past hundred years, and the status of different religious movements in Israel. Rather than looking at these six items as individual measures of confidence, I combine them into one underlying concept of confidence.[5]

Knowledge

The only indicator of students' knowledge about Israeli history and politics in the Hearts and Minds study is their familiarity with seven Zionist/Israeli leaders: Theodor Herzl, Golda Meir, David Ben-Gurion, Yitzhak Rabin, Hannah Szenes, Benjamin Netanyahu, and Henrietta Szold.[6] The majority of students knew most of these leaders, except Henrietta Szold (only 20 percent of students recognized Szold, who was the founder of Hadassah and a co-founder of the political party Ihud). Students were asked to indicate how much they admired these leaders, but one of the response options was "I don't know who this is." Thus, I assigned each student a knowledge score based on the percentage of leaders whom they knew. For example, if a student didn't check the "I don't know who this is" box for any of the seven leaders, they received a knowledge score of 100 percent. If they checked the "I don't know who this is box" for three leaders, they received a knowledge score of 57 percent.

Connection

Students were asked a series of questions about their affective connection to Israel. The six items were measured using a six-point scale anchored by 1 (strongly disagree) to 6 (strongly agree). The specific items were: (1) Israel is a home away from home, (2) Israel is the homeland of the Jewish people, (3) I have a strong connection to people in Israel, (4) I feel that Israel is my homeland, (5) When I think about Israel I feel pride, and (6) If Israel were destroyed my life would be different. Rather than looking at these six items as individual measures of connection, I combined them into one underlying concept of affective connection to Israel (just like I did with the confidence measure).[7]

Magnitude and Scope of the Gender Confidence Gap

Girls Are Less Confident Discussing Israeli Politics and History Than Are Boys

In figure 4.1, I show the percentage of students who felt "confident," "very confident," or "completely confident" on Israel-related survey items. For

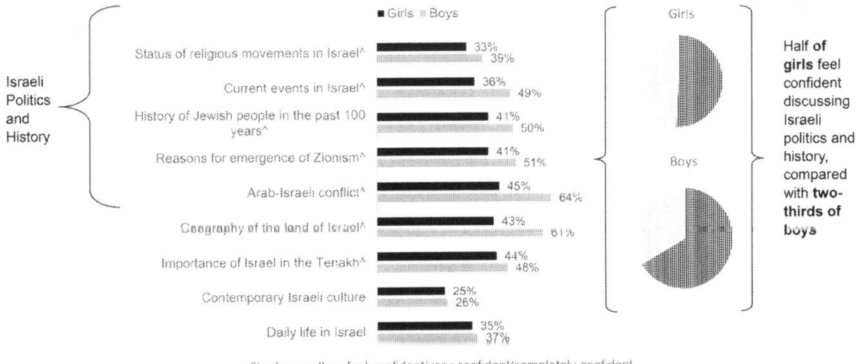

Note: Statistical differences between boys and girls are based on t-tests: ^ means that boys are more confident than girls.

FIGURE 4.1. Students' Confidence on Israel-Related Items, by Gender.

each item, I show the differences by gender. In this figure, I do not disaggregate students by their age or school denomination (I will do this in the next section). The top six items in the figure fall into what I describe as "Israeli politics and history." Again, these six items constitute what I call Israeli political and historical confidence.[8] The key finding is that there is a confidence gender gap in Jewish day schools: two-thirds of boys in day school feel confident discussing Israeli politics and history, compared with only half of girls. The gender gap is particularly pronounced when it comes to discussing current events in Israel, the Arab-Israeli conflict, and the geography of the land of Israel. In each of these three areas, girls are approximately 15 percentage points less confident than boys. Notably, girls and boys feel equally nonconfident on two items: Israeli culture and daily life in Israel. It is probably not a coincidence that the two items on which girls and boys feel similar are unrelated to Israeli history and politics.

How Does the Confidence Gap Vary by Grade Level and School Denomination?

On average, high school students are more confident in their ability to discuss Israeli historical/political issues than middle-school students. In figure 4.2, I show the percentage of students who feel confident discussing Israeli politics and history. The gender gap at both grade levels is profound. The takeaway from figure 4.2 is that girls feel significantly less confident, regardless of grade level and school denomination.

In non-Orthodox schools, eleventh/twelfth-grade students, regardless of gender, are about 10 percentage points more likely to feel confident than seventh/eighth-grade students. This means that in eleventh/twelfth grade, three of every five girls feel confident. However, in seventh/eighth grade, only two of every five girls feel confident. The trend is similar in Orthodox schools, where eleventh/twelfth-grade girls are more confident than seventh/eighth-grade girls. The fact that older students are more confident than younger students makes sense given that schools focus on teaching about the history and politics of Israel in later grades (in younger grades, schools aim to instill a love of Israel [Pomson et al., 2014]). Notably, the picture is a little different for eleventh/twelfth-grade boys in Orthodox schools: they are the only group who feel *less* confident than their younger male peers in seventh/eighth grade. It may be that as boys in Orthodox schools get older and learn more about Israeli politics and history, they realize how much more there is to learn. As a result, they become more modest in their assessment of their confidence. This would align with other research showing that people who are more knowledgeable (i.e., those who make fewer errors) exhibit less overconfidence (Lichtenstein & Fischhoff, 1977).

It is also notable that the group who feels most confident discussing Israeli politics and history are boys in non-Orthodox schools. It is unlikely that high school boys in non-Orthodox schools are more knowledgeable than the other groups, yet they assess their ability to be quite high. This is the opposite of what happens to boys in Orthodox schools who seem to become humbler as they get older. What we may be seeing is an issue of overconfidence among boys in Reform, Conservative, and community day schools.

Thus far, I have described the gender confidence gap using student-level data, which may obscure important school-level trends. To understand what school-level data can reveal, take a minute to consider the academic achievement gap between Black and white students in public schools. Overall, we know that students in the United States who identify as Black have lower test scores than students who identify as white.

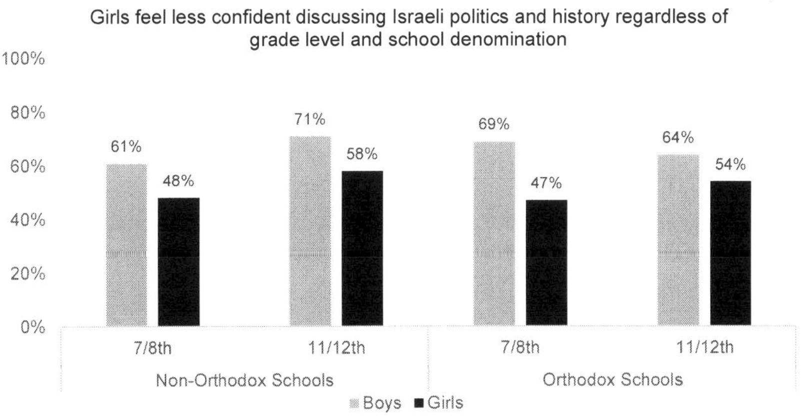

FIGURE 4.2. Students' Confidence Discussing Israeli Politics and History, by Gender, Grade Level, and School Denomination.

But the Black-white achievement gap at the school level varies. In some schools, the achievement gap is small, which means that test scores do not vary based on students' race. In other schools, the achievement gap is large, which usually means that white students have higher scores than Black students. But when we think about student achievement, we are less concerned with the actual test scores (which may be high or low). We are more concerned with how much the test scores differ based on students' race. Lower achievement gaps may be the result of district- or school-level policies that aim to equalize learning opportunities. If we care only about absolute achievement—how well kids are doing on tests—then student-level data may be enough. But if we care about educational equity—whether students across racial groups have comparable academic outcomes—then we need to think about school-level trends.

In figure 4.3, I show the school-level gender confidence gaps in 49 schools with seventh/eighth-grade students and 27 schools with eleventh/twelfth-grade students. I generate these gender confidence gaps in the following way. For each school, I first pool the scores at the school level so that my group averages are not affected by the number of observations per school. I then calculate separate confidence scores for middle school boys, middle school girls, high school boys, and high school girls (if relevant for each school). For example, if a school surveyed its eighth graders, I have a group mean for boys and a group mean for girls. If a school surveyed both eighth *and* twelfth graders, I have separate group means for seventh/eighth-grade boys and girls and eleventh/twelfth-grade boys and girls. Note that to calculate gender confidence gaps, I need enough data from girls *and* boys in each school. I only generate confidence gaps in schools where at least 8 boys and 8 girls completed surveys. This means that single-sex schools or schools with very few respondents are not included in this figure. My last step is to subtract the mean confidence score for boys from the mean confidence score for girls. The result is the "girl-boy confidence gap." A positive number means that girls are more confident than boys in that school. A 0 indicates that boys and girls have comparable levels of confidence in a school. A negative number means that boys are more confident than girls in that school.

Looking at the left-side panel of figure 4.3, you can see how 49 schools with seventh/eighth-grade students rank in terms of their girl-boy

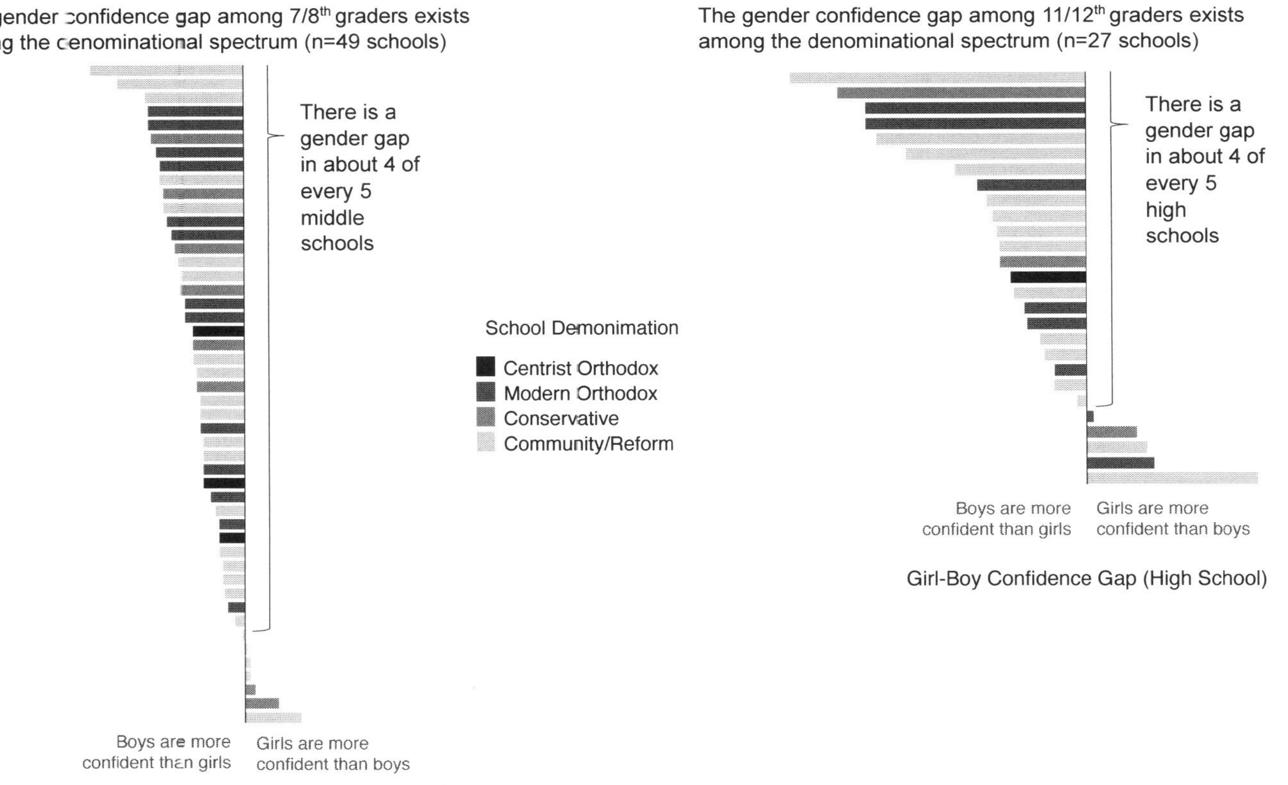

FIGURE 4.3. School-Level Gender Confidence Gaps.

confidence gap (again, these schools had at least 8 boys and 8 girls who completed a survey). There are 7 schools (14 percent) where girls are either more confident or equally confident as boys. In the remaining 42 schools (86 percent), boys are more confident than girls. In some schools, the gaps are small (e.g., schools #7 and #71), and in some schools, the gaps are quite large (e.g., schools #17 and #51). You can also see that gender confidence gaps exist regardless of school denomination. On the right-side panel of figure 4.3, you can see how schools with eleventh/twelfth-grade students rank in terms of their girl-boy confidence gap. There are 6 schools (22 percent) where girls are either more confident or equally confident as boys. In the remaining 21 schools (78 percent), boys are more confident than girls. Again, you can see that gender confidence gaps exist regardless of school denomination.

Potential Explanations for the Gender Confidence Gap

At this point, I have shown that girls are significantly less confident than boys when discussing Israeli history and politics. As a reminder, the gender confidence gap exists in about four of every five non-ultra-Orthodox Jewish day schools. The gender confidence gap is evident regardless of school denomination. This gender confidence gap is already in place among seventh/eighth graders and persists throughout high school. I now examine three potential explanations for why girls are less confident:

1. Girls are less knowledgeable
2. Girls are less connected to Israel
3. Girls are generally less confident about history and politics

In this part of the analysis, I use multilevel modeling to examine which variables are associated with students' confidence.[9] This means that when I examine which factors are associated with students' confidence, I am holding constant (i.e., controlling for) everything that happens at the school level. This means that a school's denomination, location, size, and Israel-related activities are held constant. This allows me to tease out the unique effect of student-level factors, such as students' knowledge and connection to Israel.

Are Girls Less Confident Because They Are Less Knowledgeable?

Might girls feel less confident discussing Israeli politics and history because they know less about these subjects? To figure this out, I first analyzed the data to see whether students' knowledge (based on their knowledge of seven Israeli leaders) is associated with students' sense of confidence. I found that students' level of knowledge is, indeed, positively associated with their sense of confidence ($B=0.26$, $p<.001$).[10] But I also found that girls and boys are equally knowledgeable ($B=-0.007$, $p>.10$). While there are a few gender differences on individual items,[11] on average, girls recognize as many of the Israeli leaders as boys recognize. Thus, differences in knowledge do not appear to fully explain why girls are less confident than boys.

Are Girls Less Confident Because They Are Less Connected?

Might girls feel less confident about Israel because they feel less connected to Israel? To figure this out, let's look at how students' confidence discussing Israel and their connection to Israel varies by gender, grade level, and school denomination. In figure 4.4, I show where students fall on the spectrum of confidence (x-axis) and connection (y-axis). The top of the figure shows seventh/eighth-grade students, while the bottom of the figure shows eleventh/twelfth-grade students. Students depicted in the gray icon are in Orthodox schools (Centrist and Modern) and students depicted in black color are in non-Orthodox schools (Conservative, community, and Reform).

As you can see in figure 4.4, seventh/eighth-grade boys in Orthodox schools fall in the top right-hand quadrant. This means that they feel confident *and* connected. The story is different for girls in Orthodox schools. They fall in the top left hand quadrant, which means they feel connected but not confident. Girls in non-Orthodox schools are in the bottom left-hand quadrant: this means they are neither connected nor confident. Finally, boys in non-Orthodox schools fall in the bottom right-hand quadrant. They are moderately confident and, like their female peers in non-Orthodox schools, not at all connected. In sum, girls are connected but not confident.

What is the relationship between confidence and connection for eleventh- and twelfth-grade students? First, all students except boys in Orthodox schools have shifted to the right, meaning older students feel more confident than do younger students. Again, except for boys in Orthodox schools, students have also shifted upward. This means older students feel more connected. But the confidence gender gap remains: eleventh/twelfth-grade girls, regardless of school denomination, remain less confident than boys. To answer the original question, girls' lack of confidence is not the result of a low connection to Israel—girls actually feel more connected to Israel than boys do.

Are Girls Less Confident About Their Ability to Discuss History and Politics Outside of Israel?

Might girls have lower confidence discussing Israeli history and politics because they are less confident in the ability to discuss historical and political issues more generally? To figure this out, I analyzed responses to two survey items in which students were asked about their confidence discussing US history and current events. For these two items, I only analyzed data from the US sample (because we shouldn't expect students in Canada to feel confident discussing US history and current events).

I found that girls are, indeed, significantly less confident than boys discussing US history and current events. Specifically, 52 percent of girls and 73 percent of boys feel confident discussing US current events. When it comes to US history, both groups are less confident and the gender gap persists: 37 percent of girls felt confident discussing US history compared with 62 percent of boys. To put this in perspective, imagine that a group of 200 students (evenly split between boys and girls) are hanging around during their lunch break. About 70 of those boys would be up for discussing US current events with their friends, compared with only 50 girls. If the topic of conversation was US history, about 60 boys would feel confident participating compared with only 35 girls.

Girls are not less confident about all topics. If the 200 students in the previous example were standing around discussing American culture, girls would feel just as confident about participating as boys. And if students

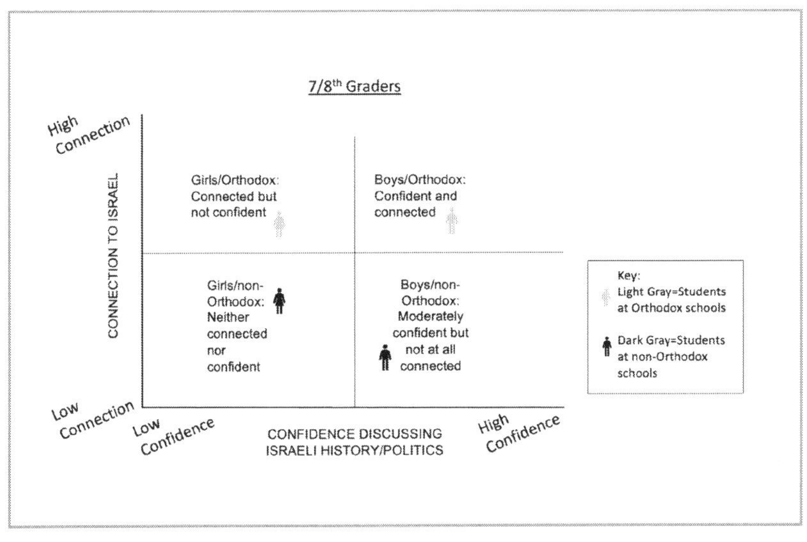

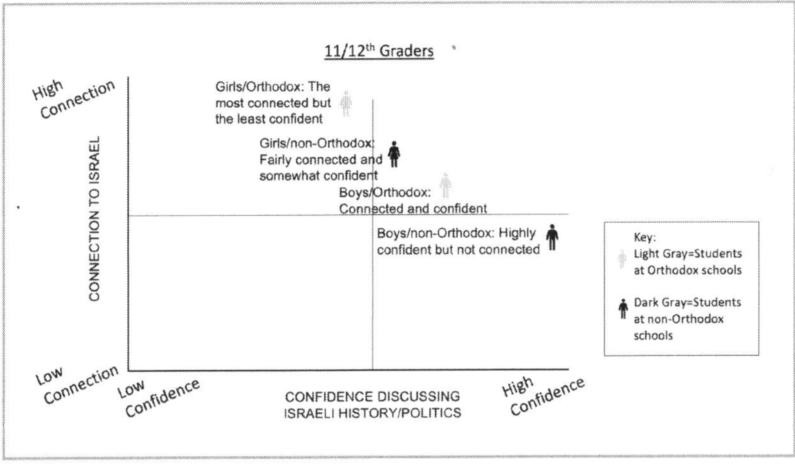

FIGURE 4.4. The Relationship between Students' Sense of Confidence and Connection.

sitting around the lunch table were discussing Jewish attitudes toward homosexuality, Jewish law (halakha), differences between Jewish religious movements (such as Orthodox, Conservative, and Reform movements), or the Holocaust (although I doubt that would ever be a lunch topic), girls would feel just as confident as boys participating. If the topic of conversation were Jewish religious customs or Jewish culture, girls would actually feel more confident than boys participating (it is notable that Jewish culture and religious customs are the more domestic realms of Judaism that tend to be female-centric). Thus, it appears that girls are specifically less confident about historical and political issues—in and outside of Israel.

To what extent do students' knowledge, connection to Israel, and confidence with US history and current events explain the gender confidence gap for Israeli history and politics? A lot. The extent to which students know about Israeli leaders, feel connected to Israel, and feel confident discussing US-based politics and history explains 55 percent of the variance in students' confidence. The remaining 45 percent is explained by other factors. (To understand what I mean by variance, consider the relationship between height and weight. People who are taller tend to weigh more, but other factors also effect one's weight. Therefore, someone's height might explain 55 percent of the variance in weight. The remaining 45 percent would be explained by factors such as diet.) Indeed, even after controlling for (or holding constant) students' knowledge of Israeli leaders, their connection to Israel, and their knowledge of US history and current events, girls are still less confident than boys.

Are Girls More Confident in Schools with High Levels of Israel-Based School Activities?

Might girls feel more confident in schools with high levels of Israel-related activity? To figure this out, I checked whether there was a relationship between students' levels of confidence discussing Israeli history and politics and the extent to which schools reported Israel-related activities as part of their school.[12] Thus, I examine how the following factors are related to students' confidence: having a full-time Israel coordinator, having a required course about Israel, having high levels of activity in the aftermath of the conflict between Gaza and Israel in 2014 (holding a special assembly, running a special program), and the extent to which Israel appears in the daily life of the school. It turns out that none of these school efforts mattered for students' sense of confidence, regardless of gender. Students' confidence appears to be uncorrelated with the level of Israel-related activity in a school. This is surprising because we might expect that students who are more exposed to Israel in school are more confident than students who attend schools that are less focused on Israel.

Discussion

Currently, Israel education in Jewish day schools is largely about getting students to feel more connected to Israel. When it comes to Israel education, none of the primary goals that teachers work toward have anything to do with cognitive learning or with cultivating an understanding of contemporary or historical events (Pomson et al., 2014). I argue that educating for the heart is insufficient.[13] While feeling connected and feeling confident are positively correlated, connection alone is not enough to get young people to feel confident. Girls feel strongly connected to Israel, but what good is this if they don't also feel confident talking about it?

The Hearts and Minds study found that some parents actually prefer that their children develop warm connections to Israel during their years in day school rather than engaging in more critical discussions that they will likely encounter on college campuses: "Some parents seek an inoculation of Zionism for their children before they encounter bitter criticism of Israel heard on some university campuses . . . they seem to feel that their children can always develop a more nuanced perspective in college or thereafter" (2014, p. 6). But prioritizing young people's affective connection to Israel may be harmful if it means young people leave high school without feeling confident about their knowledge of Israeli politics and history. The current focus in day schools on cultivating connection may actually have the opposite effect: rather than getting to college and developing a more nuanced perspective of Israel, they may choose to sit on the sidelines (Kelman et al., 2017). It's not that day schools should focus exclusively on knowledge—it's that they should help students (particularly females) feel confident about their knowledge.

Getting girls to feel more confident discussing Israeli history and politics is important for two main reasons. First, girls graduating from Jewish day schools should have the confidence to participate in conversations about Israel, whether they happen at college, at the dinner table, or in the workplace. These conversations should not be dominated by male voices. It is likely that day school graduates who go on to college will encounter a different type of narrative about Israel on their college campus than the narrative they were presented in high school. This does not mean that the goal of Israel education in day schools should be solely to cultivate students who will become ardent Israel advocates on college campuses. But it does mean that the goal of Israel education in day schools should go beyond cultivating students' love of Israel. If girls feel ill-equipped to engage in critical conversations about Israel, it may not be because they don't know enough. It's because they don't *feel* like they know enough. Thus, rather than engaging in difficult dialogues about Israel, girls may be more likely to disengage from conversations about Israel altogether.

Second, girls need to feel more confident discussing Israeli history and politics because it may help lessen the gender pay gap and leadership gap in Jewish nonprofit organizations. Currently, only 14 percent of Jewish national nonprofits are led by women—and those that are led by women tend to be smaller, social justice–oriented organizations. Women in Jewish nonprofits also earn less. According to the *Forward*'s 2015 survey of wages among Jewish leaders, which accounted for organizations' budgets and staff size, female communal leaders earned only 80 percent of what male leaders earned (Cohler-Esses, 2017; Maizels, 2017). As Maizels (2017) points out, women often don't advance into top leadership positions because they are not perceived as experts: "Women are not seen as experts, particularly in those subjects that much of the organized Jewish world values. This perceived lack of expertise may hurt women who aspire to leadership roles in the Jewish community." The problem is not that women don't have expertise—it is that they lack the self-confidence to exert their expertise (Kay & Shipman, 2014; Lundeberg et al., 1994; Orenstein, 1994; Usher & Pajares, 2008). Jewish day schools, which are often training grounds for future leaders of Jewish organizations, can do something about this by helping girls feel more confident in their abilities.

But the gender confidence gap does not simply point to a deficit in girls.

In fact, it may be that girls are more modest and possibly more accurate in assessing their knowledge. The gender confidence gap may also point to an overconfidence among boys. Overconfidence suggests an inaccurate calibration of one's ability or knowledge. Simply put, boys—especially those in Reform, Conservative, and community day schools—seem to think they know a lot about Israeli politics and history. Such high levels of confidence could be problematic. Overconfidence has been shown to have negative consequences in various fields, including incorrect diagnosing of medical patients, excessive stock market trading, poor financial decision-making, and willingness to engage in war and use coercive action (Angner, 2006; Johnson et al., 2011; Kahneman & Renshon, 2007; Kiong et al., 2016; Malmendier & Tate, 2005; Odean, 1999). It may be that boys in Reform, Conservative, and community day schools overestimate their ability to discuss Israeli politics and history and are less willing to hear alternative or new viewpoints in college or in the workplace.

From the perspective of navigating a divisive political conflict like the Israeli/Palestinian conflict, an overconfidence among men might lead to more physically aggressive actions. From the perspective of Jewish leadership, overconfidence among men may be a key obstacle to getting more women into leadership roles.

Implications for Practitioners

Although schools tend to see Israel education as working on the heart, they may want to reimagine Israel education as an endeavor in encouraging girls in history and politics (not just about Israel, but broadly). For recommendations on what teachers can do in their classrooms, I refer to a practice guide that provides teachers with recommendations for encouraging girls in math and science (Halpern et al., 2007). To encourage girls in history and politics, we need to start by changing what girls believe about their abilities in these areas. Research shows that even students with considerable competence who view their cognitive abilities as fixed or unchangeable are more likely to experience greater discouragement and lower performance and, ultimately, reduce their effort when they encounter difficulties or setbacks. Girls need to believe that their academic abilities are expandable and improvable. We then need to create classroom environments that spark initial curiosity and foster long-term interest in history and politics. We also need to expose girls to female role models who have succeeded in history and politics.

Limitations and Directions for Future Studies

In this section, I note the limitations of this study and identify seven directions for further research. First, it is unclear when the confidence gap emerges. My analysis shows that the gender confidence gap is in place by eighth grade, but when does it develop? Future studies should examine confidence among younger students. Second, my measure of how much students know about Israeli history and politics is quite narrow.[14] Although I don't find differences between how much girls and boys know, it doesn't necessarily mean that knowledge gaps don't exist. Research about political knowledge more broadly shows that men know more about politics than women (Mondak & Anderson, 2004). Thus, knowledge gaps between girls and boys about Israeli history and politics may emerge if students were asked a broader set of questions than those available in the Hearts and Minds study. My measure of knowledge may also be skewed because women are more likely than men to check off the "I don't know" option on a survey because they tend to be less confident in their knowledge (Mondak & Anderson, 2004; Rapoport, 1985). Thus, further research should examine the connection between knowledge and confidence to confirm whether girls feel less confident about Israeli politics and history even though they know just as much, or whether they actually know less. If the latter proves to be true, Jewish day schools will need to seriously consider why gender knowledge gaps exist.

Third, my analysis was highly dependent on how the confidence question was worded. An alternative wording may have provided different results. Future research should experiment with different ways of assessing confidence to ensure that the measure is valid and reliable. Fourth, this was not a longitudinal study, so I don't know how students' confidence changes over time. The variation I observed in students' confidence by grade level are two different groups of students. Future studies should take a longitudinal approach to see how students' sense of confidence changes over time.

Fifth, it is perplexing why eleventh/twelfth-grade boys in Orthodox schools are *less* confident than seventh/eighth-grade boys in Orthodox schools. This is the only group that is less confident than their younger peers, and future studies could investigate why. Sixth, I only used the student- and school-level survey data from the Hearts and Minds study because that is what was publicly available. The researchers also collected surveys with teachers, visited 12 schools, and observed trips to Israel. These additional data might offer important insights about why the gender confidence gap that I have described in this chapter exists. It may be helpful to examine the qualitative and teacher-survey data on the schools with the largest and smallest gender confidence gaps. What practices and policies might be prevalent in these schools that create these gaps?

Seventh, the Hearts and Minds study identified two types of teachers: those who believe that Israel education is best done by sharing something of themselves with their students (exemplars) and those who believe that students should learn about Israel through their own inquiry and study (explorers). It is possible that students' self-confidence varies based on the type of teacher they had. Future research should examine how students' confidence varies based on whether their teachers are exemplars or explorers.

NOTES

1. Editors' Note: The research for this chapter was conducted before the October 7, 2023, Hamas attacks on Israel and the ensuing war and its effects. Therefore, readers should be mindful of the very different circumstances in which this material was developed, while considering the ways that the findings in this chapter may remain relevant today.

2. The gender gap I describe here is a gap between boys and girls. Students in this study were only given two options to indicate their gender: female or male.

3. The survey was not administered to students at ultra-Orthodox and Chasidic schools.

4. The usable surveys represent just over 80 percent of students who took the survey. The research team excluded those who took fewer than ten minutes to complete the survey, since this did not indicate a serious enough investment of effort in a task that took on average 36 minutes to complete. The reason there are so few seventh and eleventh graders is because the original intent was to only survey students in eighth and twelfth grades.

5. I created a latent variable using factor analysis. The latent variable was inferred from the variables I observed. Latent variables are useful because they represent an underlying concept and can make it easier to understand the data. For the six items that I used to construct the latent variable, the alpha=0.85. The mean is 0 and the standard deviation is 0.91. The values range from –1.95 to 2.11.

6. The survey asked students about twenty-four different figures, including biblical figures, Jewish scholars, famous historical and contemporary figures, and celebrities.

7. For the six items, the alpha=0.87. The mean is 0 and the standard deviation is 0.93. The values range from −2.99 to 1.20.

8. I do not include the item "Importance of Israel in the Tanakh" as part of the Israeli politics and history domain.

9. Traditional ordinary least squares regression (OLS) analyses are not appropriate because students are nested in schools, thus violating a key assumption of OLS that observations should be independent. When students are nested in schools, there may be a statistical dependency among observations in the sample. For example, students attending a Jewish school in Philadelphia are more likely to be similar to each other than to students attending a Jewish school in San Francisco because they are drawn from the same communities, have the same teachers, and share similar school resources (O'Dwyer & Parker, 2014). Multilevel analysis accounts for this dependence by modeling related equations at each hierarchical level of analysis (the student and school level in the current study), resulting in a more accurate estimation of the standard errors of regression coefficients and, therefore, a more precise inference of statistical significance (Hox et al., 2017). I first test a random effects model but find that only 4 percent of the variance in students' confidence (the intraclass correlation) is between schools (at the school level). Since the intraclass correlation is very low, I use a fixed effects model with errors clustered at the school level. My model is as follows: yij=B1(genderij) + B2(gradeij) + B3 (knowledgeij) + B4 (connectionij) + αj + μij.

10. The Israel Literacy Measurement Project (Koren et al., 2015) also found that more literate students felt more confident that they could explain the situation in Israel to others than students who were less literate about Israel.

11. Girls are less likely than boys to recognize Benjamin Netnayahu, David Ben-Gurion, and Yitzhak Rabin. Girls are more likely to recognize Hannah Szenes.

12. In this model, I use OLS regression rather than a fixed effects model because I no longer want to hold constant the things that occur at the school level. Rather, I want to see which school-level factors are predictive of students' confidence.

13. Pomson et al. (2014) also argue that schools should focus more on cognitive outcomes, not just affective ones.

14. The Israel Literacy Measurement Project (Koren et al., 2015), which was a large-scale assessment of college students' knowledge of Israel, didn't collect data on respondents' gender, so I can't check whether girls and boys are equally knowledgeable.

REFERENCES

Angner, E. (2006). Economists as experts: Overconfidence in theory and practice. *Journal of Economic Methodology*, *13*(1), 1–24.

Bandura, A. (1977). Self-efficacy: Toward a unifying theory of behavioral change. *Psychological Review*, *84*(2), 191–215.

Cohler-Esses, L. (2017, December). The gender gap at Jewish nonprofits is bad—and getting worse. *Forward*.

Ehrlinger, J., & Dunning, D. (2003). How chronic self-views influence (and potentially mislead) estimates of performance. *Journal of Personality and Social Psychology*, *84*(1), 5–17.

Gallagher, A. M., & Kaufman, J. C. (2004). *Gender differences in mathematics: An integrative psychological approach*. Cambridge University Press.

Halpern, D. F., Aronson, J., Reimer, N., Simpkins, S., Star, J. R., & Wentzel, K. (2007). *Encouraging girls in math and science (NCER 2007–2003)* (Vol. 43). US Department of Education.

Hill, J. P., & Lynch, M. E. (1983). The intensification of gender-related role expectations during early adolescence. In J. Brooks-Gunn & A. C. Petersen (eds.), *Girls at puberty* (pp. 201–228). Springer.

Hox, J. J., Moerbeek, M., & Van de Schoot, R. (2017). *Multilevel analysis: Techniques and applications*. Routledge.

Johnson, D. D. P., Weidmann, N. B., & Cederman, L. (2011). Fortune favours the bold: An agent-based model reveals adaptive advantages of overconfidence in war. *PLoS ONE*, *6*(6), e20851.

Kahneman, D., & Renshon, J. (2007). Why hawks win. *Foreign Policy*, 158, *34–38*.

Kay, K., & Shipman, C. (2014). *The confidence code: The science and art of self-assurance: What women should know.* Harper Business.

Kelman, A. Y., Ahmed, A., Horwitz, I., Lockwood, J., Marom, M. S., & Zuckerman, M. (2017). *Safe and on the sidelines: Jewish students and the Israel-Palestine conflict on campus*. Report of the Research Group of the Concentration in Education and Jewish Studies at Stanford University.

Kiong, T. I. W., Hooi, L. H., Long, K. Q., & Azlinna, A. N. (2016). Managerial overconfidence, government intervention, and corporate financing decision. *International Journal of Managerial Finance*, *12*(1), 4–24.

Koren, A., Fishman, S., Krasner, J. A., & Saxe, L. (2015). *The Israel literacy measurement project: 2015 report*. Cohen Center for Modern Jewish Studies, Brandeis University.

Lichtenstein, S., & Fischhoff, B. (1977). Do those who know more also know more about how much they know? *Organizational Behavior and Human Performance*, *20*(3052), 159–183.

Lundeberg, M. A., Fox, P. W., & Punćochař, J. (1994). Highly confident but wrong: Gender differences and similarities in confidence judgments. *Journal of Educational Psychology*, *86*(1), 114–121.

Maizels, L. (2017). The old boys club is keeping women out of leadership roles in the Jewish world. *Forward*.

Malmendier, U., & Tate, G. (2005). CEO overconfidence and corporate investment. *The Journal of Finance*, *60*(6), 2661–2700.

Midgley, C., Feldlaufer, H., & Eccles, J. S. (1989). Change in teacher efficacy and student self- and task-related beliefs in mathematics during the transition to junior high school. *Journal of Educational Psychology*, *81*(2), 247–258.

Mondak, J. J., & Anderson, M. R. (2004). The knowledge gap: A reexamination of gender-based differences in political knowledge. *The Journal of Politics*, *66*(2), 492–512.

Odean, T. (1999). Do investors trade too much? *The American Economic Review*, *89*(5), 1279–1298.

O'Dwyer, L. M., & Parker, C. E. (2014). A primer for analyzing nested data: Multilevel modeling in SPSS using an example from a REL study. National Center for Education Evaluation and Regional Assistance.

Orenstein, P. (1994). *Schoolgirls: Young women, self-esteem, and the confidence gap*. Anchor Books.

Pajares, F. (2005). Self-efficacy during childhood and adolescence. In T. Urdan & F. Pajares (eds.), *Self-efficacy beliefs of adolescents* (pp. 339–367). Information Age Publishing.

Pomson, A., Wertheimer, J., & Wolf, H. H. (2014). *Hearts and minds: Israel in North American Jewish day schools*. AVI CHAI Foundation.

Rapoport, R. B. (1985). Like mother, like daughter: Intergenerational transmission of DK response rates. *Public Opinion Quarterly*, *49*(Summer), 198.

Schick, M. (2009). *A census of Jewish day schools in the United States 2008–2009*. AVI CHAI Foundation.

Usher, E. L., & Pajares, F. (2008). Sources of self-efficacy in school: Critical review of the literature and future directions. *Review of Educational Research*, *78*(4), 751–796.

Widgefield, A., & Eccles, J. S. (2000). Expectancy–value theory of achievement motivation. *Contemporary Educational Psychology*, *24*, 68–81.

5

Understanding Attitudes of Jewish Day School Students

A New Typology of Jewish Engagement

JANET KRASNER ARONSON and
RAQUEL MAGIDIN DE KRAMER

Introduction

Jewish day school attendance is one of the hallmarks of strong Jewish identity. Characteristics of day school students, however, vary widely. For Orthodox families, for whom day school is normative, a baseline level of Jewish practices and beliefs are generally assumed despite variations among Orthodox families. However, non-Orthodox families, who have a number of reasons for choosing whether or not to enroll their children in Jewish day school (Cohen & Kelner, 2007; Pomson & Schnoor, 2008), generally have a wider range of Jewish backgrounds and a corresponding variety of home-based Jewish practices and beliefs. Furthermore, particularly for older students, whether Orthodox or not, Jewish beliefs, behaviors, and attitudes do not necessarily correspond to those of their parents. Given the diversity of attitudes and practices within the day school student body, how do day school students think about their Jewish identities? How is the school experience tailored to account for those variations in beliefs, attitudes, and practices, as well as diversity in background? And what is the role of the day school in nurturing or strengthening Jewish engagement for students from different starting points? Answers to these questions undoubtedly vary based on the religious orientation of the school, its educational philosophy, and the composition of the student body.

According to Pew's *A Portrait of Jewish Americans* (Pew, 2013), almost one-quarter (23 percent) of American Jews attended yeshiva or Jewish day school in their childhood, and 25 percent of Jewish parents of minor children have children enrolled in day school. Participation in day school, however, corresponds closely to Jewish denomination: 81 percent of children of Orthodox Jews are in a yeshiva or day school, compared to 30 percent of children of Conservative Jews, 9 percent of children of Reform Jews, and 3 percent of children of Jews with no denomination.[1]

Among non-Orthodox families, the decision to enroll in day school is very much a matter of choice (as well as availability and cost). The families most engaged with Jewish life are most likely to send their children to day school (Cohen & Kelner, 2007). Pomson and Schnoor (2008) found that intermarried families and those from less traditional Jewish backgrounds are more concerned about fitting into the day school community: for intermarried families, there is anxiety about how a non-Jewish partner will be viewed within the school community. For conversionary couples, where both partners are now Jewish, there is still great concern about the cultural deficits that may impede their interactions with others (Pomson & Schnoor, 2008, p. 61). Studies of the impact of day school on students (Chertok et al., 2007; Cohen, 2007; Cohen & Kotler-Berkowitz, 2004; Dashefsky & Lebson, 2002) consistently demonstrate that day school students are more involved in Jewish life after graduation than students from similar backgrounds who did not attend day school. Whether this difference is the direct result of day school education is not clear (Dashefsky & Lebson, 2002). Students who attend day school typically come from families with stronger Jewish backgrounds, and thus any measured impact may be attributable to family and home influence rather than the outcome of the school experience.

Earlier research on day school enrollment and the impact of day school participation on adult Jewish engagement primarily focused on family or background characteristics rather than on the characteristics of students themselves. Particularly for older students (those in middle school and high school), their attitudes toward and interest in Judaism vary widely—independent of the behaviors and attitudes of their parents. To the extent that education can be tailored to students' individually (see, e.g., Bernacki & Walkington, 2018; Reber et al., 2018), understanding these concerns may facilitate better student outcomes.

The goal of the current study is to develop a typology of engagement among Jewish day school students that reflects the multidimensional nature of Jewish engagement and identity (Hartman, 2014; Horowitz, 2003; Himmelfarb, 1982). This study builds on the Jewish engagement typology (the Index of Jewish Engagement) developed for local Jewish community studies (Aronson et al., 2018) and applies this method to a dataset of over 4,000 Jewish day school students collected as part of the Hearts and Minds study of Israel education (Pomson et al., 2014). Although the focus of Hearts and Minds was on Israel education, the study collected data about many aspects of Jewish life. The present study uses that data to examine Jewish engagement among day school students more broadly. The purpose of this typology is twofold:

1. To identify the characteristics of individual students and of schools that are associated with various patterns of Jewish engagement
2. To understand the patterns of interests and attitudes among students in order to enable educators to better tailor educational activities for their students

The original Hearts and Minds study (Pomson et al., 2014) used a statistical method called cluster analysis to develop a typology of Israel engagement based upon Israel-related measures, including feelings of connection to and importance of Israel. The cluster analysis was used to categorize students into three levels of engagement, which they referred to as hyper-engaged, engaged, and detached. The study found that students who were "hyper-engaged" with Israel scored higher on other measures of Jewish engagement and motivation, such as religious and spiritual measures, compared to the lower engagement groups. Incorporating additional components of Jewish life into the typology allows us to see how these elements relate to one another and provides a broader understanding of Jewish engagement among day school students.

Data

This Hearts and Minds study collected responses from 4,030 middle and high school students in 95 North American Jewish day schools in 2012–2013

(Pomson et al., 2014). The process for school and student selection was not designed to be representative of all day school students. Table 5.1 shows the distribution of respondents by student characteristics. Details of the study methods can be found in the original report.

TABLE 5.1.
Characteristics of Student Respondents

Student Characteristics	% of Respondents
Grade	
7	5
8	58
11	9
12	28
Gender	
Male	48
Female	52
Family Denomination	
Reform	12
Conservative	26
Orthodox	10
Modern Orthodox	33
Just Jewish	13
Reconstructionist	1
Other	3
Not Jewish	2
Region	
New York City area	29
East Coast (except NYC area)	17
Midwest	9
South	14
West	9
Canada	22

Source: *Hearts and Mind*, Appendix B

Method

We created this study's typology of Jewish engagement in two stages. First, we used factor analysis, a statistical method that identifies variables that are interrelated, to identify the measures that best represented the students' attitudes about multiple dimensions of Judaism. Second, we utilized a second statistical method, latent class analysis (LCA), to combine multiple measures to create a typology of Jewish engagement, which we refer to as an index (Aronson et al., 2018). LCA looks for patterns in responses and identifies a typology or set of groups of cases that respond to questions in similar ways. In the analyses presented in this paper, the LCA technique enabled us to identify groups of students whose patterns of attitudes about Judaism across multiple dimensions are generally similar. In this paper, we refer to these patterns as "engagement styles" and we refer to the grouping of students with similar engagement styles as an "engagement class."

The resulting typology of the LCA yielded six engagement classes that categorize the ways that day school students think about their Judaism based on their responses to attitude questions. We placed each student into the engagement class that best fit that student's set of responses. Using a set of measures about schools, we examined how the styles differed based on school characteristics. We then looked at differences in classes based on student demographics and Jewish background.

Results

In the first stage of analysis, we sought to identify what we call "dimensions" of Jewish engagement. Each dimension is a single aspect of Judaism that is measured in the survey by a set of questions. The factor analysis technique was used to combine all of the attitude questions that were asked in the survey to determine which ones seemed to go together, indicating that they measured a single "factor" or dimension. We identified and labeled five factors or dimensions: Israel, community, religion, family, and universal.

From each dimension, we selected two or three items that were most representative of the dimension (that is, had the highest factor loading).

In some cases, we excluded one of the top three items because the wording was ambiguous or the item was too similar to others in the survey. The full results of the factor analysis are shown in table 5.6 (on page 110).

Table 5.2 lists the resulting eleven items that were used to represent all five dimensions. The item numbers shown correspond to the numbers used in the original Hearts and Minds report and are presented here for reference. Items that begin with a B begin with the stem "Please read each statement and mark your position relating to the statement by circling one number on the scale from 1 (strongly disagree) to 6 (strongly agree)." Response options are "strongly disagree, disagree, somewhat disagree,

TABLE 5.2. Dimensions and Measures of Jewish Engagement

Dimension/Item	Response Option
Israel Dimension	
B17. When I think about Israel I feel pride	Strongly disagree - Strongly agree
B22. I feel that Israel is my homeland	Strongly disagree - Strongly agree
Community Dimension	
B8. I feel close to other Jews in America*	Strongly disagree - Strongly agree
B5. I feel I have a strong connection to Jews wherever they are	Strongly disagree - Strongly agree
B3. I feel a part of my local Jewish community	Strongly disagree - Strongly agree
Religion Dimension	
B29. I believe that God listens to my prayers	Strongly disagree - Strongly agree
C20. Believe in God	Not at all important - Extremely important
C5. Keep Jewish law (commandments)	Not at all important - Extremely important
Family Dimension	
C2. Keep family traditions at a seder	Not at all important - Extremely important
Universal Dimension	
B11. It's important for me to have non-Jewish friends	Strongly disagree - Strongly agree
B13. I care equally about the suffering of Jews and non-Jews	Strongly disagree - Strongly agree

*Study report did not provide question wording for Canadian students

somewhat agree, agree, strongly agree." The items that begin with a C begin with the stem "From your perspective, how important is it for Jews to do the following?" Response options are "not at all important, not very important, a little important, important, very important, extremely important." To ensure that it was appropriate to retain all of these items for the next step, we ran pairwise correlations of all eleven variables. No variables were correlated at a value higher than 0.7 (Pearson's r).

The second stage of the analysis used the eleven variables as inputs to the LCA in order to identify the engagement classes. Similar to factor analysis, the researcher's judgment is required to determine the optimum number of classes that the process produces. To make this determination, we first compared "goodness of fit" measures for models with two to eight classes. The point where the goodness of fit measures do not continue to improve (decrease) suggests the number of classes in the data. As shown in figure 5.1, the model with six classes appears to be the inflection point where improvement levels off. We also verified that the resulting classes were interpretable and that all of the classes were of sufficient size to be useful for analytic purposes.

After determining the number of classes, we ran the LCA procedure using a statistical software package (Stata) to identify the composition of the classes. Based on the responses in each category, we assigned tentative names and a relative order to the six classes. Similar to the case in factor analysis, the researchers provided a name for each class that captures the

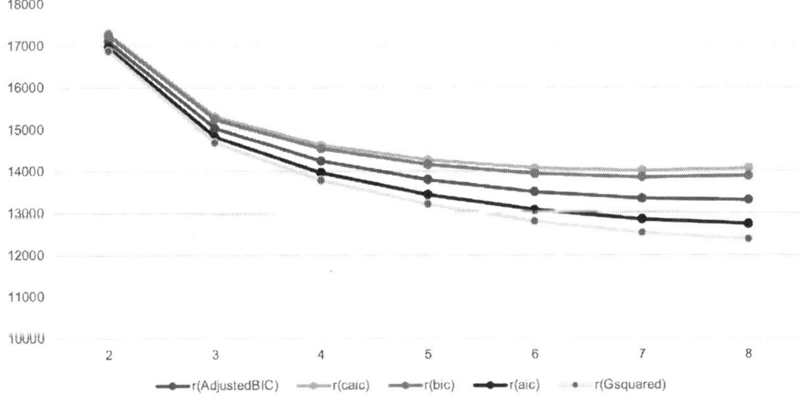

FIGURE 5.1. Goodness of Fit Measures for Classes 3–8.

presumed underlying construct that ties each class together. Considering each of the dimensions, we evaluated the degree to which the class agreed with that dimension relative to the other classes: high, low, or not at all. We named each class based on the characteristics that differentiate the classes from one another. We refer to these classes in the remainder of this paper as "Jewish engagement classes."

The resulting six engagement classes are shown in table 5.3. They include class names, the proportion of students in each class, and a brief description indicating the dimensions that are most important to each class. Based on each student's responses to the survey questions, some students fall clearly within one class, while others straddle the line between two or more classes. For this analysis, individual student respondents are assigned to the class to which they had the highest probability of belonging based on their pattern of responses.

In table 5.4, we show the proportion within each class that ranked each item highest ("strongly agree" or "extremely important").

In table 5.5, we show the complete distribution of one item from each dimension to illustrate the differences among the classes.

School Characteristics and Jewish Engagement Classes

Student populations vary among types of schools, and the distribution of classes similarly differed based on the denomination of the school and its geographic region. Figure 5.2 shows the distribution of classes for schools of each denomination. Figure 5.3 shows the distribution for each region. (All differences are significant using a Pearson chi2 test, p=0.000.) Note that the regional differences are explained, at least in part, by the fact that the New York City area includes a larger proportion of Orthodox schools than the other geographic regions. Nearly half (46 percent) of students in Orthodox day schools were classified as Immersed, compared to only 16 percent of students in Conservative day schools.

The sample included middle school students in seventh and eighth grades and high school students in eleventh and twelfth grades. In terms of engagement classes, there were statistically significant differences based on student grade and gender. As shown in figure 5.4, older students were more likely to fall in the Peoplehood class than were the younger students.

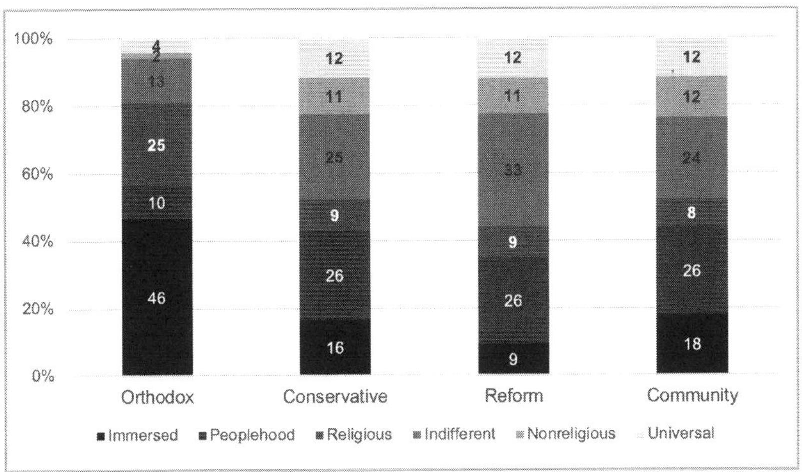

FIGURE 5.2. Jewish Engagement Class by School Denomination.

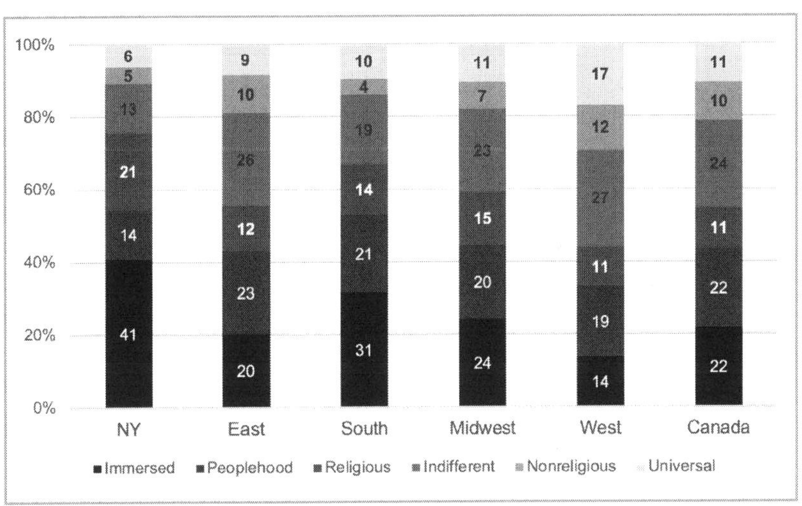

FIGURE 5.3. Jewish Engagement Class by School Geographic Region.

Specifically, 27 percent of eleventh and twelfth graders were classified as Peoplehood, compared to only 16 percent of seventh and eighth graders. A larger share of female students was in the Immersed and Peoplehood classes, compared to the male students (figure 5.5). (All differences were significant using a Pearson chi2 test, p=0.000.)

TABLE 5.3. Six Jewish Engagement Classes of Day School Students

			Dimension				
Engagement Class	Proportion of Students	Description. This group prioritizes…	Israel	Community	Religion	Family	Universal
Immersed	26%	All of the dimensions except the universal values.	High	High	High	High	Low
Peoplehood	20%	All dimensions except religious. Stronger connection to Jewish people than to Jewish ritual or belief.	High	High	Low	High	High
Religious	15%	Strongest connection to religious dimension. See ritual practice and observance as central to Judaism.	Low	Low	High	Low	Low
Indifferent	20%	Low connection to all dimensions, but prioritizes the universal values of Judaism.	Low	Low	Low	Low	High
Nonreligious	8%	Low connection to all dimensions, no connection to religious and ritual aspects. Prioritizes the universal values of Judaism.	Low	Low	None	Low	High
Universal only	9%	The only connection to Judaism is its universal values.	None	None	None	None	High

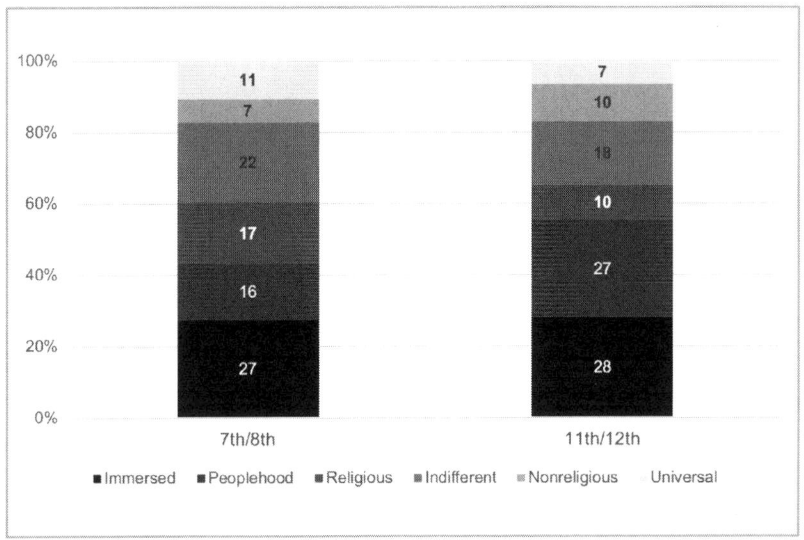

FIGURE 5.4. Jewish Engagement Class by Student Grade.

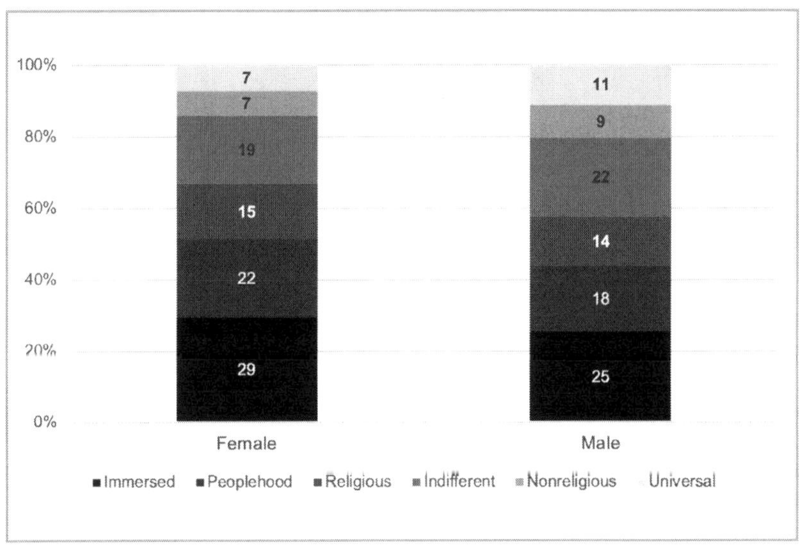

FIGURE 5.5. Jewish Engagement Class by Student Gender.

Student Jewish Background and Jewish Engagement Styles

Jewish engagement classes were strongly correlated with Jewish background characteristics (figure 5.6). Students of all Jewish denominations were represented in each of the engagement classes, but the patterns differed. The Orthodox and Modern Orthodox students were similar to one another, but more of those in the Modern Orthodox grouping were classified in the Peoplehood class. Conservative Jews had the largest share of its grouping in the Peoplehood class. (Note that denomination refers to student self-reported denomination rather than school denomination.)

TABLE 5.4. Proportion in Each Class That "Strongly Agrees" or Considers "Extremely Important" Dimensions of Israel, Peoplehood, Religion, Family, and Universality

Dimension/Item	Immersed	Peoplehood	Religious	Indifferent	Nonreligious	Universal
Israel Dimension						
B17. When I think about Israel I feel pride	60	50	11	7	15	2
B22. I feel that Israel is my homeland	61	33	17	5	9	1
Community Dimension						
B8. I feel close to other Jews in America	26	20	10	4	4	2
B5. I feel I have a strong connection to Jews wherever they are	37	31	3	2	7	1
B3. I feel a part of my local Jewish community	48	44	21	16	16	2
Religion Dimension						
B29. I believe that God listens to my prayers	54	9	32	4	0	2
C20. Believe in God	77	8	65	7	0	8
C5. Keep Jewish law (commandments)	59	7	47	3	0	4
Family Dimension						
C2. Keep family traditions at a seder	48	22	25	9	7	7
Universal Dimension						
B11. It's important for me to have non-Jewish friends	13	29	18	30	41	45
B13. I care equally about the suffering of Jews and non-Jews	29	36	26	33	49	57

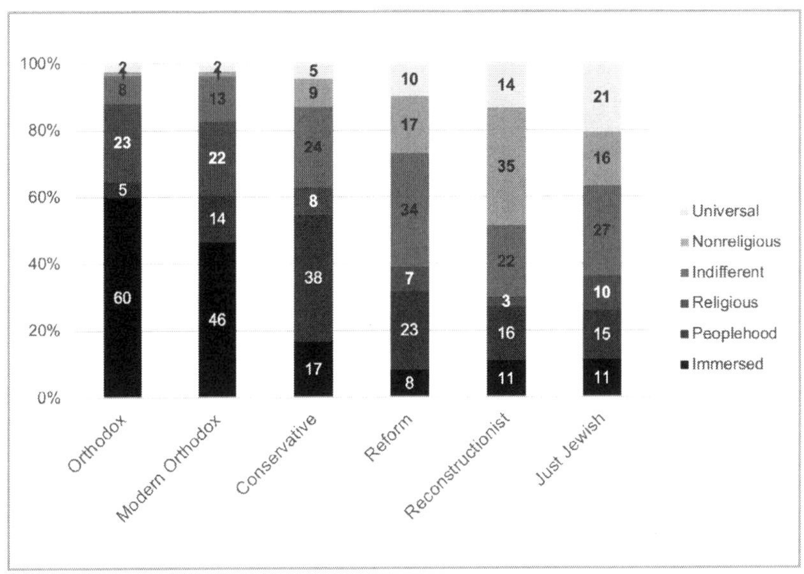

FIGURE 5.6. Student Denomination by Jewish Engagement Class.

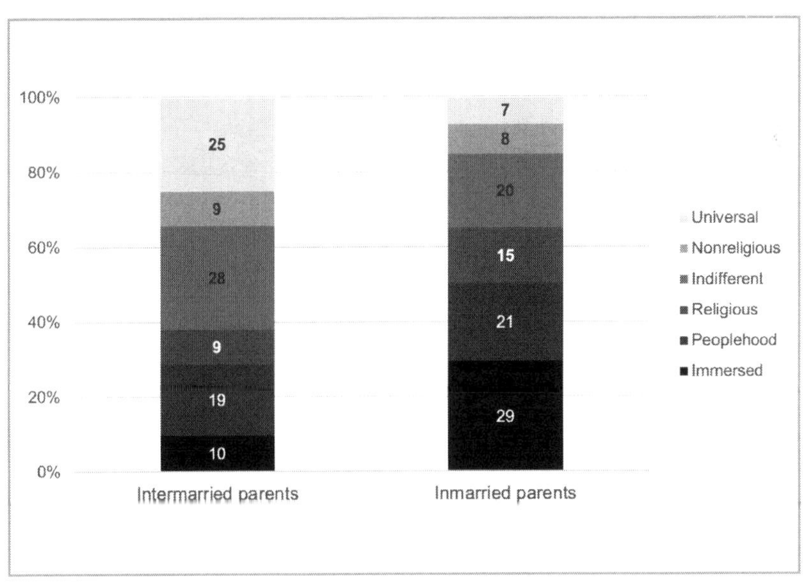

FIGURE 5.7. Parental Marriage Type by Jewish Engagement Class.

TABLE 5.5. Distribution of Responses to Each Dimension by Jewish Engagement Class

Dimension/Item	Immersed	Peoplehood	Religious	Indifferent	Nonreligious	Universal
Israel Dimension						
B17. When I think about Israel I feel pride						
Strongly disagree	0	0	1	1	1	30
Disagree	0	0	4	6	1	27
Somewhat disagree	0	1	9	12	14	15
Somewhat agree	5	6	55	51	39	24
Agree	35	43	20	23	30	3
Strongly agree	60	50	11	7	15	2
Community Dimension						
B5. I feel I have a strong connection to Jews wherever they are						
Strongly disagree	0	0	4	2	2	39
Disagree	0	0	13	11	6	43
Somewhat disagree	3	4	21	28	25	9
Somewhat agree	19	19	51	48	46	7
Agree	41	46	9	9	15	1
Strongly agree	37	31	3	2	7	1
Religion Dimension						
C20. Believe in God						
Not at all important	0	2	0	0	42	33
Not very important	0	10	0	2	43	15
A little important	0	20	0	27	10	20
Important	2	49	1	52	6	18
Very important	21	12	34	12	0	5
Extremely important	77	8	65	7	0	8

continued→

There were differences in the distribution of engagement classes for children of intermarried parents and children of inmarried parents (figure 5.7). Among children of inmarried parents, the largest share (29 percent) were in the Immersed class; among children of intermarried parents, the largest share (28 percent) were classified as Indifferent. Fully 25 percent of children of intermarried parents were classified as Universal, compared to only 7 percent of children of inmarried parents. The distribution of the other Jewish engagement classes was similar for children of intermarried and inmarried parents.

The relationship between family synagogue attendance and Jewish engagement styles appears in figure 5.8. Nearly half (45 percent) of weekly

Dimension/Item	**Immersed**	**Peoplehood**	**Religious**	**Indifferent**	**Nonreligious**	**Universal**
Family Dimension						
C2. Keep family traditions at a seder						
Not at all important	0	0	1	1	7	24
Not very important	1	2	5	4	17	20
A little important	3	14	10	25	26	21
Important	16	32	30	46	30	20
Very important	32	30	30	15	13	8
Extremely important	48	22	25	9	7	7
Universal Dimension						
B11. It's important for me to have non-Jewish friends						
Strongly disagree	8	1	6	1	3	12
Disagree	14	3	15	4	4	4
Somewhat disagree	16	9	15	10	4	5
Somewhat agree	29	24	24	26	13	14
Agree	20	34	22	28	34	20
Strongly agree	13	29	18	30	41	45

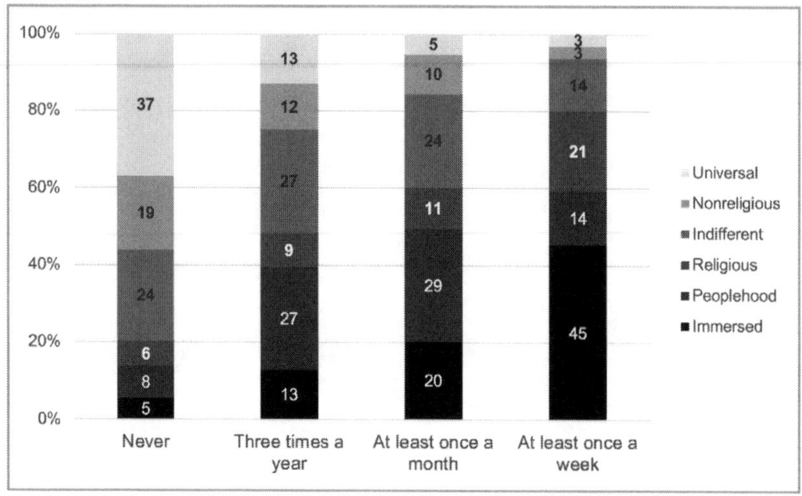

FIGURE 5.8. Frequency of Family Synagogue Attendance by Jewish Engagement Class.

synagogue attenders were classified as Immersed; one-third (37 percent) of those who never attend services were classified as Universal.

Student Connection to Jewish World and Jewish Engagement Classes

Do Jewish engagement classes correlate with the extent to which students feel a sense of belonging in the Jewish world? Students were asked to place themselves (in the center, as insiders, on the margins, and as outsiders) with respect to their relationship to Jews in America[2] (figure 5.9) and to Jews around the world (figure 5.10). In both cases, there were significant differences in feeling of belonging for those in the different Jewish engagement classes. (All differences are significant using a Pearson chi2 test, p=0.000.)

All of the Jewish engagement classes felt more central to American Jews than that of Jews around the world. Majorities of the students in the Immersed, Peoplehood, and Religious classes considered themselves to be in the center, or at least insiders, with respect to Jews in America and in relation to Jews throughout the world. For those in the Indifferent and Non-Religious classes, about three in four felt that they were in the center or insiders with respect to American Jews, but fewer than half felt that

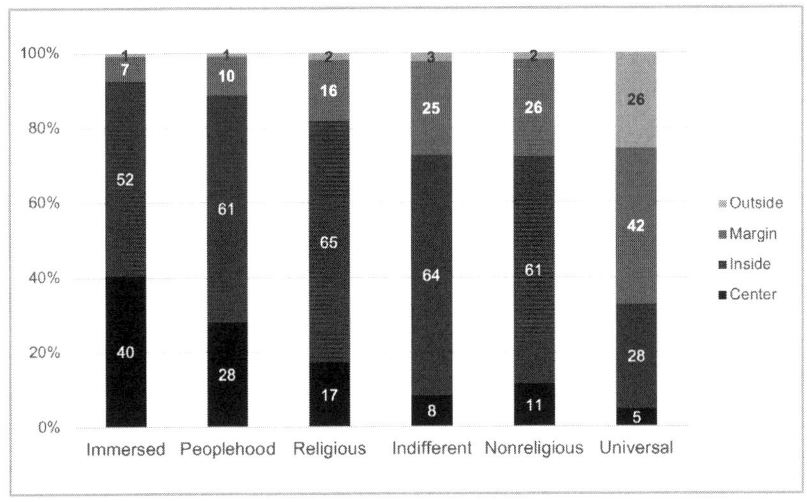

FIGURE 5.9. Perception of Relationship to Jews in America by Jewish Engagement Class.

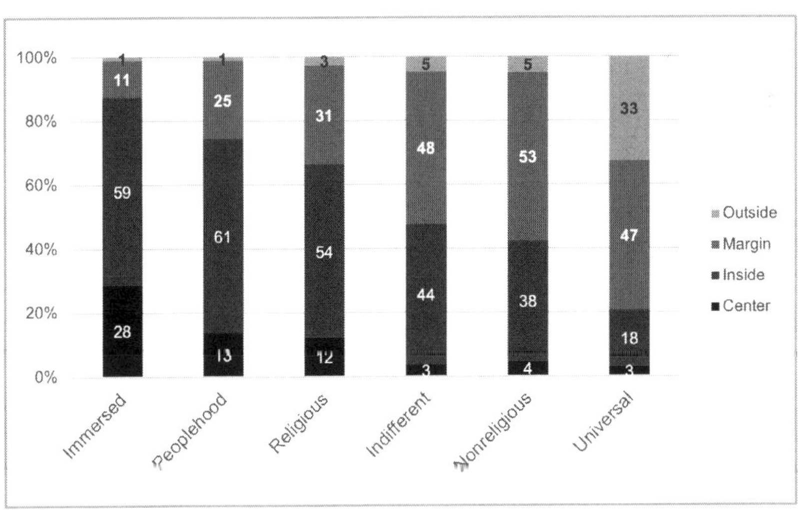

FIGURE 5.10. Perception of Relationship to Jews Throughout the World by Jewish Engagement Class.

TABLE 5.6. Factor Analysis Rotated Component Matrix*

SURVEY QUESTION	1	2	3	4	5
B17. When I think about Israel I feel pride	0.724				
B22. I feel that Israel is my homeland	0.702				
C8. Visit Israel	0.699				
B15. I have a strong connection to people in Israel	0.695				
B24. When there is a crisis or war in Israel, I pay special attention	0.678				
C9. Follow news about Israel	0.671				0.448
C10. Love Israel	0.670				
B19. If Israel were destroyed my life would be different	0.651				
B18. I'm happy when I hear that somebody famous is Israeli	0.606				
B16. Israel is the homeland of all Jews	0.591				
B23. I would like to get to know more Israelis	0.561				
B29. I believe that God listens to my prayers		0.818			
B32. I feel that I am protected from above		0.806			
C20. Believe in God		0.769			
B34. There have been moments in my life when I have felt God's presence		0.712			
B31. Observing mitzvot is a way to connect to God		0.685			
C5. Keep Jewish law (commandments)		0.649			0.461
C23. Pray in a synagogue		0.599			0.466
C7. Separate meat and dairy foods		0.573			0.481
B10. Jews, wherever they are, share a common destiny		0.548			

continued→

Extraction Method: Principal Component Analysis. Rotation Method: Varimax with Kaiser Normalization. *Rotation converged in twelve iterations.

SURVEY QUESTION	1	2	3	4	5
B8. I feel close to other Jews in America			0.639		
B3. I feel a part of my local Jewish community			0.610		
B5. I feel I have a strong connection to Jews wherever they are	0.504		0.590		
B4.When I think about the Jewish people I feel pride	0.502		0.590		
B7. There are strong similarities between Jews in different places			0.567		
B2. I would like to know more about Jews in other countries			0.560		
B25. I feel a responsibility to help Jews in need	0.488		0.544		
B9. I feel proud that people know that I am Jewish	0.433		0.542		
B30. I respect people who observe Jewish law (halakha)			0.509		
B13. I care equally about the suffering of Jews and non-Jews				-0.705	
B14. If people love each other, religion should not make a difference when they marry				-0.639	
B11. It's important for me to have non-Jewish friends				-0.635	
B6. It's important that my best friends are Jewish				0.569	
B12. It's important that Jews only date other Jews				0.560	
C3. Respect people who are different from them				-0.515	0.405
B28. When I think about making a difference in the world, I think first about helping Jews				0.413	
C2. Keep family traditions at a seder					0.527
C6. Rest on Shabbat		0.462			0.507
C4. Feel responsible for needy Jews around the world					0.483

way with regard to worldwide Jewry. Among Universal Jews, almost half (47 percent) felt on the margins, and another third (33 percent) felt like outsiders relative to worldwide Jewry.

Implications

Jewish day school students in middle and high schools have a variety of orientations toward Jewish life, and one can see these viewpoints represented in all types of schools and among students of all types of Jewish backgrounds. Considering that students of each of these types would likely respond positively toward educational messages aimed at their respective perspectives, a greater understanding of these differences can help guide effective educational interventions.

Thinking about Jewish engagement across the five dimensions of Israel, community, religion, family, and universality can help educators design programs that appeal to students who are interested in one or more of these aspects of Jewish engagement. We identified six classes, or styles, of Jewish engagement that prioritized one or more of these dimensions. Knowledge of these patterns can further tailor educational activities. For example, in our sample, only students with the Immersed and Peoplehood classes felt a strong attachment to Israel and would likely gravitate toward Israel-oriented activities. Teaching about Israel for students with other engagement styles, in contrast, should not begin with the assumption of attachment to Israel. For students in the Universal class, one approach might be to connect the study of Israel to universal values; for students in the Religious class, a more effective approach would be to connect to the religious meaning of Israel in their lives.

An additional value of this typology is that it provides insight into the way that the dimensions interact with one another. For example, as was shown in table 5.3, regardless of other dimensions, the Religious and Universal dimensions do not appear to coexist in day school students. In the only classes in which the Religion dimension is high (Immersed and Religious), the Universal dimension is low.

Correlating the typology with background characteristics reveals differences and similarities across students that might not be evident from examining individual items. To illustrate this point, consider differences in engagement classes for children of intermarried parents and children of inmarried parents (figure 5.7). Among children of inmarried parents, the largest share (29 percent) were Immersed; among children of intermarried parents, the largest share (28 percent) were Indifferent. However, each group has a similar share of students in the remaining four engagement classes. Thus, while there are noteworthy differences in engagement among students with inmarried and intermarried parents, there are far more similarities than differences.

At this point, we do not offer a diagnostic tool to assign students to categories. Nonetheless, by using questions similar to the ones listed in table 5.6, it may be possible for educators to create informal assessments of students to identify which of the dimensions interest students most. The dimensions describe here can serve as starting points so that educators can connect curriculum goals with preexisting values, beliefs, and attitudes. As well, the styles of Jewish engagement reveal the patterns that connect these dimensions with one another and with underlying student characteristics. This typology, therefore, provides new insight into how students think about their Jewish lives across multiple dimensions. Despite the fact that day school students, overall, have deeper levels of Jewish engagement than students who do not attend day school, within day schools there is a diversity of Jewish background and experience. It is not surprising, therefore, that this typology of Jewish engagement reveals a great diversity in orientation toward Jewish life among day school students.

NOTES

1. The Pew 2013 data are provided because information about Jewish education of children was not included in the Pew 2020 study, *Jewish Americans in 2020*. The share of Jewish adults who attended day school in childhood was essentially unchanged (24 percent vs. 23 percent) between the two studies. According to Pew's *Jewish Americans in 2020* survey (Pew, 2021), almost one-quarter (24 percent) of American Jews attended yeshiva or Jewish day school in their childhood.

2. We presume the question text was modified for Canadian schools, but the wording was not included in the original report.

REFERENCES

Aronson, J. K., Saxe, L, Kadushin, C., Boxer, M., & Brookner, M. A. (2018). A new approach to understanding contemporary Jewish engagement. *Contemporary Jewry*, 91–113. https://doi.org/10.1007/s12397-018-9271-8/.

Bernacki, M. L., & Walkington, C. (2018). The role of situational interest in personalized learning. *Journal of Educational Psychology*, *110*(6), 864–881.

Chertok, F., Saxe, L., Kadushin, C., Wright, G., Klein, A., & Koren, A. (2007). What difference does day school make? The impact of day school: A comparative analysis of Jewish college students. Cohen Center for Modern Jewish Studies, Brandeis University.

Cohen, S. M. (2007). The differential impact of Jewish education on adult Jewish identity. In J. Wertheimer (ed.), *Family matters: Jewish education in an age of choice* (pp. 34–58). University Press of New England.

Cohen, S. M., & Kelner, S. (2007). Why Jewish parents send their children to day schools. In J. Wertheimer (ed.), *Family matters: Jewish education in an age of choice* (pp. 80–100). University Press of New England.

Cohen, S. M., & Kotler-Berkowitz, L. (2004). The impact of childhood Jewish education upon adults' Jewish identity. United Jewish Communities Report Series on the National Jewish Population Survey 2000–2001. Report 3. www.ujc.org/njps/.

Dashefsky, A., & Lebson, C. (2002). Does Jewish schooling matter? A review of the empirical literature on the relationship between formal Jewish education and dimensions of Jewish identity. *Contemporary Jewry*, *23*, 96–131.

Hartman, H. (2014). Studies of Jewish identity and continuity in the United States: Competing, complementary, and comparative perspectives. In U. Rebhun (ed.), *Studies in Contemporary Jewry* (pp. 74–108). Oxford University Press.

Himmelfarb, H. S. (1982). Research on American Jewish identity and identification: Progress, pitfalls, and prospects. In M. Sklare (ed.), *Understanding American Jewry*. Brandeis University.

Horowitz, B. (2003). *Connections and journeys: Assessing critical opportunities for enhancing Jewish identity*. UJA Federation of New York. www.jewishdatabank.org/databank/search-results/study/539/.

Pew Research Center. (2013). *A portrait of Jewish Americans*. Pew Research Center's Religion and Public Life Project. www.pewforum.org/2013/10/01/jewish-american-beliefs-attitudes-culture-survey/.

Pew Research Center. (2021). *Jewish Americans in 2020*. https://www.pewresearch.org/religion/2021/05/11/jewish-americans-in-2020/.

Pomson, A., & Schnoor, R. F. (2008). *Back to school: Jewish day school in the lives of adult Jews*. Wayne State University Press.

Pomson, A., Wertheimer, J., & Hacohen-Wolf, H. (2014). Hearts and minds: Israel in North American Jewish day schools. https://avichai.org/knowledge_base/hearts-and-minds-israel-in-north-american-jewish-day-schools/.

Reber, R., Canning, E. A., & Harackiewicz, J. M. (2018). Personalized education to increase interest. *Current Directions in Psychological Science*, *27*(6), 449–454.

6

"Responsive Classroom" Meets the Rabbis

The Impact of DeLeT on Teachers' Community-Building Practice[1]

SHARON FEIMAN-NEMSER and

SHIRA HOROWITZ

I believe that Charney and Rambam have a lot in common... Both would hate to see a student have difficulty learning because they either learned differently or because they learned more slowly than others. I would love to see Charney engaged in a discussion with Rambam. (DeLeT intern)

A central task of teaching involves creating a safe and productive environment for learning. This covers a range of decisions and actions, from arranging the physical space to establishing a classroom culture with clear norms, routines, and expectations. The environment teachers create with and for students enables certain kinds of relationships and influences both what and how students learn.

Novice teachers often find this aspect of teaching challenging. Besides having little or no experience dealing with the myriad situations that life in classrooms presents, they are still figuring out who they want to be as teachers and what kind of classroom community they want to create. Often new teachers struggle with competing images of their role, for example, how strict or friendly to be in areas of discipline and classroom management and how to deal with what often seem like competing demands of the academic and social curricula. Preparing teachers for these critical aspects of their role and practice is a central task of teacher education.

This chapter describes how the DeLeT (Day School Leadership Through Teaching) program at Brandeis University,[2] a unique experiment in Jewish teacher education, gave a Jewish spin to this central task of teaching and how that preparation shaped the identity and practice of program graduates long after they completed the program. The study is part of a larger effort to conceptualize and document the legacy of DeLeT during the program's first decade, 2002–2012. During this time period, generous outside funding made it possible to mount a strong program infrastructure, offer full scholarships, and provide a robust curriculum that addressed both secular and Jewish aspects of day school teaching.

Several reasons led us to focus this study on how DeLeT fellows learned to create classroom communities rooted in Jewish values and experiences and how they brought that learning into their teaching. First, this focus allows us to show how DeLeT imported strong principles and practices from general education into day school teaching and teacher education. Second, it reflects DeLeT's vision of general studies teachers as Jewish educators. Third, it illustrates a noncurricular approach to integration. Most discussions of integration in Jewish education deal with why and how to form meaningful connections between general studies and Jewish studies. While DeLeT also encouraged curricular integration, it emphasized the opportunity and importance of developing and teaching a social curriculum based in Jewish values and experiences.

The chapter is organized into two parts. The first part examines what DeLeT taught and what students learned about building a (Jewish) classroom community. Data about what was taught come from course syllabi and assignments, the DeLeT Handbook, and interviews and focus groups with core faculty.[3] Data about what DeLeT fellows learned during the program come from two major assignments: a study of how mentor teachers started the year with a new class of students, which DeLeT fellows carried out in the fall, and a portfolio entry on classroom community, which DeLeT fellows created at the end of their yearlong internship in a day school classroom.

Part two focuses on the continuing influence of this preparation on the professional identity and teaching practice of two DeLeT graduates years after they completed the program. In what ways do these general studies teachers use Jewish values, texts, and experiences to build a classroom learning community and teach a social curriculum? Data for the two cases come from teacher interviews and classroom observations as well as a collection of artifacts and records of practice, such as photographs of classroom displays and samples of student work. We do not claim that these cases are representative of the hundred-plus fellows who graduated from DeLeT at Brandeis. Rather, these compelling "images of the possible" demonstrate the staying power of the program and illustrate a major affordance of Jewish teacher preparation.

Inside DeLeT

According to the DeLeT Handbook, a primary goal of Jewish day schools is to enable students "to form integrated identities as they study and experience their dual heritage and responsibilities as Americans and as Jews." To advance this mission, DeLeT sought to prepare elementary general studies teachers who "(a) take students and their ideas seriously; (b) create democratic classrooms infused with Jewish values and experiences; (c) make meaningful connections between general and Jewish studies; (d) welcome parents as partners in children's education; (e) value Jewish text study as a core Jewish activity; and (f) learn in and from their teaching."[4]

Five intersecting strands made up the DeLeT curriculum at Brandeis: fundamentals of teaching; clinical studies; subject matter pedagogy; learners and learning; and Jewish literacy and identity (table 6.1). A seminar on classroom teaching, closely coordinated with a yearlong internship, ran through the program and provided a forum for learning about planning, instruction, assessment, classroom organization, management, and culture. Subject-specific methods courses addressed the learning and teaching of core subjects in the elementary curriculum, both general and Jewish. A seminar on becoming a Jewish educator helped DeLeT students articulate and explore their personal stance on basic theological and ideological issues and consider the implications for their identity and practice as day school teachers.

A signature feature of the program was the yearlong internship. DeLeT partnered with day schools in the Greater Boston area representing a spectrum of Jewish life from Reform and Conservative sponsorship to Modern Orthodox and community day schools. Each school hosted one to three interns each year. Mentor teachers attended a summer institute and a monthly study group during the school year where they learned about the work DeLeT students were doing on campus, developed their mentoring skills, and addressed emergent problems and questions. The program also assigned field instructors who partnered with mentor teachers to help interns connect what they were learning at the university with what they were doing and learning in their internship placement.

The DeLeT curriculum rested on a set of professional teaching standards framed around eight core dimensions of teaching (table 6.2). Each standard was broken down into more specific elements that were further elaborated into developmental continua. The continua describe what it looks like to enact the standards at different levels of understanding and competence, from "pre-professional" to "approaching," "enacting," and "excelling." The DeLeT standards spell out the kind of teacher and teaching endorsed by the program. Besides helping to frame the DeLeT curriculum, the standards offered faculty, mentor teachers, interns, and field instructors a shared language for talking about teaching and a framework for assessing interns' progress and learning.

DeLeT Teaching Standards[5]

Standard 2, "Creating a classroom learning community infused with Jewish values and experiences," exemplifies a special brand of integration that DeLeT advocated, taught, and practiced—the integration of good teaching principles and practices with Jewish perspectives on the social curriculum. As the DeLeT Handbook explains, a teacher who enacts this standard "builds Jewish values and experiences into classroom life, uses Jewish texts and rituals to shape classroom culture, and connects students' personal and social responsibilities to specific Jewish values."[6]

Standard 2 has important secular dimensions as well. These include (1) establishing and maintaining clear expectations and consequences for individual and group behavior; (2) developing procedures for the smooth operation of the classroom and the efficient use of time; and (3) arranging the physical environment to support student learning. These elements help children feel safe and know what is expected of them so that they can participate appropriately as individuals and as members of the group.

TABLE 6.1. *MAT DeLeT Program at a Glance**

	Classroom Teaching	Clinical Studies	Subject Matter Pedagogy	Learners and Learning	Jewish Literacy and Identity
Summer I	Foundations of teaching	Reading practicum	Teaching reading; Teaching math; Art workshop		Studying the Hebrew Bible; Beit Midrash for Teachers
Fall	Fundamentals of teaching	Internship	Teaching Bible; Teaching Jewish holidays	Psychology of student learning [child study]	Jewish educator seminar
Winter/ Spring	Fundamentals of teaching	Internship	Teaching Science; Teaching Israel		Jewish educator seminar
Summer II	Making classroom culture	Teacher research	Teaching Jewish holidays; Art workshop	Teaching diverse learners	Philosophy of Jewish education; Beit Midrash for Teachers; Prayer and praying

*The program at Brandeis evolved as we transformed DeLeT from a freestanding fellowship in day school teaching to a graduate program that led to a master of arts in teaching (MAT) and met state requirements for initial licensure. The original thirteen-month structure with two summers of study and a yearlong internship did not change, but now the program could recruit both public school and day school candidates. Both cohorts took the same core courses required for certification. In addition, DeLeT candidates took courses to strengthen their Jewish literacy, explore their evolving Jewish identity, and introduce them to curricular materials and instructional strategies related to holidays, prayer, and Israel and to the broader purposes of day school education. Figure 6.1 reflects the version of DeLeT initiated in 2005 and maintained with some modification for the next five years.

TABLE 6.2. A good beginning day school teacher…

Standard 1: Knows children as learners	a. Gets to know children as individuals and learners, with diverse intellectual, emotional, and spiritual needs b. Refines knowledge of learning and child development through interactions with students c. Uses knowledge of children as learners in planning and teaching
Standard 2: Creates a classroom learning community rooted in Jewish experiences and values	a. Creates a classroom environment infused with Jewish values and experiences b. Creates a safe and stimulating culture of learning rooted in democratic principles and Jewish values c. Establishes and maintains clear expectations and consequences for individual and group behavior d. Develops procedures for the smooth operation of the classroom and the efficient use of time e. Arranges the physical environment to support student learning
Standard 3: Knows subject matter for teaching	a. Assesses and develops subject matter knowledge b. Acquires and uses subject-specific pedagogy c. Aligns instructional content with standards
Standard 4: Plans for student learning	a. Frames clear, developmentally appropriate, and worthwhile goals for student learning b. Designs short- and long-term plans that foster student inquiry and understanding c. Organizes coherent lessons and prepares for the "particulars" d. Uses materials and resources to make subject matter accessible to all students

continued→

Standard 5: Teaches for understanding	a. Builds on students' prior knowledge, life experiences, and interests b. Monitors and maintains students' intellectual engagement c. Adjusts instruction based on ongoing assessment d. Engages students in problem solving, critical thinking, and other activities that promote subject matter understanding e. Communicates effectively with students
Standard 6: Assesses student learning	a. Uses a variety of formal and informal assessments to monitor student learning b. Provides students with criteria and informative feedback to guide their learning and involve them in self-assessment c. Uses the results of assessments to inform future planning and instruction
Standard 7: Works with families and colleagues	a. Maintains open communication and works with families and caregivers to support student learning b. Respects and learns about families' diverse religious practices, cultural and socioeconomic backgrounds, and family structures c. Collaborates with colleagues to support and improve student learning
Standard 8: Develops as a professional Jewish educator	a. Exhibits professional judgment and behavior b. Demonstrates commitment to ongoing learning as a Jew c. Demonstrates commitment to ongoing learning as a Jewish educator and day school teacher

Teaching Standard 2

Three places in the DeLeT curriculum gave explicit, in-depth attention to teaching the understandings, values, and practices encompassed by Standard 2. It was a major focus of the fall "Fundamentals of Teaching" seminar that was closely coordinated with the internship. It was a continuing focus of the internship, which began in late August and continued through the school year. DeLeT students spent four days a week in a local day school, observing, assisting, and learning from their mentor teacher as they gradually assumed responsibilities for planning, instruction, and classroom management. So the needs and challenges of creating and maintaining a classroom learning community were always present. Finally, Standard 2 was the main focus of the final teaching seminar, "Making Classroom Culture," which took place in the second summer before graduation.

Investigating the Opening Weeks of School (September–October)

During the first two months of the school year (September–October), DeLeT students carried out a major investigation in their mentor teacher's classroom. Called "Establishing a Culture of Learning at the Beginning of the School Year," this inquiry was informed by readings and discussion in the "Fundamentals of Teaching" seminar and provided a substantive focus for observations of and conversations with mentor teachers. The overarching purpose of the assignment was to help DeLeT students begin to clarify a vision for their future classroom community by studying what their mentor teacher did to create a classroom learning community in the opening weeks of school.

The investigation had five parts: (1) an interview with the mentor teacher about their vision, values, and goals; (2) a narrative description of the first day of school; (3) documentation of classroom rules, routines, and procedures and how they were established; (4) documentation of opportunities for social participation by students; and (5) pulling it together in a coherent account. DeLeT students received detailed guidelines for carrying out each component. For instance, when they helped their mentor set up the classroom in late August, they were reminded to ask about the rationale behind the mentor's decisions about where students will sit and what to display on the classroom walls. When they reconstructed the first day of school, they were reminded to discuss "some of the most important messages that the mentor teacher communicated to the class." After documenting how classroom rules and routines were established, they were directed to "choose one rule or routine and consider how it supports or shapes student learning." While the inquiry mainly addressed general/secular aspects of teaching, DeLeT students also considered the question, "What makes this a *Jewish* classroom community?" By sharing their inquiries in their campus seminar, DeLeT students learned from one another about how different teachers built a classroom learning community in the opening weeks of school.

While DeLeT students were conducting this investigation, they read and discussed key chapters in Ruth Charney's *Teaching Children to Care: Classroom Management for Ethical and Academic Growth*, K–8 (Charney, 2002). This core text lays out the basics of building a classroom learning community grounded in an understanding of children and how they learn and a vision of a safe, respectful, cooperative learning environment. It offers theoretical perspectives and practical strategies. It rests on an approach to classroom management that promotes students' self-control and ethical conduct. Charney argues that teachers should "teach social control the same way we teach academics, as a recognized and valued part of our curriculum" (Charney, 2002, p. 17) and she shows teachers how to do that, for example, by describing how to teach expectations and formulate classroom rules with students. One of the core practices that Charney describes is "Morning Meeting," a short class meeting at the beginning of each day that builds community, reinforces academic and social skills, and gives students regular practice in respectful communication.

Learning about Building Classroom Community in Practice (September–June)

Issues related to classroom culture, organization, and management (Standard 2) were a continuing theme and focus of work between DeLeT interns and their mentors and field instructors. Interns quickly discovered that teachers do not set up their classroom community once and for all, then turn their attention to the requirements of academic instruction. Rather, classroom norms, expectations, rules, and routines must be continually reinforced, even retaught, throughout the school year.

DeLeT interns often experienced this need in January when their pupils returned from winter break and some reteaching of norms and routines was necessary. Moreover, once DeLeT fellows took on more instructional responsibilities, they confronted the simultaneous challenges of managing content while managing individuals, small groups, and the class as a whole. Mentor teachers were invaluable models and guides in their learning across the school year.

Planning for Your Own Classroom Community (July)

Standard 2 was again a central focus in the final teaching seminar called "Making Classroom Culture" offered in the second summer. Based on their conceptual and practical understanding of Standard 2, DeLeT fellows, soon to be teachers of record, began making plans for their own classroom in the fall. This meant thinking about how they could translate their vision of a Jewish classroom learning community into specific activities during the first days of school. They read *Life in a Crowded Space: Making a Learning Community* by Ralph Peterson, who advocates using "rites, rituals, and celebrations" as resources in building a classroom learning community (Peterson, 1992). They came up with a classroom ritual or celebration they hoped to introduce in their classroom. They also identified Jewish texts that embodied the norms and values they wanted to teach as a foundation for their classroom learning community.

For several years, this course included a special module called "Infusing Jewish Values into Classroom Culture." Taught by DeLeT alumna Jocelyn Segal, the module addressed these essential questions: (1) How can we apply what we learn from Jewish texts to our everyday classroom community? and (2) What does it mean and look like to create a classroom infused with Jewish values? In teaching this module, Segal drew heavily on the Jewish values curriculum she had designed for her own third-grade general studies classroom in collaboration with Orit Kent, co-designer, instructor, and investigator of the Beit Midrash for Teachers, a critical component of DeLeT's Jewish literacy strand.[7]

In this curriculum, developed into a web case called "Integrating Jewish

Values in a General Studies Classroom," Segal explores Jewish values texts with her students, using a wide variety of activities (including music, storytelling, and yoga) and structures (such as *hevruta* or paired text study and whole-class discussions). Through these activities and structures, third graders consider such classroom values as working together, respecting class members, and celebrating the uniqueness of each student.[8]

Learning Standard 2

To understand what DeLeT students learned about creating and maintaining a (Jewish) classroom learning community, we examine responses to two core assignments, one at the beginning of the internship and the second at the end. We have already described a major investigation, "Establishing a Culture of Learning at the Beginning of the School Year," which DeLeT students carried out in their internship classroom during the opening weeks of school. At the end of the internship, DeLeT students created teaching portfolios documenting their capacity to enact and reflect on core aspects of teaching. Besides a philosophy of teaching statement, there were required entries on "teaching for understanding" and "building and maintaining a classroom learning community."

We analyzed sixteen write-ups of the first investigation produced by DeLeT fellows from cohorts one and two (2002–2004) and ten portfolios created by fellows in cohorts one through five (2002–2007), paying particular attention to entries on classroom community and teaching philosophy.[9] We concentrated on work from early cohorts because they experienced a robust version of the program and because graduates from those cohorts were teaching the longest. These data offer a window on what students learned during the program about what it means and what it takes to create a classroom learning community infused with Jewish values and experiences. The lessons were conceptual and practical, general and specific, secular and Jewish.

Studying Mentor Teachers' Community-Building Practices

As they studied the opening weeks of school against the backdrop of seminar readings and discussions, DeLeT fellows began to connect the vision of a safe, respectful, productive classroom learning community, as described by Ruth Charney in *Teaching Children to Care* (2002), with the specific instructional activities and interactions they observed in their mentors' classroom. They saw how teachers embody their purposes and values in what they say and do and they uncovered the thinking behind teachers' decisions and actions. Many of their observations reflected the principles and practices they were learning about in the "Fundamentals of Teaching" seminar.

The intentionality of teaching came through as DeLeT interns helped their mentors set up the classroom, while asking them about their goals and expectations for the year. Mira, a DeLeT intern in the first cohort, wrote about her mentor teacher: "I saw how Eve's values and goals are incorporated into everything in the classroom... from the way the desks are set up to the posters on the walls."[10] Sara, an intern in the same cohort, noted: "Gail is extremely organized and has taught me to appreciate the order and structure she believes are necessary for a successful classroom... On the first day students will discuss the jobs they will have that help to create order as well as community."

Intentionality informed the way mentors established rules and routines, often in conjunction with students, as Charney advises. Here are descriptions of what three interns in three different day schools observed and understood about the values and rationale guiding the process:

> Gail asks the students to write the ground rules for the classroom after a discussion of creating a caring, safe, and respectful community. She reinforces the idea that students are allowed to make mistakes and during class discussion must treat each other with respect, stating their own opinions without criticizing others. (Sara, fifth grade)

> As in *Teaching Children to Care*, we began with their [the students'] own hopes and dreams and then, collectively as a class, devised our own set of rules that would make those hopes and dreams come true. (Jonah, first grade)

> One of the things that Ilana did on the very first day that I thought really built the classroom community was to make the rules *with* the children... with Ilana only guiding them to pick positives instead of

> negatives. These children learned that we value their ideas, that they are the ones who shape our community, and that they are responsible for making it a safe place to live in for the year. (Laura, first grade)

On a practical level, interns learned that laying this foundation takes time and requires consistency, modeling, explicitness, and often reteaching. Sam wrote: "The most important things I learned from my mentor about setting up a classroom culture at the beginning of the year are to be explicit in your expectations, to make no assumptions, [and] to be a model of respectful behavior." About the same mentor teacher, Janet wrote: "Rachel is very good about making her expectations clear... She spends time revisiting things as well as making sure her ways are consistent." And Laura described how building a classroom community was the central focus of the first month of school: "In the first month of school, our main focus seems to be building a classroom learning community. We taught specific lessons on listening and cooperation, emphasized routines and transitions, and discussed classroom rules and behavior."

Respect and community emerged as dominant values, along with responsibility, cooperation, and caring. Mentors modeled these values and helped students learn how to enact them in their relationships and interactions with one another. Jeremy explained how respect served as an umbrella value: "It [respect] applies to everyone at all times and encompasses respect for everyone's intangibles, like thoughts and ideas, as well as their physical property and space." Mira wrote that "the most important values that Elaine hopes to pass on to her students this year are the importance of community and respect and that learning happens all the time and can be fun." Jacob echoed a similar stance: "Among the values that Sara holds most sacred is the respect students exhibit toward one another and the ways in which they care for and treat one another."

As part of their investigation, interns were asked to consider the question: "What makes this a Jewish classroom community?" In their responses, they detailed what they observed and reflected on the questions this raised. Many interns began their response by noting such visible or tangible signs as the use of Hebrew and Jewish texts, boys wearing kippot, and how the Jewish calendar frames the year. Jerri produced the following list:

- Quote from Talmud on daily job chart: "Four things need to be pursued with strength and energy—Torah, good deeds, prayer, and one's daily task."
- *Boker tov* sign on the morning routine poster.
- Timeline with Jewish/Israel events.
- A poster of rules that says "Treat others the way you would want to be treated."
- Calendar with the secular and Jewish dates.

Lee noted the use of Hebrew like *derech eretz*, *kehillah*, and *kavod*, which she said "creates a sense of Jewish community, instead of just community." Yet she wondered, "What makes this classroom special in a Jewish sense?" Sara had similar questions: "How do we/should we show students that many of the Jewish values we have are shared by other religions and cultures? Do students react differently when you ask them to show *kavod* instead of respect?"

Mira explained how the teacher's identity and modeling contribute to the Jewish character of the classroom. "Since we all pray together each day, the kids see the teachers as good Jewish role models. We all come out of the prayer experience ready to begin the day fresh." She described how her mentor teacher used Hebrew or Yiddish phrases and talked about her parents who were Holocaust survivors. But the biggest influence, in her view, came from the use of Jewish commandments and values. "When something happens in a Jewish school, the teacher can always reference a Jewish story or text to teach a lesson."

Lee described how her mentor teacher created opportunities for first graders to fix what might be broken in age-appropriate ways. For instance, when a classmate was sick, she had the children send cards, which she framed as the mitzvah of helping the sick. Lee described how her mentor teacher constantly modeled respectful treatment of others by the language she used to correct student behavior: "I didn't mention a name when I told you that I do not want to see X behavior in our class anymore, because I do not want to embarrass anyone."

Some interns proposed that the Jewish character of the classroom came through indirectly. Mira suggested that the importance placed on education "makes it feel like a Jewish classroom community" and Laura claimed that having rules with consequences is a fundamental Jewish value, as she put it: "The Torah is very clear about the goals, expectations, and consequences for behavior. The message is that actions and words are what counts." Still other interns were unsure whether "being a good person, respecting others, treating people how you would want to be treated, and taking care of yourself, your things, and others are distinctively Jewish values."

Imagining Their Own Classroom Community

At the end of their internship, DeLeT fellows wrote their philosophy of day school teaching and their vision of the kind of classroom learning community they hoped to establish as teachers of record. Portfolio entries reveal the influence of Ruth Charney's approach to classroom management for ethical and academic growth as well as the community-building principles and practices of mentor teachers. Writing in the first person, DeLeT fellows conveyed a growing sense of professional agency as they moved back and forth between "big ideas" and concrete strategies. Their visions seamlessly blended secular and Jewish values, while the Jewish content of their social curricula varied in the depth of Jewish ideas and sources.

In all the portfolios we analyzed, DeLeT fellows took responsibility for teaching a values-based social curriculum as part of their approach to classroom management. *Kavod* and *kehillah* appeared in every entry, sometimes couched in terms of the three Rs—rights, respect, and responsibility—a formulation that several interns in different cohorts learned from the same mentor teacher. For some these were uniquely Jewish values. Others saw them as humanistic values translated into Hebrew. Still others claimed that grounding these universal values in Jewish sources made a difference.

Anna linked the core Jewish values shaping her classroom culture with Hebrew sayings: "Isn't it nice how we sit here together" (*hinei matov u-ma-na'im . . .*) and "love your friend as you love yourself" (*v'ahavta l'reyacha kamocha*), as she explained: "Whether sung in melody or spoken in words, these two Jewish values shaped the classroom culture and governed our eight- to ten year old community."

To develop *kehillah and kavod*, Anna taught three key responsibilities—responsibility for self, responsibility for others, and responsibility for your environment. She found it particularly challenging to foster a sense of responsibility for the classroom environment, as she noted: "By December, the classroom was a mess... Students needed to realize and to learn that without their actions, their learning environment would begin to impinge on their learning." So she introduced a new chart with jobs for each student within the classroom and instituted a "*todah*" (thank you!) list where she wrote each day the names of students who took extra initiative to keep the classroom clean.

In defining her classroom *kehillah*, Jerri used a mixture of Jewish and secular terms and standards:

> It is most important to create a classroom *kehillah* that is caring and safe, that breeds cooperation and *kavod*, that allows children to excel to their highest potential, and that assesses students and holds them accountable to clear expectations. All students should be in a place where they can succeed. In the classroom, students should feel comfortable and accepted.

Some interns emphasized the needs of individuals: "When creating classroom community, my most important goal for children is to feel valued; a child's self-esteem needs to be developed." Others stressed group unity. "As a teacher, I value group unity and want my students to feel lucky to be learning, celebrating, and growing with each other." Still others described their dual focus on individuals and the group, as Allie explained: "The focus on individuals must be balanced with the acknowledgment that we are a community of learners and that we can all learn from each other." To promote the idea that everyone is both learner and teacher, she planned to teach this saying from *Pirkei Avot* (4:1): "Who is wise? The one who learns from every person...Who is honored? The one who gives honor to others."

For some interns, the use of Jewish texts became a central vehicle for reinforcing Jewish values and promoting desirable student behavior. Tal presented an extended example in her portfolio. Returning to school in January, she saw students arguing, speaking out of turn, and refusing to work with one another. So she decided "to take time out of the academic schedule to work on the social curriculum." Taking a page from Ruth Charney, she had students brainstorm their hopes and dreams for what the classroom could look and feel like and then discuss how their actions could make these dreams come true. The next step involved generating a classroom contract that each student signed.

Two weeks later, Tal introduced a Jewish text from *B'reishit Rabbah* (100:7): "A group of people and a family resemble a head of stones. If you take one stone out, the whole [heap] totters." After discussing what it means to be in a family or a community and how each member is as important as each stone in a heap, students met in small groups to consider what makes each person special and what each brings to the class. Finally, each student wrote about and drew a picture of another student. In her community entry, Tal included a picture of a classroom display that featured the text in Hebrew and English surrounded by the students' drawings and statements about what made each person special. She concluded her entry with the following intentions:

> Next year I will establish routines and clear expectations starting on the first day of school. I believe students feel secure when there are guidelines and creativity grows within structure . . . I also plan to continue incorporating Jewish texts as introductions to working together.

Across the board, the portfolios framed classroom management in terms of a social curriculum of life skills and values that must be explicitly and consistently taught. Alice provided a particularly clear illustration of that stance:

> I teach and then reinforce social skills so that children can internalize what is acceptable behavior. I believe that these skills are not taught during a forty-five-minute period once a week, but are ongoing, and must be constantly and consistently integrated if we want children to apply them outside the confines of the classroom. Reminders must not be punitive and ill intention must never be assumed. My stance is founded on the assumption that children want to do the right thing and be part of the community and that they need our help in learning these crucial social skills.

Clearly the DeLeT fellows whose investigations and portfolio entries we analyzed developed a vision of the kind of classroom community they wanted to create and some tools and strategies for realizing their vision. Influenced by Ruth Charney and by their mentor teachers, they understood that teachers must attend to this central task of teaching in intentional and explicit ways, especially at the beginning of the school year, but also as part of an ongoing social curriculum. To varying degrees, they embraced the opportunity to frame this task in terms of Jewish/Hebrew language, values, and practices.

Enacting Standard 2

How did the teaching and learning of Standard 2 during the early years of DeLeT shape the way alumni go about building a learning community in their classrooms? To what extent do DeLeT graduates bring a Jewish lens to this central task of teaching? How did the experience of observing and co-teaching with their mentor teacher contribute to their own classroom vision and practice? In what ways do their current school contexts support or limit their ability to position themselves as Jewish educators?

Following we present cases of two DeLeT alums who have been working in Jewish day schools since they graduated from the program. Both are elementary, general studies teachers who see themselves as Jewish educators, and they offer mature examples of Standard 2 in practice. The cases illustrate how the preparation these teachers received in DeLeT laid a strong foundation for their community-building practices and how they, in turn, developed their own approach to building a classroom learning community infused with Jewish values and experiences. University-based teacher education is often considered a weak influence compared with the influence of on-the-job experience. These cases challenge this assumption.

Karen: "I Am a Jewish Teacher."

Karen has been teaching in Jewish day schools since she graduated from DeLeT in 2007. For six years following graduation, she taught kindergarten in the same school where she did her internship and where she was responsible for both general and Jewish studies. When we interviewed her, she had been teaching in an Orthodox day school in Canada. This school has a split day, with one teacher for Judaics and Hebrew and a second teacher for general studies. Karen taught general studies for half the day in second grade and half the day in kindergarten.

In her DeLeT portfolio, Karen wrote about her teaching philosophy.

> I am Jewish... I am a teacher... I am a Jewish teacher. I teach in Jewish day schools because they allow me to pass on the traditions, knowledge, and customs that I learned myself in a Jewish day school. I am a Jewish teacher because I believe that our generation needs to pass on all that we know to the next generation.

After graduating from DeLeT, Karen continues to identify as a Jewish educator. She describes herself as a general studies teacher who integrates Jewish values and identity into her classroom when she can, although officially she does not teach Jewish studies. In fact, she finds it challenging to teach in a school where Judaic and general studies are not integrated, because the integration seems so natural to her and she doesn't want to "be in a box."

» Karen's DeLeT Experience

When Karen entered DeLeT, she came with her own experience as a child in a Jewish day school. There, she remembers, "Half the day was Jewish and the other half was Canadian, and those lines didn't cross at all." Her DeLeT experience was "the eye-opener that it didn't have to be that way." Working with her mentors in kindergarten and first grade demonstrated to Karen that "of course it [Jewish values and identity] should be integrated, [and done] so seamlessly." DeLeT taught her to look beyond the black-and-white categories of "Jewish" and "not Jewish" that she had grown up with.

Karen remembers clearly seeing how her mentor teacher built a classroom community with Jewish values and identity woven in. She knows that she learned about this in her classes at Brandeis, but what she mainly recalls is "seeing it implemented in practice." Karen remembers watching her mentor teach about apologies at Yom Kippur. She remembers that anytime someone would knock something over that needed to be cleaned up, her mentor would ask, "Who's going to come be my mitzvah mensch?" She remembers that in a second mentor's classroom, the quote *"Eizehu chacham halomed mikol adam*" (Who is wise? One who learns from every person) was posted on the wall and referred to regularly. Of Jewish values and ideas, Karen says, "It was everywhere."

Looking at Karen's written work while a student in DeLeT, we can see that she was strongly influenced by her mentor's practice. In her study of how her mentor began the school year with a new class of students, she wrote:

> Hannah [Karen's mentor] loves the strong sense of Torah values that [her school] embodies. In her class, children live and breathe Torah values and these are incorporated in her class from day one. While reading, writing, and arithmetic are important things to know, being a mensch is even more important. We need to live these values, not just know them, which is not always the case in public schools. She emphasizes the importance of taking advantage of teachable moments, such as using an opportunity to discuss the importance of apologizing when a situation arises.
>
> Our classroom is a Jewish classroom in every sense of the word. It is evident from the moment you walk in the class. A lot of the rules are rooted in Jewish values, including kindness, caring, respect for classmates, for example, when someone is speaking, and respect for the classroom, for example, cleaning up without added motivation. There is also clear visual evidence that it is a Jewish class. From the *brachas* to the *birkat*, the children are immersed in Judaism.
>
> In my reflection, the rule I have chosen is calling out and talking all at once in circle . . . This rule intertwines nicely with Hannah's classroom theme of *derech eretz*. They [the students] are encouraged to respect each other and each other's space as well as the classroom and school environment. As Jews, they are encouraged to do *mitzvot*, including giving tzedakah, respecting the Torah, and caring for others. They learn the true meaning of the word *s'licha* and how to use it sincerely.[11]

» Enacting Standard 2 in Her Own Classroom

Karen has brought her stance as a Jewish educator to her own classrooms since graduating from DeLeT. In her first school, Karen found a context that supported and encouraged a culture of integration in a classroom community infused with Jewish experiences. She designed a yearlong course of study for kindergarteners integrating literacy, Jewish texts, and the social curriculum. Based around Torah stories from *B'reishit*, she taught Jewish values embedded in those stories and connected them with the social skills needed for a successful classroom community.

For example, young students in her class would often say things like, "If you play with me, I promise I'll invite you to my birthday party." When studying parshat *Lech Lecha* and God's promise to Avraham, the class explored the meaning of a promise and how to use the words "I promise." As they addressed the implications of statements about promises for their classroom community, the conversation was grounded in the Torah story they had learned, retold, illustrated, and dictated.

Karen explained that because each of these stories permeated the class for a few weeks, they became part of the structure and vocabulary. Weeks after studying the story of Noach, who was *tzaddik* (righteous), she could say, "It looks like there are people in the class who are being *tzaddik* right now; they are doing the right thing." Walking into Karen's classroom while students were studying the story of *Vayera* and the value of welcoming guests, visitors would see a large mural on the wall with figures of Avraham, Sarah, and three guests being welcomed. The visitors would often be greeted by students who might offer them a chair or something to eat or drink, enacting the values the students had learned through Jewish stories.

For the past few years, Karen has been teaching in a school with a very different culture. Judaic and general studies are taught separately by different people, and few teachers in her school take time each day to focus on building community. Yet, Karen continues to enact the stance she learned in DeLeT, employing many of the same good teaching practices that she read about and observed in her mentors' classrooms. She describes a strong commitment to building community, including taking time every day for a Responsive Classroom–style morning meeting, "a daily gathering of the class that builds group cohesion and an attentive, responsive community" (Charney, 2002, p. 45). This includes, for example, students greeting each other by name and sharing information about events in their lives.

Karen says many of her colleagues cannot understand how she can devote fifteen minutes to a daily morning meeting with so many academic demands. But for Karen, "if my kids walk out of my classroom without being able to read, I'm okay with that, but if they don't know how to be part of a community or how to share or respond to a question or apologize or greet someone, then one hundred percent I've failed as a kindergarten teacher." In her second-grade class, "The bottom line is if kids aren't feeling like they're in a safe classroom, then it doesn't matter what they're learning. So, it's worth it to take the time." Karen's comments about taking time are reminiscent of Ruth Charney's advice in *Teaching Children to Care*: "In this battle for time, we need to remember that academics and social behavior are profoundly intertwined" (Charney, 2002, p. 18).

Once again, we can look back at the investigation Karen conducted in her mentor's classroom as part of her "Fundamentals of Teaching" class and the community entry she included in her portfolio and see how the influence of DeLeT continues to this day:

> An attitude that is evident in our class is that we are all different and entitled to be different. This can be seen by having some children sit on chairs during circle, and by having different levels of help during morning work.[12]

"This illustrates perhaps some of my greatest learnings in the DeLeT program," Karen continues. "I no longer just sit back and assume that my class will act in ways that demonstrate respect. I plan each lesson knowing that although there are academic skills I wish to impart to the students, equally important are the ways in which they work together, respect each other and themselves, and learn from each other. I know that as I think about setting up my own classroom, this will continue to be a priority."[13]

Karen continues to enact her stance as a general studies teacher who is also a Jewish educator, even in an environment where that is not expected. She looks for opportunities to infuse her classroom with Jewish values and experiences whenever possible. For example, Karen teaches students to use what Charney calls an "apology of action" (Charney, 2002, p. 154) to apologize to others through actions rather than just through words.

She intentionally introduces this right before Yom Kippur. By focusing on making mistakes and apologizing, she synchronizes her social curriculum with the Jewish holiday cycle. Last winter, when Karen taught her students about Martin Luther King Jr., she wanted to make a connection to Jewish values. She invited the school rabbi to her general studies class to talk about the Jewish value of being created *b'tzelem elohim*, in God's image, and tied that to MLK's legacy. One student wrote in response to a writing prompt, "I can show it [*b'tzelem elohim*] by being very nice to people. I will not say you can't play with me or I [am] better than you because it's not nice. Also, because we were all created in God's image."[14]

Within the context of her school, this was an unusual crossing of the Jewish studies/general studies divide. For Karen, however, it is the obvious way to help students connect their own lives to others. She believes that her students related to a topic they might otherwise not have considered important because she presented it through a Jewish lens. Even in a school where the dividing line between general and Jewish studies is strong, Karen has found an appropriate way to integrate Jewish values into her classroom learning community.

Lily: A Classroom Community Infused with Jewish Values and Texts

Lily has been teaching third grade in the Jewish day school where she was originally a DeLeT intern ever since she graduated from DeLeT in 2010. She teaches general studies and has a teaching partner who teaches her students Hebrew and Judaic studies during different parts of the day.

Lily identifies herself as a general studies teacher who teaches Jewish values and Jewish identity to her students. She also considers herself a Jewish role model, as she explains: "They [my students] know I am an active Jew. I talk about my own Shabbat and *chag* practice. I actively talk about Jewish values within the school." This is welcomed and not unusual within this school's context, although Lily thinks she is the only general studies teacher who actively teaches Jewish texts. In the lower school, all the teachers are Jewish. General studies teachers are expected to be present for prayers such as *motzi*, *birkat hamazon*, and *kabbalat shabbat*, so they are seen by students in these integrated roles.

Walking into Lily's classroom, we see wall displays everywhere that mix Hebrew and English, secular and Jewish calendars, and Judaic and general studies content. The primary bulletin board has a calendar with upcoming class events, some listed in Hebrew and others in English. Posters list the third-grade class rules—"Respect for Yourself... Respect for Others... Respect for the Environment." There are clearly written examples of what behaviors are associated with each rule. One poster tells how to give feedback ("Look / Nod / Don't Argue / Think / Restate / Thank / Decide").

Above the white board are interlocking puzzle pieces with rabbinic quotes primarily from *Pirkei Avot* printed in Hebrew (e.g., quotes that could be translated as "Greet everyone with a pleasant face," "Two are better than one... for should they both fall, one can raise the other"). These puzzle pieces represent Jewish texts that Lily has chosen to study with her students each month during her general studies class time as a foundation for her social curriculum.

» Beginnings and classroom rituals: A DeLeT assignment

Lily remembers her second summer of DeLeT, just before she would take over her own classroom in the fall. In the course on "Making Classroom Culture," she learned about the power of routines and rituals to build classroom community. For the "create a classroom ritual" assignment, she developed a ritual for marking each Hebrew month. She compiled a chart of Jewish texts that she could use monthly to teach Jewish values in relation to her classroom community.

Lily also remembers that every DeLeT get-together, including the initial meeting between interns and mentors, began with a Jewish text study to set the tone. Although Lily did not refer to it explicitly, we can see the influence of the Beit Midrash for Teachers, a central part of the DeLeT program, where she studied rabbinic texts about teaching and learning with a *hevruta* or study partner in the context of a professional learning community.

» Eighteen years later: Jewish texts as foundational to Lily's classroom community

Lily has tweaked the details since that initial DeLeT assignment, but she has essentially maintained the text component of the Rosh Chodesh ritual and its structure. Over the years, she has expanded the list of texts, though she still uses many of the same texts from her original list. She organizes her teaching of the social curriculum for the year around these Rosh Chodesh text studies. In fact, Lily's curriculum map for the year includes "community" and "Rosh Chodesh texts" alongside math, reading, and social studies in her list of subject areas.

Lily begins this ritual each year in September. If Rosh Hashanah comes early enough in the school year, she uses that as her kickoff; if Rosh Hashanah comes later, she begins with Elul and explains to students that "this is the way we will normally start a new month." The first text Lily teaches is "*V'hevay mikabal et kol ha-adam b'sever panim yafot*" (Greet every person with a pleasant face) (*Pirkei Avot* 1:15). She connects this text with the way they will greet each other in class each day: They will look at each other, smile, and make eye contact.

This is then applied all year long, as Lily begins every day with a morning meeting inspired by the Responsive Classroom approach (Charney, 2002, pp. 45–46). Kriete explains the importance of such greetings: "Greeting sets a positive tone for the classroom and the day...When we make time for greeting every morning, no matter how full the schedule, we make a statement as teachers that we expect class members to treat each other with courtesy and equity and that we will do our best to make sure it happens" (Kriete & David, 2014, pp. 53). In Lily's classroom, this value is grounded from the beginning in a Jewish text from the rabbinic tradition.

What does the Rosh Chodesh ritual look like in Lily's classroom? Each month, Lily posts a Jewish text for the students to look at. She first puts the text up only in Hebrew and asks students to try to find words they know and work toward understanding. Eventually, they come up with a translation, and then discuss what this text could mean and how it connects to their classroom. After the discussion, Lily posts the quote on the class bulletin board. She will say, "I'm going to be looking for moments when you're doing this and I'll point them out," and she tries to do this throughout the year.

Most months, the text study takes place during a whole-class discussion during morning meeting. Sometimes Lily introduces the idea of *hevruta* (study partner) discussions. Students then get a written study guide that they use with a partner, with directions that include reading the text in Hebrew, reading it in English, and creating a joint interpretation of what the text could mean.

In a Rosh Chodesh discussion that Lily recorded to share with us, students explored the text "*Kol ha-malbin p'nei haveyro b'rabim, k'eilu shofech damim*" (He who publicly embarrasses his neighbor is as though he sheds blood) (*Bava Metzia* 58-b). Lily offered a translation of the translation: "When someone embarrasses their friend, it is just like they physically hurt them." In talking about what the text means, one student offered the following interpretation of "spilling blood": "Say someone spilled out an animal's blood and drained out all of its life. If you take a person, you are hurting a person. You are draining out all their happiness and strength."

After discussing the meaning of the quote, Lily asked: "What could following what this rabbi has to say look like here in our classroom if we really took it to heart?" One student said, "Let's say you are having a race with lots of people and you were first and the person who's way far behind you trips. You shouldn't laugh. You should go back and help them." Another suggested, "Don't talk behind someone's back." A third said, "You should make sure it doesn't go in your speech bubble." (Lily teaches students to distinguish ideas that belong in their thought bubbles and ideas that can be expressed in their speech bubbles.)

Finally, Lily said, "During Iyar, I'm going to be noticing how we're taking this to heart." She acknowledged that this quote is a bit more challenging to observe because it tells people NOT to do something. It's a lot easier to see students greeting one another, trying to learn from all people, and advocating for themselves and others. Since she isn't going to be looking for students "embarrassing each other," what will she be looking for during the month and the rest of the year?

Student give various answers: "Being kind." "Don't leave anyone behind if they trip and fall." "If someone with a disability comes into the school, you shouldn't put them down and make fun of them. You should be kind to them." Lily then asked, "And even if there's a moment when you see that something might embarrass them, what could you do to help?" "Don't talk about someone behind their back," a student replies.

Lily also uses Jewish texts to address prejudice, discuss partner work, and explore friendship. She explains that these topics are part of her social curriculum but she chooses to discuss them using the language of Jewish texts and Jewish values so that the texts "become part of the conversation of the classroom." When we ask Lily what difference it makes to couch her social curriculum in terms of Jewish values and texts, she explains:

> We have this rich collection of ways of talking about things that's already been written down, that we can use as a source. It's easy to talk about "it's nice to greet someone with a smile," but to have a text grounds it. This is something that's been talked about for generations and generations, and this isn't something new to us. This is something important to us as a people—this elevates the conversation a bit. For the kids, the fact that it's written down, it cements its value. It's not just something we're talking about in third grade in this school.

Concluding Discussion

The title of this chapter—"'Responsive Classroom' Meets the Rabbis"—juxtaposes two disparate sources of wisdom on teaching and learning. Ruth Charney's Responsive Classroom represents a contemporary approach to classroom management that involves teaching social-emotional skills as an end in itself and a foundation for academic and ethical learning. The rabbis offer traditional perspectives on ethical Jewish behavior. The combination reflects the Jewish spin that the DeLeT program gave to a central task of teaching—creating a safe and productive classroom learning community.

The program aimed to prepare general studies teachers who saw themselves as Jewish educators and modeled a commitment to Jewish learning and living. Such teachers would not only know how to teach their subjects and form productive relationships with students, colleagues, and families but would also be disposed to create classroom learning communities infused with Jewish values and experiences. The assumption was that a learning community in which time, space, and relationships were framed through a Jewish lens would foster ethical dispositions, teach desirable social behaviors, and strengthen students' Jewish identities.

In this chapter, we described how DeLeT helped fellows learn the theory and practice of creating a safe, respectful, Jewishly inspired classroom learning community. This was an explicit focus of instruction in two seminars on teaching and an important focus of observation, inquiry, and guided practice in mentors' classrooms. We also referred to other aspects of the DeLeT curriculum that contributed to fellows' understanding and embrace of Standard 2. These included the Beit Midrash for Teachers, which modeled the formation of a professional learning community through Jewish text study in *hevruta*, and a Jewish Educators Seminar, which supported professional and personal identity work.

We explored what DeLeT fellows learned about classroom community building by analyzing relevant samples of fellows work produced during the program. This included investigations of the opening weeks of school in mentor teachers' classrooms and classroom community entries in teaching portfolios produced at the end of the internship. We showed how fellows moved from documenting their mentors' vision and practice to describing their role in maintaining social practices and values to projecting their vision and plans for their own classroom learning community. In the process, they came to understand, albeit as novice teachers, what it means and what it takes to create a safe, respectful, well-functioning classroom environment based on both secular and Jewish values.

While DeLeT fellows were learning why it's important to be explicit and consistent in teaching expectations and routines and how to plan and run an effective morning meeting, they were also wondering what makes this a Jewish classroom community and why it matters. All embraced the use of Hebrew terms and texts to teach particular values and behaviors, especially those associated with *kehillah*/community and *kavod*/respect. A few, like Lily, saw how grounding the social curriculum in Jewish sources elevates the conversation by linking it to "something that's been talked about for generations and generations, not just something we do in our third-grade classroom."

The cases of Karen and Lily show that Standard 2 is alive and well in the classrooms of some DeLeT graduates years after they completed the program. Each has developed an integrated approach to building a classroom learning community infused with Jewish values and teaching a social curriculum grounded in Jewish texts and experiences. The rich descriptions of their community-building practice reflect a mature vision and a well-honed craft. These are not only experienced general studies teachers, but they are also reflective practitioners with a deep commitment to their professional identity as Jewish educators.

Why do these cases matter? What can we learn from this study of DeLeT at Brandeis and its short- and long-term impact on teachers' learning and practice? Two related implications stand out, one more general and the other more particular. The first speaks to questions about the kind of teacher education that makes a difference in teachers' practice and students' learning. The second concerns the specific vision of general studies teachers in non-Orthodox Jewish day schools that animated the DeLeT program.

One purpose in undertaking this study is to connect the dots between the professional preparation that DeLeT provided and the teaching and teacher leadership that graduates practiced in their schools. Demonstrating a positive program influence, especially one that represents a departure from conventional school practice, calls for an explanation. Given the low regard of university-based teacher education in many sectors and the widespread assumption that once teachers know their subjects, the rest can be learned on the job, it is important to consider what might account for this outcome.

We believe the answer lies in the kind of professional preparation DeLeT offered. Despite the belief that teacher education is a weak intervention compared with the powerful influence of school culture and teaching experience, there is mounting evidence that teacher education can make a difference when it embodies certain features. These include a guiding vision of good teaching, strong integration of coursework and fieldwork, extensive and intensive clinical experience, trained mentors, student teacher cohorts, and attention to their entering beliefs and evolving professional identity and practice.[15] On both structural and substantive levels, DeLeT embodied these features, making it a unique model for the field of Jewish education.[16]

Most people have logged ten thousand hours watching what teachers do during their years as pupils in elementary and secondary school. The familiarity with teaching, promoted by this "apprenticeship of observation,"[17] often misleads people into believing that they know what teaching entails. But watching teaching from the outside as a student does not begin to reveal the hidden world of teacher thinking and decision-making. Nor does it illuminate the complex nature of this intellectual and relational practice that must be learned and can be taught.

DeLeT took preparation for teaching practice seriously, as illustrated by our focus on the practice of creating a safe, respectful classroom learning community.[18] Standard 2 spelled out what this involves and Ruth Charney provided a coherent model, delineating specific components and offering strategies for their implementation. DeLeT fellows studied these components by investigating the opening weeks of school in their mentor teacher's classroom and connecting their emerging understanding to specific moves and strategies. With coaching and support, they practiced maintaining norms, routines, and expectations as they gradually assumed increasing classroom responsibilities. A final performance assessment examined their ability to enact component practices and conceptualize the kind of learning community they hoped to create in their own classrooms. In this way, the program laid a strong foundation for beginning teaching and for continued learning in and from teaching.

So far this account could apply to any serious teacher education program committed to preparing well-started beginning elementary teachers. But DeLeT sought to do more than bring "best practices" in teacher education to Jewish education. DeLeT opened its doors at a time when the unexpected spread of non-Orthodox day schools seemed to call for a new kind of teacher.[19] DeLeT tried to address that need by preparing general studies teachers who identified with the day school mission, modeled engaged Jewish living and learning, and created classroom learning communities infused with Jewish values and experiences.

DeLeT graduates rarely had difficulty securing a teaching position, despite the fact that many day school leaders were reluctant to hire brand-new teachers.[20] Almost everyone who sought a teaching position in a Jewish day school found one, as a full-time general studies teacher or assistant teacher.[21] This does not mean that graduates always landed in a school that embraced the integrated vision embodied in Standard 2. As the case of Karen reveals, a sharp division between general and Jewish subjects and faculty can make it harder to create a common Jewish learning environment. But, as the same case also shows, a thoughtful and committed kindergarten teacher-leader can find a way to practice this kind of integration, at least in their own classroom.

In trying to account for a teacher's practice, one must consider personal background, professional education, and school context. In this study, we highlighted the role of professional preparation in promoting a vision of a classroom learning community infused with Jewish values and experiences. We know anecdotally that this was countercultural in some of the settings where DeLeT graduates taught.[22] Hopefully, DeLeT helped them develop the vision and know-how to enact a version of this practice in the service of their students' social development and in keeping with the *L* in DeLeT, which stands for "leadership through teaching.

NOTES

1. Ruth Charney developed a humanistic, student-centered approach to building a classroom community called "Responsive Classroom." We taught this approach in the DeLeT program.

2. *Delet*, the Hebrew word for "door," also stands for Day School Leadership Through Teaching. The program was designed to open a door on a career in day school teaching. Jonathan Woocher, z"l, came up with the name in an early meeting in New York with program leaders Michael Zeldin from HUC-JIR and Sharon Feiman-Nemser, venture philanthropist Laura Lauder, Joshua Elkin, director of PEJE (Partnership for Excellence in Jewish Education), and other early supporters.

3. The faculty interviews and focus groups were conducted as part of a comparative study of DeLeT at Brandeis, the ACE program at the University of Notre Dame, and the UTEP program at the University of Chicago, three mission-drive, context-specific teacher education programs. The findings from that study are published in S. Feiman-Nemser, E. Tamir, & K. Hammerness, *Inspiring teaching: Preparing teachers for mission-driven schools*, Cambridge, MA: Harvard Education Press.

4. For a fuller discussion of DeLeT's founding vision and early history, see Feiman-Nemser & M. Zeldin, 2007.

5. We began developing the DeLeT Teaching Standards during the planning year (2001–2002), building on the development of teaching standards in general education during the l990s. The DeLeT standards were influenced by the work of the National Board for Professional Teaching Standards (NBPTS), the Interstate New Teacher Assessment Consortium (INTASC), and the elementary teacher education program standards at Michigan State University and Trinity University. Over the years, the standards were refined through contributions by DeLeT course instructors, mentor teachers, and field instructors.

6. A basic program handbook was developed during the planning year (2001–2002) with program policies, calendars, teaching standards, expectations, and rosters. Over time, the handbook was expanded and refined as we gained experience and learned what kind of shared information students, faculty, field instructors, and mentor teachers needed. This version of the DeLeT teaching standards appeared in the 2006–2007 DeLeT Handbook.

7. For a description of the Beit Midrash for Teachers and the central role it played in the DeLeT program, see Feiman-Nemser, 2006.

8. To view the web case that Segal and Kent created to make this curriculum accessible to others, see www.brandeis.edu/mandel/research/past/beit-midrash-research/jewish-values-havruta.html. The case is a further example of how a DeLeT graduate made the creation of a Jewish learning community the foundation for her social and language arts curricula.

9. When the DeLeT fellowship became the day school track in the Brandeis MAT program, we replaced the portfolio requirement with a teacher research requirement. Consequently, portfolios were only available from students in the first five cohorts.

10. Pseudonyms are used for DeLeT fellows/interns and mentor teachers.

11. Quotes are from Karen's "Investigating the Opening Weeks of School" write-up in 2006, specifically the section reporting her interview with her mentor teacher and the section on establishing rules, routines, and procedures.

12. "Investigating the Opening Weeks of School," section on "rules, routines, and procedures," 2006.

13. Portfolio entry on "classroom community," 2007.

14. Student work, Karen's classroom, 2018.

15. For empirical support, see Darling-Hammond, 2000; National Center for Research on Teacher Learning, 1991.

16. An outside evaluation of DeLeT commissioned by the Jim Joseph Foundation in 2008 acknowledged this fact, claiming that DeLeT "broke the mold" when it came to preparing teachers for Jewish day schools.

17. Dan Lortie, in his classic *Schoolteacher*, argues that the apprenticeship of observation perpetuates conventional teaching because teachers are most likely to do to students what their teachers did to them when they were students. Only strong teacher education can break the cycle by raising to consciousness the tacit beliefs about teaching that teacher candidates bring and replacing them with more defensible views.

18. For a discussion of how and why teach core practices of teaching during teacher preparation, see Grossman, 2018.

19. For a fuller discussion of how the historic context shaped the DeLeT vision, see Feiman-Nemser, 2011.

20. The yearlong internship gave DeLeT graduates a leg up. Many schools were willing to count that as a year of experience.

21. Over the years, DeLeT prepared a handful of Hebrew teachers, secondary teachers of Jewish and general subjects, and Jewish studies teachers for the elementary grades.

22. This included Reform, Conservative, community, and Modern Orthodox day schools.

REFERENCES

Charney, R. (2002). *Teaching children to care: Classroom management for ethical and academic growth*. Northeast Foundation for Children, Inc.

Darling-Hammond, L. (2000). *Studies of excellence in teacher education*. National Commission on Teaching and America's Future.

Feiman-Nemser, S. (2006). Beit midrash for teachers: An experiment in professional education. *Journal of Jewish Education*, *72*(3), 161–181.

Feiman-Nemser, S. (2011). Preparing teachers for Jewish schools: Enduring issues in changing times. In H. Miller, L. Grant, & A. Pomson (eds.), *International Handbook of Jewish Education* (pp. 937–958). Springer.

Feiman-Nemser, S., & Zeldin, M. (2007). *DeLeT (Day School Leadership Through Teaching): A five-year perspective*. Mandel Center for Studies in Jewish Education.

Grossman, P. (2018). *Teaching core practices in teacher education*. Harvard Education Press.

Kriete, R., & Davis, C. (2014). *The morning meeting book: K–8*. Center for Responsive Schools.

National Center for Research on Teacher Learning. (1991). Findings from the Teacher Education and Learning to Teach study: Final report. National Center for Research on Teacher Learning.

Peterson, R. (1992). *Life in a crowded space: Making a learning community*. Heinemann Press.

7

What Do Parents Want from Hebrew Studies in Jewish Day School Education?

SHARON AVNI

Introduction

Day schools, particularly in areas where there are competitive public schools and other strong nonsectarian private schools, are not immune from the neoliberal turn in American schooling that has led parents to become more vocal stakeholders in defining expectations and measures of their children's success (Davies & Bansel, 2007). While parental decision-making has always been an issue in day school education (Wertheimer, 2007), it has often remained at the level of enrollment choices families make between day and public schooling. But once parents have chosen day school, we know very little about what they want or expect with regard to their children's Judaic studies learning. Questions regarding their priorities and how they measure cognitive, behavioral, or affective outcomes remain unanswered. This is especially true with regard to Hebrew studies—a core component of Judaic studies at day schools—in which there is scant research on what parents want their children to know and why.

What do day school parents want their children to learn in Hebrew classes? How do they talk about these goals? How do they define a successful Hebrew educator and a successful Hebrew program? This chapter addresses these interrelated questions by presenting a case study of two fifth-grade Hebrew classes taught by a highly regarded teacher at a non-Orthodox Jewish day school located in the Northeast of the United States. The study asked parents directly what they wanted their children to know about Hebrew and how they defined successful Hebrew learning, with the findings pointing to their prioritizing *how* students feel in the language learning classroom over *what* they achieve in linguistic gains.

These findings come out of a larger ethnographic study that examined models of successful Hebrew teaching in day school contexts. The focus on parents in this study was grounded in two assumptions, one empirical and one theoretical. The first is that one of the primary reasons parents choose day schools over other public or private school options is because they want their children to receive an intensive Jewish education, which includes Hebrew language education. Hebrew, as many believe, is at the root of developing a love for and knowledge about Bible, Jewish holidays, prayer, and Israel.

The expectations for Hebrew education are also multilayered; schools teach textual Hebrew (*lashon hakodesh*) so that students can read Jewish sacred texts and participate in religious practices. They also teach Modern Hebrew, the vernacular form spoken in Israel, so that students will be able to acquire fluency. The second, more theoretical assumption is that parents have Hebrew language ideologies, or beliefs about the role of Hebrew in contemporary Jewish life and the connection between language and being Jewish (Avni, 2012a; 2012b). These beliefs underlie the decisions they make about what knowledge is deemed essential and what types of language use are acceptable. Hebrew ideologies shape and inform parents' commitments to Hebrew language learning and to Jewish education more broadly, even when the parents themselves are not proficient in the varieties of Hebrew. Therefore, Hebrew learning in the Jewish educational setting is rarely solely about the acquisition of language. Rather, it is wrapped up in a set of beliefs about what Hebrew represents in Judaism and in Jewish cultural, spiritual, and religious life. From this perspective, parents' Hebrew language ideologies form a crucial component of their expectations and the choices they make.

These two assumptions guided the two interrelated research questions about Hebrew learning in the day school setting:

1. What do parents say about Hebrew learning outcomes for their children? How do they define these learning outcomes?
2. What do these articulations reveal about parents' understanding

of Hebrew language education as a component of their children's Jewish education?

Attending to these questions requires exploring metalinguistic discourse (i.e., talk about language) as a lens for understanding how parents perceive successful Hebrew study and pedagogy. Overall, this chapter explores the ways in which various stakeholders (i.e., parents, administrator, and Hebrew teacher) talk about their definitions of successful Hebrew education, which at times challenge the taken-for-granted assumptions that language learning success is a measure of linguistic acquisition.

Theoretical Frameworks

This study bridges two areas of inquiry in day school education, Hebrew learning and school-family relations, and explores the connection between language education and family involvement. Family language policy (FLP)—an emerging field of study concerned with children's language learning as a function of parental ideologies about languages and their decisions concerning language and literacies (King & Fogle, 2006; 2013)—informs the critical role of family decision-making with respect to Hebrew learning in day schools. Much of the research into family language policy has focused on minority language maintenance, in which, for instance, the family's primary language (e.g., Spanish) differs from that of the wider English-speaking community or when parents and children have different language competences, as in the case of transnational adoptive homes (Fogle, 2013). For the case at hand, in which many day school parents have varying proficiency levels in different types of Hebrew (ranging from native fluency in Modern Hebrew to varying degrees of reading and decoding of Hebrew sacred texts), FLP scholarship reminds us that parents view language learning from a variety of sociocultural, emotional, and cognitive perspectives (Curdt-Christiansen, 2009; 2018). Put simply, parents' understanding of the importance and role of language learning in their families' lives is rarely simply a factor of what a child can or cannot do in a targeted language.

In terms of the day school–family connection, Pomson and Schnoor's study of Toronto Jewish day school families found that parents selected a Jewish day school to "fill" their own social and educational needs as much as those of their children, and that parents relied on day schools to provide Jewish knowledge, inspiration, and community. Put differently, Pomson and Schnoor's study revealed the affective and social role that day school serves, beyond the cognitive and curricular goals. Equally important, their study showed that the day school had replaced the synagogue as the families' primary point of engagement with Jewish life, what Pomson and Schnoor refer to as the "school as shul" phenomenon. "Literally and metaphorically" they write, "parents are looking for a school that speaks to them," which they take to mean "that parents want to readily understand what a school stands for and whether they can see themselves standing with it" (Pomson & Schnoor, 2008, p. 157). Although Pomson and Schnoor's study did not focus specifically on Hebrew education, it brings into stark relief the myriad needs schools meet by providing families with a sense of belongingness and reminds us to look beyond narrowly defined student learning outcomes when thinking about measures of success. For the case at hand, the affective role of the school in a family's life provides a conceptual framework for understanding parents' metalinguistic discourse about successful Hebrew teaching and successful Hebrew education.

Methodology

In recent years, case study design has become popular in research on language teaching and learning because of its descriptive power and its ability to capture the dynamic elements at work within a particular learning context (Duff, 2008). It has also shown itself to be an impactful form of research in Jewish education (AVI CHAI, 2015; Ingall, 2006; Jacobs, 2002). This qualitative case study focuses on two fifth-grade classes taught by the same Hebrew teacher at a non-Orthodox Jewish day school I refer to by the pseudonym JDS, located on the East Coast of the United States. This study draws on multiple data sources: classroom observations; semiformal interviews with parents, administrators, and the teacher; and classroom documents. In trying to identify a school that had a strong Hebrew program, I consulted with over a dozen scholars of Jewish and Hebrew education, rabbis, and parents and alumni of Jewish day schools in the Northeast United States. In the end, I chose JDS because it had a reputation as a thriving Jewish day school with a strong commitment from its families and because the administration was interested in receiving external and objective data on its Hebrew program.

I observed the Hebrew teacher at the center of this case study approximately once a week between September 2017 and February 2018. Observations were conducted in two different fifth-grade Hebrew classes, each of which lasted approximately fifty minutes. Each observation was documented in field notes about the setting, the participants, and the activities and interactions (Merriam, 1988). I interviewed the teacher three times over the course of the observations. Additionally, I conducted informal conversations with other teachers at the school and interviewed the principal of the school twice. I interviewed twenty-two parents by telephone (one parent for each family, for a total of twenty-two families out of thirty-four families in the two classes). Each of the interviews was recorded, transcribed, coded, and analyzed.

The Research Context

JDS is a non-Orthodox elementary day school serving students in grades pre-K through fifth grade in an affluent suburb outside a major East Coast metropolis.[1] The school draws families from the surrounding cities and towns, known for having a relatively strong Jewish presence, strong public schools, as well highly competitive private nonsectarian schools. Upon completion, students can continue at the JDS upper school that serves students in grades six through twelve. The school promotes its students' strong academic achievements; online school materials highlight its focus on STEM teaching, the mean SAT and ACT scores, as well as the number of Advanced Placement course offerings, in relationship to state and national statistics. In total, the lower and upper schools serve over five hundred students. Tuition at JDS in 2017–2018 was approximately $25,000 a year and there was a well-endowed scholarship program to provide financial assistance to families in need.

Hebrew language instruction is mandatory in all grades from kindergarten through twelfth grade. Between kindergarten and fourth grade, Hebrew is taught in the Judaic studies classes. Starting in fifth grade and continuing through the upper school, Hebrew is separated from Judaic studies, which means students have Hebrew as a designated subject at least five classroom periods a week, or approximately five hours of Hebrew instruction a week. The TaL AM curriculum is used in the lower school and Bishvil Ha-Ivrit (formerly NETA-CET) is used in grades six through twelve. Students study Hebrew Bible in fifth grade and use MATOK, a Bible curriculum developed by educators at JTS. Spanish is introduced in the eighth grade, and students have the option of either pursuing this foreign language or taking a STEM track.[2]

JDS identifies the teaching of textual and Modern Hebrew as important goals in the school's mission to provide a strong Jewish education to students. According to the fifth-grade teacher at the focus of this study:

> One of our primary goals is to introduce our children to Hebrew as a second language, as the language of the Jewish people, as a vehicle to connecting with the Jewish people, with the state of Israel, [and] with their heritage when it comes to everything from prayer to text to Torah text. Another goal, or complementary goal, to that end, is to be able to speak. It's a living language. And so to master it as students who are comfortable conversing, writing, [and] reading as they build their identity as young Jews.

The lower school Hebrew curriculum is carefully laid out so that each year builds on the language learning progress from the previous year. Some of the fifth-grade Hebrew curriculum learning outcomes include: using correct subject/verb/adjective agreement; identifying command forms of regular verbs; writing paragraphs and stories; expanding vocabulary; improving correct use of present, past, future, and infinitive verbs; expanding knowledge of the Hebrew number system; and improving comprehension skills. In spite of the more affective goals the teacher cites previously, this curriculum is focused on developing knowledge about language structures—the nuts and bolts of how the Hebrew language works. In that regard, it focuses heavily on learning Hebrew syntax (how words are combined into larger units to achieve intended meanings); it is not a curriculum focused on communicative competence. By the end of fifth grade, the learning outcome is that students will learn how to produce strings of words that conform to the syntactic (or grammatical) rules of

Hebrew. This curriculum lacks specificity about teaching Hebrew in the four modes of expression—listening, speaking, reading, and writing. It also does not fully address levels of language function—communicative tasks that students perform, such as asking for and responding to information, narrating past activities, describing events, and expressing opinions.

This study focused on one teacher, Morah Marsha, who has been a full-time teacher at JDS for seven years, and who was part time for several years before joining the full-time faculty. Morah Marsha is American-born and moved to Israel as a young adult, where she taught English at various educational settings. She has a BA in English and an advanced certificate in language education. She is not a native Hebrew speaker; she acquired Hebrew through her own formal Jewish education, as well as through living in Israel for several years and marrying an Israeli. Morah Marsha identifies herself as a practicing Jew and mostly aligns herself with the Conservative movement. Her children attended JDS. Our conversations over time revealed her strong Jewish identification, her involvement in her local Jewish community, and the ways in which her family's life was integrated with Judaism. Yet, at the same time, Morah Marsha was deeply enmeshed in American culture. In my observations, I noted that she was able to easily converse with the students about pop music, current movies, children's books, cultural events, restaurants, and sports happenings. Morah Marsha was in her early fifties and shared many of the characteristics of her students' parents; she was well educated and middle class.

Findings

Searching for Community

Like the families in Pomson and Schnoor's study (2008), JDS parents, when asked about Hebrew study as a factor in their choice of day school for their children, mentioned the importance of the day school in providing a sense of community for them and their children. While some families specifically identified themselves as Conservative, Reform, Modern Orthodox, or with the neologism "Conservadox," others identified their Jewish affiliation based on a range of Jewish practices and lifestyle choices, including keeping kosher, celebrating Shabbat (by attending synagogue, lighting candles, having Friday night dinner together), visiting Israel, and sending their children to Jewish summer camps. Some parents were themselves graduates of Jewish day schools, while others pointed out that the decision to enroll their children at JDS was because it was important to the grandparents or spouses, and because of the generous financial aid the school offered. All of the parents I spoke with felt highly committed to Jewish life and felt that being Jewish was a defining identity for their families.

The principal also noted a dramatic shift in parents' desires for a sense of community and belongingness at the school. Parents looked to the day school, not the synagogue, as the center of their Jewish activity. As the principal stated:

> More and more, I think we see a trend that there are families that don't join synagogues. That was unheard of twenty years ago in a day school...They just went hand in hand...We're seeing this kind of growing number of people who say, "The school fits the bill for me for everything. Why do I need a synagogue? The school gives me community. The school gives me identity. The school gives my kids the foundation in everything we could possibly want. I don't need to also go to a synagogue."

The notion of connectedness was salient in many interviews. Parents spoke about their desire for schools to provide a space in which Jewish observance and belongingness could interconnect. In response to a question about the importance of day school education to her daughter's development, one mother stated:

> We wanted her to have a life that made sense Jewishly. We wanted our religious observance to be in concert with what she was learning at school. We wanted her to have friends who live her life system a little in their lives in a similar way. We wanted them to be, you know, committed and connected.

This sentiment about connecting home life to school, as well as connecting to other Jewish youth, echoed many of the other reasons that parents gave. When asked directly about the importance of learning Hebrew in their decision-making process, not one of the parents interviewed explicitly identified Hebrew as one of the main reasons they were sending their children to JDS. Moreover, only one parent touched on the additive cognitive advantages of knowing a second language as a significant factor in their choice. Instead, parents prioritized the importance of the school providing an environment in which students could be with other Jewish youth in the process of learning about Judaism and building a Jewish identity. As I will discuss in the remainder of this chapter, parents' metalinguistic discourse about learning textual and Modern Hebrew reflected this objective and was less focused on specific Hebrew language learning outcomes.

Learning Textual Hebrew

Interviews with parents revealed it was not a priority to learn Hebrew as a matter of faith or in order to study sacred texts. Instead, they indicated that what was important to them was for their children to develop a comfort with religious practices and in the process make personal meaning. Hebrew was at times tangential to this goal. For example, when asked whether his daughter's learning of textual Hebrew was important to him, one father, himself a graduate of Jewish day school, responded:

> The learning of the language is not necessarily what is driving [the decision to send her to day school]. It is not the number one priority as far as her Judaic learning for us... Let me just find the words. I mean, it's about the meaning of the text, of the values of the text, and how that it is relatable and drives their choices as opposed to the language that the text presents itself in.

This provocative comment brings an important dynamic into focus: the tension between accessing texts in translation and the fealty to the immutability and untranslatability of the Hebrew word. The latter perspective has dominated Hebrew educational practices. Many Jewish thinkers and educators have shown an aversion to and antipathy for the use of translation as an inferior form of mediation.

Literary scholar Ruth Wisse, for example, writes that "Hebrew alone can give children unmediated access to their heritage," whereas "English leaves them forever at the mercy of second-rate interpreters" (Wisse,

19993, p. 273). According to this moral hierarchy, "those who can read it [Torah in Hebrew] are rightly recognized by those who cannot as more 'authentically' Jewish" (p. 272). Dichotomizing discourses also impute to translation practices a corrosive effect that leads to assimilation and discontinuity (Avni, 2012c). However, in this father's comment we see that he is less concerned with reading in the original Hebrew than he is with his daughter being able to create personal meaning from the text. In other words, making meaning and engaging in the content took priority over the language in which the meaning was written.

Other parents also placed an emphasis on participation, interestingly often pitting Hebrew rote reading against the ability to make a deeper connection to the text. In responding to what a successful Hebrew learning experience looks like, one mother captured this tension by saying:

> I think, for us, it looks like that the child comes away with an ability to participate in services in a deeper level and doesn't just feel like they're repeating something that they don't understand. It's more that they have a good understanding of what they're saying, why they're saying it, and that they can participate in Jewish religious life.

Yet another parent stressed that knowing about Jewish practices and wanting to be part of a religious community was more important than Hebrew language proficiency when they considered choosing a day school education for their children:

> We wanted them to learn and care about, you know, being Jewish and the holidays and the customs and all of that... I would say it's less about language and becoming proficient in the language as it is about just knowing stuff.

In follow-up questions with this parent, she made it explicitly clear that her day school expectations had less to do with concrete language learning outcomes and more to do with whether her daughter felt good about what she was learning and what she actually knew. When asked if she felt happy with her daughter's Hebrew achievements so far, the mother responded: "Yes. I think she does well. I think also, most importantly, she enjoys it."

Finally, one mother acknowledged that knowledge of textual Hebrew was not a priority to her, but that she was surprised by how much the learning of trope—the musical pronunciation associated with the cantillation marks (accents) used for the ritual public chanting of the Torah—was important to her daughter. The astonished mother stated:

> Please don't judge me when I say that it [learning textual Hebrew] is really not important to me, because to Sarah [my daughter], it is extremely. I mean this was our fourth consecutive week attending shul [synagogue] because she wanted to practice her trope. She wanted to hear it. She wanted to read it. She's like so excited about it . . . you are asking me my opinion, but ultimately it's their life and I want to expose them to it. I want to expose them to everything and have them make their own decisions about what's important to them. Yes, I would love it if they were able to go to shul and follow it. I go to shul and I can't read or write [Hebrew], so I have to read the English side, which they don't even have in the Uptown shul, and so it's more boring. So I'm happy that they have the ability to be able to read and then one day follow it and use it.

Because the Torah scroll has no punctuation, no vowels, and is written in a font that differs from prayer books, trope helps Torah readers pronounce the words correctly, put the emphasis on the right words and syllables, and pause at the proper places. Trope helps readers convey the meaning and the emotion of the text, much like musical notation on a score. It is a literacy skill that must be explicitly acquired, a process that the students at JDS begin in fifth grade once a week in a separate class taught by a different teacher. Over the course of my classroom observations, I overheard many student conversations in which they expressed their excitement and pride in mastering this technical skill and putting it into practice.

Though it is clear that this mother does not share the daughter's enthusiasm for reading trope (and attending Saturday services), her discursive moves express an appreciation of this technical literacy skill. If this mother is bewildered by her daughter's newfound interest, she nonetheless appreciates that her daughter will have the literacy tools to be able to participate in religious life in the future. To some degree, this sentiment is a rejoinder to those preceding that prioritize meaning over form and question the dispensability of Hebrew. Whereas parents indicated that knowledge of textual Hebrew was not their top priority and disavowed rote learning, they recognized the importance of acquiring Hebrew literacy skills so that their children would have the possibility to be part of the synagogue practices of Torah reading. These seemingly contradictory stances seem to suggest that parents still ascribe value to some aspects of technical Hebrew reading, especially if it leads to being an active participant of the synagogue community.

Learning Modern Hebrew

Parents' views about Modern Hebrew also were at odds with prevalent discourses about the importance of language for building a connection to Israel. Pomson and Wertheimer's (2017) finding that most non-Orthodox parents placed greater priority on Modern Hebrew for the purposes of communication over textual Hebrew for prayer and studying sacred texts did not emerge in my data. When responding to questions regarding the importance of learning Modern Hebrew, one father remarked:

> I mean, ideally, what I would want for my students is to be able to read … no, to write in complete Hebrew sentences, which I think most of them have, to speak in complete Hebrew sentences, which I don't think most of them have, and to understand a bit of spoken Hebrew, not to be able to hear a conversation between Israelis and understand it, but to understand when someone talks to them and knows that they're American, in Hebrew … I think the main goal for me and why I sent my kids here was for them to just have a strong sense of their Jewish selves, and a love for Israel, and just to be future Jewish leaders.

This comment must be read in light of the parents' strong support of Israel. In spite of some of their expressed misgivings about the Israeli occupation and their awareness of the growing chasm between American and Israeli Jews, they did not dismiss or reject the importance of learning about Israel. Nonetheless, they did not view their children's degree of Modern Hebrew acquisition as a measure of their commitment to Israel or their love of the country. As the father indicates, his main objective was for the students to have a general familiarity with the language as a means for them to develop a strong sense of themselves as American Jews, which would serve as a basis for their having a strong sense of identification with Israel.

Another parent directly addressed the question of the necessity of Modern Hebrew fluency when talking about her goals for her son. Rather than seeing Hebrew as the end product, she saw it as a means to living a full and committed Jewish life.

> So I strongly felt that I wanted my kids to be able to attend JDS to get that foundation and connection to Israel and understanding of traditions and values and halakha [Jewish laws] and as well as exposure to the language. But whether they walk out of there speaking Hebrew or not is not my main objective . . . I'm trying to think how to phrase this. It's more for me like if they were to leave JDS in fifth grade, I want to make sure that their connection to Judaism is strong enough that they're going to still do things that are related to Israel and to the Jewish religion and beliefs. I want to make sure that they understand that they should marry somebody Jewish. That they should continue to attend services and the importance of the holidays and the traditions that have been set forth before us. That they feel part of a community of Jewish learners and part of the Jewish community.

What is important to note is that the mother clearly affirms her commitment to Israel and Judaism. However, she is not focused on her daughter being able to speak fluently; rather, her expectation is that the school will equip her daughter with the foundation and knowledge to commit to Jewish life, defined here through marriage choice, ritual observance, and feeling part of the broader community. Simply put, proficiency in Modern Hebrew is not in and of itself sufficient or even required for this objective.

When asked about the importance of being proficient in Modern Hebrew, other parents struck a more pragmatic note. One parent responded:

> That [being fully proficient in Modern Hebrew by fifth grade] probably wasn't going to be the reality. They weren't probably going to come out

> with real good conversational Modern Hebrew. But at least it's a start and then if they do go to Israel or if they do go study abroad, at least they have something to start with.

Echoing what other parents said, this father expressed tempered expectations regarding Modern Hebrew, hoping that Hebrew study at JDS would provide a foundation for learning more Hebrew in Israel one day in the future. To be clear, parents did value the importance of Modern Hebrew as part of a day school education, in general. In fact, interviews revealed that some parents considered it a crucial component of the Jewish day school curriculum. It is therefore curious and arguably paradoxical that while parents viewed the presence of Hebrew as indispensable to Jewish day school education, their children's actual acquisition was more open to negotiation and not necessarily a priority (Avni, 2012a). In short, parents did not view their own children's acquisition of Modern Hebrew fluency (or the acquisition of Israeli-accented Hebrew) as one of the primary measures of a successful Jewish day school education.

Teacher Qualifications

Pragmatic goals for children's Hebrew learning also emerged as a theme in conversations regarding Morah Marsha's nonnative Hebrew skills. Morah Marsha recognized that her accent and level of Hebrew fluency were a concern for some parents and was even sympathetic to their perspective. In one interview, she reflected:

> I totally understand it. Students with Israeli parents are not that happy about that. And I understand that. If I lived in Israel and an Israeli was teaching my kid English, I wouldn't be that happy, so I do get it, and I've talked to [the principal] about it.

She unapologetically acknowledged that her "Hebrew is not perfect" and that earlier in the day of our interview, she had gone to one of the Israeli teachers at JDS to ask what a word in a Hebrew song meant. She told a story about making a Hebrew mistake on a handout and one of the Israeli parents fixing it, and recounted an episode when an Israeli parent of a new student at the school called the principal to complain about her not being a native Hebrew speaker. In narrating this story, she proudly told me:

> At back-to-school night, she [the parent] told [the principal], "I take back whatever I said. My daughter's so happy. She's learning." So I was really happy to hear that.

Describing the Israeli mother's transformation, Morah Marsha attributed the change to two pedagogical approaches: (1) her ability to skillfully position the new student as the Hebrew expert in the class, and (2) her ability to make a personal connection with the student and have the student see that Hebrew class was a place where all students of different levels could contribute and grow. By doing so, Marsha positioned the "outsider" student as a Hebrew resource, thereby giving her an opportunity to integrate with her new classmates, and made the student feel at home in the new surroundings. In an interview, the parent of the new student had the following to say:

> I was highly disappointed when I moved here and learned that most teachers were not [native Hebrew speakers]. I would have hoped and prayed that they would have hired native Hebrew-speaking teachers because I feel like they would know it [Hebrew] better... I don't know if I necessarily feel the same way now. Just because you're a native Hebrew teacher doesn't make you better as a teacher. You know, it just gives you an advantage. I guess the only thing that bothers me really, now that I'm thinking about it, it is the dialects. You know it's like the *shabbas* versus *shabbat*. You know, like it's old Hebrew.

This Israeli parent conveyed her evolving perspective regarding the necessity of having native Hebrew teachers. While she did indicate she was initially disappointed, she came to see that effective teaching is more than just knowing a language as a native speaker. Particularly revealing, though, are her comments regarding what she calls the different "dialects" between American and Israeli Jews, referring to American Jews' tendency to use the Ashkenazi pronunciation of Hebrew, while Israelis use the Sephardic pronunciation. What she laments is not only the accent but also that Americans use a pronunciation that represents "old world" Yiddish-inflected Judaism in her mind.

In general, native English-speaking parents were less concerned about Morah Marsha's lack of native Hebrew proficiency. One mother interviewed was not at all concerned that Morah Marsha was not a native Hebrew speaker:

> Mother: Not in the least. Obviously, you may speak to Israeli parents that may feel differently... But I have no concerns about that at all. Certainly, I learned foreign languages from teachers who were not native speakers growing up and I didn't feel like that slowed me down at all.
>
> Sharon: So there're other things that are more important to you than the actual accent or the—
>
> Mother: Yeah... And in a way, sometimes non-native speakers have a better understanding of grammar and mistakes than native speakers who are used to doing things in a colloquial way and they don't have as much knowledge of the grammar.

This debate between the advantages and drawbacks of native and non-native language teachers is not new in language pedagogical circles (Llurda, 2006; Rampton, 1990). Broadly speaking, the argument goes that non-native teachers, as learners of the target language themselves, have greater teacher language awareness (Andrews, 2008), meaning that they can provide a better learner model, teach language-learning strategies more effectively, supply more information about the target language, better anticipate and prevent language difficulties, and benefit from their ability to use the students' mother tongue (Medgyes, 1992). What these advantages highlight is that a person who has consciously learned a language often has a better understanding of the structure of the language than a native speaker who can use it correctly, but cannot necessarily explain how the language works. For example, many non-native English-speaking teachers and learners can describe the grammatical differences in the use of the past tense versus the present progressive in sentences like "I lived in New York" and "I have lived in New York," whereas native English speakers cannot easily explain the difference in the use of these tenses.

Coupled with this advantage is the idea that a teacher from the same cultural and linguistic background as the student is in a better position because of shared language and cultural norms, an idea put forth by one mother:

> In some respects, there might be an advantage to that, because . . . some kids could be intimidated when a native Israeli who tries to speak all the time, and maybe sometimes even difficult to understand when they go from Hebrew to English and so on. And I had a whole bunch of those when I was growing up. And they can be hard on you too.

Another parent, who spoke at length about her child's Hebrew learning experience prior to being in Morah Marsha's class, shared similar beliefs:

> The problem [Hebrew] teacher last year was like fresh off the boat from Israel, and I think that was part of the challenge, certainly from a cultural perspective as well as from a communications perspective. Although this year my younger daughter has Morah Yael, a native Israeli, and that seems to work, but general feedback from my kids has always been that they find it more challenging to work with Israelis . . . they don't understand their English, let alone their Hebrew.

Yet another parent dismissed Hebrew fluency as a requirement for teachers, claiming that this knowledge set was beside the point when it came to defining a good Hebrew teacher. She stated:

> I think it's completely irrelevant, because I think it's really about the teacher. It's about connecting with the kids. It's about knowing the kids' strengths and weaknesses, and it's about teaching the content so that the kids can evolve. And we had Marsha a couple of years ago as my son's Hebrew teacher, and she really took great care with him, and was a great resource for him, and that was third grade. So it was a little bit of a different level, a little more hands-on. So I don't have any issues with having a non-native Hebrew speaker being a Hebrew teacher.

Finally, the school principal, acutely aware of the native versus non-native debate, had much to say about it based on her experience as an administrator at the school for many years.

> Listen, in an ideal world, we want a native Israeli who is also a master teacher. That's the ideal. And they [families] do not want an American teaching Hebrew. What I have come to observe in my time here . . . is that it is beyond rare to find that person today. And so when we tiptoe out and say we are going to take this person who is a native Israeli, and we're going to invest in them, and we're going to give them all of the professional development possible because they're bright and they have the Hebrew, so they'll learn the pedagogy, we have gotten burned over time. Because the truth of the matter is, it's a very special person who can teach. It's temperament and it's class management. And what we have found in my tenure here is that often Americans whose Hebrew is very good end up stronger teachers because they were teachers to start. And they have the classroom management. They have the understanding of the whole child in child development oftentimes. They understand the culture here and what [it is] that American parents are generally looking for when they sign on the dotted line and spend that amount of money. They understand there is political savvy, and symbolic gestures that happen as part of that experience. So again, it's not that I will look for the American to do it, because at the end of the day, our hope is that we find Israelis who fit this bill. We have just found it harder and harder to do that.

The principal acknowledges that having a native Hebrew-speaking teacher for Hebrew classes is the ideal scenario, but that finding an Israeli who has pedagogical expertise, pedagogical content knowledge, understanding of American children, capacity to interact with highly demanding American parents, and an educator's disposition is difficult to find. From her experience, giving more weight to Hebrew knowledge over pedagogical know-how has led to disappointment and failure. What this honest reflection underscores is that while the native versus non-native debate is a pedagogical question, it must also be evaluated in light of the consumer orientation of schooling. In the current marketplace of school options, parents have choices as to where to send their children and have expectations for what their tuition dollars are buying. Thus, the principal knows that all her teachers, including the Judaic studies and Hebrew teachers, need to be strong educators who can navigate the broader expectations of what working in a private school entails.

Hebrew and Meeting Students' Learning Needs

The debate about what a Hebrew educator needs to know about pedagogy in general, and language pedagogy more specifically, as well as about the culture of the school and the families, extends to discussions about students' learning needs. When the Hebrew language classroom is brought up in Jewish educational discourse, it is often done so with the "ideal" learner—a student without any special learning needs, social struggles, or cognitive challenges—in mind. Yet, the reality of classrooms today is that a growing number of students are neurodivergent and/or have a range of specific learning challenges that include one or more of the basic psychological processes involved in understanding or using spoken or written language, which may manifest itself in an imperfect ability to listen, think, speak, read, write, spell, or do mathematical calculations.

While it has long been recognized in the field of learning disabilities that foreign or second language study poses unique challenges to students with special learning needs, this concern has only recently begun to emerge in discussions in the day school context, which often has limited resources to address these challenges (Uhrman, 2017). Teachers who once dismissed students who struggled to learn Hebrew for their lack of motivation or behavioral problems now have a more nuanced understanding of the types of challenges learning-disabled students have when learning an additional language, including challenges with phonological awareness, learning the basic sound units of language (phonemes), dyslexia, and not recognizing or being able to manipulate these basic units of sounds and words efficiently, all of which can lead students to have difficulty with the actual perception and production of language necessary for basic comprehension, speaking, and spelling. Keenly aware of this issue, the principal implied that one of the selling parts of a Jewish day school in general is that it can offer "small classes and more support" than a public school. Specifically with regard to Hebrew study, she had the following to say:

> We also have this conversation when we talk about students with extensive learning profiles for whom learning a second language is truly difficult. Learning English is difficult for them oftentimes. So you have a language processing disorder, you have some other types of challenges, spending half of your day in another language is truly torture. So we have talked in kind of broad terms over the years about whether there will be a day when, based on our strategic plan, we run some type of alternate track where Judaics is done in English, completely in English.

One of the central themes that emerged in the interview with Morah Marsha was her capacity for differential instruction, which at its core is about addressing students' varied learning needs and developing personalized instruction so that all students within a given classroom can learn effectively, regardless of differences in ability, interest level, and learning profile. Morah Marsha directly addressed the cognitive and social load of Hebrew learning and her need to build lessons that addressed the different learning abilities in her classes:

> For some students, I need to make it manageable, and for others who need it to be challenging, I need to make it challenging. When I write my lessons I always try to think about what the lowest level student in my class is going to do and what the highest level is going to be doing during that lesson. I don't always succeed with that, but that really, that guides a lot of my lesson planning.

Parents at JDS linked the definitions of successful teaching with differentiation in instruction. One mother defined a successful educator as "someone who peeks into, or counts the needs of the individual learner." Another mother went as far as claiming that her child has remained at JDS because of Marsha's capacity to effectively address his specific learning needs:

> Mother: So, my oldest has a learning disability and they have been, and especially Morah Marsha, has been his lifesaver. He has a learning

disability and they have just been tremendous in modifying and giving him what he needs so he's still able to follow along in class and get what my desires are out of it.

Sharon: So she's been really instrumental in helping him with that?

Mother: Beyond. Beyond. If it wasn't for her, I don't know that we would still be at the school.

Sharon: Oh really?

Mother: The academics and stuff are challenging and she's been able to make it something that he still enjoys and something that [is] still manageable so he feels safe and comfortable, as opposed to overwhelmed and stressed. I am really saying it from the heart. She has been a very instrumental part in my son's desire to stay at the school and his connection to Judaism...we have been very, very lucky.

This mother's effusive praise of Morah Marsha underscores that she measured success in the Hebrew class less in relation to the amount of Hebrew her son was learning and more in terms of his ability to participate in class.

Marsha's ability to create a safe, nonthreatening, and enjoyable learning environment was mentioned by many parents. Not surprisingly, Marsha herself identified it as one of her strengths, saying that beyond teaching language, one of the ways she defined successful teaching was to create the conditions in which students:

> learn and retain what they learn...where the material is somehow important to them, important for them to share, and important for them to think about in the future. Or, even if they kind of look back on the learning with a good feeling. Not necessarily knowing exactly what went on, nothing specific, but have a good, positive feeling about their learning. I think that's important.

Some language educators may raise their eyebrows reading this sentiment. Because one of the primary reasons a foreign or second language is taught is in order to give students the capacity to read, speak, write, and listen to the language, it raises questions about how Hebrew proficiency is valued. Language instruction is not typically measured in metrics of feeling, but by students' ability to use the language with some degree of accuracy in terms of function and context. Yet Morah Marsha's reflection indicates that other measures are equally important.

With regard to utilizing Hebrew teaching class to build connections with students, engage them in learning, and provide a strong model of Jewish adult behavior, parents judged Morah Marsha as extremely successful. In asking one mother to give her opinion about whether Morah Marsha was a successful Hebrew teacher, she stated:

> Definitely, yes. She's kind of well known to be a very high-quality educator and I think she does all of the things that I said, which is that she keeps the kids engaged. Sam [her son] never says, "Oh, I hate Hebrew" or "I hate doing the work for this class." It just doesn't happen. So I think that Morah Marsha really does a great job of keeping the energy high.

Implicit in this sentiment is that Morah Marsha had successfully broken the mold of the boring Hebrew teacher and turned her class into a period of the day that students looked forward to. For his mother, Sam's absence of negativity about learning Hebrew is a measure of success.

Other parents spoke directly about her warm, caring, and uplifting personality. I often witnessed her effectively comforting upset children in the hall and speaking to students during and in between classes about extracurricular activities, including their sport competitions and family events. She was very familiar with the students' families, including older and younger siblings, and their parents' professions. Because she taught students for several years in a row at the school, she was able to bring up stories and events from previous years, as she did often in reminding students that they had learned a particular topic in second grade that they were revisiting in fifth grade.

One parent was able to capture Morah Marsha's capacity to connect with the students beyond the Hebrew classroom:

> She's delicious. She's smart. She's caring. She goes above and beyond with the children if they don't understand... I'll never forget this story. One summer my daughter did not go to sleepaway camp and she knew that and she called me several times to find out if my daughter wanted

> to go out to lunch with her. And she followed through. She called her several times to find out if she was available. She met her at Barnes and Noble. Above and beyond.

Another parent talked about Morah Marsha's ability to use her understanding of the students to get them to be better students and to love learning:

> She just gets my kid, and she pushes her. She holds her accountable. She has said to her, "I know you can do better than this," or, "I know you can do this and work, and I'll help get you there." And she's cool, like for my daughter's... and free enough from our entire family's perspective, but from my ten-year-old daughter's perspective... she has street credibility... She's cool. She's fun. She's funny.

Her "street credibility" earned her the respect and admiration of the students, as well as the parents. Noticeably absent in these complimentary responses to questions about what makes Marsha a successful Hebrew teacher is her pedagogical content knowledge or the specific students' Hebrew learning outcomes. Nonetheless, parents did address her ability to model successful Jewish adulthood as something that they believe will have a significant lifelong impact on their children, perhaps even more than any specific linguistic gains. As one mother mentioned:

> She mixes her love and knowledge of Judaism with her love of American culture. She knows Bible and the latest teen craze. She shows the kids that you can sing a Hebrew song and make it cool, like a TV show. She shows that you can look fashionable, be a strong person, and value education. My daughter responds to that, and looks up to her.

Concluding Thoughts

In identifying the ways in which day school parents perceive success in their children's Hebrew learning, this chapter challenges assumptions that stakeholders measure effective language teaching by students' linguistic gains in the target language. One of the central findings is that there is a disconnect between what parents perceive as the idealized vision of

Hebrew success in the day school context and personal hopes and goals for their own children. Though Hebrew knowledge is important to the parents, they view Hebrew learning success as a function of linguistic proficiency (i.e., what students can or cannot do with the target language in different contexts) *and* according to nonlinguistic goals, including cultivating a strong sense of communal belonging, providing a meaningful foundation for future Jewish learning and growth, and addressing students' learning needs. One would hope that these goals would align with students' progress in Hebrew language learning, but by and large parents seem to be saying that they do not, and at times, are even in direct opposition. By surfacing these more affective goals parents have for their children's Hebrew learning, this chapter offers a new perspective on the dynamics of Hebrew education and the various meanings that families attach to Hebrew nativeness and Hebrew learning goals, and point to a more capacious notion of successful Hebrew education in the day school setting.

How do these findings inform our understanding of the measurements of a successful Jewish day school education? Would we find similar responses to parents' perceived notions of success and educational achievements in other Jewish content areas? Is there something unique about Hebrew education, and language learning in general, that leads parents to prioritize affective considerations over linguistic gains? Pomson and Wertheimer (2017) note that schools do not make an explicit case for why it is important to learn Hebrew in explaining why parents and students in their study were unpersuaded that Hebrew is necessary for text study or for communication. Perhaps there is a more nuanced explanation for this lack of prioritization. It could be that parents recognize the importance, but view their priorities through the lens of their children's overall learning experiences. Without additional research, it is impossible to know whether the stakeholders in this present study are anomalous or whether their responses, as uneasy as they may be for Jewish educators, reflect an underexplored dimension of day school education. These questions, nevertheless, suggest the need for further research into the ways in which different stakeholders perceive, act on, and talk about what successful Jewish education entails on the cognitive, social, and psychological level.

NOTES

1. The name of the school and the names of all teachers and parents mentioned in this chapter are pseudonyms.

2. TaL AM is a Hebrew language and Jewish heritage curriculum designed for elementary school grades. Bishvil Ha-Ivrit is a Hebrew language program for students in grades six through twelve.

REFERENCES

Andrews, S. J. (2008). Teacher language awareness. In N. H. Hornberger (ed.), *Encyclopedia of language and education* (pp. 2038–2049). Springer.

AVI CHAI Foundation. (2015). *How schools enact their Jewish mission. Twenty case studies of Jewish day schools*. http://avichai.org/areas/case-studies/.

Avni, S. (2012a). Hebrew as heritage: The work of language in religious and communal continuity. *Linguistics and Education*, *23*, 323–333.

Avni, S. (2012b). Hebrew-only language policy in religious education. *Language Policy*, *11*, 169–188.

Avni, S. (2012c). Translation as a site of language policy negotiation in Jewish day school education. *Current Issues in Language Planning*, *13*(2), 76–104.

Cohen, S. M., & Kelner, S. (2007). Why Jewish parents choose day schools. In J. Wertheimer (ed.), *Family matters: Jewish education in an age of choice* (pp. 80–100). University Press of New England.

Curdt-Christiansen, X. L. (2009). Invisible and visible language planning: Ideological factors in the family language policy of Chinese immigrant families in Quebec. *Language policy*, *8*(4), 351–375.

Curdt-Christiansen, X. L. (2018). Family language policy. *The Oxford handbook of language policy and planning*, 420–441.

Davies, B., & Bansel, P. (2007). Neoliberalism and education. *International Journal of Qualitative Studies in Education*, *20*(3), 247–259.

Duff, P. (2008). *Case study research in applied linguistics*. Taylor & Francis.

Fishman, S. B. (2007). Generating Jewish connections: Conversations with Jewish teenagers, their parents, and Jewish educators and thinkers. In J. Wertheimer (ed.), *Family matters: Jewish education in an age of choice* (pp. 181–210). University Press of New England.

Fogle, L. (2013). Parental ethnotheories and family language policy in transnational adoptive families. *Language Policy*, *12*(1), 83–102.

Ingall, C. (2006). *Down the up staircase: Tales of teaching in Jewish day schools*. Jewish Theological Seminary of America.

Jacobs, B. (2002). Where the personal and the pedagogical meet: A portrait of a master teacher of Jewish history. *Journal of Jewish Education*, *68*(1), 73–86.

King, K., & Fogle, L. (2006). Bilingual parenting as good parenting: Parents' perspectives on family language policy for additive bilingualism. *International Journal of Bilingual Education and Bilingualism*, *9*(6), 695–712.

King, K., & Fogle, L. (2013). Family language policy and bilingual parenting. *Language Teaching*, *46*(2), 1–13.

Kress, J. S. (2007). Expectations, perceptions, and preconceptions: How Jewish parents talk about "supplementary" Jewish education. In J. Wertheimer (ed.), *Family matters: Jewish education in an age of choice* (pp. 143–180). University Press of New England.

Kress, J. S. (2011). Parents and Jewish educational settings. In H. Miller, L. Grant, & A. Pomson (eds.), *International handbook of Jewish education* (pp. 901–915). Springer.

Llurda, E. (ed.). (2006). *Non-native language teachers: Perceptions, challenges and contributions to the profession* (Vol. 5). Springer Science & Business Media.

Medgyes, P. (1992). Native or nonnative: Who's worth more? *ELT Journal*, *46*(4), 340–349.

Merriam, S. B. (1988). *Case study research in education: A qualitative approach*. Jossey-Bass.

Olssen, M., & Peters, M. A. (2005). Neoliberalism, higher education and the knowledge economy: From the free market to knowledge capitalism. *Journal of Education Policy*, *20*(3), 313–345.

Pomson, A. (2007). Schools for parents: What parents want and what they get from their children's Jewish day schools. In J. Wertheimer (ed.), *Family matters: Jewish education in an age of choice* (pp. 101–142). University Press of New England.

Pomson, A., & Schnoor, R. F. (2008). *Back to school: Jewish day school in the lives of adult Jews*. Wayne State University Press.

Pomson, A., & Wertheimer, J. (2017). *Hebrew for what? Hebrew at the heart of Jewish day schools*. AVI CHAI Foundation.

Prell, R.-E. (2007). Family formation, educational choice, and American Jewish identity. In J. Wertheimer (ed.), *Family matters: Jewish education in an age of choice* (pp. 3–33). University Press of New England.

Rampton, B. (1990). Displacing the "native speaker": Expertise, affiliation and inheritance. *ELT Journal*, *44*(2), 97–101.

Ross, R. R. (2012). Forms and patterns of parent participation at a Jewish and Catholic school. *Journal of Jewish Education*, *78*(1), 5–33.

Selvi, A. F. (2014). Myths and misconceptions about nonnative English speakers in the TESOL (NNEST) movement. *TESOL Journal*, *5*(3), 573–611.

Tomlinson, C. A. (1999). Mapping a route toward a differentiated instruction. *Educational Leadership*, *57*(1), 12.

Uhrman, A. L. (2017). The parent perspective: Disabilities and Jewish day schools. *Journal of Jewish Education*, *83*(1), 4–26.

Wertheimer, J. (ed.). (2007). *Family matters: Jewish education in an age of choice*. University Press of New England.

Wisse, R. (1993). The Hebrew imperative. In A. L. Mintz (ed.), *Hebrew in America: Perspectives and prospects*. Wayne State University Press.

8

Three Conceptions of Rabbinics

Understanding Teachers' Thinking

JOSHUA S. LADON

During a Jewish studies department meeting at the high school where I worked, I once shared a Hanukkah teaching from the twentieth-century Haredi rabbi R' Yitzhak Hutner (*Pachad Yitzhak*, *Hanukkah* 3). In the essay, Hutner argues that the Seleucid (he says "Greek") proclamation forbidding Torah study for the Jews, at the outset of the Hanukkah story, led to the rise of disagreement within the Jewish tradition. He draws a historical connection between the Hanukkah story and the emergence of the proto-rabbinic leaders known as the *zuggot* (pairs), whose tenure is described in the first chapter of *Mishnah Avot*, as evidence that the ban on Torah study led the sages to forget Torah, ultimately leading to multiple divergent viewpoints.

Hutner's primary audience understands the Oral Torah as having been handed down in perfection from generation to generation and sees disagreement as a reflection of misunderstanding or loss of Torah. While his essay eventually articulates support for the value of disagreement and the many faces of the Torah, his starting point, and that of his community, is that disagreement in the tradition is a problem that needs to be explained, because it suggests the Torah's disunity.

My colleague, who had spent several years in Jerusalem studying in a coed center for Jewish studies, was surprised by this teaching. "I don't understand," she replied. "I thought *mahloket* [disagreement] is a central pillar of Judaism." What seemed obvious to Hutner—that disagreement within Torah is a theological historical problem to be explained—was a view that she had not previously encountered. Within her own educational background and current community, Torah and its reception is understood to be, and is celebrated as, multivocal.

This anecdote illuminates just one of the challenges encountered when engaging teachers' thinking about the subject matter of "rabbinics." The name itself is imprecise, designating a field that has a range of definitions, from a narrower focus on the study of the Babylonian Talmud to a broader focus on postbiblical texts and the legal and interpretive works that those texts then generate. In fact, rabbinics is not only a designation of a school subject but also, in some Jewish settings and some educational conversations, a stand-in for "the Jewish tradition" as a whole. This is important because, as a result, the implicit and explicit notions of rabbinics take on an added layer of gravitas, as teachers explore, with their students, central ideas of Judaism and how to live a Jewish life.

Later, while working on the "Students' Understanding of Rabbinics" research project (Cousens, 2016; Levites, 2020a; Levites, 2020b), I had the opportunity to interview ten teachers of rabbinics in Jewish day schools (grades six through twelve).[1] These faculty had varied training (rabbinical school, doctoral programs, education training programs) and ranged religiously in their own practice. They included six men and four women. Their schools were diverse geographically (from across the United States) and denominationally (from Modern Orthodox, Conservative, and community schools). The interview protocol asked a series of questions about their notions of expertise in rabbinics and invited them to "nominate" those they understood as experts in the field of rabbinics.

As I interviewed the teachers, and then read and reread the transcripts, I noticed that, as they described expertise in rabbinics, they also employed and sometimes articulated divergent notions of rabbinics itself. What I have in mind is not merely the variety of names under which the study of rabbinic texts is organized in Jewish day schools, such as Talmud, Mishnah, Gemara, *Torah Sheba'al Peh* (Toshba), and Rabbinics. Rather, they seemed to employ three more fundamental conceptualizations of the subject—what I will call, in this chapter, three "conceptions of rabbinics." Some of the teachers articulated ideas that place them squarely within one particular conception of rabbinics, while others' ideas traversed the three. Sometimes ideas were expressed more explicitly, and sometimes more implicitly. But what is most important here is that these three ideas, three conceptions of rabbinics employed by these Jewish day school instructors, seem quite distinct. This chapter is an effort to capture these three conceptions, as they emerge from the interviews.

Teacher Thinking and the Jewish Studies Curriculum

Because Jewish day schools are run independently and autonomously from one another, there is little consensus over what should be taught to Jewish students. A broad range of curricular models exist with little formal coordination. Schools can be categorized around the way they present Jewish material. At the high school level, many Orthodox schools offer some form of rabbinics, often called Gemara or *Torah Sheba'al Peh* (Oral Torah) as well as classes in *chumash* or Tanakh and Jewish history. In the non-Orthodox world, high schools primarily fit into two categories, either offering one thematic Jewish studies course (that employs rabbinic texts in conversation with other ancient and modern Jewish texts) or two discipline-based courses of rabbinics/Gemara and Tanakh. By virtue of their disciplinary offerings, schools begin to shape the notions of Judaism and Jewish study for their students (as well as faculty, staff, parents, and community members). Those notions of Judaism are further shaped by the faculty students encounter, explicitly through content, and implicitly through the "hidden curriculum" (Snyder, 1973; Giroux & Purpel, 1983).

In addition to a lack of communal governance over curriculum, the Jewish tradition itself lacks a coherent authoritative structure that might dictate specific content knowledge requirements for children. As Judaism is neither dogmatic in nature (Schechter, 1972; Kellner, 2006) nor governed by a unified church (Halbertal, 1997; Hayes, 2017), there are relatively few guideposts regarding what should be taught to students. *Mishnah Avot* 5:21 offers specific ages at which one should progress through various life-cycle events, including learning sacred texts, starting with Torah at age five. Franz Rosenzweig, in conceptualizing his Lehrhaus in 1920, imagines a curriculum that brings the estranged Jew from outside the tradition, inside (Rosenzweig, 2002). These two radically different contexts highlight the challenge. What should be the curriculum?

This lack of consensus is deeper than simply a dispute about what books to study; within the last two decades, scholarship on the teaching of classical Jewish texts has deployed the idea of distinct teacher "orientations" within the teaching of Tanakh (Holtz, 2003) and rabbinics (Levisohn, 2010), which themselves build on Pam Grossman's exploration of English teachers' approaches to their subject (see Grossman et al., 1989; Grossman, 1991; Grossman & Shulman, 1994).[2] As Grossman and Shulman (1994, p. 5) write, "In teaching a text, teachers act upon assumptions about the nature of text, the nature of literature, what it means to read a text, how one marshals evidence to support a particular reading of a text, and the very nature of evidence itself." Bound up in teacher orientations are the teacher's notions of the domain itself, what is important about the domain, and how best to represent it.[3]

Drawing on Grossman, Barry Holtz frames the teacher's orientation as that which "encompasses aspects of both the knowledge and belief sides of a teacher's relationship to the subject matter" (2003, p. 47). By fleshing out nine orientations to the teaching of Tanakh, Holtz creates a selection of ways teachers conceptualize their fields. Focusing on rabbinics, Jon Levisohn (2010) likewise places an orientation at the heart of what it means for the teacher to conceptualize his or her subject. It includes "conceptions about the subject's boundaries, its central challenges, and its purposes... of what the subject is about and why it is worth teaching and learning" (Levisohn, 2010, p. 8). He arrives at ten distinct orientations to the teaching of rabbinics.

Notably, Levisohn also asks a definitional question about the project of identifying orientations: Are orientations "mutually exclusive and immutable categories," or are they instead "a rough approximation of a collection of ideas about the purposes and practices of teaching the subject that typically, but not necessarily, hang together" (p. 11)? He calls the former the "strong view" of orientations and the latter the "weak view," and specifically uses the term menu to advance the weak view, which is defined in looser terms than a map. Just as cuisines have overlapping ingredients and techniques, have been influenced by neighboring cuisines, and have been shaped over time, so too with orientations. They are not exclusive terms.

Levisohn's orientations drew upon a set of interviews and focus groups with instructors of rabbinics in various settings, from which he developed these "collection[s] of ideas about the purposes and practices of teaching the subject" (2010, p. 11). Each orientation also includes ideas about the subject itself, not just about the purposes of teaching it and the relevant pedagogic practices to emphasize. For example, what Levisohn calls the Jurisprudential Orientation moves legal material within rabbinic texts to the foreground and non-legal material to the background, in the implicit or explicit belief that rabbinics is, at its core or essence, a set of legal arguments.

Yet, as I listened and relistened to what the teachers in our study were saying, I heard something different—three distinct ways of thinking about the subject itself that, while not unrelated to Levisohn's orientations, feel more fundamental. I do not mean that they are more fundamental in an architectural sense; I am not proposing that these three conceptions are the foundational layer upon which the ten orientations are then constructed. Nor do I mean that they are more fundamental in an existential sense, as if teachers, who might be promiscuous with respect to orientations, are existentially committed to particular conceptions of the subject. We have little evidence for either of those claims. What we do have, on the other hand, is data that emerges from a different set of conversations with teachers of rabbinics than the ones that Levisohn undertook, in response to different prompts. And those data indicate three conceptions of the subject that, we might say, intersect with Levisohn's orientations but do not line up neatly.

It is tempting, when encountering Holtz's map of orientations for teaching the Bible, Levisohn's menu of orientations for rabbinics, or these three conceptions of rabbinics, to see them as permanent, fixed, underlying structures. I want to caution against such an approach. While these different orientations and conceptions can be used as tools to aid in the professionalization of teaching, helping teachers on their way to be more conscientious and intentional pedagogues, what is evident from this research is that the subject is fluid, shaped by the training and experiences of the teacher, the needs and capacities of their students, and the milieu in which the material is taught. If anything, the existence of conceptions and orientations reflect a notion that teacher thinking is matrixed, bound up in the relationships they have with their own teachers, the material, their students, and the communities in which they teach.

The Use of Metaphors

Becca, who teaches rabbinics at a Midwestern community high school, wanted her students to take hold of Torah. She meant this quite literally: She reported that she has each one of them commit to "doing *hagbah*"—raising the Torah after ritually reading the week's portion—during at least one Torah service during the year. But this embodied practice has metaphorical and symbolic meaning. She said, "I feel like that is symbolic of my goal, which is, I want them to have the experience of knowing that it's theirs and they have got a firm grasp of it, so that they actually can say, 'This is mine.'" Becca's desire for her students to physically embody a "firm grasp" of the Torah, raising it as a symbol of their acquisition, was a powerful articulation of her pedagogic ambition, which also, at the same time, telegraphs a notion of what "Torah" or "the Torah" is, or indeed, what the entire Jewish tradition is. The Torah is not simply the written scroll they grasp. As a rabbinics teacher, she is drawing a deep connection for the students between the content of her class and the physical artifact in their hands. The notion of taking hold of Torah requires it to be graspable. You must be able to wrap your hands around it, and to wrap your head around it. In some sense, then, Torah is finite and bounded.

This is not the only metaphor for Torah (in the expanded sense). In the rabbinic tradition, Torah is compared to a tree, water, and the desert, among others. Just as different notions of Torah in the rabbinic tradition reflect different values, so too, teachers' notions of Torah are reflected in their craft and through their language, assignments, and curricular choices. Teachers' metaphors offer insight into their beliefs and understanding (Pajares, 1992). Metaphors used by teachers reflect epistemologies about the world, and these metaphors shape the knowledge and understanding of students. Lakoff and Johnson (1980) explain that metaphors allow for understanding of aspects of concepts through other concepts as well as between one domain and another. Lakoff (1989) argues further that conceptual categories are built out of human experience of those categories, in contrast to classical notions of universal structure. Thus, conceptual categories reflect the use of "imaginative processes (metaphor, metonymy, mental imagery) that do not mirror nature" (Lakoff, 1989, p. 371).

In the data that form the basis for this chapter, teachers at times intentionally employed their own metaphorical language in talking about rabbinics, like Becca did previously. At other times, they used metaphorical language unconsciously, but in a way that provides insight into their thinking. More specifically, what emerges from the data is a set of three conceptions of rabbinics, each of which is expressed through its own distinct metaphor: (1) rabbinics as a canonized corpus, (2) rabbinics as an ecology, and (3) rabbinics as a thought process.

To be clear, these three conceptions of the subject—these three metaphors—are not intended as a comprehensive taxonomy. It is possible that a different group of teachers might yield other conceptions. Furthermore, as noted previously, there is not a one-to-one correspondence between teacher and metaphor; among the teachers interviewed, there are some whose description of expertise fall squarely in one category, but for many, their descriptions scatter across these notions. For analytical purposes, however, we will examine each one separately.

Rabbinics as a Canonized Corpus

One view of rabbinics sees it as a corpus of interrelated texts developed by the rabbis that emerged around or following the destruction of the Second Temple in Jerusalem in the year 70 CE. Significantly, the outer limit of the corpus might be found many centuries in the future. Moshe, a Modern Orthodox rabbi and PhD, said,

> The corpus of Jewish text study, let's say written between the year 0 and the year 1800—all the text written in that period that are not biblical or philosophical—are what I would define as rabbinics.

For Moshe, the rabbinic project is primarily a premodern endeavor with clear boundaries. He further clarified that midrash presents a question. While its authorship is postbiblical and written by the same population that wrote the Talmud, codes, and responsa, its preoccupation with biblical texts and its homiletic nature seem too far afield to be considered rabbinics. For Moshe, rabbinics is also defined by genre as much as by origin.

> Talmud, Mishnah, Jewish law—they all share the same essential structures—questions, answers, the move that I mentioned before about how you solve problems. None of that is within midrash. And I think it's because the essential structures of midrash are common with . . . with [inaudible] Bible [more] than with rabbinics.

Rabbinics, then, is essentially legal in nature.

In this teacher's thinking, however, the corpus of rabbinic texts shares more than just an origin, or a bounded history, or a genre. We could say that, as a corpus (a body), it shares a biology. Saiman (2018) suggests that the texts "add up to [a] system that can be engaged as a self-standing entity" (p. 13). Earlier in the interview, Moshe mentioned psychologist and educational theorist Jerome Bruner as central to his own thinking. According to Bruner, "Grasping the structure of a subject is understanding it in a way that permits many other things to be related to it meaningfully. To learn structure, in short, is to learn how things are related" (Bruner, 1977, p. 7).

For Moshe, the use of corpus can be understood as more than just a turn of phrase but an intentional expression highlighting the literature's physiology and shared DNA.

For those who conceptualize rabbinics as a corpus, mastery over its content and understanding how this content is related becomes the primary focus of study. Rabbinics as corpus is associated with valuing breadth of knowledge and the ability to quote material. Noah, a rabbinics teacher with a master's in education, serves as a Judaic studies department head at a community school in a Western state. He recalled his own education, saying, "I had teachers who could do brilliant things with the material that we were using. I just don't know enough about how much they knew."

These teachers, however, are not experts in his view. They don't know enough. Noah, like Moshe, valued mastery over any usage of the material.

By contrast, Noah described another former teacher as an expert by pointing to his recall of important material, or if lacking recall, his ability to quickly access the relevant information. Noah fondly remembered this expert's ability to "give an answer, citing his sources. Occasionally he would need to look something up. But he would be able to tell a student,

'Go downstairs, grab this book for me.' Because he knows what the book is, he just wants to make sure that he's getting the quote exactly right. And then he'll flip open to it and share the passage..."

This practitioner could be compared to a master surgeon, who could theoretically explain where something in the tradition is found before guiding the hands of a young protégé to its location.

Teachers expressing this particular view often value knowledge of the textual connections inside the rabbinic corpus. Moshe said, for example, "Nonexperts often will see a citation from one source to another and they'll need to look up the citation and understand what is going on there. And I think expertise means an ability to pick up the citation almost instantly."

Identifying citations was especially important to Moshe, who described the rabbinic tradition as a series of "intertextualities," or overlapping and interlocking textual references. By instantly identifying and understanding these references, one has greater knowledge of the corpus and its internal workings. Reflecting on her own lack of expertise, Becca, a Conservative rabbi teaching at a Midwestern community school, shared a similar sentiment. Describing a colleague, she explained how expertise requires a thirst for uncovering the tradition. The colleague would always want to understand more, turning to as many points of reference as possible. "I look up the *pasuk* [verse]," she said. "He reads the entire chapter."

The teachers who conceptualized rabbinics as a corpus also tended to emphasize the notion of solving problems. Just as a doctor might study anatomy to be better equipped to make clinical decisions, so too one who has broader mastery over the corpus of rabbinic material can solve the problems that arise. Several teachers used the term problem without a clear or consistent definition other than to suggest that experts know how to solve these problems. Ilan, a Modern Orthodox rabbi teaching in a pluralist high school, described a colleague who consistently strived to identify all of the problems that later interpreters have with a particular passage in the Talmud. This colleague would ask, "How do they articulate those problems? And how do they resolve those problems? And to see how that deeply impacts even a *peshat* [plain sense] reading of the text." Knowledge of these problems illuminate the network of texts that make up rabbinic discourse around a particular subject.

Examples of these problems could include (1) an unclear *sugya* (passage) that seems illogical or missing something, (2) inconsistencies or contradictions between sources, or (3) discord between ethics and Jewish law (for example, the legal problem of *agunot*, women whose husbands refuse to grant a divorce). The first two kinds of problem can generate considerable inquiry and creative interpretation in order to bring the different parts of the body into alignment. Ilan extolled those teachers who were able to draw out the different layers and voices in the text to illuminate a rabbinic concept. He admired:

> their ability to see a concept in its most umbrella nature—meaning to say, to not just see something within the confines of the *sugya* [passage] and the later text on it . . . The wealth of knowledge and research and their ability to bring in so many different examples . . . Each new voice and layer contributed to a broader understanding of the concept.

This conception of rabbinics as a canonized corpus sees rabbinics as a body of knowledge that is bound together and whole. It is a notion that is well founded in rabbinic literature. Those who consider rabbinics in this manner are likely to emphasize mastering the breadth of the tradition, venerating experts with encyclopedic ownership of the texts. In emphasizing breadth, the sea of Talmudic interpreters becomes a focus of study, more so than in other conceptions. Being able to map out and understand how Talmudic texts are in conversation, seeing lines of connection that have not previously been identified, and noticing how layers of interpretation interact become central educational goals in this notion. This focus on layers of interpretation demonstrates how a conception of a discipline shapes larger encounters with the tradition. While Talmudic discussion is neither exclusively legal nor does it regularly offer legal decisions, it later becomes a constitutive text for rabbinic legal decision-making (Fishman, 2011). By emphasizing the corpus and placing rabbinic interpretation of Talmud within the focus of study, one is naturally drawn into an emphasis on the legalism of the tradition.

Rabbinics as an Ecology

In contrast to the conception of rabbinics as a corpus, there are those who see rabbinics as a constellation of texts and ideas, written by a diverse population, across time and geography, sharing key characteristics regarding authorship and form. Rabbinics, in this view, is an expanding field, not just a set of intellectual qualities. It is also not necessarily a single thing. For some with this view, rabbinics is an umbrella term for a variety of genres of literature. Talmud, midrash, Midrash Halakha, Aggadah, and codes are all subspecialties within this broader category. The language of ecology, a community of interrelated groups that share time and space and interact with their environment, helps capture this notion of rabbinics (Odenbaugh & Pfeifer, 2005). Rabbinics is thus a network of actors, texts, and ideas shaped by its context and shaping its context. It is an ecology that has continued and evolved. It is an ecology with a history.

This view was shared by a number of faculty who had completed academic graduate work in the field. Shira, a PhD in rabbinics, who has taught at a number of non-Orthodox day schools, offered a glimpse of this notion through an encounter with its opposite. Describing an experience with her haredi family, she retold a popular yeshiva myth that she had heard from members of her family:

> There's some story, some big rabbi . . . that put up *marei mekomot* [a list of sources for a class] on the yeshiva wall or something . . . and someone played a joke and it was Purim or something and took it down and put up all these random pages that the people should study for the *shiur* [class]. And everyone studied and it made no sense. And the rabbi took it down and they were laughing—the kids who knew the joke that they had put up a fake one. And he looked at it and he closed his eyes for two minutes and then he gives a brilliant *shiur* connecting the dots between these presumably randomly chosen *sugyas* [sections of text].
>
> And that's supposed to be so impressive that the person knows . . . not just this random Joe, but this is the height of serious knowledge. He knows everything just by being told the page. Everything in the world is really, truly connected. So he can make these brilliant connections between them and weave this web. And I personally find it really

> unimpressive and inorganic and it's just about "Wow—he's memorized everything and can concoct patently artificial connections."

Shira's description of the closed system mirrors the descriptions of the corpus view. Drawing connections between the texts and noting the allusions (what Moshe called "intertextualities") demonstrates that everything is connected. Shira described an encounter with her brother-in-law:

> It's a closed system of knowledge in that if you throw in a curveball, they wouldn't know what to do. They would be like, "What do you mean?" In the way that when I asked my brother-in-law, who was then a teenager and in yeshiva, and learning sixteen hours a day, and I said something to the effect of, "Can you entertain that maybe Rashi is wrong?" And he laughed out loud as though I had just told a really funny joke. And the conversation did not proceed. There was no way in which I was going to explain it to him. That he could just be wrong. Maybe there's a different way to read it. He was like, "No, Rashi says it. What do you mean in a different way? That's absurd."

For Shira's brother-in-law, there is no chance that part of the corpus is incorrect. If it were unclear, or conflicted with another source of equal authority, it would create a problem to be solved. For Shira, however, Rashi can be wrong and the system will not be broken. In fact, it may actually become more interesting for her. And the fact that the text is not part of a larger, systemic canon, but an artifact of rabbinic creativity, enables her to investigate the lives, world, and ideas of the rabbis using tools that originate and exist outside the corpus.

Similarly, Ilan shared a story about an ongoing argument with his brother about the extent to which rabbinic texts are imbued with the humanity of the rabbis. If the text is imbued with the human desires and needs of the rabbis, then it is fallible, and opinions can be contextualized and perhaps even discounted. While Ilan sees "the rabbis as deeply human," his brother argues that "the actual study of Torah and the fear of understanding the Torah wrong is actually what enables them to not be *nogeia b'davar* [have a conflict of interest]."

For both Ilan and Shira, rabbinic texts can be fallible and thus disconnected from a complete system. In their views, the humanity of the tradition is what is to be valued. Earlier in the interview, Ilan pointed out his admiration for the rabbis' ability to understand the human condition and speak to the needs of different humans. For Shira, canonical thinking limits the tradition. While she recognizes the cleverness of drawing connections between various locations within the textual corpus, she does not believe that this connection making or problem resolving leads to deeper understandings. Rather, these connections often feel showy; they are "superficial" and "vapid." A closed-corpus approach limits the breadth of intellectual pursuit that rabbinics enables. But in the ecological view, on the other hand, rabbinics expands as new forms and subjects of inquiry emerge.

Consider Shira's description of hearing a lecture by Yale professor Christine Hayes at the Association for Jewish Studies (AJS) annual conference:

> She thinks about who the people are. Who produced this text. She draws in historical knowledge and sociological knowledge. And whatever other sorts of things she can get her hands on... And I was so impressed, at this last AJS she was talking about humor in the Talmud. And she made this comment like, "Don't get me wrong, I'm not saying I find it funny. Or that... I just have the hunch that they found it funny." She said there is research on what was considered funny, because you can reconstruct that based on when there's laughter described as a response to certain things in ancient performances and different things like that. And I was so taken. She was like, "No, no, no, scientifically this was funny to them"... It's really using lots of different tools to use these texts to think about who the rabbis were. And to think about what... to essentially connect it to the larger question of, What is religion? What is Judaism? What is expression? And what are we going to make of these people and this text and these laws? So, what is law? She asks big questions and she uses the Talmud effectively to answer them.

For Shira, Hayes's inquiry is paradigmatic of great rabbinics. She wants to understand the world of the rabbis in service of answering larger questions about our world today. But in order to understand the rabbis, she relies on deep knowledge of rabbinic literature with a fluency in a host of tools to illuminate that material. In this model, rabbinic literature does not have fixed boundaries from its surrounding ancient neighbors. Further, the scope of what one does in rabbinics is expansive, amplified by the study of sociology, law, history, and so on.

Another story further rounds out this view. A class with Hebrew University professor Menahem Kehana, instilled in Shira the idea that broad knowledge of the world is required for fleshing out rabbinic texts and meaning with potentially no boundary. She shares:

> He knows the entire world through the lens of Midrash Halakha... And there was a class that he was giving about *Sifrei Bemidbar* and a guy was doing a presentation in class and it had to do something with the Mishkan and gold. And they smelted the gold for something, something. And the midrash says this or that. And Kahana stops him and says, "Have you been there?" And the guy says, "Have I been where?" And Kahana says, "Have you been when they smelt gold?" And the guy rolls his eyes and says, "No I haven't." And he says, "Well, I have. I had to go to a factory because I needed to find out what this midrash meant. And you are completely wrong about what it means." Things like that. If it comes up, he's got to know about it. Though, theoretically, everything—agriculture, gold smelting, history, philology, astronomy, anything... literary tropes, law. There are so many different angles. That's what I mean.

In this story, rabbinics becomes a gateway for intellectual pursuit across disciplines. If one is learning history, philology, or astronomy, in service of understanding rabbinics, they are doing rabbinics. Rabbinics is an expanding ecology not simply because its primary texts continue to be written in the form of responsa and interpretations, but because the field of rabbinics continues to expand. For example, learning Persian was not part of rabbinics until scholars started to learn Persian in service of finding greater understanding of the Babylonian context.

At the heart of this conception of rabbinics is an ever-expanding set of tools for analyzing the text. Lest one imagine that this toolbox is only associated with academic approaches to the interpretation of rabbinic texts, this conception is present even among avowedly "religious" teachers. Nati, a Modern Orthodox rabbi, described the process of reading a midrash:

> [When] I'm learning all the *midrashim* on *Akedat Yitzhak* [the binding of Isaac in Genesis 22] . . . I'm not just learning the midrash. I'm thinking about "How does this matter? How does this affect larger theological issues? How does this affect political issues in Judaism?". . . That is a person who has expertise where they have in their, I won't say fingertips, that's too extreme, but they have in their toolbox or in their brain, they're able to process a number of areas in Jewish thought at the same time, and that matters to them.

For the conception of rabbinics as ecology, the goal of uncovering meaning that is both in the text and of personal significance requires a broad range of conceptual frameworks and technical skills to draw out knowledge.

It is telling that Nati drew an example from midrash. Whereas Moshe suggested midrash should be a part of the discipline of Tanakh. Within the ecology conception, midrash is a key artifact of rabbinic creativity. Adina, a PhD at a Modern Orthodox school, observed that midrash was generally absent from her school's curriculum in part because it provides an opening for broad dissent. She described how her colleagues would express insecurities about midrash because it would elicit students' inquiry into material about which they did not feel prepared. "The kids have so many questions. I don't know how to answer them," her colleagues would share. The open-endedness of rabbinics as ecology lacks the secure boundaries of rabbinics as corpus. For Adina, a broader academic understanding of midrash provides her with the confidence to engage the endless multivocal possibilities of rabbinic midrash. For her, reading midrash leads to "understanding the world of the rabbis, appreciating the literary artistry, being able to understand the layers of meaning encoded in these texts, and not worrying about [historical accuracy]."

Rabbinics as a Thought Process

While rabbinics presents itself to the student through the form of different texts, some see those texts as products of rabbinic minds. In this conception, rabbinics is a mode of thinking more than a body of texts. That the tradition began rooted in orality further shapes this conception.

Rabbinics does not just happen through texts but in the interpretive process over the texts, the conversations that are animated by rabbinics, and ultimately the thought processes engendered by the study of rabbinics. The literature that has emerged around *hevruta* study, which aims to identify the ways that the study of rabbinic texts engenders particular interpretive behaviors and lived values and emphasizes the acts of study, speaks to this particular notion. Further, it can be compared to the notion of mathematics as problem solving (Ernest, 1989), which sees mathematics as "a process of enquiry and coming to know, not a finished product, for its results remain open to revision" (p. 250). Its emphasis is on the back and forth of rabbinic discourse and the emphasis on a method of critical thinking for uncovering truth.

For many of the teachers in this study, cultivating fluency in rabbinic thinking was deemed important for understanding how to analyze the texts. David, however, described a vision of expertise and pedagogical practices that suggest an emphasis on cultivating thought processes through interaction with content. Describing the qualities of rabbinics experts, David offered two related qualifications: (1) the ability to hold multiple complex arguments or views at one time and (2) the ability to use known information to predict what might happen in another related situation. He described an expert as someone who has:

> The ability to hold on to multiple, different pieces of information simultaneously and on multiple levels. Meaning that it's not just "this person says this, this person says this, and this person says this"—but rather a person says "A" because they come and they operate within this world with this values context. Person B believes this because they come from this world and they operate here. Person C becomes this and then... So, it's the multilayers of understanding about each person...What this person might argue in a new context that is perhaps parallel or perhaps identifying where the analogies work and where the analogies don't work. To be able to effectively anticipate what a ruling might be or what a thought might be.

For David, this kind of expert embodies a rabbinic way of thinking. They are able to hold on to distinct opinions within complex arguments. The rabbis featured in these texts are representatives of larger theoretical schools of thought cultivated in a particular context. The expert is able to capture the complex logical opinion, the contextual information that gave rise to the opinion, and fit it into a philosophical school. In addition to identifying and holding all of this information, it informs future understanding and decisions. The expert in rabbinic thinking uses this information to predict how situations will unfold elsewhere or interpret the text according to these different understandings of the material. In this respect, rabbinic thinking lives in the upper realms of Bloom's taxonomy (Bloom et al., 1984), where one can analyze multiple distinct notions, evaluate the values or ideas behind the positions, and then create using those values.

David's description of a conflict that arose regarding student placement for his advanced class proved particularly instructive about his conception of rabbinics. In his community day school, the norm was to place students with higher Hebrew capabilities in advanced "text" classes, taught in the original. But David felt frustrated by this, preferring students with higher intellectual and logical capacities over students with advanced language skills. In the current model, he explained, "You end up having a bunch of kids who have really strong Hebrew because they're Israeli, but their intellectual capacity for being a tenth grader is not as developed." Language fluency, David notes, does not prepare one for navigating the advanced thinking found in rabbinic literature. Rather, rabbinic literature requires students of a certain intellectual prowess who will be better prepared to be inducted into the material.

Marc offered similar sentiments, suggesting that students with "for lack of a better term, pure intelligence" are more likely to excel in rabbinics and noting the challenge of making the texts meaningful for a population with varied cognitive abilities. The grappling with the logical rigor described by David and Marc mirrors a growing body of literature expressing similar concern about Talmud study in Orthodox settings in America and Israel (Oaks & Handelman, 2003) as well as subjects like math and physics, and speaks to the nature of the domain. Just as one with stronger fine motor skills may be better prepared to play guitar or paint, one with stronger abstract thinking skills may be better prepared for rabbinics. While these are certainly skills that one can acquire and develop, raw talent certainly helps. In this type of classroom, study focuses on inducting the student into the thought processes. David links his aim to Joseph Soleveitchik's philosophy as expressed in *Halakhic Man* (Soloveitchik, 1991), hoping students will begin "seeing the world through Talmudic glasses." He wants students to express their own experience through the language of the Talmud studied in class. In describing a unit about transformation that drew on material from the second chapter of tractate *Megillah*, he explained how he ultimately wants his students to describe their own encounter with transformation, either personally or through popular culture. "And, if they're able to write about it at that level," he says, "then what we're seeing is the text that they're studying and the life that they are experiencing... lining up more directly." For David, this unit was not a study of the second chapter of *Megillah* but about the idea of "transformations." The assignment required students to apply texts, in order to help those students to see their lives through rabbinic categories.

Other teachers, too, referred to the desire for students to cultivate the ability to understand how the rabbis think, and in particular, the capacity for holding multiple opinions. Noah, who earlier articulated his conception of rabbinics as corpus, spoke glowingly of the multiple opinions at play in rabbinic texts, especially in the Mishnah. He liked being able to bring new students into the world of the rabbinic disagreement and debate.

> That it's like, "Okay, we're going to pray." Great. But when are we going to pray? We're going to bring out different opinions. And mostly what they see in the Mishnah is, you just see a list of opinions. It doesn't explain why. It doesn't say who's right or wrong. Except for on some occasions. There's just a lot of different possibilities out there...
>
> With the Mishnah it's...you can kind of see how the halakhic system works. That you basically have a democracy. And I kind of point out the whole "*Torah tziva lanu Moshe*" (The Torah that Moses commanded us)... It's ours. We own this document. And we have to figure out what to do with it. And that it's not that God told us all, "Okay, here is every little detail of how to do everything." You have differing opinions on how to best do this. And we have to go with what we think is best. That

> that argument sounded the best. Or that had the majority, so that's what we're going to do. And that that's what Judaism is.

Noah, who earlier described mastery of the corpus as the ideal, here prioritizes the navigation among divergent opinions as "what Judaism is."

Adina, who earlier adopted the conception of rabbinics as ecology, articulated the added value of learning midrash for developing students' thinking. The complex nature of midrash, its attention to language, its use of multiple meanings, and its multiple takes on the same topic push students to reconsider the notion of textual meaning and require abstract thinking skills. For Adina, midrash enables:

> creativity when it comes to reading and not having the misconception that there could ever be one absolute meaning. Midrash by itself doesn't necessarily do that, but particularly when a midrashic passage has multiple opinions and positions, it destabilizes the sense that there is one reading that's possible. In terms of helping kids feel, both in terms of their relationship to Torah, but also in terms of their relationship to ideas, that there are many ways to think about a problem, many access points, is not only critical for them, but also for the society that we're trying to build.

Like Shira, others also pointed to the complexity of this literature as the reason why it was personally so enthralling and meaningful.

Conclusion

Gershom Scholem's essay "Revelation and Tradition as Religious Categories in Judaism" (1972) sets out a conflict embedded in the teaching of Judaism. On one hand, Judaism is a collection of texts that represent revelation with God at Sinai. On the other, Judaism is the application of these texts to life, which, over time, becomes enshrined as something to be studied with deep reverence. In what ways might the conception of rabbinics as corpus conceptualize revelation and application? Moshe, who separated midrash from rabbinics, will likely emphasize a legalism in ways that Adina, who sees rabbinics as an ecology and has a doctorate in midrash, may not. One's conception of rabbinics may well influence one's parameters of what counts as revelation and creativity.

The fact that rabbinics may be conceptualized in these different ways offers a challenge to Schwab's (1973) and Bruner's (1977) notions of discipline structure. Both assume a stable, essential disciplinary structure, which forms the basis on which teachers should make instructional decisions. But a discipline like rabbinics, as this paper has shown, lacks agreement about its disciplinary structure. This suggests that educators need to be responsible for thinking deeply about their own conceptions of their subject, and perhaps too, for developing their capacity for thinking about a subject beyond their own conceptions. Encountering multiple conceptions, such as have been presented here, offers a way to approach their implicit biases about their subject and more effectively uncover the "hidden curriculum" in their classroom (Snyder, 1973; Giroux & Purpel, 1983), at least in respects to teachers' notions of the Jewish tradition.

Beyond this point, we ought to consider the cultural contexts that seem to valorize some conceptions differently than others. Among the three conceptions of rabbinics presented in this study, the conceptions of rabbinics as corpus and of rabbinics as ecology tend to emerge from traditional Orthodox institutions and from academic environments, respectively, and were represented more broadly than the third conception, rabbinics as thought process. Each cultural context has its own, mostly implicit ideas about what counts as legitimate knowledge.

Indeed, these teachers' conceptions of rabbinics were derived from their own experiences of being students, particularly at institutions of higher learning—universities and*yeshivot*. Many of the teachers described experts that were one or two degrees of separation away (Levites, 2020a). While we were fortunate to interview a pool of teachers who were diverse with regard to gender and educational background, the sample is likely overly diverse when compared to the broader field. And it is worth considering that even if the sample is diverse, there are only a handful of locations one can study rabbinics. In comparison to literature, for example, the field is tiny. This is significant because it leads to a limited number of modes offered to students.

Before we consider what students might know, it is valuable to map what students might have access to knowing. In this study, we were not able to interview a teacher working in the field who had graduated from HUC or RRC. While we had a number of non-Orthodox teachers, they were educated at settings that recognized the binding nature of Jewish law in ways that Reform and Reconstructionist Jews do not. This research begs questions about how teacher representation and the expression of that knowledge reinforces itself so as to only offer students a sliver of the intellectual field that is rabbinics, and ultimately, what it means to be Jewish.

It is possible that all three conceptions presented in this chapter could lead to classroom teaching that looks relatively similar in certain respects. It is possible, for example, that all three conceptions could produce classrooms where learning how to read rabbinic texts in the original languages is taken seriously. But even in a classroom where students are expected to learn in the original, a teacher's conceptions of rabbinics—which, as we have noted, is often bound up with how that teacher conceptualizes the Jewish tradition in general—may lead to different types of assignments and ultimately the type of success in the classroom that will be privileged.

In fact, which kinds of knowledge are privileged as legitimate may lead to decisions about who has access to the classroom in the first place. Consider David, who argued with his administrator about who should be in the advanced rabbinics course. David's department head wanted to put students with strong Hebrew in the class without a focus on their cognitive skills. David had a preference for students with strong abstract thinking skills over "secular Israelis who happen to have strong Hebrew." This is similar to Marc, who saw rabbinics as conceptually difficult, mentioning that students with sharper "IQs—logic and reasoning skills" would be better at rabbinics. This discussion about placements is natural and normal, not nefarious, but what is striking is how it is linked to the teacher's conception of the subject and ultimately their conception of legitimacy regarding lived Judaism. If not the secular Israelis with strong Hebrew, who are the students that will make up David's advanced rabbinics class?

As readers consider these three conceptions of rabbinics, they may find themselves disagreeing with one or another, or perhaps find themselves gravitating to elements of all three. This discussion does not aspire to offer a comprehensive taxonomy of how teachers think about rabbinics, or about the tradition. Rather, it is a step toward illuminating larger questions about what we are teaching students and hopefully offers a tool for enabling teachers to think about their own implicit and explicit values.

In describing the purpose of the menu of orientations for teaching rabbinics, Levisohn hopes that the menu will "serve as a framework for discussion among teachers about the practices of teaching rabbinic literature—discussion that is more nuanced and more specific, that is less ideological and more pedagogical" (2010, p. 80). By exploring a menu of orientations, one may transcend one's own predilections in the service of meeting the variety of students who sit in one's classroom. "Ideological" discussion about teaching focuses on what a teacher believes is correct or right; "pedagogical" discussion, by contrast, focuses on how to engage with a subject with particular students.

The addition of this paper is a deeper push for teachers to bring to their classroom heightened awareness of their own perspectives. It is an argument for the idea that our ideologies, even ones of which we are not conscious, bleed into our teaching. This does not emerge from a desire to eliminate some notion of teacher bias, but from a desire to strengthen teachers' capacities to be conduits, opening pathways for their students into the material. An investigation into their own notions of the tradition allows teachers to engage their students with broader confidence. In this capacity, they may step into the role of concierge, stewarding different students through the myriad ways one may encounter, embrace, and respond to the rabbinic tradition.

NOTES

1. The "Students' Understanding of Rabbinics" research project was a partnership between the Jack, Joseph and Morton Mandel Center for Studies in Jewish Education at Brandeis University and the William Davidson Graduate School of Jewish Education at the Jewish Theological Seminary. The primary focus of the research project was students' understanding and experience of the subject; these teacher interviews generated background data for subsequent interviews of students. The project was also interested in the possibility of creating an expert/novice study (Nelson & Schunn, 2009), which is why the teacher interviews asked about notions of expertise, although in the end that proved impractical.

2. Holtz and Levisohn's use of orientations has led to a range of studies including focus on specific orientations in practice (Levisohn, 2008; Cousens et al., 2008; Greenstein, 2009), teachers' orientations in practice (Tauber, 2010; Greenberg, 2017), proposed new

orientations for Bible or rabbinics (Gutoff, 2015), and proposed orientations for different areas of Jewish education such as Jewish thought and Israel education (Galili-Schachter, 2011; Gottlieb, 2013).

3. Grossman describes teacher orientations as stemming from Lee Shulman's seminal work (1986) on Pedagogical Content Knowledge (PCK), which provides a framework for thinking about the way the professional skills of teaching interact with the content of the subject being taught and its translation into curriculum. It is the capacity to provide "representation of those ideas, the most powerful analogies, illustrations, examples, explanations, and demonstrations—in a word, the ways of representing and formulating the subject that make it comprehensible to others" (Shulman, 1986, p. 9).

REFERENCES

Apple, M. W. (1990). *Ideology and curriculum*. Routledge and Kegan Paul.

Baldwin, J. (1985). A talk to teachers. In *The price of the ticket: Collected nonfiction, 1948–1985* (pp. 325–332). Joseph.

Berkowitz, B. A. (2017). Different religions?: Big and little religion in rabbinics and religious studies. In E. Alexander & B. A. Berkowitz (eds.), *Religious studies and rabbinics* (pp. 39–53). Routledge.

Bloom, B. S., Krathwohl, D. R., & Masia, B. B. (1984). *Taxonomy of educational objectives: The classification of educational goals*. Longman.

Bruner, J. S. (1977). *The process of education*. Harvard University Press.

Chase, W. G., & Simon, H. A. (1973). Perception in chess. *Cognitive Psychology*, *4*(1), 55–81. https://doi.org/10.1016/0010-0285(73)90004-2/.

Chi, M. T. H., Feltovich, P. J., & Glaser, R. (1981). Categorization and representation of physics problems by experts and novices. *Cognitive Science*, *5*(2), 121–152. https://doi.org/10.1207/s15516709cog0502_2/.

Cochran-Smith, M., & Lytle, S. L. (2009). *Inquiry as stance: Practitioner research for the next generation*. Teachers College Press.

Cousens, B. (2016). *"A text that is never resolved": Skills, knowledge and personal meaning in students' experiences of rabbinic literature* (Phase 1, pp. 1–26). Mandel Center for Studies in Jewish Education, Brandeis University, and William Davidson Graduate School of Jewish Education, JTS.

Cousens, B., Morrison, J. S., & Fendrick, S. P. (2008). Using the contextual orientation to facilitate the study of Bible with Generation X. *Journal of Jewish Education*, *74*(1), 6–28. https://doi.org/10.1080/15244110701874019/.

Ellis, V. (2007). Taking subject knowledge seriously: From professional knowledge recipes to complex conceptualizations of teacher development. *The Curriculum Journal*, *18*(4), 447–462. https://doi.org/10.1080/09585170701687902/.

Ernest, P. (1989). *Mathematics teaching: The state of the art*. Falmer Press.

Fishman, T. (2011). *Becoming the people of the Talmud: Oral Torah as written tradition in medieval Jewish cultures*. University of Pennsylvania Press.

Gafni, I. (2009). The modern study of rabbinics and historical questions: The tale of the text. In R. Bieringer, F. García Martinez, D. Pollefeyt, & P. Tomson (eds.), *The New Testament and rabbinic literature* (41–61). Brill.

Galili-Schachter, I. (2011). Pedagogic hermeneutic orientations in the teaching of Jewish texts. *Journal of Jewish Education*, *77*(3), 216–238. https://doi.org/10.1080/15244113.2011.601450/.

Giroux, H. A., & Purpel, D. E. (1983). *The hidden curriculum and moral education: Deception or discovery?* McCutchan.

Gottlieb, O. (2013). Media studies orientations for Israel Education: Lessons from in treatment, homeland, and Z-cars. *Journal of Jewish Education*, *79*(1), 49–69.

Greenberg, G. P. (2017). *Exploring the curriculum narratives of Jewish day school Bible teachers*. (Publication No. 10250904. Doctoral dissertation, Northeastern University). https://www.proquest.com/openview/172c22617bad8eb8ebdc93c5df51cd1c/1?pq-origsite=gscholar&cbl=18750/.

Greenstein, E. L. (2009). A pragmatic pedagogy of Bible. *Journal of Jewish Education*, *75*(3), 290–303. https://doi.org/10.1080/15244110903079284/.

Grossman, P. (1991). What are we talking about anyhow?: Subject-matter knowledge of English teachers. In J. Brophy (ed.), *Advances in research on teaching: Teacher's knowledge of subject matter as it relates to their teaching practice* (Vol. 2, pp. 245–264). Jai Press.

Grossman, P. L., & Shulman, L. S. (1994). Knowing, believing, and the teaching of English. In T. E. Shanahan (ed.), *Teachers thinking, teachers knowing: Reflections on literacy and language education* (pp. 3–22). National Council of Teachers of English.

Grossman, P. L., Wilson, S. M., & Shulman, L. S. (1989). Teachers of substance: Subject matter knowledge for teaching. In M. C. Reynolds (ed.), *Knowledge base for the beginning teacher* (pp. 23–37). Pergamon Press.

Gutoff, J. (2015). Toward a moral-imaginative pedagogy of Talmudic narratives. *Journal of Jewish Education*, *81*(3), 312–339. https://doi.org/10.1080/15244113.2015.1063034/.

Halbertal, M. (1997). *People of the book: Canon, meaning, and authority*. Harvard University Press.

Hayes, C. E. (2017). *What's divine about divine law?: Early perspectives*. Princeton University Press.

Holtz, B. W. (2003). *Textual knowledge: Teaching the Bible in theory and practice*. Jewish Theological Seminar of America.

Kellner, M. M. (2006). *Must a Jew believe anything?* Littman Library of Jewish Civilization.

Lakoff, G. (1989). *Women, fire, and dangerous things: What categories reveal about the mind*. The University of Chicago Press.

Lakoff, G., & Johnson, M. (1980). *Metaphors we live by*. University of Chicago Press.

Lave, J., & Wenger, E. (1991). *Situated learning: Legitimate peripheral participation*. Cambridge University Press.

Levisohn, J. A. (2008). Strengthening research on the pedagogy of Jewish studies: Introduction to a suite of articles on teaching Bible. *Journal of Jewish Education*, *74*(1), 3–5. https://doi.org/10.1080/15244110701872179/.

Levisohn, J. A. (2010). A menu of orientations to the teaching of rabbinic literature. *Journal of Jewish Education*, *76*(1), 4–51. https://doi.org/10.1080/15244110903534510/.

Levites, A. (2020a). *Student's understanding of rabbinics* (Final Report, pp. 1–60). Mandel

Center for Studies in Jewish Education, Brandeis University, and William Davidson Graduate School of Jewish Education, JTS.

Levites, A. (2020b). Worth knowing: Talmud study and the intellectual values of high school students at liberal Jewish day schools. *Journal of Jewish Education*, *86*(1), 65–93. https://doi.org/10.1080/15244113.2020.1710810/.

Nabokov, V. V. (2008). *The real life of Sebastian Knight*. New Directions.

Nelson, M. M., & Schunn, C. D. (2008). The nature of feedback: How different types of peer feedback affect writing performance. *Instructional Science*, *37*(4), 375–401. https://doi.org/10.1007/s11251-008-9053-x/.

Odenbaugh, J., & Pfeifer, J. (2005). Ecology. In S. Sarkar (ed.), *The philosophy of science: An Encyclopedia* (pp. 215–225). Taylor & Francis Ltd.

Pajares, M. F. (1992). Teachers' beliefs and educational research: Cleaning up a messy construct. *Review of Educational Research*, *62*(3), 307–332. https://doi.org/10.3102/00346543062003307/.

Rich, J. M., & Schwab, J. J. (1968). Structure of the disciplines: Meaning and significances. In *Readings in the philosophy of education*. Wadsworth.

Rosenzweig, F. (2002). *On Jewish learning*. N. N. Glatzer (ed.). University of Wisconsin Press.

Saiman, C. N. (2018). *Halakhah: The rabbinic idea of law*. Princeton University Press.

Saks, J., & Handelman, S. A. (2003). *Wisdom from all my teachers: Challenges and initiatives in contemporary Torah education*. Urim Publications.

Schechter, S. (1972). *Aspects of rabbinic theology*. Schocken Books.

Scholem, G. (1972). Revelation and tradition as religious categories in Judaism. In *The messianic idea in Judaism and other essays on Jewish spirituality* (pp. 282–303). Schocken Books.

Schwab, J. J. (1973). The practical 3: Translation into curriculum. *The School Review*, *81*(4), 501–522. https://doi.org/10.1086/443100/.

Schwab, J. J., & Schwab, J. J. (1982). Education and the structure of the disciplines. In I. Westbury & N. Wilkof (eds.), *Science, curriculum, and liberal education: Selected essays* (pp. 229–274). University of Chicago Press.

Shanahan, T., Grossman, P. L., & Shulman, L. S. (1994). Knowing, believing, and the teaching of English. In *Teachers thinking, teachers knowing: Reflections on literacy and language education* (pp. 3–22). National Conference on Research in English.

Shulman, L. S. (1986). Those who understand: Knowledge growth in teaching. *Educational Researcher*, *15*(2), 4. https://doi.org/10.2307/1175860/.

Snyder, B. R. (1973). *The hidden curriculum*. MIT Press.

Soloveitchik, J. D. (1991). *Halakhic man*. Jewish Publication Society of America.

Stern, D. (2012). Rabbinics and Jewish identity: An American perspective. *Jewish Thought and Jewish Belief*, 7–26.

Tauber, S. M. (2010). *Facilitator, co-learner, community-builder: The congregational rabbi as a teacher of adults in liberal synagogues* (Publication No. 3458673. Doctoral dissertation, The Jewish Theological Seminary of America). https://www.proquest.com/openview/6c0d810b769e5f18b9f977a193729c5b/1?pq-origsite=gscholar&cbl=18750/.

Wimpfheimer, B. S. (2011). The dialogical Talmud: Daniel Boyarin and rabbinics. *Jewish Quarterly Review*, *101*(2), 245–254. https://doi.org/10.1353/jqr.2011.0001/.

9
Four Approaches to the Instruction of Halakha

YAAKOV JAFFE

It is almost a truism that Jewish education—indeed, all education—is predicated on a commitment to three things: the development of certain skills and abilities in students, the acquisition of some scope of content knowledge on the part of those students, and the cultivation of a series of beliefs and commitments within those students. Though this organizational system of education is well known and is explicit in Bloom and Adler's writings on general education, Jewish schools still often do not crystallize for themselves where the balance lies between the three strands of Jewish education that all coexist chaotically at the same time in a Jewish school. Schools are not explicit to themselves and to the parents: where the priorities lie, where greater time investment should be made, and whether skill development, knowledge acquisition, or conversation on beliefs should be the focus of the curriculum. This chapter will focus on the subject halakha, Jewish law and custom, using the topic of halakha as a microcosm or case study for the more general questions Jewish schools face: Is the focus on growing students' knowledge base *about* Judaism, on developing students' ability to *live* Judaism, or on ensuring a *commitment* to Judaism long term? We will also ask whether schools are self-aware about the priorities, making aligned choices to bring the priorities into practice, or whether instead schools make decisions at times oblivious to how those choices might reflect on broader goals.

Halakha, or Jewish law, is one of the major curricular areas in American Jewish day schools. Most students will at some point study halakha, the performances, rituals, and customs that Jews practice as part of their

Jewish living. The study of halakha has been part of Jewish education in some form for centuries, although it is only in the last few decades that Jewish schools have begun to plan and carry out its formal instruction as a distinct area of study. The scholarly literature about the topic, mostly developed over the last fifty years, demonstrates four major conceptual modes and models for how schools can engage in halakha instruction. Each emerges from a particular stance as to the nature and even the ultimate purpose of halakha teaching and learning, and so the study of the different approaches sheds important light on the broader goals of day school education. The topic is thus of interest to halakha educators, and also those who develop and analyze other types of Judaic studies curricula (such as Bible or rabbinics), and those who study alignment in Jewish education more broadly, as we consider the extent to which theories of Jewish education correspond to actual classroom applications and student outcomes.[1] This chapter examines how a Jewish day school's stated vision or approach to halakha instruction impacts or aligns with the curricular, school structure, or classroom decisions related to halakha. To that end, we focus on Modern Orthodox high schools and their choices within a matrix of different approaches to halakha teaching.

Four Approaches

The prevalent and predominant approach to halakha education in the literature sees halakha as a subject whose purpose is to teach students the content knowledge they will need to apply in practice outside the classroom (Eisenberg, 1976; Goldmintz, 1996; Harari & Wolowelsky, 1987; Jaffe, 2014). Stated differently, the ultimate purpose of the study of halakha is preparing students for a life when they will keep all the laws and customs of Judaism correctly, although schools move toward this purpose through the study and teaching of a set of key content knowledge. A second approach agrees that the aims are lifelong practice, but also believes that the educational discipline or subject focuses more on the real-life learning of halakha, the learning of procedural knowledge in real life and not in the classroom (Krakowski et al., 2012; Soloveitchik, 1994). This approach sees the quintessential halakha class as a teacher-led trip to purchase food from

Starbucks or to immerse vessels in a mikvah; as an engineering exercise to build a sukkah or route an *eruv*. It looks at a daily prayer service, a *Purim Megillah* reading, or a Saturday night Havdalah held in the school as prime examples of halakha education because students can learn the skills of Jewish living through participating in those actions in a very real way.[2] Historically, this approach to halakha education is the oldest one, even explicated in the Talmud (*Sukkah* 42a).

I have previously drawn attention to a third approach, which is alluded to elsewhere in the literature, that sees halakha education as part of general Jewish cultural literacy, purely focused on the study of Jewish content like a class of Bible or rabbinics (Jaffe, 2009).[3] Still others take a fourth view and argue that the primary purpose of halakha study is to enable students to acquire perspectives, beliefs, and values about Judaism through the study of halakha, more than to study halakha itself.

Ironically, a school's selection of one of these four models ("learning for future practice," "observational learning," "cultural literacy," and "halakha as philosophy") do not neatly divide into type of school or denomination of students. For example, ultra-Orthodox schools often engage in less observational learning around holidays (such as Purim, Passover, or Sukkot) as they anticipate the student body engaging in observational learning at home; in contrast, it is community, pluralistic, or nondenominational schools that are most likely to have school on the holidays in order to model halakhic practice through observational learning. Meanwhile, the "cultural literacy" approach is also championed by some Orthodox schools (Jaffe, 2018), and is not limited to schools that are less invested in halakha as an essential practice.

A somewhat lengthier summary of these perspectives can be found in Schwartz (2012). His work is a valuable collection of recent literature, especially of those in Hebrew, but it suffers from two significant problems. First, he fails to maintain the distinction between the discipline halakha and the related disciplines of rabbinics, Mishnah, and Talmud. Second, he often bifurcates similar approaches to a degree of nuance or subtly, which is not helpful to researchers and practitioners, as some of his approaches overlap with each other nearly completely.

Contrasting the Four Approaches

What are the practical differences between the various approaches? The literature provides some illustrations of areas in which the different approaches contrast, and what the trade-offs, positives, and negatives of each specific approach are.

One of the earlier attempts to map a program of halakha instruction for the American day school movement was undertaken by Yehudah Eisenberg of the Torah Education Department of the World Zionist Organization with the Board of Jewish Education of New York in 1975–1976 (Eisenberg, 1975 and 1976). His introduction clearly reveals his assumptions about the nature of halakha teaching in the day school. Eisenberg notes that the objective of the discipline is "to study the laws well in order that they be put into practice" (1975, p. 8; 1976, p. 5). Thus, the primary goal of halakha teaching is to teach content to students that can enable them to produce a desired behavior as an outcome. The focus is not on the teaching of pure content, and it does not merely consist of watching adults; instead, content is studied in a classroom setting for the sake of using it in future practice.

The curricular decisions made by Eisenberg are governed by this assumption as well. Skill learning requires more review and less depth than content learning and so the system involves much repetition of material from year to year. Eisenberg notes that in the early twentieth century, halakha teachers generally taught the same basic halakhic content each year, covering the full corpus of Jewish law and custom nearly every year in order to review them with enough regularity for students to have instant recall and be able to put them into practice. After a brief criticism about how unrealistic such an approach is, Eisenberg retains the system where the entire corpus of Jewish law and custom is meant to be covered multiple times across schooling, in place of learning those topics more deeply. He makes minor tweaks to the previous system but avoids a major revision: topics are covered in detail every three or four years (instead of every year) and are reviewed three times in a K–12 system (instead of twelve times). But there is no major break from the assumption that halakha is the teaching and learning of a large corpus of basic content that is intended for practice. The two major concerns with this approach, raised repeatedly by Eisenberg and elsewhere in the literature, is that this superficial study lacks the depth to facilitate the development of lasting structures and deep understandings of the discipline, while it also can be a cause for boredom in the classroom.

Supporters of observational and experiential learning of halakha are drawn to it because it addresses two unique challenges posed in the study of halakha. First, the study of halakha involves the application of a large amount of background knowledge principles to a case in question, but students first confront the situation before mastering the background knowledge, constituting a major barrier for even entry into basic halakha study. This is true on two levels—both that students do not know the structures of the *specific* subtopics of halakha and also that they do not know *general* principles of halakhic decision-making (see Goldmintz, 1996, p. 57; Krakowski et al., 2012, p. 6). The second challenge is that halakha classrooms promote high levels of passivity because they involve less student originality and more rote learning. Halakha classes teach the appropriate, best, conventional way of Jewish acting in a given situation, assuming that every question has one best answer, and consequently there is less room left for student originality. The range of acceptable options is narrower in halakha than in other areas of Jewish life, so students' own views or instincts are often rejected in the end, even when there is a difference of opinion among earlier authorities. Thus, an experiential learning approach helps remove student passivity in halakha study and the need for background knowledge, because halakha is liberated from classroom format; rather, it is learned in a way that is alive and applied to real life.

There are two challenges posed to the observational learning approach. First, on a practical level, it is not always possible for schools to provide real-world opportunities for students to watch and learn about each arena of Jewish law and custom. How can a school that is closed on Passover authentically provide observational learning for the complete family Passover seder? Beyond this practical reason, which does not render this model nonviable but would only limit its applications, others raise concerns with this model on a theoretical level by invoking the problem of transfer. In halakha, students are asked to "transfer" (see Niedelman, 1991, pp. 322–329) the localized rulings they have experienced in the past to new situations that arise in their own lives in the future.

Students learn one example of a law and are expected to extrapolate from that example to real-life cases that are similar but not identical. Yet, no matter how many modern-day cases are experienced in school, there are an almost infinite number of cases and applications that students are never presented with. Can students be expected to transfer the customs of a Passover seder that takes place on a Wednesday night to the customs of the seder on a Saturday night? Or the customs of the 9th of Av that commences on Monday night as opposed to the end of Shabbat? If they have never been sick on a Shabbat or a fast day, if their stove pilot light has never gone out, if they have never paid attention to the order of the Torah reading on the sixth day of Chanukah, then the student has no observational learning experience of these situations and no way to transfer the old knowledge learned to new, but analogous situations when they first occur.

In an effort to respond to some of the concerns with the first two approaches, the "cultural literacy" approach changes the primary student outcome and sees the study of halakha as a pure content discipline within Jewish education, totally divorced from any sort of preparation for practice. It believes that halakha is a vital part of the study of Judaism, and students should learn this content even if they will never observe the specific laws and customs. The content is studied for its own sake, and students master the unique structure and grammar of the discipline, and not merely as an end to practice. This allows teachers to overcome the superficiality and breadth-over-depth focus that has plagued the earlier approaches, thereby increasing retention and meaningfulness of the material studied. They teach halakha in a way that maximizes engagement and understanding, and not in a way that maximizes exposure to every last detail. The primary cost of this approach is that students study fewer topics as a trade-off for the focus on deeper structures. But adherents of this approach are less concerned with student behavioral outcomes and more focused on learning and knowledge goals, so they are less concerned with studying fewer topics.

Fundamentally, this alternative perspective sees halakha as a corpus of declarative knowledge (see Rosenak, 1987, p. 39). Most educators in previous decades have granted that halakha exists in two planes (as declarative knowledge and as procedural knowledge) but argued that its role in the Jewish school was primarily as utilization or procedural knowledge, learning "rules and regulations" and when they apply. Jay Goldmintz once summed up the earlier approaches to halakha teaching as "the teaching of the commandments geared as it is to the very question of actions and beliefs in day to day life" (1996, p. 61; although contrast Goldmintz in Rimon, 2005). The "cultural literacy" approach breaks with this understanding and sees halakha mostly as declarative knowledge. In this regard, an apt parallel would be science instruction. Science instruction includes both declarative content knowledge and also laboratory procedural knowledge, but most schools spend more time or energy on the former, not the latter; when it comes to halakha, schools in the past would focus on the procedural knowledge, not the underlying principles.

Under this approach, the teaching and learning methodology for halakha would also include the underlying structures and grammar of the discipline and the generalization of rules and concepts to new cases, so students will be prepared to conduct this transfer process on their own. This sets a higher bar for teachers, who will require extra effort to teach concepts in such a way that students can truly acquire the knowledge and then be able to apply it correctly to new cases not addressed in the studied case law. But the story of education is replete with examples of greater depth and deep structures yielding better long-term outcomes than a blind focus on complete, comprehensive breadth.

Recently, Yosef Tzvi Rimon has advocated widely for this approach to the teaching of halakha (Rimon, 2008, p. 11). Rimon has authored many halakha curricula for use in the United States and argues that his curricula move the study of halakha forward because it focuses on students learning the underlying principles of the law, and not just the rules of the law (Rimon, 2005). However, though the explicit *claim* of Rimon's program is to revolutionize the study of halakha into the study of a content discipline instead of a study of practical halakha for life, the curriculum Rimon *actually* develops does not differ greatly from the work of earlier curricularists in its focus on the procedural knowledge that is used in practice. Rimon's curriculum is a cautionary tale for us, then, about how schools can claim or even plan to have one approach to teaching halakha that is later belied by the curriculum they actually put into place.

Lastly, many schools focus their halakha curricula around beliefs and attitudes, creating a class where Jewish *values* are taught and presented as normative, in lieu of Jewish law and custom. These halakha classrooms are prone to focus on topics like the "history of halakha" (the study of the religious and historical process wherein old debates are resolved and new realities are tackled), "philosophy of halakha" (the philosophic constructs that explain why halakha remains a relevant corpus through the passage of time), "reasons for the *mitzvot*" (the explanation of the deeper reasons why Jews chose particular practices), and "Jewish ethics."[4] Adherents of the first three views in the literature would not countenance these topics becoming the dominant focus of a class entitled "halakha." These topics might be addressed as special asides within the regular halakha class but could not dominate the lessons. Yet, many schools demur and say that halakha's true purpose in a Jewish school is the promulgation of beliefs and values, and not preparation for a life of enacting certain behaviors.

The trade-offs of this approach are self-evident: Imagine a biology class where the focus is not the corpus of biological knowledge known to scientists but instead the history of important figures in biology and their views. Surely the students in the class would emerge more knowledgeable in the fields of intellectual history and the history of science, and possibly even more passionate about biology, but they would also have less knowledge of the science itself. They would be very well prepared to study the religious and cultural assumptions of sixteenth-century Italy, for example, but not very well prepared to do further research into the field of biology. Similarly, the history of halakha is an appropriate topic for a Jewish history class (it highlights the role of authority in the Sephardic world, the role of mysticism in Jewish life, and the orientations of the divergent academies in different generations, etc.), but it runs counter to the goals of halakha per se. Yet, adherents of this fourth approach reply that halakha retains its meaning for the modern audience only when it is treated as a manifestation of Jewish philosophy, and they ask teachers to engage with this approach and not with the ones that speak less to students.

Study Methodology

This study investigates the extent to which a school's stated vision or approach to halakha instruction impacts or aligns with the curricular, school structure, or classroom decisions related to halakha. Though our study focused on Modern Orthodox high schools[5] in the United States, the general problem of the alignment between conceptual framework and curricular/classroom choices is applicable to all types of schools and all ages in all countries. We sought out to answer the following research questions:

1. First, we question whether there are indeed four approaches to halakha that are all manifested in American Modern Orthodox high schools. Though four approaches have been suggested by theoreticians, we can ask whether the approaches appear in schools, and whether some are limited to only a very small number of schools.
2. Second, we explore the extent to which different approaches exist and whether the self-report of a particular approach aligns with a school also manifesting a certain cluster of determinants consistent with the ideals of their approach. Here we ask whether the various schools that have chosen one approach to halakha instruction make similar choices about the ways they go about teaching halakha.

Surveys were sent via email to all forty-four Modern Orthodox Jewish high schools in the United States. Two-thirds of the schools (n=30) were coeducational (some may have had separate classes for boys and girls but had one administration and leadership for boys' and girls' divisions) and 14 single gender. These 44 schools were naturally divided equally between the New York metropolitan area (22 schools) and the rest of the United States (also 22 schools). Thirty schools (68 percent) indicated a willingness to participate in the study; 38 surveys were returned from 28 schools. The demographic distribution of the class of respondents roughly approximates the distribution in the population at large, with 14 schools outside the New York metropolitan area and 14 inside responding, and with 23 of the schools that responded being coeducational (82 percent) and 5 of the schools being single gender (4 of them male and 1 female).

In light of the analysis in the previous pages, we hypothesized that a school's stated approach to halakha instruction would impact a series of other halakha choices, as illustrated in table 9.1.

The survey first asked each respondent what their approach to halakha education was, and then asked various questions about classroom, structural, or curriculum choices that may have reflected that choice. The survey was addressed to the administrator in each school who was most involved in the halakha program and was filled out by that administrator or a lead teacher in the department, or sometimes both. The text of the halakha education survey appears in the Appendix to this paper.

Results

We answer the first research question in the affirmative, finding that the same dominant visions that were prevalent in the literature were the same ones held by most schools, with some of the more minor visions and approaches in the literature only accepted by a smaller number of schools. Specifically, we found more schools adhering to the first two visions on our conceptual map ("observational learning" and "learning for practice") than the second two ("cultural literacy" and "halakha as philosophy"). Thirteen respondents (39 percent) considered the primary purpose to be

TABLE 9.1. Instructional Choices for the Halakha Classroom, as Determined by a Broader Approach to Halakha Education

Learning, for Practice	Observational Learning	Cultural Literacy	Halakha as Philosophy
Topics studied are practical for students at some point in their lifetime	Topics studied are practical for students when studied	Topics are chosen based on interest (practical or not) or illustrative capacity	Nonpractical topics are chosen to illustrate ideals and values
Standard exams, focused on practical	Performance-based assessments	Standard exams, focused on theory	No assessments; journaling or essays
Legal-handbook texts	No textbook used	Theoretical texts	No textbook used
Standard instructional time	No scheduled classroom time	Standard instructional time	Informal discussions or regular classroom time
Teacher teaches material	Teacher arranges activities	Teacher develops/ organizes material	Teacher leads discussion
Some theory, much detail	Little theory/ background	Little detail when topics are covered	Focus on theory, less on rules or details

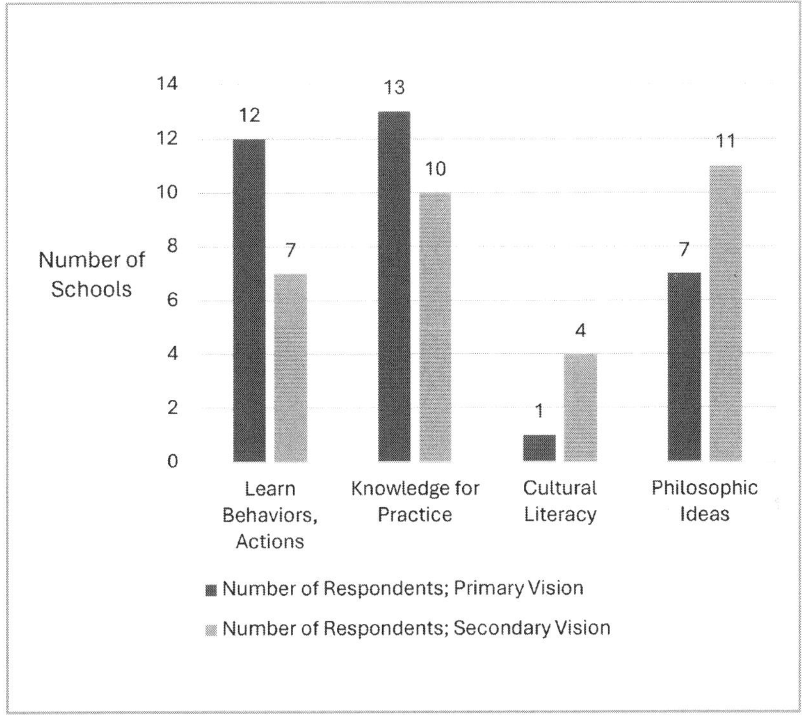

FIGURE 9.1. Primary and Secondary Visions of the Nature of halakha Instruction.

the teaching of a corpus of knowledge that is critical to know to be eventually put into practice, while 12 respondents (36 percent) considered the primary purpose of halakha to be the teaching of a certain set of behaviors and scripts for action. Thus, 75 percent of all respondents identified with one of the first two tracks, or visions, of halakha education, both of which focus on future halakha practice as the primary purpose of the study of Jewish law and custom. A smaller number of respondents (n=7, or 21 percent) believed that the primary purpose of halakha education was to convey a series of beliefs or philosophical notions about Judaism. Only one respondent in our survey group adopted the one remaining vision of halakha education, seeing halakha education as the study of critical texts that make up the corpus of Jewish knowledge. Refer to figure 9.1, which illustrates the different primary and secondary visions that were identified by the survey respondents.

There was no relationship between espoused primary vision and espoused secondary vision, and our analysis will focus on the stated primary vision for halakha education espoused by the survey responder. To be sure, the visions that were more popular as primary visions dropped off when respondents were asked to share what their secondary vision was, because none could select their primary vision for their secondary vision.

When considering the second research question, whether self-identification with a specific vision correlates with a set of determinants or other choices that reflect that vision in the classroom, we found that not a single classroom or curricular choice in our entire survey correlated with any of the visions of halakha instruction expressed by the specific school. Even composite scores that were developed to sum together questions in an effort to create greater statistical power for statistical analyses failed to yield any significant correlation with any of the espoused visions. Espoused vision had no effect on all other measures, including, but not limited to, total number of topics studied ($p=.182$), number of years of halakha study ($p=.852$), number of minutes of instruction per week ($p=.647$), a composite score for time spent on study ($p=.767$), whether there was a dedicated classroom teacher ($p=.618$), the learning speed ($p=.525$), type of text used ($p=.957$), whether exams involve supplying law for prompted cases ($p=.384$), whether exams ask students to reply to unknown scenarios ($p=.260$), whether exams ask students to merely summarize the material learned ($p=.284$), how the school conceptualized the role of the teacher ($p=.325$), how the school conceptualized the role of the student ($p=.904$), and a composite score asking how much time was spent on extra excursuses into the deep structures and grammar of halakha beyond the mere study of the practical laws ($p=.870$). In sum, our results demonstrate a wide variety of choices of general approaches to halakha instruction, but no alignment between classroom choices and underlying vision.

Most of these Modern Orthodox schools offered an independent class of "halakha," where students had a specific teacher and specifically scheduled classroom time for the study of this discipline ($n=24$, or 63 percent).[6] A smaller number did not offer a specific halakha class, but instead taught halakha as part of the Talmud class ($n=9$, or 24 percent); a still smaller number had no formal classroom-based halakha program at all ($n=5$, or 13 percent). Yet, contrary to the expectations borne out of the literature, having no formal classroom-based halakha program had no relationship with the espoused vision of halakha instruction. Evidently, schools' choices about their master schedules were largely uninformed by the conceptual approach they espoused regarding the study of halakha.

A small number of respondents (n=2) used no textbook or sourcebook at all in their teaching of halakha, relying on teachers' lecture or modeling for course content. This choice also showed no correlation with the espoused approach to halakha instruction. Most schools used a classical text composed before the year 1900 (15 respondents) or used handout sheets or sourcebooks that provided excerpts of many of those same classical sources (14 respondents). A very small number (n=2) used contemporary handbooks of Jewish law and custom intended for the student or lay audience. In this regard, we see that the instruction of halakha is approached as other Judaic studies subjects, where students study using *classical* texts, and not in the matter of general studies subjects like science or history, when a *contemporary* text is used to summarize and teach information. When asked which classical texts were used, *Mishnah Berurah* or *Shulchan Arukh* were most prevalent—few schools used *Arukh HaShulchan* or Rambam as their point of departure. Again, the textbook chosen has no statistical relationship with the self-identified vision for halakha education; many surveys were misaligned on this point.

Further statistical analysis sought to compare responses to questions not related to vision, and to determine a relationship between responses to those questions. Here, a series of relationships was evident. Number of topics studied was related to the type of text being used (p=.037), with the use of a more rigorous text (e.g., a classical text as opposed to sourcebooks or handouts) statistically related to a greater number of topics studied. As we noted previously, use of a text, especially a rigorous one, is indicative of a school adopting the "learning for practice" vision or the "cultural literacy" vision, and the selection of more topics, even ones not practical to students at the time of study, is further consistent with the school having an unarticulated, unstated, affinity toward a vision of "learning for practice" or "cultural literacy." Types of textbooks and number of topics are not connected on a *practical* level, and thus it is reasonable to attribute the relationship to an underlying commonality in *conceptual* approach that drives both questions.

Number of topics studied also correlates with frequency of analysis of deep structures ($p<.05$). As noted previously, we predicted that schools espousing the "observational learning" vision would study fewer topics and fewer extended structures, and schools espousing the "halakha as philosophy" vision would also study fewer topics and on the aggregate fewer extras than schools espousing "learning for practice" or "cultural literacy." These analyses indicate that schools do have a consistent unstated or subconscious vision about halakha that leads those schools toward certain curricular and classroom decisions, even if they are not themselves aware what their underlying visions might be.

The questions that were correlated (text used, number of topics studied, and also exams with prompts of situations, time spent for study, and use of extras) are a cluster of questions that are indicative of those that subconsciously see halakha as "material studied by students to use later in life" ("learning for practice"), though the responders did not all mark the same vision for study in the first section of the survey. This leads schools to either move toward more rigorous textbooks, more time for halakha instruction, and a greater number of topics to be studied or to move away on the spectrum from all these questions: away from text, moving instead toward study of fewer topics, using less time, and learning in a more superficial way.

This finding corroborates a hypothesis that structural, curricular, or classroom halakha decisions are linked to each other; schools have radically different ways of thinking about and conceiving halakha instruction, and this *does* impact how they structure their halakha programs. Schools do, indeed, answer these specific questions in different ways, based on how they understand the purpose of halakha instruction, but this understanding is only inchoate for many of the schools and not reflective in their enunciated vision or approach to halakha study.

Applications

The clearest conclusion from this study is directly applicable to halakha, although equally relevant to all Judaic studies. Jewish day schools must continue to devote time and energy to articulate and surface the unstated assumptions around instruction that are underlying school choices if they wish for student learning and student outcomes to match their mission and goals for instruction. Were there no underlying common approaches to halakha, even of the unstated variety, then the demonstrated consistency and correlation would be unthinkable or impossible. But because there is an intuited approach that does drive curricular or classroom choices, schools must embark on a path toward surfacing and formulating their specific approach and vision. These results are significant in that they ought to spur school leaders to become more mindful of the way they want their school to approach halakha instruction, to ensure what actually takes place in the school accurately reflects the desired outcomes of the underlying vision.

In their defense, educational leaders drafting school curricula may not be experts in each curricular area that they choose to plan and designate for their school's study, and many of them may not have an awareness of the literature around the various discrete approach to halakha instruction. The literature on halakha teaching remains small, especially when compared with the literature on Tanakh or Talmud study, and one hopes that increasing the published literature available for public consumption may increase awareness about the importance of alignment in halakha education, thereby achieving greater consistency.

One final warning is important in this regard. Increasingly, publishing houses and national organizations have been generating new, externally developed curricular materials that they in turn market to schools on the basis of sharp graphics, eye-catching colors, or beautiful photography and artwork. Purchasing curricular materials on this basis fails to recognize that the underlying approach or vision about the teaching of the subject might be different among the schools, and that the text or curriculum should vary by vision and approach instead. Because of the wide variety in approach among schools, publishers and external curricularists must be more transparent about their own theoretical constructs and how it impacts their view of education and curriculum, before assuming that materials or curricula can translate readily from one environment or school to another.

Our research has also uncovered many descriptive statistics about the way halakha is taught in this country at the time this chapter was written. Some of these observations can be thought-provoking for schools drafting new master schedules or classroom curricula from scratch. These questions do not relate to our primary research questions and hypotheses, but they are still valuable for practical application. It is helpful to share a snapshot of some findings on the state of halakha education because it also raises questions about the future of halakha education.

The question of the most appropriate text for use in halakha instruction is one gaining much attention in recent years. At the time of this research, classical texts were still used by the slim plurality of school surveyed, but sourcebooks and source sheets of classical texts were used by a near equal number of respondents. Based on our research, we would recommend that schools committed to the teaching of halakha as part of Jewish cultural literacy might want to continue to use classical texts or at the very least source sheets of classical texts, but schools that see Jewish law education in terms of providing students with the knowledge needed to live an adult Jewish life would probably have little reason to use complex texts, and might instead prefer more succinct, colorful, modern textbooks that restate the law in clear and accessible language. Schools seeking to focus on the Jewish values and ethics might forgo use of a text entirely.

One question addressed throughout the literature, and summarized previously, is the amount of time to be designated in a school week for the study of halakha. In a short school week, often with fewer than forty teaching hours, school schedulers must find time for at least four general studies subjects, along with Bible, rabbinics, halakha, and whatever other Judaic studies topics or electives schools wish to schedule. Some schools, particularly those that prefer the observational approach to halakha instruction, take the attitude that no instructional time should be designated for halakha (13 percent), while others solve the scheduling problem by asking the Talmud teacher to cover the teaching of halakha, without setting aside separate time for halakha instruction (24 percent). Nearly half of schools that have formal halakha classes alleviate some of the scheduling pressure by scheduling halakha classes in fewer than four years of high school, offering a different subject area using the same time in other years. Some also schedule halakha for fewer class meetings per week in an effort to leave more time for other subjects. Schools are thoughtful in giving halakha enough time for the subject to be credible, while also deprioritizing it compared to other traditional Judaic studies demands.

Halakha instruction is often the forgotten subject in Jewish schools, hiding behind the more important subjects of Bible and rabbinics, and the more engaging subjects of Jewish thought and Jewish history. Yet, it continues to play an important role in Jewish education, and schools must give the discipline greater proactive attention, both in terms of the vision, approach, and alignment, and in terms of the resultant curricular and classroom decisions. In many ways, the Jewish future will be built around the continued dedication of the next generation of Jews to Jewish law and custom, and halakha education is the vehicle through which Jewish education reaches that critical place.

Appendix: Halakha Education Survey

Section 1: Theoretical Approach to Halakha

For the next four questions, please rate how much this statement reflects your thinking about the purpose and nature of halakha education:

1. The purpose of the study of halakha is to expose, teach, and familiarize students with a series of behaviors and scripts of acting they need for their lives as religious Jews.

__ STRONGLY AGREE	__ NEUTRAL	__ SOMEWHAT DISAGREE
__ SOMEWHAT AGREE		__ STRONGLY DISAGREE

2. The purpose of the study of halakha is to develop a set of beliefs, ideals, and perspectives about G-d and Judaism within the students.

__ STRONGLY AGREE	__ NEUTRAL	__ SOMEWHAT DISAGREE
__ SOMEWHAT AGREE		__ STRONGLY DISAGREE

3. The purpose of the study of halakha is to teach students knowledge needed in order to live a halakhic life.

__ STRONGLY AGREE	__ NEUTRAL	__ SOMEWHAT DISAGREE
__ SOMEWHAT AGREE		__ STRONGLY DISAGREE

4. The purpose of the study of halakha is to teach students information and content of another branch of Jewish knowledge as part of the content of Judaism that they should know as literate Jews. It is a subject whose material and content is important just like any other subject.

— STRONGLY AGREE
— SOMEWHAT AGREE
— NEUTRAL
— SOMEWHAT DISAGREE
— STRONGLY DISAGREE

5. Of the preceding approaches in questions one through four, which approach best captures how you see halakha instruction? 1 2 3 4

6. Which approach does the second best job in capturing how you see halakha instruction? 1 2 3 4

Section 2: Classroom Choices for the Teaching of Halakha

In this section, some questions ask for a selection from multiple-choice responses, others ask for a short free response.

7. What grades do you teach halakha to, if any? *Check all that apply.*

— a. 9 — b. 10 — c. 11 — d. 12

8. In your school, do students take an independent subject, called halakha?
   a. Our school does not have a formal halakha class.
   b. Students study halakha with their Talmud teacher, as a sub-subject of Talmud.
   c. Students study halakha as an independent subject with an independent teacher.

9. How many years of halakha do your students take in high school?

— a. 1 — b. 2 — c.3 — d. 4

10. How many instructional minutes per week does each student have in their schedule for halakha?

a. less than 45 min b. 45 min–1 hr c. 1–2 hrs d. more than 2 hrs

11. Do you use or read any sefer, text, or textbook for the study of halakha?
   a. Yes, we use a classical text of Jewish law written before the year 1900 (up to and including *Mishnah Berurah*).
   b. Yes, we only use a textbook written in the past century for use in schools.
   c. No, we do not use any sourcebook or textbook at all; all sources shared are distributed via handout or are projected on the board.
   d. No, we do not use any sourcebook or textbook at all.

12. If you gave one of the first two responses to Question 11, please type the name of the primary text or sefer your students use in their study of halakha: ________________.

13. Does your halakha class include assessments?
   a. No, the class is not graded.
   b. The class is graded based on participation but not assessments.
   c. Yes, the predominant assessment is a traditional content-based exam.
   d. Yes, but we use projects and nontraditional assessments to gauge student achievement in this class.

14. Which statement is typical of your assessments? *Check all that apply*.
   a. Students are asked to summarize or restate what they have learned.
   b. Students are given a case or situation they studied and asked to supply the law.
   c. Students are given an unknown case or situation and asked to apply what they have learned to this new situation.

15. Can you give an example of what a typical question might be?

16. Besides what is done in your classroom, is there anything else that goes on in school that helps you achieve the goals of halakha instruction? If so, explain what.

17. Do students ever study "history of halakha" (how the forces of history caused the halakha to come to be what it is today) as part of studying a particular topic?

  a. No. (Students learn the laws, not where they came from.)
  b. Sometimes. (Students learn it occasionally, but it is not a focus of the curriculum.)
  c. Regularly. (Most of the topics students learn contain a lesson or partial lesson on how this halakha historically came to be what it is.)

18. Do students ever study reasons why we follow one halakhic position over others (Klalei Hapsak)?

  a. No. (Students learn the laws, not the process of reaching halakhic rulings.)
  b. Sometimes. (Students learn it occasionally, but it is not a focus of the curriculum.)
  c. Regularly. (Most of the topics students learn contain a lesson or partial lesson on the process for choosing one position to be the accepted one halakhically.)

19. Do students ever learn why the Torah set up a particular mitzvah or rule (Taamei Hamitzvot)?

  a. No. (Students learn the laws, not their reasons.)
  b. Sometimes. (Students learn it occasionally, but it is not a focus of the curriculum.)
  c. Regularly. (Most of the topics students learn contain a lesson or partial lesson on reasons for why the Torah wanted us to follow one rule or another.)

20. Do students ever discuss general rules of halakha (such as what to do in case of doubt, or what becomes permitted in a case of duress, or how the law applies differently to minors, etc.)?

  a. No. (The class focuses on the main topics in each unit, and doesn't spend time on general rules.)
  b. Sometimes. (In the course of study of a particular topic, students learn how this topic relates to general rules of halakha.)
  c. Regularly. (E.g., our year begins with a unit on general rules of halakha.)

21. How often do you relate the halakha that is the focus of your topic to other areas of halakha that you are not studying at this time (like relating the laws of Pesach to the laws of separating challah or eating in the sukkah)?
   a. Regularly (approximately once a week).
   b. Periodically (approximately once a month).
   c. Very rarely, if at all.

22. What statement best captures how you see your role in the classroom?
   a. I teach content that the students don't yet know.
   b. I describe problems and situations for students to contemplate and consider.
   c. I help students learn key texts on their own.

23. What are you looking for students to do in halakha class?
   a. Read primary texts and predict what the law should be.
   b. Respond to theoretical thought-questions with predictions what the halakha should be.
   c. Learn the prescriptions for proper action that is found in classical sources.

24. Halakha is a study of what to do in specific situations. How many specific or discrete situations will students study in any given lesson?
   a. One situation per lesson.
   b. Multiple situations per lesson.
   c. One situation takes more than one lesson.

25. Do you feel your teaching of halakha involves depth or is superficial? Which of the following statements best captures the goals of your class?
   a. Little depth: Students' focus is knowing what to do in specific situations, so we don't dig too deeply into the halakha.
   b. Depth: Students learn the topics in depth so they will be interested, but the focus is that students should know what to do.
   c. Depth. Students study topics in depth so they understand the topic well and are not just memorizing details of what to do.

26. If you provide depth, what does that include? Does this mean you spend time on reasons for halakha? History of halakha? Parallels and further applications of each halakha? Give a brief illustration of how you dig more deeply into the halakha.

Section 3: Topics That We Study

Questions 27 and 28 are the final questions of the survey. Please remember to click submit after answering these questions to submit your survey.

27. Please place a check next to each topic that students study in your school's halakha program, over the entire four years of high school. Please only include things that are actually studied, not things you might spend fifteen minutes reviewing in advance of the holiday or special occasion.

__ Laws of Prayer
__ Meaning of the Prayers
__ Sanctity of the Synagogue
__ Laws of Tzitzit
__ Laws of Tefillin
__ Laws of Mezuzah
__ Laws of Netilat Yadayim
__ Laws of Brachot
__ Positive Mitzvot of Shabbat (Kiddush, Candles)
__ Cooking on Shabbat
__ Eruv and Carrying on Shabbat
__ Other Prohibitions on Shabbat
__ Laws of Cooking on Yom Tov
__ Laws of Chameitz and Cleaning for Pesach
__ Laws of the Seder
__ Laws of Kashering for Pesach
__ Laws of Rosh Hashanah
__ Laws of Yom Kippur
__ Laws of Sukkot
__ Laws of Lulav
__ Birkat Kohanim
__ Laws of Tisha B'Av and the Three Weeks
__ Laws of Purim
__ Laws of Chanukah
__ Laws of Yom Ha'atzmaut
__ Separating Terumah and Maaser
__ Tearing Kriya When Visiting Israel
__ Laws Related to Serving in the IDF
__ The Holiness of Israel, Mitzvah to Live in Israel
__ Laws of Shemitah
__ Eating Milk and Meat Together
__ Identifying Kosher Animals
__ Kibbud Av Va-em
__ Purchasing from Non-Kosher Vendors

continued→

__ Eating Blood and Salting Meat
__ Laws of Contact Between Genders
__ The Jewish Marriage Ceremony
__ Taharat Hamishpacha
__ Construction/Nature of a Mikvah
__ Laws of Children and Family Planning
__ Laws of Brit Milah, Pidyon Haben
__ Baby Naming
__ Charging Interest
__ Orlah, Shatneiz, Reishit Hageiz
__ Laws of Mourning
__ Laws of Tzedakah
__ Hashavat Aveidah
__ Tvilat Keilim
__ Leshon Hara
__ Gentile Cooking, Milk, Bread, Wine
__ Entering a Church
__ 13 Principles of Faith
__ Making a Fence Around the Roof
__ Permitted Haircuts and Shaving
__ Medical Ethics, Organ Donation
__ Rabbinic Authority
__ Kohanim Entering a Cemetery

28. Essential topics: Having read the preceding list, check off the eight or fewer most critical topics you study in halakha.

NOTES

1. The term halakha has been used to mean different things over the centuries of Jewish teaching and learning, including in the modern literature. It is sometimes used to describe the *method* through which rabbinics, Oral Law, or Talmud are studied, such as when the texts of the Talmud are studied in an effort to extrapolate actionable, legal content, instead of as its own *subject* of Jewish law and custom. Consequently, some of the literature that may at first seem to be about halakha, the subject, is in fact about halakha, the style of Talmud study, and so is outside the scope of this paper (see Lichtenstein, 2003; Levisohn, 2010). Similarly, it is also outside the scope of this discussion to consider the hotly contested contemporary question about whether the Talmud should be studied from an analytical/philosophical mode (sometimes called "conceptual Gemara") or as an artifact of halakha (sometimes called "halakhic Gemara"), because then halakha is the modifier or *method* of Talmud study and not its own *subject*.

2. This approach also takes two basic nuanced forms—learning mimetically through observation or learning through crafted and preplanned problem-based activities—but the core insight is the same: Jewish law and custom must be taught authentically, through

student practice and real-world halakha activity. Even schools that teach halakha in the classroom might partially agree with this view; most schools adopt this approach, at least in part, when considering the prayer services conducted in school.

3. This view can take many subforms. For the ultra-Orthodox, halakha is part of Jewish cultural literacy because it is part of the large corpus of "Torah," which they believe descended from the Almighty at Sinai. In contrast, others might consider halakha part of Jewish cultural literacy because the system of halakha is a central facet of the corpus of literary accomplishment of the Jewish people over the last two thousand years and an essential part of Jewish history. Still others might take a more Maimonidean approach that halakha is the repository that captures the inner core of Jewish worldview (see *Temurah* 4:13, Mekhilta to *Shemot* 18:20, Soloveitchik, 1983).

4. "Jewish ethics" is rarely studied for the purpose of students learning procedural knowledge to carry out in their own in life but is instead studied to promulgate philosophic values of Judaism. Moreover, the ethic is rarely codified in traditional legal texts, but is instead derived by modern authorities or the students themselves from the values promulgated by non-legal traditional texts, so the study becomes one of ethical/moral/philosophical values and ideals, not discrete legislated laws and customs. Student discussion dominates much more than the reading and study of classical texts. Prizma's Moot Beit Din program is a particularly current example of a halakha program whose focus is not on the law but on the derived ethics.

5. We define Modern Orthodox schools as those that express commitment to both (1) the normative, traditional practice of Jewish law and either (2) the value of secular knowledge or (3) the state of Israel.

6. When taught as a class, halakha was almost always treated as a regular class in the schedule, with more than an hour of instruction per week—be it two periods (n=12, or 32 percent) or more than two periods (n=18, or 48 percent). Only one respondent said their halakha program met for merely one forty-five-minute period per week, less than the standard number of meeting times for a regular high school class.

REFERENCES

Adler, M. J. (1982). *The Paideia Proposal: An educational manifesto*. Simon & Schuster.

Bloom, B. S. (1956) *Taxonomy of educational objectives*. Allyn and Bacon.

Eisenberg, Y. (1975 and 1976). *Halakha curriculum.* World Zionist Organization. [Hebrew].

Goldmintz, J. (1996). On teaching halakha. *Ten Da'at (9)*1, 55–62.

Goldmintz, J. (2005). Introduction. In Y. T. Rimon (ed.), *Shiurei Hilkhot Shabbat.* Herzog Teachers College. [Hebrew].

Harari, R., & Wolowelsky, J. B. (1987). Developing a yeshivah high school curriculum in halakha. *Ten Da'at (2)*2, 17–19.

Jaffe, Y. (2009). Towards a new paradigm for the study of halakha. *Ten Da'at 20*, 83–87.

Jaffe, Y. (2014). Halakha education for the present or the future. *Jewish Educational Leadership*, *13*(1), 18–20.

Jaffe, Y. (2018). The Yeshivat Har Etzion approach to the study and teaching of halakha. *Alei Etzion*, 95–102.

Krakowski, M., Kramer, J., & Lev, N. (2012). Empowering students through problem- and project-based learning. *Jewish Educational Leadership*, *10*(2), 4–8.

Levisohn, J. (2010). A menu of orientations to the teaching of rabbinic literature. *Journal of Jewish Education*, *76*, 4–51.

Lichtenstein, A. (2003). Why learn Gemara? In *Leaves of Faith* (pp. 1–17). Ktav Publishing House.

Niedelman, M. (1991). Problem solving and transfer. *Journal of Learning Disability*, *24*(6), 322–329.

Rimon, Y. T. (2005) *Shiurei Hilkhot Shabbat.* Herzog Teachers College. [Hebrew].

Rimon, Y. T. (2008). *Shemita: From the sources to practical halacha*. Maggid Books.

Rosenak, M. (1987). *Commandments and concerns: Jewish religious education in secular society.* Jewish Publication Society.

Schwartz, Y. (2012). Approaches in teaching halakha. *Shma`atin*, *182*, 85–98. [Hebrew].

Soloveitchik, H. (1994). Rupture and reconstruction: The transformation of contemporary Orthodoxy. *Tradition*, *28*(4), 64–130.

Soloveitchik, J. B. (1983). *Halakhic man.* Jewish Publication Society.

Vygoda, S. (2005). Petikha. In Y. T. Rimon, *Shiurei Hilkhot Shabbat.* Herzog Teachers College, 2005. [Hebrew].

10

Signature Pedagogy and Constituent Authenticity

A New Model of Authentic Activity in Jewish Day School Classrooms

MOSHE KRAKOWSKI

Introduction

Since the late 1980s, education researchers have argued that classroom learning practices should be more *authentic*: connected to ordinary real-world practices recognizable to practitioners in a particular field. In the decades since, an abundant literature has addressed how to instantiate this form of "authenticity" in different domains, via approaches such as experiential education, inquiry learning, and problem-based learning.

In this paper, I will suggest that pedagogical practices in American haredi[1] boys' elementary schools may be understood as possessing a different form of authenticity from that which has been conceptualized in the research literature until now. The paper argues that haredi pedagogy functions very similarly to Lee Shulman's concept of signature pedagogy (Shulman, 2005a). Using an in-depth analysis of one sample of first-grade boys'[2] *chumash* (the first five books of the Hebrew Bible) instruction in a haredi school (drawn from a broader group of sixty hours of videotaped observations collected in three schools), I map Shulman's notion of signature pedagogy to a specific feature of American haredi pedagogy that I term "constituent authenticity." Shulman's understanding of signature pedagogy was developed in relation to professional education. In those contexts, he explored how professional schools socialize students into larger communal structures; they may therefore be seen as *authentically* belonging to those structures. That is, they possess "constituent authenticity" as a constituent part of broader practices that exist and that possess social and cultural importance to stakeholders in the school beyond the school day itself. I argue that as a signature pedagogy, boys' *chumash* represents a distinct first stage of a broader communal practice that spans school, culture, and community and that, as a result, it is a constituent of a socially *authentic* activity.

It is true that boys' participation in first-grade *chumash* does not reproduce real-world engagement in *chumash* in the same way that traditionally authentic activities (such as problem-based learning) reproduce other domains. But analogy to Shulman's signature pedagogies suggests that perhaps they don't have to. First-grade *chumash* is not *like* real-world *chumash*; it *is* real-world *chumash* precisely because it is a constituent part of a broader communal practice.

Authenticity

In a seminal paper, Brown, Collins, and Duguid (1989) argued that classroom practices are authentic to the degree that they would be recognized by practitioners outside the classroom as the same practices in which they themselves engage. The rationale Brown et al. give for using authentic practice in classrooms is that knowledge divorced from its context of use is extremely weak, and that designing practices that are recognized as authentic by outsiders places that knowledge in a broader context of practice, enabling deeper, stronger learning.

In the decades since, this situated approach to school activity has dominated educational research (Putnam & Borko, 2000), particularly in the domain of science, where authenticity is understood as a tool that enculturates students into a community of practice. Different approaches to authenticity have been explored, including students' actual participation in adult practices outside the classroom, and the simulation of those practices in the classroom (Barab & Hay, 2001; Hay & Barab, 2001; Radinsky et al., 1998, 2001). Some have suggested that authenticity is not a feature of any particular pedagogical strategy but is an emergent property of the interactions between the learner, task, and environment (Barab et al., 2000; Rahm et al., 2003). Others have focused on how authentic norms can foster authentic identities (Cobb et al., 2009; Gresalfi, 2009), and on how students' identification with classroom practices impacts their perception of the nature of those activities (Sfard & Prusak, 2005). The entire pedagogical and curricular technique of problem-based learning is designed to embed learning in authentic contexts of use, so that students will be more likely to engage with and retain the information (Dean & Kuhn, 2007; Kanter, 2010; Strobel & van Barneveld, 2009).

But what does it mean for knowledge to be divorced from its context of use, and what counts as an *authentic* context of use? What makes school memorization or a teacher's lecture inauthentic? The answers to these questions depend on the relationship between the knowledge acquisition practices that take place in school and the *culture* in which that knowledge is used. To unpack the term authenticity we need to first make a number of sociological judgments about culture, identity, and activity: What does it look like when knowledge is used meaningfully (in any context)? How is knowledge embedded in non-school contexts of use? What purpose, or purposes, does school or societal knowledge serve those who learn it?

These questions address authenticity by asking about the culture that would make some knowledge practice authentic to an individual or group. Another way to approach the same set of issues is to ask how authenticity contributes to learning. Is it simply a pragmatic tool for better or broader knowledge recall and use, or is there something inherently valuable in engaging in a learning practice that is connected in some way to an "authentic" culture? The two approaches in fact ultimately converge; whether we open with cultural or pedagogical questions, our analysis will focus on how activity and meaning intersect to promote learning in the classroom.

These questions have an added dimension when we turn to Jewish day school education. Little work has addressed what it would mean to make classroom practices authentic in Judaic studies classes, yet Jewish subject matter's connection to religion, culture, and practice is central to the purpose of Jewish day schools. In past work (Krakowski et al., 2012; Krakowski, 2017), I have examined how Modern Orthodox day schools have used pedagogical models such as problem-based learning to help develop certain forms of Jewish identity. In this chapter, I will examine the relationship between classroom and culture through an exploration of a very different model of authentic practice in the classroom.

Although authenticity can certainly be expressed in the simulation of adult practices (as in problem-based learning), it may also be expressed through practices that explicitly enculturate students into society, even when these practices do not resemble a mature version of the same activity. This model of authenticity has been well articulated in the context of professional education (though without explicit reference to the concept of "authenticity").

In the course of a decade-long study for the Carnegie Foundation, Lee Shulman (Shulman, 2005a) developed a construct called "signature pedagogy" to describe a cluster of key similarities in professional instruction across several different fields. For Shulman, the key features of professional schools are that they use pedagogies that are pervasive and uniform in their fields; involve fixed routines and rituals; are visible and interactive; and inculcate particular "habits" in students (Shulman, 2008). Shulman argues that professional schools employ signature pedagogies precisely because such schools require more than just student understanding; they demand education for practice and serve to socialize students into a profession's culture and epistemology (Shulman, 2005b). Precisely because *all* students in a particular professional school will be joining the same profession with the same expectations, their initial learning practices can be considered *a part of* that profession.

Religious Education in Orthodox Jewish Classrooms

Religious schools, connected as they are to religious communities of practice, provide fertile ground for exploring questions about culture, socialization, and authenticity. Indeed, socialization has been widely noted as a goal of religious schooling: as Rapoport, Garb, and Penso note, "religious educational frameworks act simultaneously as educational institutions and as religious socializing agencies" (Rapoport et al., 1995, p. 48). In Orthodox Jewish communities, schooling functions explicitly to enculturate and socialize; content knowledge is important, but becoming a productive member of Orthodox Jewish society is primary (Krakowski, 2008a, p. 322; 2013).

Since the last quarter of the twentieth century, American Orthodox Jewish religious education may be broadly divided into two distinct approaches, enacted by the two major American Orthodox denominations (themselves umbrella categories that may be subdivided into many other finer-grained denominational groups): Modern Orthodox and ultra-Orthodox. Broadly speaking, Modern Orthodoxy values secular Western culture and knowledge and Modern Orthodox institutions generally seek to synthesize Jewish religious knowledge, thought, and practice with full participation in Western culture and society. Ultra-Orthodoxy, on the other hand, views such synthesis as problematic and generally leans toward some measure of isolation. Ultra-Orthodox schools therefore typically provide a minimal secular education intended to permit students to eventually maintain gainful employment, but assign no intrinsic value to secular culture and knowledge.

Both yeshivish and Chasidic schools share this perspective on secular education, but they express it in different ways: in general, Chasidic schools offer less secular education than do yeshivish schools. This isn't because they disagree about the purpose of secular education, but because they have different cultural expectations of the types of occupations community members will hold.

In nearly all ultra-Orthodox schools in the United States (and in many Modern Orthodox schools as well), boys begin studying *chumash* in or before first grade, learning to read and translate biblical Hebrew and learning the basic content of biblical stories and laws. By third or fourth grade, boys at most schools start to add the study of Mishnah, a late ancient code of Jewish law that forms the backbone of the Talmud, and in fifth or sixth grade they begin to study Gemara, the complex text full of arguments, analysis, and discussion, that together with the Mishnah makes up the Talmud. Although ultra-Orthodox men are expected to continue to study other subjects (such as practical Jewish law, ethical instruction, the Prophets and other writings of the Bible, and the weekly *chumash* portion) throughout their lives, Talmud remains the dominant subject of study.

Given their commitment to full participation in Western society, Modern Orthodox Jewish high schools have struggled to make the religious curriculum meaningful to students in a context where secular academics and college prep are more dominant realities for the students (Bieler, 1986; Goldberg, 1981; Heilman, 1992; and see, e.g., Pomson, 2011, in the related context of liberal Jewish day schools). Student engagement in religious subjects such as Talmud and Jewish law (halakha) is particularly low, as the vast network of Jewish laws and regulations often seems arbitrary and confusing to students, something externally imposed over their regular lives (Weiser & Bar-Lev, 1989). In this context, authentic practices may offer a mechanism to engage students in halakha in a way that builds connections between the text-based legal codes and practices that are personally important and relevant to them (see, e.g., Krakowski, 2017).

Ultra-Orthodox schools, in contrast, do not typically suffer from this kind of pervasive lack of student engagement in religious material (even if some individual students are indeed disengaged).[3] Moreover, these schools view their mandate more as an "inculcation of ultra-Orthodox worldview and culture" (Krakowski, 2008b, p. 17) than specific content knowledge acquisition. Ultra-Orthodox schools serve the most traditional and stringent elements of Orthodox Jewry in America. Beginning in elementary school and increasingly in high school, most of the long school day is spent on religious study, while a small portion of the day is reserved for basic secular education. Boys in these communities are expected to continue to engage in religious study throughout the rest of their lives in very prescribed ways. The material that they study in school, therefore, has a clearly articulated context of use, one that is central to the entire endeavor of boys' ultra-Orthodox education. In this sense, the entire program of education is deeply tied to a clear model of authentic knowledge use outside the classroom.

Given the centrality of religious study for men in this community, the acquisition of religious study skills is fraught with importance and pressure. Religious study is so central, in fact, that students who fail to learn how to read biblical and mishnaic Hebrew or who fail to acquire complex Talmud study skills (reading Aramaic, following complex legal arguments, researching the competing textual interpretations of medieval commentators) are at risk of dropping out of the community entirely, a phenomenon known to members of the American ultra-Orthodox community as "going off the *derech*" (going off the path). (See Goldberg, 2004, in particular, on the impact of failing to acquire Hebrew reading fluency on behavioral problems in Orthodox contexts.) This illustrates the deep connection between the content studied in school and the culture of the community; failure to acquire religious studies content holds tangible social and cultural meaning in students' lives.

Signature Pedagogy and Constituent Authenticity

Much like religious study in ultra-Orthodox communities, when students enter a professional school, they choose to join a professional community. Students in such schools follow a trajectory from the periphery to the interior while being enculturated in the community's norms and dispositions. In both cases, because the learning trajectory students follow is already defined as normative by the surrounding community, and because students' expectations for future use of knowledge are clear, the authenticity of classroom practices does not necessarily reside in these practices' similarity to an external, "real-world," set of practices, but rather in constituting a *component* of such external practices. In contrast to models of authenticity that require classroom activities to simulate or replicate authentic practices, I term this very different type of authenticity constituent authenticity.

Signature Pedagogy: A Model of Authentic Activity in Professional Education

In a ten-year study of professional education for the Carnegie Foundation, Lee Shulman has extensively addressed problems related to *authentic* classroom activity without ever using the term. Professional education is explicitly designed to prepare students to engage in a community of practice. Professional education is often overlooked in the research on the authenticity of school practices, but it represents an archetype of educational practice situated within a larger cultural superstructure. Professional education is genuinely embedded in an authentic context of use and it explicitly socializes students into the norms and practices of a given field—one that school practitioners assume all students will enter once they complete their schooling. Students attending professional schools are learning material as part of a clear community of practice they are participating in the culture, without ever leaving school.

Shulman has used the term signature pedagogy to describe key similarities in professional instruction across a wide range of fields (Shulman,

2005b). In the Carnegie study, his team observed that certain instructional formats, such as the Socratic case-study dialogue of the first-year law school classroom or the medical rounds of doctors-in-training, are clearly and unambiguously identified with particular fields. Though this distinctiveness is what makes them "signature," these pedagogic approaches also share certain characteristic features (Shulman, 2008):

- They are pervasive and uniform in their fields.
- They involve fixed routines and rituals.
- They are visible and interactive.
- They each inculcate particular "habits" in students.

Such habits differ between professions. For example, legal training develops habits of mind (thinking like a lawyer), while medical training develops habits of practice (acting like a doctor), while clergy training creates habits of the heart.

Shulman argues that signature pedagogies are found in professional schools precisely because professional schools require more than just understanding; they demand education for practice (Shulman, 2005a). That is to say, professional schools exist not only to teach foundational content in a discipline but also to help students adopt the identities of their chosen fields. Because the students will all enter the same profession after graduation, identity formation can be developed in a uniform and consistent manner. In such contexts, pedagogy must include mechanisms for socialization into a profession's culture and epistemology. As Shulman writes, "[Signature pedagogies] implicitly define what counts as knowledge in the field and how things become known. They define how knowledge is analyzed, criticized, accepted, or discarded. They define the functions of expertise in a field, the locus of authority, and the privileges of rank and standing" (Shulman, 2005b, p. 54).

There is, therefore, something inherent to the features of signature pedagogy that helps situate the learning activity within a broader culture that gives meaning to the activity. Without explicitly using the terminology of norms and dispositions, it is clear that this is indeed what Shulman is referring to. Habits of mind, practice, and heart *are* norms and dispositions (which indeed are sometimes termed habits of mind, e.g., Gresalfi, 2009, p.

364). Thus, what is significant for my purposes about Shulman's research is that it identifies those features of learning environments that situate learning activities within the broader culture that students are joining—that is, it identifies how to make activities a constituent part of a broader authentic set of cultural practices.

How do these specific features embed learning activities in an authentic professional culture? The norms and dispositions inculcated by professional education differ by profession, but in each the pedagogical structure is pervasive and uniform (as suggested by Shulman's term signature). This uniformity is an essential element of enculturation—regardless of which law school an individual attends, she will have had roughly the same formative experiences and will have adopted characteristic "habits of mind" (Falk, 2006) that will smooth her transition into the community of lawyers. These fixed routines and rituals structure learning *explicitly and visibly* along specific preset norms of behavior and attitude. Ritualizing learning practices in a public manner provides a platform for explicit affiliation with a community of practice.

These features do not need to simulate adult practices. Though context of use is essential to the learning process, most professional training bears little resemblance to real-world activities within the profession itself. Law schools, for example, do an excellent job of teaching students to *think* like lawyers, but law school activities don't actually resemble those found in everyday professional legal practice. Indeed, the Socratic methodology found in these classrooms has been criticized for this reason (e.g., Hyland & Kilcommins, 2009).

Despite the criticism, these signature features socialize students and provide them with the essential skills to progress to more advanced stages of learning, and ultimately to mature participation in the authentic activities of the domain. Precisely because attending a professional school signifies students' intention to have a clear end point of full participation in a particular community of practice, the skill-building aspects of student activities do not need to resemble actual mature practice—there will be plenty of time for that later. The fact that students now act *within* the larger cultural superstructure of lawyers and doctors allows them to work on essential skills in a context that renders that work meaningful. It is critical that lawyers develop certain habits of mind and modes of reasoning (e.g.,

Harner, 2011), but these foundational skills might not be easily acquired if the classroom actually resembled the real world. (Indeed, this is a common challenge for teachers in traditionally authentic classrooms; see Krakowski, 2017.)

To be clear: I am not arguing that any practice, no matter how retrograde, can be magically made meaningful and useful for learning if students all expect to participate eventually in a common culture. Rather, each profession has certain skills that are central to its practice but that cannot be acquired by simulation. These signature features embed skill-building practices in a cultural setting. Shulman's heuristic of signature pedagogy offers a particularly clear example of constituent authenticity that provides a road map to the types of features essential to making a classroom skill-building activity an explicit component of a broader cultural context. The public and signature nature of these educational structures serves to unify and reify abstract notions of what it means to be a member of a professional community of practice, while students engage in practices that might be useful for learning but may also otherwise be boring or nonmeaningful.

This is the case for *chumash* as well; without a larger cultural superstructure in which there is a clear end point of full participation in a particular community of practice, *chumash* learning might just be drilled practice and interleaved repetition—tasks that are notoriously difficult and discouraging for many students. However, as I will argue in the following section, boys' *chumash* learning in first grade is the authentic first (formal)[4] stage of a larger cultural activity—one that extends from childhood through adulthood. Boys in *chumash* class begin the process of enculturation into the practices of the Orthodox Jewish world, while acquiring the basic skills necessary to advance within that context.

This cultural framework relieves much of the tension between meaningfulness and learning. In constituently authentic classrooms, activities are not made meaningful by emulating meaningful activities; they are intrinsically meaningful because they define and shape what it means to be a member of this community. Because students live within this culture, meaning does not need to be artificially provided, and as such, types of learning structures that might in other contexts be repetitive, rote, and meaningless can be introduced without automatically stifling student engagement and interest.

Chumash in Ultra-Orthodox Schools

The description of *chumash* learning provided in this section comes from a broad ethnography of three boys' ultra-Orthodox elementary schools, two Chasidic and one yeshivish, in which sixty hours of videotaped observation were collected from eleven classes spanning first through eighth grades.[5] Classroom activities were broken into units for analysis in ways that emphasize the cultural features of classroom practices, closely examining the socializing and worldview-orienting features of classroom scripts, routines, and activities.

Elementary Chumash *Study*

There are two parts of the ultra-Orthodox school day, religious and secular, and they are not given equal weight; religious study takes up the morning and early afternoon while secular study (e.g., math and language arts) takes up only the late afternoon. In the religious part of the day, examined here, the central units analyzed were related to the study of *chumash* and the study of Gemara, which make up the bulk of classroom activity for younger and older students, respectively. Aside from these two subjects, classes also focus on prayer, Jewish law, the weekly Bible portion, and the Prophets. One particularly significant unit of activity, ubiquitous throughout the day and frequently intertwined with many other activities, consists of brief explicit lessons in morals, ethics, and spirituality. I have argued elsewhere (Krakowski, 2008a; 2013) that these religious classroom activities are generally more complex and contextually connected than their counterparts in the secular part of the day and that these schools deliberately strip secular learning activities of larger worldview significance.

Here, I'd like to focus on just *chumash*, the central learning activity in first grade. In *chumash*, students learn to read the Hebrew text, translate it, recognize the grammar, and understand the story of the text. The process involves aspects of lecture, singsong reading, call and response, translation of text, partnered reading, and drilling of Hebrew vocabulary and grammar concepts. These components are intermingled with one another, and the rebbe (religious instructor—always male) will often cycle through them numerous times.

To demonstrate how *chumash* socializes students while providing a structure for important foundational skill acquisition, I provide a close reading of an excerpt of a videotape in a first-grade yeshivish classroom.[6] In this excerpt, students review verses from the *chumash* story of Noah and the flood, which deal with how the wickedness of man prompted God's decision to destroy the world. The excerpt, six and a half minutes long, focuses on their treatment of one verse (out of four that they reviewed that day) that describes the wickedness of the "sons of the Elohim," who were kidnapping women to be their wives: "And the sons of the Elohim saw the daughters of men, that they were good, and they took wives for themselves from among all that they chose" (Genesis 6:2).

Throughout the class, the rebbe circulated throughout the room, holding flash cards with two or three Hebrew words from the text, color-coded to indicate the different parts of the Hebrew word that translate into separate English words, or to indicate the word's root, tense, or gender.

For this verse, the rebbe begins by asking an individual student to identify the root of the Hebrew word "and they saw" (*va-yir'u*, from the three Hebrew letters *reish*, *aleph*, and *hei*) by pointing to a previous verse that contains a word with the same root. He points out the function of three additional Hebrew letters contained in the word *va-yir'u*: the prefix *vov*, which means "and," and the *yud*-prefix/*vov*-suffix combination that renders the verb third-person plural ("they"):

Rebbe: Alright—I need a smart person; look in the next *pasuk* [verse], I need the *shoresh* [root] letters of the next *pasuk*'s first word. I don't want you to read the first word yet, I want three *shoresh* letters of the next word; don't get tricked by the beginning or the ends of the word. Don't be tricked, I want three letters of the first word in *pasuk beis* [verse 2]. Look in *pasuk beis*, I want the three *shoresh* letters. Take a moment to look; don't be tricked by the beginning letters or last latter, the prefix or suffix letters. I need three letters for the *shoresh*. Reuven Benyamin,[7] you want to try it?

Student: *Reish, aleph, hei*.

Rebbe: Beautiful! That's the right answer! *Reish aleph hei*. How many boys knew *reish aleph hei*? Raise your hand—beautiful! *Reish aleph hei* are the three *shoresh* letters. Alright, Reuven Benyamin, now comes the hard question: What does it mean, *reish aleph hei*? What's the word?

Student: "Saw."

Rebbe: Beautiful, excellent, SAW. Reuven, very nice. Let's say *pasuk beis* together—everyone—and the *vov* at the end makes it THEY, the *yud* with the *vov* at the end has nothing to do with AND. I want Levi to say the *pasuk* AND Shimshon. But does that *vov* at the end make it AND? No, it makes it THEY.

At the rebbe's instruction, the class chants/sings the verse together in Hebrew, interspersed every few words with the English translation they have previously learned. The capitalization is meant to indicate the cadence of the chant in which the verses are read:

Rebbe: Okay, alright, let's say *pasuk beis* together:

Students all together, slowly with the rebbe: *Va-yir'u bnei haeloKIM*—and the sons of the rulers SAW, *es benos haADOM*—the daughters of the MAN, *ki TO-vos heina*—that they were good. *Vayikchu lahem nashim*—and they took for themselves wives, *miKOL asher BA-CHARU*—from whoever they CHOSE.

The rebbe then points out that another Hebrew word from the verse, "they chose" (*bacharu*), also has a *vov*-suffix denoting the third person plural:

Rebbe: And here's the word *bacharu*. *Bacharu* means "chose," the *vov*—THEY chose, the *vov* at the end makes it "they." The *vov* at the end makes it "they." Okay, the *vov* at the end makes it "they," except, Yosef Chaim, can you tell me again where does it say the word THEY? Where does it say—which part of the word makes it THEY?

Student: The *vov*.

The rebbe asks first one and then the other half of the class (previously grouped as the "cholent pots" and "lukshen kugels") to chant the verse together again:

Rebbe: Alright, I want only my cholent pots—just the cholent pots—to say *pasuk beis*, not the lukshen kugels, just the cholent pots; let's say *pasuk beis*. Go ahead, all of my cholent pots.

Half the class together, with only a little help from the rebbe: *Va-yir'u bnei haeloKIM*—and the sons of the rulers SAW, *es benos haADOM*—the daughters of the MAN, *ki TO-vos heina*—that they were good. *Vayikchu lahem nashim*—and they took for themselves wives, *miKOL asher BACHARU*—from whoever they CHOSE.

Rebbe: Okay, alright, cholent pots, that was very good, but I think that the lukshen kugels sound a little more heated up, I think they're gonna do a fine job too. Alright, I want my cholent pots, okay, this side of the room, lukshen kugels, I mean.

Half the class together, with only a little help from the rebbe: *Va-yir'u bnei haeloKIM*.

Rebbe: Way to go, lukshen kugels! And the sons of the rulers SAW, *es benos haADOM*—the daughters of the MAN, *ki TO-vos heina*—that they were good. *Vayikchu lahem nashim*—and they took for themselves wives, *miKOL asher BACHARU*—from whoever they CHOSE.

The rebbe now turns to the content of the verse, placing it in context of the following biblical verse ("And the Lord said, 'My spirit will not abide in man forever, for he too is flesh, and his days will be one hundred and twenty years'") and of a rabbinic story associated with the biblical character Enosh (Genesis 5:6–11):

Rebbe: Alright, this did not make *Hashem* [God] very happy—both sides, the lukshen kugels did very nicely, yes—*Hashem* was not very happy with what he saw, when people were kidnapping, and not only that they were kidnapping other people's wives, no problem they were [unintelligible], they were *chas ve-shalom* [God forbid] killing the husbands to steal their wives. That's terrible! People were doing *avodah zorah* [idol worship], and they were stealing each other's wives, and they were killing. What happened to the beautiful world that *Hashem* created?

Hashem was not very happy with the people. *Hashem* was a little bit upset. And so *pasuk gimmel* [verse 3], let's take a look what *Hashem* said. *Hashem* said, "I'm gonna give the world one hundred and twenty years to do *teshuva* [to repent] and I hope by then they will change their bad ways and become good again. I'm hoping that after one hundred and twenty years that the people will do *teshuva*," right? They're not gonna live forever otherwise. What is *Hashem*, Shloimeh Zalman, gonna send if they don't become good again? What's *Hashem* gonna send to the world?

Student: A *mabul* [flood].

Rebbe: A *mabul*. *Hashem* is gonna send a flood, right. As a matter of fact, what happened in the time of Enosh? Already when the *avodah zara* started, what did *Hashem* do? Dov?

Student: He destroyed one-third of the world.

Rebbe: He destroyed one-THIRD of the world. He was hoping—if I destroy just part of the world, the other parts will do ______?

Students together: *Teshuva*.

Rebbe: *Teshuva*. And did they do *teshuva*?

Students together: No.

Rebbe: Shloimeh Zalman, and did they do *teshuva*?

Student: No.

Rebbe: No. They did not. Okay, let's take a look at *pasuk gimmel*.

In reviewing this verse, the rebbe focused on the grammar and meaning of two particular words, asked the class to chant the verse and its translation several times, and briefly discussed its meaning in the context of the larger biblical story. In other classes where students learned new verses, rather than continuing the process of gaining proficiency in previously seen verses, the singsong would have been conducted in a call-and-response format, with the rebbe singing and translating each clause, and the students repeating it after him, and they would have repeated it many more times. Though not demonstrated in this excerpt, *rabbeim* also frequently ask specific individual students to read all or part of a verse, and they focus on other aspects of grammar, such as tense and word gender. Finally, students are regularly grouped in pairs (the traditional *hevruta* structure) to read and translate a set of verses to each other in the same singsong format.

What Is Learned in *Chumash* Study?

This excerpt illustrates many of the distinctive features inherent in first-grade *chumash* learning: a choral reading structure, frequent repetition, a public and interactive pedagogical structure, and pervasive enculturating content. These features address a number of different implicit and explicit learning goals. One way of dividing these goals is in terms of those that deal with reading fluency, grammar, and vocabulary, and those that deal with the relationship between classroom and culture.

Chumash Reading Fluency

First, how effective is this approach in giving students actual competency in reading *chumash*? Because the goal of *chumash* instruction includes comprehension and language learning, and students ultimately use the *chumash* text in sophisticated analytical ways, reading automaticity is essential to free up cognitive space for interpretation and analysis.

There are no current statistics available for success and failure rates of *chumash* competency in ultra-Orthodox schools; this is a small community, and they are studying a subject of interest only to community members. Moreover, success or failure in this domain is readily apparent within the community, and community members generally do not feel the need for outside analysis. Anecdotal evidence makes clear that some individual students do fail to grasp the essential skill of reading and translating *chumash*.[8] Nonetheless, many aspects of *chumash* activity structures mirror methods that have demonstrated efficacy in other literacy contexts, giving us good reason to believe that these methods may be generally effective here as well.[9]

a. *Practice*: The choral reading structure, with its emphasis on frequent repetition of the words and translations, broken up by clauses and phrases, accomplishes one thing that is unanimously agreed to be essential for fluent reading: practice. Over the course of one class that introduces a new verse, students may repeat, either together or individually, the verse ten to fifteen times, providing the practice and repetition that is essential for the development of reading automaticity (Samuels, 1988, p. 759).

b. *Fluency*: *Chumash* study combines aspects of the unassisted repeated reading method (Samuels, 1979) with modeling and reading-while-listening (Heckelman, 1969), a relatively common combination (e.g., Allington, 1983; Dowhower, 1987). In particular, the emphasis on the repetition of specific demarcated phrases with appropriate intonation (given by the singsong) may have benefits for fluency as well as comprehension (see Kuhn & Stahl, 2000). Finally, in *chumash* learning, the teacher provides a content explanation prior to modeling and repeated reading to foreground comprehension, something that has also been found to be effective in promoting reading fluency (Hoffman, 1987).

c. *Retention*: Practice in learning *chumash* is also structured to aid in retention, in that the practice is typically spaced and repeated over numerous days, taking advantage of the spacing effect (Cepeda et al., 2006). For example, in the previous excerpt, students were cycling back to verses they had explored throughout the previous week. Similarly, by varying the skill to be practiced frequently throughout the session (for example, switching from vocabulary translation to reading practice to content description to grammar), the practice is substantially interleaved, another feature that is generally understood to improve retention (Taylor & Rohrer, 2010).

d. *Flexibility*: Finally, the structure of *chumash* learning is very flexible and provides substantial opportunities for differentiation. Students of differing abilities may be asked to read individually with greater or lesser frequency; when *hevruta* occurs, pairs may be grouped to facilitate individual attention. Further, students can be asked to practice in a variety of ways, including writing on the board or drawing, singing together, and reading out loud.

Why are these features important? Many of them, while efficacious, are also—for lack of a better term—boring. Spacing or interleaving material may be demonstrably better than other methods of retention in the lab, but they aren't particularly motivating or intrinsically meaningful; the process is not tied to specific content in meaningful ways. And yet, to build skill automaticity, there are few better methods than practice and structured repetition. I argue, however, that this dilemma is resolved by the larger superstructure of enculturation within which these activities are situated.

Enculturation

Students in *chumash* class learn a wide range of content, much of which directly relates to fundamental conceptions about the world, their religion, and the nature of the *chumash* text they are studying. Much as the pedagogical structure of math instruction can have an impact on student dispositions regarding math and conceptions of what it means to do math, the way in which students study *chumash* significantly impacts student conceptions and dispositions regarding *chumash*. Specifically, *chumash* learning inculcates two types of dispositions in students: dispositions regarding the nature of the *chumash* text and dispositions regarding students' own relationship to the *chumash* text.

» Dispositions regarding the nature of the *chumash* text

Conceptions regarding the nature of the *chumash* text are primarily epistemological; they relate to students' understandings of the nature of the knowledge they are acquiring in *chumash* class. Naturally, this epistemology reflects ultra-Orthodox beliefs regarding the Bible. Just as a Christian scholar or an academic Bible scholar would study *chumash* content in ways that reflect their underlying assumptions about the text, the way in which these students are asked to engage with the text reflects ultra-Orthodox assumptions.

a. *The meaning of the text is fixed and mediated by tradition rather than open to individual interpretation*: As in the previous excerpt, *rabbeim* in ultra-Orthodox classrooms present the meaning of the biblical text according to traditional readings expressed in rabbinic commentaries, rather than, for example, a careful individual reading of the text.

For example, the rebbe translates the evil *b'nei haelohim* as "the children of the rulers," and while the word elohim does mean "ruler," it more frequently means "God" or "gods," an obviously problematic interpretation from an Orthodox Jewish perspective, but one that makes more sense textually given the contrast to the daughters of man. The rebbe, it turns out, is following the first of two interpretations given by the medieval commentator Rashi. Similarly, the rebbe explains their wickedness in terms of killing husbands, kidnapping their wives, and engaging in idol worship. Of those, only "kidnapping wives" has any possible source in the text itself ("and they took for themselves wives, from whoever they chose"). Again, this is a reference to a midrashic[10] gloss on the story. Finally, his description of God destroying a third of the world in previous times, in order to get the rest of the world to repent, also derives from a midrashic source, rather than the text itself. In ultra-Orthodox *chumash* study, these traditional interpretations of the text are presented as truth, and the contrast between what is actually written in the text and the story the students are taught creates an implicit understanding that the text must only be understood through traditional sources—not on its own.[11]

b. *The text is assumed to be a literal description of events*: A pervasive underlying assumption in elementary ultra-Orthodox *chumash* study is that all of the events truly happened the way they are described (unless tradition specifically dictates that the text is allegorical). In the previous excerpt (along with the broader story), the rebbe's presentation assumes that the narrative actually happened as described—that the flood really covered the entire world, killing everything but Noah and the animals (who all miraculously fit on the ark). In lessons on the following verse, students learned of giants on Earth who mate with normal humans, and in other verses in this section they learned of God's direct communication with Noah. All of these remarkable occurrences are taught as actual historical events, shaping students' understanding of the text.[12]

» Dispositions regarding students' own relationship to the *chumash* text

The second type of disposition inculcated in first-grade *chumash* learning relates to students' own personal interaction with *chumash*.

c. *It is the practice that is of value, not its component skills*: By integrating vocabulary, grammar, and reading practice with the study of the text itself, ultra-Orthodox schools send an important message regarding the purpose of *chumash* study. One might imagine that students would not begin in-depth study of the *chumash* text until they have mastered biblical grammar and have acquired basic vocabulary. This is, in fact, the way that some Modern Orthodox and Conservative schools teach *chumash*. Alternatively, one might focus on the stories contained in the *chumash* and not bother with Hebrew at all—there are schools that do this as well.

Blending the activity in this way retains an element of authenticity; despite the fact that singsong choral reading is not found outside of this context, engagement with the authentic text itself in order to learn grammar and vocabulary publicly points to the ultimate mature expression of *chumash* learning. Students' *chumash* skills will not be needed for some other content, or for wider knowledge of grammar systems; rather, they are expected to continue to study this exact text throughout their lives.

d. *The text has active moral and religious implications:* Finally, *chumash* content contains many basic principles, norms, and beliefs that structure how ultra-Orthodox community members understand the way that the world works; these are expressed as relevant in the children's present lives as well as being historical truths. For example, in the story of Noah, the students are taught that God gets angry or happy with people based on their good and bad actions, repentance can change God's mind to forestall punishment, people can die because of their sins, that if you act badly bad things will happen to you, and that taking revenge is a sin. They are also taught theology through this textual study. In one of the subsequent verses, "God was sad unto His heart," the rebbe makes a special point of stressing, and having the students repeat, that God doesn't really have a heart—this is just an expression. These and many other lessons organically contained within the *chumash* learning structure shape student understandings of their own lives in relation to the lesson of the *chumash* text.[13]

To sum up: the structure and content of this activity adds a tremendous amount of complexity to the otherwise straightforward task of learning how to read and translate biblical Hebrew in order to be able to study *chumash*. Students do repeatedly practice vocabulary and grammar, but they practice in a singsong pattern, from the text itself, while learning moral and theological lessons, developing a narrative and communal identity around the text based on both its content and the epistemology of its study.

Authenticity Reconsidered

Is the practice of *chumash* in ultra-Orthodox school an authentic practice? Not if we require authenticity to faithfully replicate, or simulate, the ordinary practices of adult *chumash* study. In adult practices there is no singsong chanting of the verses, the grammar and translation are already known, and the basics of reading need no practice. Yet *chumash* study is clearly authentic in an entirely different sense: as a pedagogical practice deeply embedded in a very specific context of use, which it works to reinforce in myriad ways, epistemologically, theologically, and structurally.

Chumash *Learning as a Signature Pedagogy: Signature Pedagogy as Constituent Authenticity*

Although it appears in an early elementary rather than a professional educational context, *chumash* learning accords closely with Shulman's description of signature pedagogical structures. A boys' first-grade classroom in almost any ultra-Orthodox school will include some variant of this activity, practiced in essentially the same way. The pedagogy is therefore pervasive and immediately recognizable: upon entering the classroom a visitor familiar with ultra-Orthodox schools will have no doubt what is being studied, without looking at the *chumashim* on the desks for confirmation. Aside from uniformity of practice across different schools and classrooms, *chumash* learning is relatively uniform in its execution, maintaining the fixed routines and rituals that Shulman describes as essential to signature pedagogies.

The activity is also public and interactive, requiring a high degree of performance and engagement. (Which is not to say that it is necessarily always effective at this task. As with all pedagogical structures, students are capable of nonparticipation and weak engagement.) Finally, as demonstrated previously, *chumash* learning inculcates distinctive habits of heart, practice, and mind (or, *dispositions*).

Like professional education, *chumash* study also possesses constituent authenticity. Because the students are part of a broader Orthodox culture that has clearly articulated normative expectations for students' lives (and within which *chumash* study is an essential practice), their participation in *chumash* class in first grade is given meaning by that broader culture. As noted at the outset, because the larger meaning of the activity is provided by a broader superstructure, the activity becomes *part* of real-world *chumash*, rather than an emulation of it.

Because it adheres to a clear set of cultural expectations, the study of *chumash* significantly impacts the narrative that students develop about what it is they are doing when they study *chumash*. As described previously, this narrative is explicitly and implicitly communicated in classroom practices. Students acquire norms relating to the methodology of *chumash* study, the relevance of its content, and the relevance of its practice to their lives. Just as in professional schools, the end goal of instruction is clear—knowledge use in the context of the professional community students will eventually join—the end goal of *chumash* learning in ultra-Orthodox schools is clear as well: participation in the full spectrum of adult ultra-Orthodox religious life. This provides significant authenticity to classroom pedagogy and activity, not because it resembles mature *chumash* learning, but because it is embedded in a larger cultural context in which the practice of *chumash* learning will be utilized.

Beyond Chumash

The role of signature pedagogy in creating constituent authenticity has implications for the acquisition of foundational skills in a variety of domains in Jewish education. Adults in haredi communities study *chumash* (and other texts that draw on *chumash*) for a variety of reasons and in a variety of ways: in order to acquire a deeper understanding of their religion, to support in-depth Talmud study, to deduce religious and ethical principles, and to fulfill the religious requirement of Torah study. Boys in first grade are expected to engage in all of these practices eventually, but they first need to acquire a basic fluency with the text. Because the most effective way to acquire fluency is through this type of repetition and choral reading, and those practices don't resemble adult practices, a different approach is needed to make the practices religiously meaningful. Constituent authenticity is a particularly good fit in this regard precisely because the activity structures need not closely resemble authentic practices. Because foundational skills must be automatic in order to replicate authentic activities (one cannot model the practices of a historian, a poet, or a literature expert without first knowing how to read, for example), it is not possible to simulate authentic adult activities while first developing these skills.

This is where Shulman's account of signature pedagogy serves as a productive point of departure. To develop foundational skills in any Jewish studies domain, activities must include the type of structured repetition that promotes fluency. But to make those practices meaningful they need to include some element of public performance, be uniform across contexts, and should involve fixed routines and rituals. These elements help create a group culture around the learning practice that can explicitly point to an assumed future engagement in the practice. To those features I would add a clear account of the epistemology of the learning practice (e.g., What is the nature of this knowledge?) and a clear articulation within classroom discourse of the expected contexts of use, both of which are found in *chumash* study.

Chumash learning in ultra-Orthodox Jewish schools serves as an exemplar of what this might look like at the elementary level, while professional education is an exemplar of more advanced constituent authenticity. In both, foundational skills can be acquired in ways that do not replicate or simulate real-world practice, yet are meaningful due to the broader cultural context within which the learning practices are embedded.

This is something that can be profitably employed in a wide range of Jewish educational contexts, provided that schools and communities can identify common expectations for their students. If schools that struggle to make religious studies meaningful can identify common experiences and expectations *beyond* school, they can also start to create pedagogical models that explicitly point to that broader context of use. If important foundational skills can be embedded in signature pedagogies that are meaningfully associated with mature practices, then students may experience religious subjects as intrinsically meaningful, rather than as an external imposition.

NOTES

1. Haredi here refers to both Chasidic and yeshivish schools. Two of the schools in this study were Chasidic and one yeshivish. The example provided in this paper comes from the yeshivish school, but it is consistent with the findings from the two other schools, as well as the many other yeshivish and Chasidic schools in which I have conducted research.

2. The cultural and religious expectations for boys and girls in haredi society are quite different, and consequently, so is their education. Because of this, analyses of pedagogy for boys and girls in haredi schools must be conducted separately.

3. Engagement problems in haredi schools tend to occur in secular classes, where it is difficult to make the material meaningful while the structure of the school and the community worldview all signal that the secular material is not meaningful. See Krakowski (2013) for more on this.

4. The enculturation certainly takes place in numerous informal contexts before schooling begins as well.

5. The universality of these practices is apparent in that nearly every American haredi school that I have observed, including both Chasidic and yeshivish schools, has utilized some version of these practices, with minor adaptations.

6. There are subtle, but significant, differences between schools in the two streams of ultra-Orthodoxy, yeshivish and Chasidish, but in regard to this excerpt, other than the English—rather than Yiddish—language of instruction, I have observed no significant differences. Because this excerpt is in English it is simply easier to discuss in the paper.

7. All names used are pseudonyms.

8. Note my earlier observation that those who do fail to acquire this skill are at risk of dropping out of the community entirely. Although even then, they may still acquire much of the ancillary content—the moral, theological, epistemological, and identity-building aspects, which may be retained without further participation in the community.

9. In addition, it is assumed by school leaders that *rabbeim* will teach in this way, and if they need help, they are given training and mentoring to successfully teach this way. This reflects the belief by those with the most at stake that these methods actually work. This doesn't guarantee that they are correct, but it does offer some indication, especially given the literature on these methods in other contexts.

10. Homiletic and exegetical discourses on the biblical text dating back to the third century.

11. This feature of *chumash* practice paves the way for later components of *chumash* learning that students will encounter as they age. As part of the graduated approach toward skill development in *chumash*, students will later learn Rashi script and start to read these very same Rashis on their own (most schools begin this process around the third grade). In most schools, students in the upper years of elementary school are exposed to a greater range of medieval commentaries, but because their focus at that point is Talmud, this is one area where girls (who do not study Talmud) receive a more robust religious education than boys.

12. In theory, *rabbeim* have a good deal of agency in determining which midrashic tales are incorporated into the text, but in practice, over dozens of haredi schools in all sorts of haredi communities, I have seen the same midrashim utilized, with minimal variation—perhaps a function of *rabbeim* making use of the same curricular materials.

13. Although many students will ultimately develop much more nuanced understandings of midrash, this typically does not come through formal instruction in school, but through exposure to more sophisticated commentaries when studying *chumash* as adults.

REFERENCES

Allington, R. L. (1983). Fluency: The neglected reading goal. *The Reading Teacher, 36*, 556–561.

Barab, S. A., & Hay, K. E. (2001). Doing science at the elbows of experts: Issues related to the science apprenticeship camp. *Journal of Research in Science Teaching, 38*, 70–102.

Barab, S. A., Squire, K. D., & Dueber, W. (2000). A co-evolutionary model for supporting the emergence of authenticity. *Educational Technology Research and Development, 48*, 37–62.

Bieler, J. (1986). Integration of Judaic and general studies in the Modern Orthodox day school. *Jewish Education, 54*, 15–26.

Brown, J. S., Collins, A., & Duguid, P. (1989). Situated cognition and the culture of learning. *Educational Researcher, 18*, 32–42.

Cepeda, N. J., Pashler, H., Vul, E., Wixted, J. T., & Rohrer, D. (2006). Distributed practice in verbal recall tasks: A review and quantitative synthesis. *Psychological Bulletin, 132*(3), 354.

Cobb, P., Gresalfi, M., & Hodge, L. (2009). A design research perspective on the identities that students are developing in mathematics classrooms. In B. Schwartz, T. Dreyfus, & R. Hershkowitz (eds.), *Transformation of knowledge through classroom interaction* (pp. 223–243). Taylor & Francis.

Dean Jr., D., & Kuhn, D. (2007). Direct instruction vs. discovery: The long view. *Science Education, 91*, 384–397.

Dowhower, S. L. (1987). Effects of repeated reading on second-grade transitional readers' fluency and comprehension. *Reading Research Quarterly, 22*, 389–406.

Falk, B. (2006). A conversation with Lee Shulman—signature pedagogies for teacher education: Defining our practices and rethinking our preparation. *The New Educator*, *2*, 73–82.

Goldberg, H. (1981). A critique of the American Jewish day school. *Tradition*, *19*(4).

Goldberg, S. J. (2004). *The relationship between English (L1) and Hebrew (L2) reading and externalizing behavior amongst Orthodox Jewish boys*. New York University Press.

Gresalfi, M. (2009). Taking up opportunities to learn: Constructing dispositions in mathematics classrooms. *Journal of the Learning Sciences*, *18*, 327–369.

Harner, M. M. (2011). The value of "thinking like a lawyer." *Maryland Law Review*, *70*, 390.

Hay, K. E., & Barab, S. A. (2001). Constructivism in practice: A comparison and contrast of apprenticeship and constructionist learning environments. *The Journal of the Learning Sciences*, *10*, 281–322.

Heckelman, R. (1969). A neurological-impress method of remedial-reading instruction. *Intervention in School and Clinic*, *4*, 277.

Heilman, S. C. (1992). Inside the Jewish school. In S. L. Kelman (ed.), *What we know about Jewish education: A handbook of today's research for tomorrow's Jewish education* (pp. 303-330). Torah Aura Productions.

Hoffman, J. V. (1987). Rethinking the role of oral reading in basal instruction. *The Elementary School Journal*, *87*, 367–373.

Hyland, A., & Kilcommins, S. (2009). Signature pedagogies and legal education in universities: Epistemological and pedagogical concerns with Langdellian case method. *Teaching in Higher Education*, *14*, 14.

Kanter, D. E. (2010). Doing the project and learning the content: Designing project-based science curricula for meaningful understanding. *Science Education*, *94*, 525–551.

Krakowski, M. (2008a). Dynamics of isolation and integration in ultra-Orthodox schools: The epistemological implications of using *rabbeim* as secular studies teachers. *Journal of Jewish Education*, *74*, 317–342.

Krakowski, M. (2008b). *Isolation and integration: Education and worldview formation in ultra-Orthodox Jewish schools*. Northwestern University.

Krakowski, M. (2013). Worldview construction and identity formation in ultra-Orthodox Jewish elementary schools. *Diaspora, Indigenous, and Minority Education*, *7*, 21–38.

Krakowski, M. (2017). Developing and transmitting religious identity: Curriculum and pedagogy in Modern Orthodox Jewish schools. *Contemporary Jewry*, *37*(3), 433–456.

Krakowski, M., Kramer, J., & Lev, N. (2012). Empowering students through problem- and project-based learning. *Jewish Educational Leadership*, *10*(2), 4–8.

Kuhn, M. R., & Stahl, S. A. (2000). Fluency: A review of developmental and remedial practices. *Ann Arbor*, *1001*, 48109–1259.

Pomson, A. (2011). Day schools in the liberal sector: Challenges and opportunities at the intersection of two traditions of Jewish schooling. In H. Miller, L. Grant, & A. Pomson (eds.), *International handbook of Jewish education* (Vol. 5, pp. 713–728). Springer Netherlands. http://dx.doi.org/10.1007/978-94-007-0354-4_40/.

Putnam, R. T., & Borko, H. (2000). What do new views of knowledge and thinking have to say about research on teacher learning? *Educational Researcher*, *29*, 4–15.

Radinsky, J., Bouillion, L., Hanson, K., & Gomez, L. (1998). *A framework for authenticity: Mutual benefits partnerships*. American Educational Research Association.

Radinsky, J., Bouillion, L., Lento, E. M., & Gomez, L. M. (2001). Mutual benefit partnership: A curricular design for authenticity. *Journal of Curriculum Studies*, *33*, 405–430.

Rahm, J., Miller, H. C., Hartley, L., & Moore, J. C. (2003). The value of an emergent notion of authenticity: Examples from two student/teacher-scientist partnership programs. *Journal of Research in Science Teaching*, *40*, 737–756.

Rapoport, T., Garb, Y., & Penso, A. (1995). Religious socialization and female subjectivity: Religious-Zionist adolescent girls in Israel. *Sociology of Education*, *68*, 48–61.

Samuels, S. J. (1979). The method of repeated readings. *Reading Teacher*, *32*, 403–408.

Samuels, S. J. (1988). Decoding and automaticity: Helping poor readers become automatic at word recognition. *The Reading Teacher*, *41*, 756–760.

Sfard, A., & Prusak, A. (2005). Telling identities: In search of an analytic tool for investigating learning as a culturally shaped activity. *Educational Researcher*, *34*, 14–22.

Shulman, L. (2005a). Pedagogies of uncertainty. *Liberal Education*, *91*, 18–26.

Shulman, L. (2005b). Signature pedagogies in the professions. *Daedalus*, *134*, 52–59.

Shulman, L. (2008). Pedagogies of interpretation, argumentation, and formation: From understanding to identity in Jewish education. *Journal of Jewish Education*, *74*, 5–15.

Strobel, J., & van Barneveld, A. (2009). When is PBL more effective? A meta-synthesis of meta-analyses comparing PBL to conventional classrooms. *Interdisciplinary Journal of Problem-Based Learning*, *3*, 4.

Taylor, K., & Rohrer, D. (2010). The effects of interleaved practice. *Applied Cognitive Psychology*, *24*, 837–848.

Weiser, S., & Bar-Lev, M. (1989). Talmud instruction in the yeshiva high school: Difficulties and prospects. *Niv Ha-Midrashiya*, 22–23.

11
Orienting Students to Engage with Pluralism
A Cultural Approach[1]

SUSAN L. SHEVITZ

The Challenge of Socializing Newcomers

Every organization, whether as intimate as a family or as large as an army, faces the challenge of socializing newcomers, i.e., helping them acquire the social knowledge, skills, and attitudes necessary to negotiate and succeed in the new environment. Orientations can help new participants sense the culture of a new setting by conveying, both implicitly and explicitly, how people are supposed to perceive, feel, and act in the new setting.

But what about orienting students to schools or other settings that are intentionally and robustly pluralistic, where they aim for what I will call engaged and generative pluralism by exploring differences in people's perspectives, policies, and programs? How might they convey what everyone shares while encouraging the differences? This is the problem that is discussed in this paper as we explore the orientation on the first day that freshmen and transfer students attend what we are calling Tikhon Academy.

Tikhon is a pluralistic Jewish day high school in a suburb of a large Jewish community. With two other researchers, I conducted a multi method study of Tikhon early in its history to understand how pluralism was conceptualized and enacted in a school that was widely known for its commitment to pluralism as central to its religious and educational approach. Assuming that the challenge of interpreting and enacting pluralism would be most visible when Tikhon first worked with its students, we focused on the experience of the incoming freshmen throughout the year and into the next.[2] I returned in their senior year to interview, survey, and observe the same students discussing real-life dilemmas related to pluralism in Jewish schools in order to learn how their understanding of and commitment to pluralism had changed over their four years in the school. This article describes and analyzes the ways in which Tikhon's orientation tried to prepare students to begin their education in a pluralistic setting.

Challenges of Pluralistic Settings

Pluralism is generally understood to be a theory or system that recognizes more than one ultimate principle. As both a philosophy and a practical methodology, it has the potential to address the chasms and rancor among people, not by asking them to relinquish their own ways but rather by being able to share their own beliefs and practices while encountering others' beliefs and practices with openness, empathy, respect, and a readiness to engage around how they differ as well as about what they share.

As a framework for describing and analyzing pluralism, I elsewhere proposed a continuum with several points (Shevitz, 2006): (1) Demographic pluralism is a precursor to pluralism, not an actual expression of it. It means that an organization respectfully includes participants who have fundamental religious, ethnic, racial, economic, and or other differences, though it still operates according to a single ideological perspective. We include it on the continuum because organizations that start with diversity may begin to actively use their diversity as an element of their programs. (2) Coexistence pluralism actively uses the setting's diversity by helping students express their own and learn about each other's beliefs and practices. It tries to foster student interactions about their differences in an environment designed to help them understand and work—coexist—despite holding different truth-claims that may even be mutually exclusive. Some, notably political theorist Michael Walzer (1997), refer to this as tolerance. (3) Engaged pluralism more purposefully uses participants' differences by helping them articulate their own ideas as well as grapple with others' even—or especially—about sensitive issues that are often avoided. It is highly interactive and leaves open the possibility that by dealing with difficult issues, new understanding or action might emerge.

When it does, it is (4) generative pluralism because new insights can lead to new approaches that potentially challenge the status quo.

Tikhon's commitment to engaged and generative pluralism challenged and could even undermine what most of its incoming students had and would continue to experience in other educational and/or community settings. To take young people who for the most part grew up in settings that were singular in their understanding of Jewish life and introduce them to a multiperspectival and multivocal approach that encourages the exploration of both their differences and similarities is not a simple task. Psychosocial and practical dilemmas abound. How are students to relate to the Jewish practices and beliefs with which they were raised? Are they and their families open to exploring alternative ways of being Jewish? Will students feel safe enough to question their assumptions and explore new possibilities? How will their social networks be affected? How would decisions about varied Jewish practices be determined? These are questions that the freshmen might face over their years at Tikhon. But as they first entered the building, we informally asked the newcomers what they thought pluralism meant. Most said that they hadn't thought much about it, while a few students mentioned having "different kinds of Jews coming to school together" or "having Orthodox, Reform, and Conservative services." In light of these realities, Tikhon had to consider how it could best prepare students for its pluralistic perspective and practices. Orientation was where the formal process of socializing students to pluralism first took shape.

Freshman Orientation

Background about Tikhon and Its Students

The scene the freshmen saw as they arrived at school in 2005 could hardly have been imagined just a few years back. From forty-seven students in the ninth and tenth grades when it opened in 1997, Tikhon grew to enrollments well above two hundred by the mid-2000s. It soon outgrew its first two rented buildings and in autumn 2003 it moved into its twenty acre campus that is large enough for several buildings that are surrounded by ample grounds and sports fields. Light-filled interior spaces include spacious classrooms, laboratories, gyms, a black box theater, a common room where the school community gathers for assemblies, a dining hall and kitchen, and many cozy spaces for people to talk and hang out.

The class of 2010 was the first that would spend its full four years at the new campus. Students came from thirty-five different communities. Sixty were from six different day schools and, of these, fully half the students came from a school affiliated with the Conservative movement. The other students were roughly evenly split between independent and public schools.

The school was so young that its original name, "The New Jewish High School," was carved into the building's façade under the name Tikhon Academy. Many students still referred to Tikhon as "New Jew." Rabbi Aaron Levy, a pseudonym for the founding head of school and a passionate spokesperson for pluralism, was on sabbatical and would be at school only sporadically throughout the year. His absence would reveal the place of pluralism at the school. Would it fade into the background without, to use a teacher's phrase, "his constant pushing the [pluralism] envelope?" We were about to find out.

A quick glance at the gathering students suggested varied Jewish commitments. Some boys and an occasional girl wore *kippot* [skullcaps], a statement that conveyed both more and less traditional observance, because in traditional settings boys are required to wear these but it is taboo for girls to wear them. This announced that some girls were assuming religious practices that until recently were exclusively male and remain so in traditional settings. *Tzitzit*, the four-cornered garment with attached fringes, mandated in the Bible (Numbers 15:37–41) and worn by traditional males, peeked out from underneath a few boys' shirts. Some girls dressed according to traditional Jewish practice, with skirts reaching below the knees and sleeves below their elbows, but most wore clothes that would be seen in most any affluent high school. The admissions office corroborated these impressions, reporting that fifty-six families claimed Conservative affiliation, twenty Reform, eighteen Orthodox, two Reconstructionist, and eight "other." (Several checked two or more categories.) Many of the students were greeting friends from their elementary schools and summer camps, but there were some who didn't seem to know any others.

Orientation Activities and Experiences

Teachers, assisted by some upperclassmen and alumni, quickly began to lay the groundwork for the first day of an orientation that would also include an overnight stay at school. After some welcomes and icebreakers, students engaged in *hevruta* learning, a method that they would experience throughout their years at Tikhon. *Hevruta* is a traditional Jewish approach to text study in which pairs of learners carefully investigate texts as a prelude to a more thorough, full group discussion that is traditionally led by an illustrious religious leader (Holzer & Kent, 2013). A teacher laid out Tikhon's rules for *hevruta* study and later led the group discussion. In her words:

- You have to be open to learning, to really looking at the text and listening to your *hevruta* partner carefully.
- You have to be supportive of your *hevruta* partner; it might be a challenging time for him or her.
- Everyone has responsibility for exploring the text.
- There are always multiple interpretations that are supported by the text.

These themes, especially openness and multiple interpretations, would recur throughout the day and, though the students could not yet know it, throughout the next four years as well.

After the *hevruta* learning, the group went outside for community-building games. One game introduced the possibility of students' touching each others' hands. Because physical contact between the genders is unacceptable to the most traditional students, and because many of the others were likely unaware of this, the teacher warned that before holding the hand of someone nearby they should ask whether that is okay. She then generalized the lesson: "It is very important not to assume anything." Avoiding a long explanation of the different kinds of behaviors regarding male and female interactions within different Jewish groups, she called attention to a central feature of Tikhon: while the students may all look more or less the same, they have different religious requirements. She was also signaling that in a pluralistic environment each student had to be respectful of the other students' personal boundaries and comfort levels.

Lunch followed. Saying the traditional blessings after the meal, *birkat hamazon*, was another potentially divisive event. The more traditional students would not consider the prayer acceptable with a female leading the opening recitation, while other students would be offended if the girls were told they could not do this. The group was instructed to do the prayer "the Tikhon way," though this was also the practice in other settings: both a male and a female would chant the opening phrases after each other, allowing students to respond to whichever prayer leader they preferred. While this dilemma could have been an opportunity to engage students around their differences, the teachers preferred to reinforce a sense that there was a legitimated Tikhon approach.

Students then had time to socialize and receive important information about the nuts and bolts of life at Tikhon. At two o'clock they convened in the large space called the *beit midrash*, the traditional name for a house of study, and at Tikhon the name of the large room in which big events took place, for the first session of a trimester-long course, "Pluralism Lab," that all freshmen were required to take.

Quotations from traditional texts in Hebrew and English covered the walls. Students were told about two categories of commandments: behaviors that structure a person's relationship to other people (*bein adam l'havero*) and those that regulate a person's relationship with God (*bein adam lamakom*). The teacher animatedly explained that these texts deal with "what we [Jews] have in common." In their community, he claimed, there are "fifty-six synagogues, fifty-six different ways of doing Jewishness." He then questioned students about the main movements of Jewish religious life and made the point that most often people order them Orthodox, Conservative, and Reform and very rarely in the inverse order. "Why," he asked, "does this happen?" He poked holes in students' arguments. For example, when someone said that "we see Orthodoxy as more religious, closer to the source, the Bible," he countered that "actually, Reform Jews observe seven days of Passover and this is closer to the biblical instruction than the Orthodox community's eight days." The point, he went on, was that students will participate in Pluralism Lab to explore "how we interpret Jewish law and why we need to have these conversations. They are really about what we believe . . . What we believe determines what we do."

This teacher was challenging the assumption that a single belief system is closest to the truth, and that the others should be measured by their distance from that truth. "Different approaches are legitimate," he continued, and "if taken seriously, they will lead to actions that reflect that [belief system]." This reinforced the message that there can be multiple legitimate interpretations based on the same textual evidence.

The teacher segued into the next activity. In small groups, students grappled with dilemmas about Jewish observances that are important to the school community, mostly policies about *kashrut* (dietary laws) and prayer. These are among the more obvious areas in which the school has to decide policy in the face of competing interpretations and commitments. A teacher probed students' assumptions by asking why the school needed a food policy. A student responded, "So all people can eat here and since we have Orthodox students, it will be easier for them." A different teacher then reminded the students that at Tikhon teachers and other students will push arguments further: "We do not want a double standard and we do not want to check people's kitchens. So how do you think our *kashrut* policy can create community?" Students discussed what it means to be a "united," respectful community that includes everyone. They then learned that Tikhon's *kashrut* policy is complex because the school tries to balance the needs of the community and of individuals in it. They were told that all of the school's communal events were to be strictly kosher, i.e., have a *heksher* (kosher certification by a rabbi) and there was a list of acceptable certifications. But students could bring lunch from home, whatever the *kashrut* standards of their families, as long it was dairy and not meat or shellfish. He then added details based on Jewish law but without explaining the laws: "Because it is hot you cannot order pizza to be delivered at school, but you can bring cold pizza for lunch as long as it does not have any meat." The *kashrut* policies were then and remained a source of confusion for many students and parents over the years.

The teacher then recalled the "old days" when Tikhon's building did not have a kitchen. Students lobbied to be allowed to eat at local restaurants and make their own decisions about what to eat. In this way, students could follow their families' *kashrut* standards, but they would also have to figure out how to be sensitive to their classmates' needs, especially those with stricter *kashrut* practices. The teacher reminded students, "In the new building, the kitchen has rabbinic supervision, but the lunchroom doesn't." Another teacher said, "There are no cookie police here...We are always compromising...*Kashrut* can be a big, divisive issue, so our policy is a compromise."

Similarly, the group discussed prayer requirements: freshmen were required to attend one of several types of services twice a week and on the other days they could go to a service or another group for some sort of serious reflection. Once again, the history of this policy's origin was explained: some students had argued to the administration that because Tikhon was a pluralistic school they should not be forced to go to prayer services. A teacher reminded students that there would be times in their lives when they will attend synagogue services and they should know the "etiquette of prayer." Another continued that at a pluralistic school, students will be judged not "according to someone else's standard in issues of religiosity but by their own standard." The session ended with a teacher again pointing out that compromises are made. How and why specific decisions are made was unclear and students would see the requirements for prayer change over their years at school.

At a Prayer Fair later in the afternoon, students learned about the available options: (1) the "*mechitzah minyan*," where males and females sit in separate sections as practiced in Orthodox settings and all prayers are led by males, (2) a "traditional-egalitarian *minyan*" that follows the traditional liturgy, though the males and females sit together and have equal roles in leading the service, and (3) a "liberal-egalitarian *minyan*" that includes selections from the liturgy as well as other inspirational readings. On days when students were not required to go to a *minyan* there would be many choices, including meditation, humor, yoga, journaling, and listening to music. "These activities," a teacher explained, "are not set in stone. [In the past,] students initiated other approaches and some of these have fallen by the wayside, but some are still available. You may decide after a trial period that you want to switch to another *minyan* but then you have to commit yourself to one for a trimester."

Students then rotated in small groups to hear more about each prayer option from teachers and the older student facilitators. The Orthodox and Conservative teachers responsible for these services, with some comments by upperclassmen, explained what was unique to each service. A teacher who is a Reform rabbi described how Tikhon's liberal *minyan* was established. In Tikhon's first or second year a student who was Jewish by patrilineal descent (in traditional circles, only people born of a Jewish mother or converted by a traditional rabbinic court are considered Jewish) told the head of school that she wanted a liberal prayer service in which she, as a patrilineal Jew, would be counted in the *minyan* and allowed to lead services. Based on their understanding of Jewish law and practice, neither the egalitarian nor the traditional *minyan* could allow this. Levy saw the validity of her position and a liberal *minyan* was soon formed. The story as told was historically inaccurate. As reported years later by Levy, "There were just not enough people at first to create a liberal *minyan*." He explained that he still felt regret that he was "less creative in finding solutions than he might have been." By the following year the problem disappeared: the school was large enough to support a liberal *minyan*. This oft-told story serves as one of Tikhon's founding myths: a tale based in history that conveys a lesson deemed important, but is not necessarily historically accurate. In any case, the teacher again reminded the students, "If we are not offering what you need, please come to us and we will accommodate."

As the day wound down, students learned more about the day-to-day expectations and procedures, including the advising system, homework, absences, tests, use of technology, and the like, and had time to interact informally with each other. After dinner there were more community-building activities led by the upperclassmen who, at the end of the evening, shared pointers for having a good first year and then gave the all-important instructions for the rest of the night: boys were to stay on one floor, girls on the other, and no one was allowed outside.

A Cultural Framework for Thinking about Orientation

Levels of Culture

Edgar Schein's classic work on organizational culture shows how a culture forms and is maintained (Schein & Schein, 2017). As founders of an organization face challenges, they draw on often unarticulated assumptions about the nature of things. Solutions that work well enough are considered valid and are then taught to new members as the correct way to perceive, think, feel, and behave in relation to those problems and quickly become taken for granted. They shape the pattern of beliefs, values, and norms that become the bedrock of its culture.

Accordingly, there are three levels of culture. (1) The first level, artifacts, or what people see and hear when they encounter the organization, are plentiful but cannot be accurately interpreted on their own. Examples of artifacts from the orientation include Tikhon's architecture, the Hebrew heard and seen, the role of older students, how students addressed teachers and how teachers interacted with each other, quotations on the walls, and so on. (2) The second tier consists of espoused values. These can be more or less aspirational or operational and are expressed through more formal, official pronouncements of why things are done a certain way. Materials that students received before, during, and after they applied, whether online or on paper, are replete with espoused values. At orientation they were most often expressed by the teachers' explanations, such as students have to respect everyone and ask about their religious practices, or that the school is flexible and will respond to students' needs. (3) The third level consists of the underlying beliefs that shape leaders' assumptions and cannot be easily deciphered. They are deeply embedded, taken for granted, and relate to all aspects of the organization.

The content of a culture falls into three categories: (1) assumptions about how the new entity can survive in the external environment (e.g., assumptions about mission, goals, strategy, structure, systems, processes, ways to detect and correct errors, etc. (2) practices for how to achieve integration within the organization (e.g., issues about common languages and concepts, group boundaries and identity, nature of authority and relationships, and allocation of rewards and status); and (3) assumptions about how the world works (e.g., general assumptions about human nature, the natural world, reality, relationships, time and space, etc. (Schein & Schein, 2007).

At orientation, for example, students heard official rationales for the *kashrut* policy, among them that people are responsible for themselves ("there are no cookie police here"). This value was based on an underlying assumption about human nature: that people are good and can be relied upon to do the right thing. (I can assert this only because I have ample corroborating evidence from other artifacts, espoused values, including interviews with Tikhon's founders and other leaders. Underlying assumptions cannot be inferred from minimal data.) A strong culture has considerable alignment among the artifacts and espoused values that people perceive in their day-to-day experience, and these exemplify the beliefs that have become taken for granted. Even small things can be expressing fundamental ideas.

Everything students experienced during orientation—how it was organized and used available time, the rooms' setups, what content was presented and how it was presented, how teachers and students interacted, how support staff were treated, and all else, conveyed information about Tikhon's culture. Students' experiences over the next days, weeks, and months would confirm, modify, or negate their early impressions as they experienced more of the culture, with all its contradictions and complexities. For example, a lot of prime time at orientation was spent discussing Jewish rituals and prayer. Were these actually the central features of Tikhon's formal and informal curriculum? Was there room for expressions of Jewish life that were unrelated to ritual practice, such as culture? Would teachers generally be as accessible as they were during orientation? Would students' requests be taken as seriously as the anecdotes conveyed? Did pluralism only relate to Tikhon's Judaic curriculum? Would Tikhon be so heavily focused on analysis and argumentation? Students' cumulative experiences would provide the answers to such questions.

Conveyed and Missing Messages about Pluralism

Perhaps the most consistent and powerful message of the day was that at Tikhon pluralism was pervasive. Students heard the term in many different discussions. Activities were designed to introduce them to Tikhon's values and actions, and these almost always related to pluralism. Students repeatedly heard:

- It is essential to recognize others' religious, intellectual, and emotional diversity.
- Students should inquire about other people's needs, commitments, and preferences instead of assuming things about each other.
- There are multiple views of texts.
- Individuals' understanding of texts should influence their actions.

- Students are expected to engage with ideas, and the school will push students by asking them to explain their positions.
- Compromises that do not trample any group's sensibilities are valued.
- The school is responsive to students' voices.
- By exploring their different ideas, students might generate new ways of thinking and/or behaving.

Pluralism was never defined. Similarly, content that might have been expected was missing, such as aspects of Jewish life beyond ritual observance, spoken Hebrew, Israel, and references to general studies and to contemporary society. As researchers, we wondered about several observations:

- Jewish religious and ritual life dominated the program. Were other aspects of Jewish life valued?
- America's diversity, as well as its historical or contemporary realities, was not mentioned. Was this considered irrelevant to Tikhon's pluralistic mission?
- The word community was applied to various groups of people: the freshman class, students, faculty and teachers, families and their congregations, local, national, and worldwide Jewry and the Jewish people.
- What did the term really mean? What were the unimportant and actual links between the school and these other groups?
- Tikhon was already known for its strong emphasis on "cognitive pluralism," defined by the teachers who prepared Tikhon's 2005 self-study for accreditation as "the ability to understand, hold, and grapple with multiple, even contradictory, interpretations and perspectives" (p. 47). Teachers at orientation repeatedly made the point that teachers would "poke holes in their thinking and [push students] to further their ideas." What about freshmen who were not at this stage of cognitive development or whose strengths were in other types of intelligence? (See Gardner, 1983; Piaget, 1997.)
- While there was some physical movement, the arts and sports were absent. This seemed to demonstrate Tikhon's emphasis on cognitive pluralism. Over the next years, students would learn that the arts and sports were also important at Tikhon.

Concern for Community

Throughout the orientation, the faculty tried to foster a sense of community by using Tikhon's often specialized phrases that emanated from the vocabulary of Jewish ritual life, such as *minyan*, *tefila, davening*, *hevruta*, etc. Sometimes the phrases also emphasized commitment to the school's traditions, such as "doing *birkat hamazon* the 'Tikhon way.'" Teachers seemed to want to create a sense of belonging by telling stories about the school's quirkiness in its earliest years: the overcrowded building that briefly housed the school, students' assertiveness, and much else. For example, instead of simply explaining *kashrut* policy, students heard a rambling story from when Tikhon was young and students wanted to get lunch on the nearby street that was home to many fast food restaurants. Teachers explained why they allowed students to eat in them and also about the dilemmas that the policy created. The underlying message was that Tikhon trusted its students to do the right thing. Other stories demonstrated the need to be sensitive to people's food restrictions because they were, a teacher explained, a "community and need to consider everyone's needs." It seemed that the faculty was trying to show the students that they had to consider both the needs of a group and the needs of the individuals whose positions differed.

At the same time, I wondered about the teachers' stories about events from Tikhon's first years. Were they trying to forge a connection between new students who were entering a campus that looked like other independent schools with the school's pioneering spirit, when the head of school had the goal of creating "new kinds of Jews"? Or perhaps the focus on Tikhon's past was an expression of teachers' own nostalgia for the days of yore? Either way, the desire to connect the freshmen with Tikhon's past was clear as incidents were recalled and interpreted.

Events like orientation often show people's standing within a community. On that day at least, Tikhon's heroes were not the high achievers or top athletes. They were individuals who challenged the system by asking for a different prayer experience, being sensitive to each other, organizing to get permission to eat in neighborhood joints, or being able to engage with teachers who would push them to express their opinions.

The Efficacy of Tikhon's Orientation

A Taste of Tikhon's Pluralistic Culture

It would be naive to think that a concept as complex and slippery as pluralism could be encapsulated in orientation, a day when adolescents were understandably concerned with the immediate questions of whether they will fit in, find friends, like teachers, and succeed in their new setting. In follow-up research with these students in the second semester of their senior year, I learned that it took time—for some, four years—for them to understand what pluralism is (a few students claimed that they never got there) and that they had varied routes to comprehending it. Activities outside the classroom—*shabbatonim* (on- and off-site retreats over the Sabbath), discussions with individual teachers, special activities and trips—were often cited as most influential, although specific classes and conversations with peers and teachers also had large roles. It was the cumulative effect of many different experiences that led to understanding what pluralism means, even though students were actually practicing aspects of pluralism from the start.

Clear Messages Supporting Tikhon's Pluralism

While students could not know it that late August day, their orientation was a fair representation of key aspects of Tikhon's culture at that time. To return to Schein's schema, they were bombarded with artifacts and assertions about values that for the most part were in alignment. In many ways, they heard about and experienced the emphasis on cognition and analysis, multiple interpretations, and the need to think for themselves. They were to be engaged and generate new approaches. There was less concern about social and emotional aspects of students' lives than about their ideas and intellectual capacities.

Four clear messages emerged in the course of the day. Though students were not presented with a clear definition of pluralism, it was evident to them that pluralism was a central feature of their new school. They were being prepared to engage with it. To use an outdated metaphor: orientation positioned students' antennae to pick up pluralism's waves in much the same way that radio receivers grasp radio waves.

A second message was more subtle. Whether intentional or not, Tikhon's pluralism seemed to be rooted in its Jewish religious mission. References to general studies and the wider community for the most part were absent, and the Jewish content was primarily about rituals and practices. Pluralism's urgent message to the wider society was not addressed. By the time they graduated, some students were questioning these gaps.

Tikhon also transmitted a third message: it valued students who would, to use the educators' favored phrases, "seriously engage with ideas," be ready to "live in the gray zone of ambiguity," and express their views while "being open to others' perspectives." This meant that students were to respect other people's positions and be sensitive to their classmates' needs. The emphasis on becoming comfortable with multiperspectival thinking is consonant with what is known about adolescents' cognitive development. A major task of adolescence is for young people to move from concrete to abstract thinking. With its insistence on learning to have opposing views and developing a commitment to an idea even when realizing there are counterarguments, Tikhon wanted to nudge students beyond early adolescents' concrete, binary cognition.

The fourth message was also subtle. On the one hand, students heard how individuals had successfully caused changes at Tikhon and that they, as individuals, needed to take responsibility for their learning. Teachers had even explained that Tikhon wanted them to be the best kind of Jew they could be from whichever approach to Judaism they were committed to. This is the language of individual influence and fulfillment. At the same time, they frequently heard the word community and were often reminded that as members of a diverse community they needed to be sensitive to others' beliefs and practices and, by extension, perhaps sometimes subjugate their own preferences for the needs of the group. It seemed to be assumed that a group would always be able to figure out some way of respecting both the individual and the collective when some difficulties arose.

By highlighting both the community and the individual, Tikhon was expressing a basic rationale for the existence of pluralistic schools and organizations. Commitment to the Jewish people had sharply declined over the last decades, while insularity and conflict among Jews with different commitments keeps growing. Many sophisticated observers of Jewish life believe that there is an urgent need to educate people who will be able to bridge the gap among Jewish groups and work together productively on shared concerns. While no one at orientation preached this message, students heard anecdotes suggesting that cooperation and collaboration were both desirable and possible.

Implications Beyond Tikhon, Orientation, and Pluralism

There are two broad implications of Tikhon's orientation that relate to other kinds of educational settings—and beyond. The first demonstrates the potential of using a cultural perspective when planning, as well as analyzing, events. The second focuses on the potential of pluralism to address contemporary divisiveness within the Jewish and American contexts.

Applying a Cultural Lens

Organizational culture theory provides a powerful lens to both describe and, more importantly, plan events such as orientation, whether in schools or other organizations. Occasions such as assemblies, promotion celebrations, meetings, and graduations can be seen as ceremonies replete with rituals to help people begin to perceive the organization's rules, roles, standards, values, and beliefs.

Ceremonies involving longer-term group members, whether post-sports celebrations, activities on the last night of summer camp, or fundraising galas, can recount and celebrate aspects of a culture, thereby reinforcing commitment to the group. Everyday events are equally important: how people address each other, how dissent is expressed, whose achievements are touted, who defers to whom—all express and reinforce the organization's values. Tikhon used formal and informal, didactic and experiential approaches. It is easy to imagine other ways to structure a high school orientation and to critique some of the ways Tikhon's was implemented. But based on what we learned about Tikhon in this research over the next years, orientation showed that a strong culture had developed early in the school's existence.

Ceremonies might best be thought of as cultural bonanzas. Like much else in a setting, they are effective when artifacts, espoused values, and beliefs are for the most part in alignment, as they were at Tikhon. When they are not, the messages transmitted will be inconsistent, unclear, and confusing—even if the event itself was enjoyed. This suggests that people responsible for designing ceremonies and other events need an understanding of the culture. Had I asked the teachers and students who planned Tikhon's orientation to describe its underlying beliefs and assumptions, I'd probably have gotten confused stares or rambling accounts of some practices. But it was fascinating to see the faculty's near unanimity about key aspects of the culture as they repeated the same phrases that I came to understand expressed Tikhon's underlying assumptions: (1) people are by nature good and can be expected to do the right thing, (2) truth is determined through argumentation and analysis (rather than by empirical methods or received tradition), and (3) changes must be made by advocating for one's own needs.

The cultures of some organizations have more ambiguities and incongruities than Tikhon's. For example, there are schools that claim to be pluralistic because their students come from families whose Jewish commitments differ but teach Jewish content from a single, perspective or camps that advertise that their highest value is developing campers' *menschleikheit* (human decency and kindness) but might maintain tight control of staff and campers, thereby conveying a pessimistic message about human nature: without oversight and control, people will be lazy or undependable. Such misalignment or lack of clarity needs to be addressed, though this is a complex process. In such a case, ceremonies of all kinds can be part of a cultural change process by intentionally demonstrating and articulating the aspirational values even as the organization looks more deeply at its underlying assumptions and beliefs.

Missing Content

Sometimes what is absent is as significant as what is present. Tikhon was established at time when there was increasing fragmentation and polarization within the Jewish community as well as in Western society. Yet Tikhon's orientation exclusively referred to Jewish content and concerns. Recognition of what was going on in the wider society was curiously absent. Trying to understand this, I later learned that there were attempts in Tikhon's first years to bring students together with those of a Catholic high school for intergroup deliberations; however, this was discontinued because of scheduling problems, time constraints, and concerns about socioeconomic disparities. While there were other opportunities for students to become involved with the wider community, such as through internships and travel, these were not presented as part of Tikhon's pluralism. The espoused value of preparing students to apply their pluralistic perspectives in the wider society, as well as in the Jewish community, was at odds with the artifacts, i.e., what actually went on, and suggests that some basic assumptions about the relationship of the Jewish and general worlds were at work.

Pluralism's Potential

It is obvious that the divisiveness and acrimony observed throughout the world when Tikhon oriented the class of 2010 is today far more extreme. We are constantly seeing evidence of the continuing dissolution of broad consensus around values and beliefs within and among different factions of society. The desire, capacity, and opportunity for people from disparate groups to communicate, let alone work toward shared goals, is increasingly rare, and no sector of society, including cyberspace, is immune to these realities. Some groups try to impose their own beliefs and practices on others, using whatever sources of power on hand, as the rancor on local, regional, national, and international levels intensifies.

At the same time, some pluralistic schools such as Tikhon as well as other settings are attempting to educate people to become constructive forces in their communities. There are successful examples of people and groups who bridge the chasms between themselves and those with whom they disagree about fundamental issues. They have found ways for people to hear each other, respect their commonalities and differences, and move forward productively.[3] Addressing Tikhon's limited engagement with societal dilemmas, some leaders at Tikhon specifically claim that because the students developed a pluralistic stance in the safe environment of a small, all-Jewish school, they would be prepared to apply this in the more diverse settings at college and beyond.

It would be a mistake, however, to infer from orientation that the primary rationale for Tikhon's pluralism was as a response to civic or religious tensions. For the head-of-school and at least some of the faculty, pluralism is a theological stance. It is part of the divine economy and deeply rooted in their religious beliefs. Over the coming years, students would encounter biblical, rabbinic, and other texts, as well as interpretations of various rituals that demonstrated this. To use two frequently cited rabbinic metaphors: God spoke in seventy voices at the revelation at Sinai and each person perceived it in a unique way. Similarly, the manna in the wilderness tasted different to each Israelite, each according to their individual reality. No one can claim to have "the truth." To fully understand Torah, people need others' insights.

As early as the first day of orientation Tikhon tried to show as well as tell its students that they could live together productively in a highly functional community with their differences, and not in spite of them. To return to the radio metaphor from the perspective of the theory of organizational culture: orientation began to transmit words, values, and behaviors related to Tikhon's pluralistic mission. No one thought that the students at this time would recognize a pattern among these elements. But intentional, ongoing transmissions about essential aspects of Tikhon's culture made it more likely that students would come to understand and perhaps appreciate diversity and would integrate Tikhon's commitment to generative pluralism in their lives.

NOTES

1. This chapter is part of a larger research project conducted under the auspices of Brandeis University's Mandel Center for Studies in Jewish Education.

2. Drs. Rahel Wasserfall, Shirah Hecht, and I observed activities in and out of the classroom; had ongoing conversations with educators, administrators, other staff members, and lay leaders; conducted semistructured interviews and focus groups with students and teachers; read curricula, newsletters, meeting notes, and other documentation; and surveyed the students.

3. For descriptions of attempts to enact pluralism in disparate settings such as public square, interreligious civic programs, and Jewish classrooms, see: Holzer & Kent, 2013; Marom, 2003; Kress, 2012; Mosher et al., 2023; Pierce, 2023; and Shevitz & Wasserfall, 2009.

REFERENCES

Erikson, E. (1998). *The life cycle completed*. W. W. Norton.

Holzer, E., & Kent, O. (2013). *A philosophy of hevruta: Understanding and teaching the art of text study in pairs*. Academic Press.

Marom, D. (2003). Before the gates of the school: An experiment in developing educational vision from practice. In S. Fox, I. Scheffler, & D. Marom (eds.), *Visions of Jewish education*. Cambridge University Press.

Mosher, L., Pierce, E., & Rose, N. (2023). *With the best of intentions: Interreligious missteps and mistakes*. Orbis Books.

Novak, W. (1997) *Visions at the heart: Lessons from Camp Ramah on the power of ideas in shaping educational institutions*. Council for Initiatives in Jewish Education.

Piaget, J. (1990). *The child's conception of the world*. Littlefield Adams.

Pierce, E. (2023). *Pluralism in practice*. Orbis Books.

Pomson & H. Dietcher (eds.), *Jewish day schools, Jewish community: A reconsideration*. Littman Library.

Schein, E., & Schein, P. (2017). *Organizational culture and leadership* (5th ed.). Wiley.

Shevitz, S., & Wasserfall, R. (2009). Building community in a pluralist high school. In A. Pomson & H. Deitcher (eds.), *Jewish day schools, Jewish community: A reconsideration* (pp. 37–394). Littman Library.

Tikhon working committee. (2005). *Self-study prepared for accreditation*.

Walzer, M. (1997). *On toleration*. Yale University Press.

12 Designing Schools Around Five Dimensions of Community

SHIRA HAMMERMAN

Introduction

Time and time again, Jewish day school advocates, professionals, and scholars reinforce the centrality of community within schools through action papers, communications, and value propositions. The word community is mentioned over 120 times in the landmark *A Time to Act* report (The Commission on Jewish Education in North America, 1990), which has influenced Jewish educational policy and funding for more than twenty-five years (Krasner, 2016). Its relevance to Jewish day schools was reaffirmed in a national survey in which 40 percent of participating schools specifically referenced community in their mission statements, and many more referred to actions and terms that can be associated with community (American Institute for Research, 2015). Some go so far as to suggest that community is the "*raison d'etre* for Jewish day school education" (Pomson, 2009, p. 25).

In their emphasis on community, Jewish day school leaders echo scholars of general education who call for the development of schools that are designed "as communities" rather than "as organizations" (Sergiovanni, 1993, 1994). These researchers suggest that the dominant approach to school design overly aggrandizes linear planning, negotiations based on self-interest, and centralized leadership models. In contrast, seeing schools as communities refocuses educational institutions on relationships, mutual responsibilities, and empowerment models of leadership, with the belief that this creates supportive contexts for teaching, learning, and emotional growth.

While this rallying call has the potential to infuse Jewish day school life with added energy and meaning, its power as an organizing principle is limited by the lack of clarity that is inherent in the term community and the lack of data regarding the lived experience of community in Jewish day schools. Theorists have worked for many years to make sense of the social relationships that comprise communities, often using Tonnies's (1887/2002) continuum of social relationships as a starting point. Tonnies refers to relationships that are based on kinship, neighborhood, and friendship as *Gemeinschaft* and describes such relationships as generally homogeneous and close-knit, yet involuntary and taken for granted. He refers to relationships that are designed with an instrumental purpose in mind as *Gesellschaft*. These relationships are completely voluntary, functional, rational, and strategic without regard to personal characteristics or family of origin. Durkheim (1893/1984) makes a similar distinction in analyzing the social cohesion that connects individuals in society. He distinguishes between mechanical solidarity, which refers to shared experiences, thinking, and lifestyles that bond homogeneous groupings, and organic solidarity, which develops when interdependence necessitates individuals to work together. In more recent years, theorists have complemented these traditional notions with depictions of communities that are abstract (James, 1992), symbolic (Cohen, 1985), and even imagined (Andersen, 1983/2006; Kanno & Norton, 2003; Wenger, 1998). Modern day schools bring to life this full range of conceptions, and leaders must understand the complexity of their shared social context if they are to build and sustain school community in intentional ways.

This chapter adds analytical weight to the notion that Jewish day schools be designed as communities by considering: What does school community look like from a teacher's perspective? What happens to a teacher's sense of connection when everyone else seems to know one another? When the writing on the wall is a foreign language? When the standard of dress and other cultural norms are unfamiliar? Do these differences prevent an individual from feeling accepted among colleagues? What might schools think about when integrating staff members into a school community? In doing so, this chapter highlights connections that bond day school teachers to their institutions and to one another, identifies five dimensions that provide entry points into school community, and provides direction for school leaders who seek to engage the full gamut of stakeholders into a shared social context.

Why Design Schools as Communities?

Harnessing community as an organizing principle for Jewish day schools aligns with research that demonstrates the benefits of strong school community, draws upon a cultural propensity within Jewish tradition toward inherently strong communal connections, and complements shared cultural norms that abound in many day schools.

Designing schools around a shared social context is supported by a large body of empirical work that documents the positive influence of school and teacher communities on students, teachers, and society. Strong school community is said to lower dropout rates (Bryk & Driscoll, 1988; Bryk et al., 1993; Osterman, 2002), improve student attitudes toward school (Battistich et al., 1995; Goodenow, 1993; Solomon et al., 1996), increase academic motivation (Battistich et al., 1995; Goodenow, 1993; Osterman, 2002; Solomon et al., 1996), raise commitment to community norms and values (Solomon et al., 1996), increase student self-esteem and sense of autonomy (Osterman, 2002; Solomon et al., 1996), increase math achievement (Bryk & Driscoll, 1988), improve prosocial attitudes and behavior (Bryk and Driscoll, 1988; Osterman, 2002; Solomon et al., 1996), and teach students to live in a multicultural democracy (Furman, 2002). In addition, teachers in schools with high communal engagement report increased enthusiasm and devotion (Bryk et al., 1993), as well as higher levels of participation, collegiality, collaboration, student-teacher relationships, social comfort across departments (Oxley, 1997), morale, and satisfaction (Bryk & Driscoll, 1988). Professional development has been found to be more effective in contexts where collegiality is the norm (Little, 1982); teacher commitment, retention, effectiveness, and development are higher when teachers feel supported by administrators (Rosenholtz & Simpson, 1990) and colleagues (Papay & Kraft, 2017; Ronfeldt, 2017); change efforts are more successful when they are supported by relational trust (Bryk & Schneider, 2002); and student achievement increases when teacher social capital (Leana & Pil, 2017) and a sense of collective teacher efficacy (Eells, 2011) is developed.

The cultural context of Jewish day schools makes them particularly apt for such a design. A deeply rooted notion of Jewish community emphasizes the responsibility of individual members to attend to the goals of the collective (Roth, 1977). This has yielded a plethora of Jewish communities that can be described as strong in that they are both "value communities" and "functional communities" and a source of social capital for their members (Coleman, 1988; Coleman & Hoffer, 1987). They are value communities in that individuals share value consistency even if they are not brought together by the structures of the community, and they are functional communities in that the close-knit relationship among community members reaches across generations to create, reinforce, and perpetuate social norms and sanctions. Within the North American context, a sophisticated network of institutions creates the potential for individuals to interact with one another within multiple Jewish settings, including synagogues, youth groups, summer camps, and community centers. Jewish day schools are often integral parts of these networks (Pomson, 2009).

The impact of this phenomenon is apparent in the emphasis on Jewish values and Jewish continuity among day school stakeholders (Ackerman, 1969; Bieler, 2001; Cohen, 1974; Geffen, 2005; Goldman, 2003; Kaplowitz, 2002; Roth, 1977). The expectation that schools supplement their academic focus with social education is not unique to the Jewish community, but the extent to which broader communal and social goals have taken hold in Jewish day schools (Pomson, 2009) is remarkable, in contrast to the contemporary emphasis in public schools on student academic achievement. Jewish day schools are seen as much more than sites of academic study; rather, schools are expected to enculturate students into Jewish society, preserve Jewish values, and foster strong Jewish identities (Aron, 1992; Cohen, 2007; Dashefsky & Lebson, 2002; Fox et al., 2003; Himmelfarb, 1984; Phillips, 2000).

In many cases, Jewish day schools seeking to strengthen communal ties among stakeholders benefit from the increased level of student homogeneity and interconnection that frequently characterizes Jewish day schools relative to nonsectarian counterparts as a result of voluntary enrollment, normative social standards, and association with a broader Jewish society that elevates communal affiliation and action. Parents, particularly in Orthodox day schools, choose day schools for their children because they want to maintain their family's commitment to Judaism (Cohen & Kelner, 2007), and they are likely to choose day schools because of a comfort level with the traditions, norms, and values of the particular school (Cohen, 1999). Many teachers, even some who do not teach Judaic subjects, cite Jewish character as a reason why they work in day schools (Feiman-Nemser et al., 2014; Pomson, 2000). Furthermore, Jewish day schools often have structures that are associated with collegiality and strong professional teacher communities. They are generally not constrained by the same government regulations as public schools, are often small (Schick, 2014), and have teaching arrangements that require some level of collegiality or collaboration (Pomson, 2005).

Addressing Diversity in Jewish Day Schools

Previous research provides limited direction for organizing schools around the concept of community. Many schools are fraught with microcommunities within departments (Siskin, 1994), balkanization between communities (Hargreaves, 1994), and the formation of informal groupings (Datnow, 1998) that impinge on a broader sense of school-wide community. Critics describe the notion of community as being at odds with contemporary society. They claim that its actualization excludes those who do not espouse the community's shared goal, idea, or commitment and raises the possibility of discrimination, intolerance, and uniformity within our schools (Achinstein, 2002; Feinberg, 2006; Furman, 1998; Furman & Starratt, 2002; Hargreaves, 1994; Lima, 2001; Noddings, 1996; Shields & Seltzer, 1997).

Day schools are not immune to these challenges. Even with the homogeneous tendencies cited previously, Jewish day schools retain elements of diversity. First, an increasing number of "community day schools" or transdenominational Jewish day schools have opened across the country in recent years (Schick, 2014). These schools are built on the principles of pluralism (Kay, 2009); though stakeholders within these schools share a commitment to pluralism and, often, a common Jewish heritage, they often vary in their religious practice, religious values, and synagogue affiliation.

Even day schools that cater to a particular Jewish denomination most likely do not have a completely homogeneous school community. Just as Lesko (1988) and Shields and Seltzer (1997) discovered in their respective studies on Catholic schools and highly ethnic schools, seemingly homogeneous schools are generally more diverse than they appear to be. Demographics suggest that the faculty in all schools may be more diverse than the student body and thus more likely to struggle with the normative nature of community. Teachers are less likely than parents to choose a school because they are drawn to its traditions, norms, and values (Pomson, 2009). The demographics of teachers in Jewish day schools suggest that there is diversity among the faculty and that a number of teachers in Jewish day schools are not directly affiliated with the religious community that they serve (JESNA, 2008; Schick, 2014). The mandate of Jewish day schools to teach both general and Judaic studies makes it particularly common for there to be religious and cultural differences among their faculty members (Goldberg et al., 2009). These cultural and religious differences can lead to variation in the teachers' philosophies, opinions, and objectives that may put teachers at odds with the school's normative values (Goldberg et al., 2009), educational work (Muszkat-Barkan & Shkedi, 2009), and teacher community (Dashevsky & Ta'ir, 2009) and increases the potential for microcommunities (Siskin, 1994). Researchers also found a range of precollegiate Jewish education among Judaic studies teachers (Gamoran et al., 1998).

The broad spectrum of teachers who work at Jewish day schools can detract from communal connections by putting some teachers at odds with the school's religious, educational, or ideological positions. School leaders must address this variability to actualize community as an organizing concept for Jewish day schools and require additional guidance to design schools around the concept of community so as to engage the full spectrum of stakeholders.

To address this dynamic, I draw upon the reflections of a diverse group of teachers from Tehila Yeshiva,[1] a small, Centrist-Orthodox Jewish day school (as categorized by Schick, 2014) in the New York City metropolitan area. I selected ten teachers to represent the variation across as many dynamics within the professional network as possible, including gender, religious affiliation, teaching assignment, and professional experience (see table 12.1). I conducted in-depth interviews and observations and reviewed documents to gather data on the teachers' experiences of community in school and at home. In addition, each participant was asked to create two visualizations (Ingall, 2006) to illustrate what community looks like from his or her perspective. My analysis explores the similarities and differences in the ways these teachers talk about their experiences of community in order to provide a better understanding of what community means to

Jewish day school teachers, how community is realized in educational institutions, and how community can be conceptualized to further support Jewish day school educators.

Five Dimensions of Community

The experiences, stories, and depictions of Tehila Yeshiva teachers point to five dimensions of community that potentially serve as entry points for Jewish day school teachers: geographic, occupational, interpersonal, inspired, and resonant. Each dimension of community highlighted in teacher interviews sheds light on a different connection that bonds people to their institutions and to one another. The teachers' descriptions help explain how community is simultaneously *Gemeinschaft* and *Gesellschaft* (Tonnies, 1887/2002), solidified (Durkheim, 1893/1984), and networked (Kadushin, 2012; Rainie & Wellman, 2012; Simmel, 1922/1955), concrete and abstract (James, 1992), symbolic (Cohen, 1985), and even imagined (Anderson, 1983/2006). Together, these dimensions encompass the variety

TABLE 12.1. *Participant Table*

	Gender	Jewish	Orthodox?	Years @ Tehila	Boys/ Girls	Lower/Middle School	GS/JS/JH*
Mr. Hirsch	M	Yes	Yes	1	B/G	MS	JH
Ms. Coin	F	No	No	4	G	5th grade	GS/Other
Ms. Greene	F	Yes	No	~20	B/G	LS	GS
Mr. Glazer	M	Yes	No	~6	B	5th grade	GS/Other
Mr. Murphy	M	Yes	No	1	B	LS	GS
Rabbi Eisenmann	M	Yes	Yes	5	B	5th grade	JS
Rabbi Gold	M	Yes	Yes	~15	B	LS	JS
Ms. Laden	F	No	No	1	B/G	MS	GS
Morah Perl	F	Yes	Yes	~6	B/G	MS	JS/JH
Morah Rubin	F	Yes	Yes	~6	G	5th grade	JS

*GS refers to general studies, JS refers to Judaic studies, and JH refers to teachers on the general studies faculty but who also teach about Jewish history in social studies. Those who are marked as "other" spend part of the day working in the office, gym, or guidance departments.

of ways in which teachers are drawn into adult relationships within schools and provide a starting point for developing schools as multidimensional communities.

Geographic Community

Geographic community arises through attachment to shared space. It is the most concrete manifestation of community, in that it is defined by its topographical and physical properties and is affected by spatial characteristics such as size, density, and land use. This dimension highlights the role of location, distance, landscapes, public space, and physical boundaries in facilitating connections among people and institutions. From this perspective, community is tangible; it has a shape that is largely preestablished without input from those who exist within it; and it is experienced primarily in the here and now. For many, the *a priori* nature of geographic community creates an almost automatic connection for people within them that resembles a traditional *Gemeinschaft* (Tonnies, 1887/2002).

In line with examples from elsewhere in the literature, the physical and spatial character of Tehila helps shape how its teachers experience community (Datnow, 1998; Hargreaves, 1993; Siskin, 1994). The concrete and thus recognizable nature of these spaces may contribute to the prominence of geographic proximity in portrayals of community. Among Tehila teachers, geographic community is the most widely discussed dimension of community. Of the nine teachers who created illustrations of their communities, seven depicted specific physical locations.

Geography affects the school's relationship to the neighborhood that surrounds it and the relationships within the school. While the external geography shapes school policies and demographics, the school building itself takes on the role of a geographic community for teachers, students, and others who spend the majority of their time within its classrooms and offices. Teachers who live outside the local neighborhood primarily consider Tehila Yeshiva to be a "different" or "separate" geographic community from where they live. They describe the Tehila community as being bound by the gate that surrounds the parking lot and comprised of all teachers, students, administrators, parents, and others who spend time in the school.

Within the school's geographic community, teachers note strong connections to individuals with whom they interact regularly. They highlight school size, physical placement of classrooms and communal spaces, and scheduling as influential in developing proximity of time and space. In comparing Tehila to other schools, teachers associate its smallness with a stronger sense of community. Even so, most teachers note that they only interact with a small number of colleagues on a regular basis and, therefore, feel more strongly connected to particular colleagues. Interactions among teachers often take place as they pass one another in the hall or within classrooms, and are, therefore, limited to groups who frequent the same halls, classrooms, offices, meeting spaces, teacher lounges, and copy rooms. Tehila's layout is limiting in this regard because the building is divided among three floors by grade level, and each floor is further divided into a boys' wing and a girls' wing, separated by doors that are closed during school hours.

Proximity of time plays a significant role in the extent to which teachers connect with one another. This is particularly true at Tehila because most teachers work on a part-time basis. In almost all cases, Judaic studies teachers work in the morning and general studies teachers work in the afternoon, making cross-disciplinary interactions extremely difficult.

This is exacerbated by the fact that many teachers have second jobs or outside responsibilities that require that they spend minimal time in the school beyond their teaching hours. The teaching schedule itself provides few breaks and limited time for interactions, particularly among Judaic and lower school teachers. Ms. Laden, a middle school general studies teacher, identifies the importance of shared time and space when explaining her close relationship with other non-Orthodox middle school teachers: "And do we talk to each other as much as I might talk to somebody else who is completely Orthodox? . . . I think it just is much more a situation of if you're just sitting in the teachers' lounge during given times."

Occupational Community

Occupational community is a connection among people who share specialized purposes. These purposes range from task-specific, procedural objectives to long-term, big-picture visions. The instrumental nature of occupational community resembles a *Gesellschaft* (Tonnies, 1887/2002) in its emphasis on voluntary, functional, rational, and strategic relationships and yields an organic solidarity (Durkheim, 1893/1984) that develops when interdependence necessitates that individuals work together.

The work of occupational community is to advance the goal that unites them, either through shared practice or parallel efforts. From this perspective, community is functional; it is task-oriented; and it is frequently shaped by organizational structure and microcommunities (Siskin, 1994). In schools, it is enacted through formal and informal communities of practice (Lave & Wenger, 1991), collegial relationships, and contractual obligations. Focusing on the work-oriented associations that comprise occupational communities builds upon a well-developed literature on teacher communities and communities of practice in schools that touches on various ways that schools build collaboration, collegiality, and community with an overarching aim of improved student outcomes (Lave & Wenger, 1991; Little & McLaughlin, 1993; Louis et al., 1996; McLaughlin & Talbert, 2001; McLaughlin & Talbert, 2006; Rosenholtz, 1991; Talbert & McLaughlin, 1994).

Occupational community primarily develops around and within professional enterprises. School administrators initiate the formation of occupational community within schools through their hiring processes and contractual obligations. While some organizations prefer to hire staff members who share ideologies, past experiences, and outlook, many bring together individuals who have little else in common outside their work-related tasks and goals. This is the case in Tehila, where staff members are of different stages of life, religious affiliations, educational backgrounds, and prior work experiences.

Occupational community within Jewish day schools is largely self-contained. All staff members work toward an organization-wide purpose of educating students. In contrast to public schools that are supervised by district and state officials, Jewish day schools operate under the auspices of their own boards to create policies that directly reflect stakeholders' interests. When done effectively, this results in a sense of collegiality that comes from shared purpose. Almost all Tehila teachers experience this collegiality in the working relationships they have with all administrators, faculty, and support staff. As Rabbi Gold, a lower school Judaic studies teacher, explains, "We're in the same school; we work as a team. The school works as a team."

The depth of these collegial connections is limited by the instrumental nature of the group's shared purpose. Mr. Hirsch, a middle school Jewish history teacher, identifies this dynamic in the Tehila occupational community when reflecting on the meaning of the word colleague. He clarifies, "If we go to a staff meeting, I would consider all those people my colleagues, but I clearly have different relationships with each person in the building."

Often occupational community is a conglomeration of communities of practice (Lave & Wenger, 1991) and microcommunities (Siskin, 1994) that share a more specialized purpose than the broader community. These groups may splinter based on structural and organizational dividing lines. For example, Rabbi Eisenmann, a fifth-grade Judaic studies teacher, describes his department as having its own goals: "As a group of *rabbeim* (rabbis) . . . everybody thought the goals are common goals, and the goals are basically to instill a love of learning, and a love of *Yiddishkeit* (Judaism)."

At other times, professionals build relationships around shared approaches to work, regardless of departmental affiliations or formal structuring patterns. The most frequently noted microcommunity at Tehila developed primarily without formal school support after Mr. Glazer, a fifth-grade general studies teacher, implemented a team-based approach to classroom management where students sat in squads with appointed captains and all classroom activity was done collaboratively and scored in an ongoing competition. Mr. Glazer became an informal mentor to several teachers over his tenure, including seven of the ten study participants, as they observed, tried, and adapted this method. "The Mr. Glazer System," as Rabbi Eisenmann refers to it, has been implemented by both new and veteran teachers, in girls' classes and boys' classes, in Judaic studies and general studies, and in lower and middle school grades.

Interpersonal Community

Interpersonal community is the chain of relationships linked by shared connections across dyads. It is shaped by its membership and their actions rather than physical boundaries or institutional norms. This dimension emphasizes the importance of mutual associations, friendship, responsibility, and acts of care as tools for bringing people together (Noddings, 1988). From this perspective, community is about relationship, it is primarily interactive, it varies in intensity across a school, and it builds in intensity over time so that even the most utilitarian associations can become friendships (Little, 1993). In contrast to previously discussed dimensions of community, it is created and sustained by its participants rather than by its physical and institutional structures. Collectives of this sort provide a sense of comfort and support but, due to the unpredictability of human relationships, often require ongoing maintenance to ensure stability. While some interpersonal communities are marked by social solidarity that bonds their membership into cohesive groups (Durkheim, 1893/1984) resembling a traditional *Gemeinschaft* community (Tonnies, 1887/2002), others link individuals and groups into larger social networks that connect multiple groups and individuals (Kadushin, 2012; Rainie & Wellman, 2012; Simmel, 1922/1955).

The social relationships at the heart of interpersonal community are a fundamental aspect of school life (Bryk & Schneider, 2002; Noddings, 1988; Waller, 1932/2014) and go beyond the work-oriented connections within an occupational community. Several teachers talk about the "camaraderie" that exists among the teachers at Tehila Yeshiva. Morah Rubin, a fifth-grade Judaic studies teacher, observes the camaraderie in the chatter before staff meetings begin; Rabbi Eisenmann identifies the camaraderie among the *rabbeim*, who share personal stories at recess, tell personal jokes, and partake in family celebrations; and Mr. Glazer uses the same word to describe his relationship with the other men on the general studies faculty.

These social relationships are marked by a sense of mutual responsibility. When asked why community is important, Rabbi Gold associates being part of a community with fulfilling a duty, because "we're responsible for one another, you know? You can live in . . . an apartment building with hundreds of other people and you have no connection to them. But a community, you feel *ahrayus* [responsibility] for each person, you know?" Examples of this from within the school include Morah Rubin's willingness to help her general studies counterpart, Ms. Coin, when scheduling conflicts arise, an assertion made by Mr. Murphy, a lower school general studies teacher, that he and his close group of five colleagues "look out for one another," and Ms. Laden's ongoing "soup dates" with her mentor. Morah Perl, who teaches both middle school Judaic studies and Jewish history, gives the most concrete example of this phenomenon in describing a faculty-wide gift-giving initiative. While many teachers reserve gifts for close colleagues, Morah Perl speaks fondly of one individual who is driven by the communal connection to "always, always give" even though he has never received a gift from the initiative and barely interacts with most recipients.

Mutual responsibility often develops into deeper ties of friendship and care among small groups of colleagues. Ms. Greene, a longtime lower school general studies teacher, is one of several who describe professional bonds that develop among teachers as seeds of friendship. She fondly reminisces about afternoon mah-jongg games played with colleagues, a weekly practice that continued for several years. Mr. Hirsch explains that "what starts off as a professional relationship" can develop into a "personal relationship" as colleagues spend more time together. This, in turn, changes the nature of the professional relationship because "the nature of what you can say to somebody changes because the scope of what you're talking about, and also what's more acceptable in the way they look at you, changes for most people."

Inspired Community

Inspired community is a connection based on shared values, principles, standards, beliefs, and other sources of motivation and direction. These ideas are useful starting points for envisioning Jewish educational pursuits (Fox et al., 2003) because they inspire a collective by providing a sense of meaning, guiding behavior, and creating a "*Gemeinschaft* of mind" (Tonnies 1887/2002, p. 42). Being driven by shared convictions leads community members down related, though not necessarily identical, paths, and may lend toward tangible shared action. From this perspective, community is about shared starting points. It is abstract, almost spiritual, and it builds upon motivations and growth with less focus on a specific outcome.

Inspired community is similar to occupational community in that both are connected by shared motivations. However, the nature and role of the shared motivations differentiate these dimensions from each other. The goals that shape occupational community are based on an anticipated end result, and community members unite in pursuit of the end result that they mutually desire. In contrast, inspired community is based on a shared starting point: a conviction, perspective, or value that provides shared inspiration to community members.

While both geographic and occupational community are primarily bound by preset structures, the boundaries that shape inspired community can be animated from within the institution. When cultivated within an existing collective, they foster a unifying sense of spirit and significance that entwines with school culture. As such, inspired community materializes in schools through both values, principles, and expectations that are said and those that are left unsaid. Charters, mission statements, standards, curriculum, subject matter, teaching schedules, and written policies provide a snapshot of the stated values and expectations that formally connect the school community; the sights and sounds of a school's halls, offices, and classrooms provide evidence of unstated values enmeshed in school culture; and actions taken by community members to bring these ideas to life demonstrate the extent to which various inspirations are truly shared within a community.

Shared values, principles, standards, and beliefs can define a collective in much the same way that a professional contract defines the goals and responsibilities of an institution's workers and a map defines the physical parameters of a neighborhood. Ms. Laden refers to values that function in this way as a "page" to which all community members have been directed by rules, standards, and normative expectations. As she describes, "At Tehila, there's a whole set of shared values that you don't get elsewhere. And I'm not saying that you don't have values other places, but it's just that here everybody is on the same page."

Beyond Ms. Laden's "page," many collectives are bound by shared values that are unwritten and ambiguous. Mr. Hirsch identifies various "senses" that might serve as "centerpieces" for the school and identifies these as the "heart" of the school. Like the heart, the school's values ideally work internally to give life to a preexisting form. By establishing normative behavior for the community, these informal inspirations provide further definition for the collective. Rabbi Gold describes shared beliefs about appropriate dress and related observances as "social standards." While "there's no rule" that states these standards as community boundaries, it is generally known within and around the school that it is "socially uncomfortable" for families who do not fit within these standards.

Like other matters of the heart, values, principles, standards, and beliefs that shape inspired community can be elusive and decentralized. They become embedded into a collective's culture, but their abstractness can make them hard to identify, define, or measure in any concrete way. As a result, community members vary in their connectedness depending on the values they espouse and the roles they play in actualizing those values. As a teacher, Mr. Hirsch finds it difficult to pinpoint a unifying value system among the professionals at Tehila Yeshiva. While all teachers and administrators are brought together by their physical proximity, professional purpose, and the charter values that they have accepted as affiliates of the school, he does not see them as being inherently linked by one value system. For Mr. Hirsch, being on the "same page" as established by the school's charter and mission is only a starting point for developing inspired connections. He would like to see something more.

Resonant Community

Resonant community is a connection based on how people see themselves relative to others. It unites some collectives around abstract beliefs while dividing others into outsiders and insiders. Resonant community sometimes consists of strangers who share an affiliation or identification with a larger cause but have never interacted in a common time, space, or relationship. From this perspective, community is subjective and symbolic (Cohen, 1985); it does not require tangible interaction or connection (Anderson, 1983/2006; Kanno & Norton, 2003; Wenger, 1998); it is the remnant or abstraction of real connections that resonate with individuals across time and place (James, 1992).

Resonant community forms as individuals build connections around intersecting aspects of their senses of self. Mr. Hirsch associates with places that were significant during his childhood, Mr. Glazer associates with compatriots thousands of miles away because they are part of his country, and Mr. Murphy associates with Tehila students based on a shared religious identity, even before he has met them. In each of these cases, participants form connections with strangers based on perceived commonalities rather than face-to-face interaction.

The self-defined nature of resonant community has several effects on their structure and composition. It yields boundaries that are less recognizable and more pervious than those of other dimensions of community, it yields memberships that are diffuse and, at times, lacking in internal cohesiveness, and it generates community formation around points of connection that are of particular salience to members. The demarcations across resonant community are often unspoken, unspecified, or even unknown on any conscious level. Even those who co-associate within a resonant community are not always entirely in agreement as to who belongs in the collective and who does not, or how to relate to some who share their mutual affiliations.

Resonant community exists at varying levels of abstraction and imagination. It is possible for some individuals to experience affiliation in a very tangible and concrete way, while other individuals experience the same affiliation as symbolic. For example, some Tehila teachers describe their connections to Jewish people and institutions beyond the school as based in real, ongoing interactions; others talk about their connections, or lack of connections, with Jewish people and institutions as existing only on a conceptual level, without concrete manifestations. While the former participate in inspired and interpersonal aspects of Jewish peoplehood, the latter are connected to Jewish life only as resonant community.

While resonant community can be seen as imagined because it lacks cohesion or clear, objective boundaries, the influence that it has on affiliates has real and tangible consequences. Once individuals associate with a resonant community, this affiliation guides future actions. Often these judgments are the result of subjective responses to various cultural markers, including language, behavior, and appearance. Morah Perl describes this tendency to judge outsiders based on cultural differences as a "barrier." She explains: "In this world or in this school or in this community, those types of things, those silly religious-looking or -acting things, are somehow a demarcation." These barriers provide shape to resonant community.

Within schools, resonant community shapes both climate and learning content. The pictures of famous rabbinic role models that Morah Perl displays, the Jewish melodies that Rabbi Eisenmann sings during class transitions, and the Jewish psychologists that Ms. Laden identifies during class discussion reflect a resonant attachment to Jewish peoplehood. Incorporation of the Pledge of Allegiance into morning routines, celebration of national holidays, and lessons on American heroes reflect a resonant attachment to national identity. Creating illustrated stories to send to Africa, using Olympic teams to decide class groupings, and encouraging students to care for earthquake victims in other countries reflect a resonant connection to worldwide community.

Resonant community can play a particularly important role within parochial schools, in which a significant percentage of stakeholders identify with the same religion. A parochial school's affiliation with a dominant religious peoplehood can create a dynamic where those who do not share that affiliation feel like outsiders to the dominant resonant community. Mr. Murphy describes his discomfort with the thought of teaching at a Catholic school, given his Jewish affiliation. He explains, "When searching for a job, I was applying to the archdiocese and one of the things that I was nervous about was going in being a Jew. That to me would be weird." In contrast, he assumed that his mutual affiliation with Jewish peoplehood would make Tehila a more comfortable place for him to work: "So it's—even for me being a Reformed [*sic*] Jew in an Orthodox setting it's a little uncomfortable but at least . . . I am a Jew, so I feel like there is a bond."

Intersection Across Dimensions

Each of the five dimensions of community can be described on its own terms but intersect within collectives. This intersection seems to happen at a distinctively high rate within a day school setting, as Mr. Hirsch illustrates with a comparison of his childhood experience in public school to his students' day school experience. While physical proximity created a geographic connection between Mr. Hirsch and his childhood neighbors, the lack of shared goals and values leads Mr. Hirsch to conclude that, in comparison to Tehila students, "there's no sense of community where I grew up, really." The intersection between inspired and geographic community that Mr. Hirsch identifies at Tehila is further enhanced by crossover with resonant and interpersonal community. As Ms. Laden describes: "They go to the same summer camps . . . they don't have the different religions that take them to different places on the weekends . . . They'll do Shabbat with each other. So they're really connected religion-wise . . . And that's the basis of their ethics, morality, values. They're connected in that way, much more so than a regular public or private school." Ms. Coin describes this multidimensional experience of community as all-encompassing: "You start young, and you're all living together; it's not just a small part of your life; it is your life." As a result, "You can just see that everybody's connected, and that everybody is in it together, and you can kind of feel the love that everybody has for each other."

TABLE 12.2. *Five Dimensions of Community as Experienced by Teachers**

	Mr. M.	Mr. G.	Ms. L.	Mr. H.	Ms. C.	Ms. G.	Rabbi E.	Rabbi G.	Morah R.	Morah P.
G (I)	1	2	2	2	3	2	1	2	2	3
G (E)	1	1	1	1	1	1	2	3	3	3
O	2	3	2	2	2	2	2	2	2	2
Inter	2	2	2	2	3	2	3	2	2	3
Insp	1	1	2	2	1	2	3	3	3	3
R	2	1	1	2	1	2	3	3	3	3
Total	9	10	10	11	11	11	14	15	15	17

*G (I): Internal Geographic Community; G (E): External Geographic Community; O: Occupational Community; Inter: Interpersonal Community; Insp: Inspired Community; R: Resonant Community

Experiencing Multidimensional Community in Schools

As shown in table 12.2, each Tehila teacher shares an experience of community that is multifaceted, nuanced, and inclusive of all five dimensions described in this study, though the dimensions present themselves to varying extents in each participant's story. Some teachers' experiences of community are consistent across all five dimensions. Morah Perl, Ms. Greene, and Mr. Murphy stand out as having particularly consistent experiences of community.

Morah Perl has a consistently high experience of community, Ms. Greene has a consistently midlevel experience of community, and Mr. Murphy has a consistently low experience of community. In contrast, other teachers' experiences vary from low to high depending on the dimension of community in question. Ms. Coin and Mr. Glazer stand out as having particularly inconsistent experiences of community across the dimensions. While Mr. Glazer describes himself as largely isolated from resonant and inspired community at Tehila, he has become a leader in the school's occupational community by mentoring teachers in classroom management. Similarly, Ms. Coin has almost no connection to Tehila's resonant, inspired, and external geographic community but has significant presence in the school's internal geographic community and has developed close friendships with a variety of school stakeholders.

The multidimensional nature of community can limit the influence of religious and cultural affiliation on teachers' social experiences, even within the relatively closed, homogeneous setting of an Orthodox day school, so that alignment and misalignment with the school's religious and cultural milieu do not determine acceptance within a school community. Teachers who are outsiders in one dimension of community can be insiders in others and retain social mobility within the school community by balancing low cultural or social capital in one dimension of community with higher cultural or social capital in another dimension. For example, Ms. Coin came to the school without a Jewish background, little knowledge of Jewish values, culture, or history, and no significant connection to Jewish life. Given her lack of social and cultural capital, one would expect that her sense of community at school would be particularly weak. However, Ms. Coin has offset her diminished capital in those areas by increasing her presence in the school's occupational and geographic communities. She expanded the number of roles she plays at school and spends more time in varied locations within the school, putting herself in closer physical and temporal proximity to a wider range of colleagues. She has also developed friendships with colleagues that extend beyond the school through shopping trips and shared life cycle events. As a result, her experience of community is on par with others who came to the school with significantly more social and cultural capital.

Teachers who are engaged by multiple dimensions of the school community describe deeper communal experiences than those who do not. This may explain why Mr. Hirsch's experiences of community at Tehila are significantly weaker than those of other Orthodox teachers, even though he generally identifies with his colleagues' inspired and resonant communities. The other Orthodox teachers benefit from interaction among all five dimensions of community: physical proximity, job responsibilities, social opportunities, values, and cultural identity. Mr. Hirsch does not. He is the only Orthodox teacher without prior connections to Tehila's local community or constant proximity to students and families. The other Orthodox teachers also benefit from being part of the strong Judaic studies department that draws them further into the school's interpersonal and inspired communities and enables them to connect over shared work, shared locations, and shared schedules. Their bonds are so strong that they describe themselves as a family. Rabbi Eisenmann explains, "Amongst the *rabbeim* . . . we have a good friendship . . . both inside and outside school. Rabbi Yankel . . . was commenting at my *chasana* (wedding). He said, 'I feel like this is just one of the family.'" As a general studies teacher, Mr. Hirsch does not benefit from multidimensional community to the same degree and does not share the *rabbeim*'s deep collegial connections.

While data suggest a lack of consensus regarding the value, prominence, or influence of any particular dimension, some dimensions are easier to engage with than others. Teachers access geographic and occupational community through employment and require only an interest and introduction to access the school's interpersonal community. Beyond that, factors such as personality, prior experience, perspective, and tenure can shift the balance between being a community insider and being a community outsider. As a result, professionals who find themselves at odds with some aspects of school life can integrate into the school community via another dimension. For example, when told that her interactions with male teachers were incongruous with school norms, Ms. Laden was able to distance herself from the school's inspired community without feeling distanced from its interpersonal or occupational communities. Similarly, Ms. Greene accepts Tehila's increasingly strict dress code as part of the requirements of her occupational community, even though it is at odds with her personal values, and Ms. Coin views the unique rituals, rules, and customs that she has encountered at Tehila as "an anthropologist" in order to engage in the school community despite being uninvolved in its inspired and resonant dimensions.

The inspired and resonant dimensions of community pose larger barriers for those whose backgrounds, value systems, and cultural affiliations and markers are not aligned with those that are prevalent in the school. As table 12.2 shows, there is a dichotomy between the experiences of teachers with prior connections to Orthodox Jewish values and traditions and the experiences of the teachers who lack those connections. Those who enter the Tehila community with connections to its Jewish heritage, values, and doctrine are likely to feel more immediately at home, and teachers with connections to the school's local geographic community, where most of the school's families live, benefit further. In some cases, school norms are so elusive that even teachers who have been accepted into some aspects of school life cannot break the boundaries the norms create. Mr. Hirsch suggests that those who entered Tehila as outsiders "can't give themselves completely because they don't fit in completely." Ms. Coin notes that cultural differences create challenges. In describing her motivation to succeed, she acknowledges that "I can only do so much, since I don't know... Hebrew and that kind of thing, so I can't be active in certain areas." Yet, she continues to sidestep many boundaries to find a comfortable place for herself at Tehila.

With rare exceptions, Tehila teachers who appear left out of the school's inspired and resonant communities have developed strong connections within the school based on shared space, shared professional goals, and/or shared friendships. Comparing the experiences of Mr. Glazer and Morah Perl provides an example of this phenomenon. As depicted in table 12.2, Mr. Glazer's total experience of community at Tehila is weak, while

Morah Perl's total experience of community at Tehila is high. Morah Perl's Orthodox background, prior experiences in Jewish day schools, and affiliation with the local Jewish community put her in closer alignment with more colleagues than do Mr. Glazer's non-Orthodox background, prior experiences in public school, and current identification as "just Jewish." They have both developed connections with the teachers in their physical proximity, with colleagues who have become friends, and with others in the school who share their personal identifications. While Morah Perl's cultural and social capital allow her to play a more central role in the lives of students and teachers as part of their inspired community, Mr. Glazer has strong occupational connections within the school and stands out among his colleagues as the only teacher to seek a mentor role within the school community.

Multidimensional Community and School Design

Developing a framework that conceptualizes community as multidimensional adds nuance to our understanding of schools as communities (Sergiovanni, 1993, 1994). By identifying multiple entry points into school community, the framework highlighted here provides practical insight into how to design schools so as to maximize opportunities for teachers to form connections that will benefit the school and the students and is of particular usefulness to Jewish day schools that support diverse teacher populations within environments grounded in religious tradition and culture. Each dimension of school community provides school leaders with a different lens through which to align school character with goals, induct new teachers more successfully, and examine school procedures and structures.

Geographic Community

Looking at schools through the lens of geographic community guides educators to consider how the physical structure and placement of the school encourage or inhibit teacher connections: How does the school's size and layout influence connections among teachers? Does the schedule allow for teacher interactions within a shared space, particularly among part-time staff? Do public spaces exist for meeting and congregating? How are spaces divided? Which classrooms, halls, offices, and meeting rooms are placed in close proximity to one another? Who crosses paths with whom over the course of a day? Do the decor and furnishings encourage interaction and relationship-building by providing welcoming places to sit and talk?

Occupational Community

Looking at schools through the lens of occupational community guides educators to consider how the objectives and organizational structure of the school encourage and inhibit teacher connections. Are the school's goals widely shared among teachers and other stakeholders, including new members? How do they inspire or inhibit a sense of cohesiveness across departments, roles, and positions? How are staff programming, professional learning opportunities, meetings, and school celebrations used to encourage teachers to connect as a community of practice beyond their departments and roles? What interferes with the teachers' cohesiveness?

Interpersonal Community

Looking at schools through the lens of interpersonal community guides educators to consider how the social and relational dynamics of a school strengthen and weaken teacher connections. Does the school provide substantial opportunities for interactions among teachers? How can the school foster social connections and encourage teachers to care for, trust, and support one another? What social divisions stand in the way of community development and how can they be mitigated? Who are the leaders within the school's social networks and how can they help strengthen community?

Inspired Community

Looking at schools through the lens of inspired community guides educators to consider how values, principles, standards, and beliefs shape relationships within their schools. What are the driving inspirations among school leaders? Where do they come from and why are they important? How do they materialize within the policies and culture of the school? How are these inspirations used to draw teachers and other stakeholders to the school and motivate teachers and other stakeholders within the school? What does the school do to connect with teachers and other stakeholders who do not share the driving values, principles, standards, and beliefs of school leaders?

Resonant Community

Looking at schools through the lens of resonant community guides educators to consider how the fusion of identity groups within the school fosters or prevents a sense of communal connection. What identifications are prevalent among school leaders, teachers, families, and other stakeholders? To what extent do school stakeholders identify with a shared identity group? What initiatives are in place to foster a cohesive identity group among stakeholders and what impedes this effort? What cultural markers define groups within the school and how can they be explained to and traversed by outsiders to the prevalent identity group? To what extent do prevalent identifications meld well together? To what extent do they clash with one another? How are teachers being taught to better understand those who affiliate with different identity groups? What programs are in place to support stakeholders who are uncomfortable with prevailing identity groups? What programs are in place to foster a sense of openness and comfort across identity groups?

Multidimensional Community at Work in Jewish Day Schools

Jewish day schools are potential sources of communal connection for teachers, students, administrators, board members, and families. They serve as places of physical congregation; provide space for shared ideas, goals, and actions; foster relationships among people; and preserve age-old values, traditions, and identifications. School design that considers the multidimensional nature of community helps ensure that school professionals find their place within the school, deepen their connections to the school over time, benefit from the positive and collaborative social context, and develop as effective educators.

Bringing the multidimensional nature of community to the attention of teachers encourages individual educators to reassess and reimagine their roles in the school and teacher communities so as to encourage those connections. It is empowering for teachers who perceive themselves as outsiders in certain dimensions of community to appreciate their contributions in other dimensions of community. Simultaneously, it is eye-opening for teachers who perceive themselves to be insiders in dominant dimensions of community to understand the breadth and depth of the collective of which they are a part so that they welcome the contributions and leadership of all colleagues.

Capitalizing on the intersection among communal dimensions that often exists at Jewish day schools can facilitate distinctively deep, multifaceted connections among stakeholders while further cultivating the sense of commonality, collegiality, and connectedness that has been shown to foster both academic and nonacademic learning in schools. Understanding and intentionality within the cultivation process can mitigate situations in which the benefits of communal connections are outweighed by the detriments of narrow-mindedness, uniformity, and the potential for division between "outsiders" and "insiders." The five dimensions of community highlighted in this study provide a solid foundation for shaping day schools that bring stakeholders together for the benefit of students, teachers, and communities.

NOTES

1. All names are pseudonyms. General studies teachers are referred to with the titles Ms. or Mr.; Judaic studies teachers are referred to with the titles *Morah* (teacher) or Rabbi.

REFERENCES

Achinstein, B. (2002). Conflict amid community: The micropolitics of teacher collaboration.

Teachers College Record, *104*(3), 421–455.

Ackerman, W. I. (1969). Jewish education—For what? In M. Wallach (ed.), *American Jewish Year Book* (pp. 3–36). Jewish Chronicle Publications.

American Institute for Research. (2015). *Jewish educational leadership in day schools*. Unpublished raw data.

Anderson, B. (1983/2006). *Imagined communities: Reflections on the origin and spread of nationalism*. Verso.

Aron, I. (1992). The teacher's role in curriculum reform. *Studies in Jewish Education*, *6*, 155–173.

Battistich, V., Solomon, D., Kim, D., Watson, M., & Schapps, E. (1995). Schools as communities, poverty levels of student populations, and students' attitudes, motives, and performances: A multilevel analysis. *American Educational Research Journal*, 32(3), 627–658.

Bieler, J. (2001). Cornerstone for a vision for Jewish day school education. *Journal of Jewish Education*, *67*(3), 36–38.

Bryk, A. S, & Driscoll, M. E. (1988). *The high school as community: Contextual influences and consequences for teachers and students*. National Center on Effective Secondary Schools.

Bryk., A. S., Lee, V. E., & Holland, P. B. (1993). *Catholic schools and the common good.* Harvard University Press.

Bryk, A. S., & Schneider, B. (2002). *Trust in schools: A core resource for improvement.* Russell Sage Foundation.

Cohen, A. P. (1985). *The symbolic construction of community*. Routledge.

Cohen, S. M. (1974). The impact of Jewish education on religious identification and practice. *Jewish Social Studies*, *36*, 316–326.

Cohen, S. M. (1999). Money matters: Incentives and obstacles to Jewish day school enrollment in the United States. In Y. Rich & M. Rosenack (eds.), *Abiding challenges: Research perspective on Jewish education* (pp. 251–274). Freund Publishing House.

Cohen, S. M. (2007). The differential impact of Jewish education on adult Jewish identity. In J. Wertheimer (ed.), *Family matters: Jewish education in an age of choice*. University Press of New England.

Cohen, S. M., & Kelner, S. (2007). Why Jewish parents send their children to day schools. In J. Wertheimer (ed.), *Family matters: Jewish education in an age of choice*. University Press of New England.

Coleman, J. S. (1988). Social capital in the creation of human capital. *The American Journal of Sociology*, *94*(S), S95–S120.

Coleman, J. S., & Hoffer, T. (1987). *Public and private high schools: The impact of communities*. Basic Books.

Dashefsky, A., & Lebson, C. (2002). Does Jewish schooling matter? A review of the empirical literature on the relationship between Jewish education and dimensions of Jewish identity. *Contemporary Jewry*, *23*, 96–131.

Dashevsky, I., & Ta'ir, U. (2009). Mutual relations between *shlihim* and local teachers at Jewish schools in the Former Soviet Union. In A. Pomson & H. Deitcher (eds.), *Jewish day schools, Jewish communities: A reconsideration* (pp. 155–171). Littman Library of Jewish Civilization.

Datnow, A. (1998). *The gender politics of educational change*. Falmer Press.

Durkheim, E. (1893/1984). *The division of labor in society*. Free Press.

Eells, R. J. (2011). Meta-analysis of the relationship between collective teacher efficacy and student achievement. *Dissertations*, *133*. https://ecommons.luc.edu/luc_diss/133/.

Feiman-Nemser, S., Tamir, E., & Hammerness, K. (2014). *Inspiring teaching: Context-specific teacher education for the 21st century*. Harvard Education Press.

Feinberg, W. (2006). *For goodness sake: Religious schools and education for democratic citizenry.* Taylor and Francis Group.

Fox, S., Scheffler, I., & Marom, D. (2003). *Visions of Jewish education*. Cambridge University Press.

Furman, G. C. (1998). Postmodernism and community in schools: Unraveling the paradox. *Educational Administration Quarterly*, *34*(3), 298–328.

Furman, G. C. (2002). *School as community: From promise to practice*. State University of New York Press.

Furman, G. C., & Starratt, R. J. (2002). Leadership for democratic community in schools. In J. Murphy (ed.), *The educational leadership challenge: Redefining leadership for the 21st century* (pp. 261–288). National Society for the Study of Education.

Gamoran, A., Goldring, E., Robinson, B., Tamivaara, J., & Goodman, R. (1998). *The teachers report: A portrait of teachers in Jewish schools*. Council for Initiatives in Jewish Education.

Geffen, R. M. (2005). Breaking through the self-fulfilling prophecy about Jewish education. *Journal of Jewish Education*, *71*(2), 227–228.

Goldberg, S. J., Krohn, B., & Turetsky, M. (2009). Teacher perspectives on behavior problems: Background influences on behavioral referral criteria and definitions of rebellious behavior. In A. Pomson & H. Deitcher (eds.), *Jewish day schools, Jewish communities: A reconsideration* (pp. 324–340). Littman Library of Jewish Civilization.

Goldman, S. (2003). Jewish education—A crucial imperative. *Journal of Jewish Education*, *69*(1) 80–83.

Goodenow, C. (1993). Classroom belonging among early adolescent students: Relationships to motivation and achievement. *Journal of Early Adolescence*, *13*(1), 21–43.

Hargreaves, A. (1993). Individualism and individuality: Reinterpreting the teacher culture. In J. W. Little & M. W. McLaughlin (eds.), *Teachers' work: Individuals, colleagues, and contexts* (pp. 51–76). Teachers College Press.

Hargreaves, A. (1994). *Changing teachers, changing times: Teachers work and culture in the postmodern age*. OISE Press.

Himmelfarb, H. (1984). The impact of religious schooling: A synopsis. *Studies in Jewish Education*, *2*, 255–288.

Ingall, C. K. (2006). *Down the up staircase: Tales of teaching in Jewish day schools.* The Jewish Theological Seminary of America.

James, P. (1992). Forms of abstract "community": From tribe and kingdom to nation and state. *Philosophy of the Social Sciences*, *22*(3), 313–336.

JESNA. (2008). *Educators in Jewish schools study*. JESNA Learnings and Consultation Center.

Kadushin, C. (2012). *Understanding social networks: Theories, concepts, and findings*. Oxford University Press.

Kanno, Y., & Norton, B. (2003). Imagined communities and educational possibilities: Introduction. *Journal of Language, Identity, and Education*, *2*(4), 241–249.

Kaplowitz, T. (2002). Community building: A new role for the Jewish day school. *Journal of Jewish Education*, *68*(3), 29–48.

Kay, M. A. (2009). *The paradox of pluralism: Leadership and pluralism in pluralistic Jewish high schools*. Unpublished doctoral dissertation. New York University Press.

Krasner, J. (2016). American Jewry at risk: "A time to act" and the prioritization of Jewish education. *Contemporary Jewry*, *36*(1), 85–123.

Lave, J., & Wenger, E. (1991). *Situated learning: Legitimate peripheral participation*. Cambridge University Press.

Leana, C. R., & Pil, F. K. (2017). Social capital: An untapped resource for educational improvement. In E. Quintero (ed.), *Teaching in context: The social side of educational reform* (pp. 15–35). Harvard Education Press.

Lesko, N. (1988). *Symbolizing society: Stories, rites, and structure in a Catholic high school*. The Falmer Press.

Lima. J. A. (2001). Forgetting about friendship: Using conflict in teacher community as a catalyst for school change. *Journal of Educational Change*, *2*(2), 97–122.

Little, J. W. (1982). Norms of collegiality and experimentation: Workplace conditions of school success. *American Educational Research Journal*, *19*(3), 325–340.

Little, J. W. (1993). Professional community in comprehensive high schools: The two worlds of academic and vocational teachers. In J. W. Little & M. W. McLaughlin (eds.), *Teachers' work: Individuals, colleagues, and contexts* (pp. 137–163). Teachers College Press.

Little, J. W., & McLaughlin, M. W. (1993). Introduction: Perspectives on culture and contexts of teaching. In J. W. Little & M. W. McLaughlin (eds.), *Teachers' work: Individuals, colleagues, and contexts*, (pp. 1–8). Teachers College Press.

Louis, K. S., Marks, H. M., & Kruse, S. (1996). Teachers' professional community in restructuring schools. *American Educational Research Journal*, *33*(4), 757–798.

McLaughlin, M. W., & Talbert, J. E. (2001). *Professional communities and the work of high school teaching*. University of Chicago Press.

McLaughlin, M. W., & Talbert, J. E. (2006). *Building school-based teacher learning communities: Professional strategies to improve student achievement*. Teachers College Press.

Muszkat-Barkan, M., & Shkedi, A. (2009). Ideological commitment in supervision of Jewish studies teachers: Representing community. In A. Pomson & H. Deitcher (eds.), *Jewish day schools, Jewish communities: A reconsideration* (pp. 270–288). Littman Library of Jewish Civilization.

Noddings, N. (1988). An ethic of care and its implications for instructional arrangement. *American Journal of Education*, *96*(2), 215–230.

Noddings, N. (1996). On community. *Educational Theory*, *46*(3), 245–267.

Osterman, K. F. (2002). Schools as communities for students. In G. Furman (ed.), *School as community: From promise to practice* (pp. 167–196). State University of New York Press.

Oxley, D. (1997). Theory and practice of school communities. *Educational Administration Quarterly*, 33(S), 624–643.

Papay, J. P., & Kraft, M. A. (2017). Developing workplaces where teachers stay, improve, and succeed. In E. Quintero (ed.), *Teaching in context: The social side of educational reform* (pp. 15–35). Harvard Education Press.

Phillips, B. A. (2000). Intermarriage and Jewish education: Is there a connection? *Journal of Jewish Education*, *66*(1/2), 54–66.

Pomson, A. (2000). Who's a Jewish teacher?: A narrative inquiry into general studies teaching in Jewish day schools. *Journal of Jewish Communal Service*, *77*(1), 56–63.

Pomson, A. (2005). One classroom at a time? Teacher isolation and community viewed through the prism of the particular. *Teachers College Record*, *107*(4), 783–802.

Pomson, A. (2009). Jewish schools, Jewish communities: A reconsideration. In A. Pomson & H. Deitcher (eds.), *Jewish day schools, Jewish communities: A reconsideration* (pp. 1–28). Littman Library of Jewish Civilization.

Rainie, L., & Wellman, B. (2012). *Networked: The new social operating system.* MIT Press.

Ronfeldt, M. (2017). Better collaboration, better teaching. In E. Quintero (ed.), *Teaching in context: The social side of educational reform* (pp. 71–89). Harvard Education Press.

Rosenholtz, S. (1991). *Teacher's workplace: The social organization of schools*. Teachers College Press.

Rosenholtz, S. J., & Simpson, S. (1990). Workplace conditions and the rise and fall of teachers' commitment. *Sociology of Education*, *63*(4), 241–257.

Roth, S. (1977). *The Jewish idea of community.* Yeshiva University Press.

Schick, M. (2014). *A census of Jewish day schools in the United States: 2013–2014*. AVI CHAI Foundation.

Sergiovanni, T, J. (1993). *Building community in schools*. Wiley, John, and Sons.

Sergiovanni, T. J. (1994). Organizations or communities? Changing the metaphor changes the theory. *Educational Administration Quarterly*, *30*(2), 214–226.

Shields, C. M., & Seltzer, P.A. (1997). Complexities and paradoxes of community: Toward a more useful conception of community. *Educational Administration Quarterly*, *33*(4), 413–439.

Simmel, G. (1922/1955). *Conflict and the web of group affiliations.* K. H. Wolff & R. Bendix (trans.). The Free Press.

Siskin, L. S. (1994). *Realms of knowledge: Academic departments in secondary schools*. Routledge.

Solomon, D., Watson, M., Battistich, V., Schapps, E., & Delucchi, K. (1996). Creating classrooms that students experience as communities. *American Journal of Community Psychology*, *24*(6), 719–748.

Talbert, J. E., & McLaughlin, M. W. (1994). Teacher professionalism in local school contexts. *American Journal of Education*, *102*(2), 123–153.

The Commission on Jewish Education in North America. (1990). *A time to act: A report of the Commission on Jewish Education of North America*. University Press of America.

Tonnies, F. (1887/2002). *Community and society*. Dover Publications.

Waller, W. (1932/2014). *The sociology of teaching*. Martino Publishing.

Wenger, E. (1998). *Communities of practice: Learning, meaning, and identity*. Cambridge University Press.

13
Sometimes Seen
The Experience of Latine Students in Jewish Day Schools

ERIK LUDWIG

"Educational institutions operate in contradictory ways, with their potential to oppress and marginalize coexisting with their potential to emancipate and empower."[1]

Introduction

"We don't see color, just students," says the head of a Jewish day school as we talk in the hallway. At a different Jewish day school, one teacher explains to me that she doesn't implement a multicultural curriculum because, as she authoritatively puts it, "there are no diverse students in my class." As it turns out, both the head of school and the teacher are wrong. The teacher is wrong in a straightforward sense: she is not aware of the backgrounds and identities of some of her students who identify as ethnic minorities, but they are present in the classroom. The head of school is wrong in a slightly more nuanced sense: his confident normative claim about how "we," i.e., the adults at the Jewish day school, treat students is contradicted by the experience of some of those students, who know that the institution is not "colorblind."

Both of these moves are familiar—the move of the teacher who is not aware of diversity and the move of the educational leader who wants to treat students as the same even when they are not. When educators are uncomfortable talking about race, they often alleviate their discomfort by describing a faithfulness to colorblind pedagogies. And when that "hallway talk" reaches the classroom, it can have the effect of telling racially diverse students, "you are not seen." Jewish day schools can thus fall into the trap of enacting the two contradictory dynamics that Solórzano and Yosso (2002) describe in the epigraph to this chapter; they have the potential to marginalize as well as to empower.

The racial and ethnic diversity of contemporary Jewish day schools is an outgrowth of the historic and contemporary diversity of the Jewish people. Some demographic studies have indicated that approximately 8 to 15 percent of North American Jewry can be classified as non-white (Kelman et al., 2019; Pew Research Center, 2021; Tobin et al., 2005). While the exact percentages are the subject of scholarly debate, and the scholarly debate itself is complicated by shifting definitions (e.g., most non-white Sephardic Jews do not consider themselves to be "Jews of color," although many do), every observer agrees that the numbers have increased and will continue to increase over time. At the same time, teachers in Jewish day schools who are part of a Jewish culture that sometimes promotes colorblindness and meritocracy as a way of addressing racial, cultural, and ethnic differences are likely to replicate these normative beliefs in their classrooms. These educators may well have the best of intentions, believing that colorblind pedagogies support classroom equality. What they miss is the ways that colorblindness may actually normalize whiteness, implicitly demanding that racially diverse students assimilate white cultural norms and expectations. Colorblind approaches may thus result in students in Jewish day school classrooms operating with a kind of racial deficit, which has the potential to lead to students' academic disengagement in Jewish day schools as it has done in public schools (Valenzuela, 1999).

These concerns generate research questions such as the following: How do racially diverse students experience Jewish day school environments, which are overwhelmingly white and Ashkenazi? How do racially diverse students perceive teacher-student relationships in these schools? How do racially diverse students in Jewish day schools see themselves relative to white students? And most practically, how do they experience pedagogical practices that strive to support their academic engagement and success?

Unfortunately, there is very little research on the experiences of racially diverse students in contemporary Jewish day schools. This chapter will offer a modest contribution to our knowledge base of the subject, by exploring how six Latine students talk about their experiences as students at David Ben-Gurion Jewish Day School.[2] The students in this study talked about how they felt cared for by teachers and felt a sense of belonging at school. They are also aware of ethnic differences between them and their white peers and are eager to have those differences acknowledged. Attending to these students' perspectives will contribute to culturally responsive pedagogies for the particular environment of the contemporary Jewish day school.

Background: The Promise of Religious Schooling

Students of color experience schooling differently than their white peers, in general. Despite the introduction to some schools of the principles and practices of multicultural education, as a way of navigating differences in the cultural knowledges of majority and minority students, it remains the case that schooling can have a negative effect on the academic engagement of minority youth (Ferguson, 2000; Fordham & Ogbu, 1986; Jeynes, 2010; Noguera, 2003). Literature on the academic achievement of minority students has provided ample evidence that racially diverse students, particularly Black and Latine students, occupy a tenuous space in the classroom (Ferguson, 2000; Fordham & Ogbu, 1986; Gregory et al., 2006; Ladson-Billings, 2009; Morris, 2007; Noguera, 2003; Ogbu, 2003; Tatum, 1997; Valenzuela, 1999, 2008). The negative effects of schooling are punctuated by a high school dropout rate that remains significantly higher for Latine students (14 percent) and Black students (8 percent) than it is for white students (5 percent; Pew Research, 2014).

However, there is some evidence that K–12 schools under religious auspices may provide more effective resources for many racially diverse students than public or independent schools (Jeynes, 2005). Black and Latine students in majority white, religious schools achieve at higher levels than do their counterparts in nonreligious schools (Jeynes, 2002; Roorda et al., 2011). Why might this be the case? It is hard to know for sure, but some research suggests that it may be the result of religious schools' ability to foster affective relationships through a set of shared values between teachers and students that permeate school culture and support the formation of caring teacher-student relationships (Bryk et al., 1993; Rothstein et al., 1999). Further, the structure of religious schools, particularly the ability of teachers to construct extended relationships—what students talk about as family-like relationships that are perceived by students as a form of teacher caring—also appear to have a positive effect on motivation and academic engagement of racially diverse students (Bryk et al., 1993; Gay, 2010; Howard, 2002; Jeynes, 2002, 2010; Neal, 1998; Sander, 2001).

Racially Diverse Students and Jewish Schools

The discussion in the preceding section about religious schools in general provides some grounds for optimism about the experience of racially diverse students in Jewish schools in particular. There is reason to believe that the benefit of attending religious school would be present in Jewish schools because the benefit for racially diverse students appears resilient across student characteristics (Jeynes, 2002), which may suggest that it is connected to teacher practices and in the ways that religious schools' structure fosters academic engagement.

Beyond these general characteristics of religious schools, the specific nature of Jewish day schools provides further reasons that the experience of racially diverse students may be more positive than at other schools. Jewish schools may be more likely to provide the kind of culturally responsive pedagogies that benefit racially diverse students. After all, the emphasis on affirming a particular subculture is part of the *raison d'etre* of Jewish day schools. Furthermore, the contemporary pluralistic Jewish school in particular (as opposed to denominational Jewish day schools) envisions an education that welcomes and affirms diverse Jewish expressions. It is possible—not certain, but possible—that this appreciation for and celebration of intra-Jewish religious diversity might carry over to an appreciation for and celebration of intra-Jewish ethnic diversity. Finally, Jewish day schools may operate with a welcoming and inclusive attitude on the basis of the premise that "we are all Jews here" (even if, in many contemporary Jewish day schools, that may not be accurate).

On the other hand, precisely because of the premise that "we are all Jewish here," it is also possible that teachers at Jewish day schools may shy away from any acknowledgment of ethnic diversity, as noted previously, in the belief that such an acknowledgment might undermine the core mission of reinforcing intra-Jewish solidarity. Teachers or administrators might even operate with the assumption that identity is a zero-sum game, and that embracing or exploring diverse ethnic identities will inevitably dilute the focus on Jewish culture, history, and practices. And finally, the specific history of the American Jewish community—with its postwar material and cultural success, and its embrace of liberal values—may encourage an implicit inclination among educators or school leaders toward the norms of colorblindness and meritocracy.

Which of these two narratives is more accurate? Are racially diverse students better off in Jewish day schools than they would be in non-Jewish schools, or on the other hand do the particular cultural characteristics of Jewish day schools present even greater obstacles to their flourishing? We cannot answer the question definitively. We do not have enough data on Jewish day school students' characteristics in general (race, socioeconomic status, household composition, etc.), nor do we have the necessary understanding of students' experiences in Jewish schools in general, nor do we have anything like the kind of comparative data that would yield an authoritative answer to the overly simplistic binary question of whether racially diverse students are "better off" in Jewish day schools. However, this chapter is an initial step toward understanding some of the dynamics that racially diverse students experience.

Research Design

The research was completed at David Ben-Gurion Jewish Community Day School, which is a composite profile of an accredited pluralistic Jewish school serving kindergarten through eighth grade in suburban California. The typical student at David Ben-Gurion is white and Ashkenazi, although approximately 7 percent of students are racially diverse. The head of school and the majority of faculty are white women from Ashkenazi ancestry. The rest of the faculty are a combination of white Ashkenazi men, white non-Jewish women, and non-white non-Jewish women and men, in descending order of frequency. The third through eighth grade Latine students discussed in this chapter (n=6) were purposefully selected to achieve diversity in gender and grade level (see table 13.1). All of these

Latine students identify as Jewish and as Spanish speaking. Five of the students self-disclosed that they had a Latine parent. While specific data on Latine students' socioeconomic status was not gathered, there is evidence in the way students dressed, as well as conversations about parents' professions, vacation travel, and home neighborhoods, that they are from similar socioeconomic backgrounds as their white classmates. Four of the six students would be considered academic high achievers based on their GPA. The teachers who participated in this study were selected because their classrooms included students whose data would be used in the research. All five teachers discussed by students are white women and have taught previously at David Ben-Gurion for a minimum of four years. The teachers' styles and pedagogical practices are highly individualized, although there is a loose attempt to connect assignments and pedagogy to the school's moral and ethical values of chesed, Klal Yisrael, tikkun olam, and tzedakah.

Data collection included interviews with students and their teachers as well as classroom observations during the course of a full school year. Semi-structured interviews were guided by a standardized set of protocols and provided an understanding of students' perceptions about teacher

TABLE 13.1. *Student Participant Demographics*

Name	Gender	Grade	GPA
Rubén	M	6	3.2
Alejandra	F	5	4.0
Octavio	M	5	4.0
Lenore	F	4	4.0
Juan	M	4	2.8
Raquel	F	3	3.9

practices, school culture, and what characteristics could be attributed to caring teachers. Each student was interviewed individually and then group interviews were held—which included the six students as well as some others who are not represented in this chapter—in groupings by grade level: third through fourth grade, fifth through sixth grade, and seventh through eighth grade. The individual student interviews lasted approximately sixty minutes and the group interviews took approximately seventy-five minutes. Classroom and campus observations were completed for students in the study and for teachers whose students were participating in the study. The observations took about sixty minutes each and provided an opportunity to establish congruence between what students shared in their interviews and what was visible in the experience of students in the classrooms. After all of the student data had been collected, semi-structured interviews with teachers were held using protocols based on the same set of interview questions as the student interviews. The teacher interviews, which took approximately sixty minutes each, provided a deeper understanding of how teachers perceive the classroom as a caring environment and the activation of pedagogical practices that reinforced caring teacher-student relationships. These student and teacher interviews, and classroom observations, yielded a rich dataset that was then carefully analyzed.

The voluminous amount of data from these interviews and observations generated a strong understanding of the perspectives of these students and their teachers. However, it is also important to avoid generalizing from the findings from this qualitative inquiry. In the end, the analysis provides a window into the experiences of six Latine students whose lives have been shaped by cultures, religions, and beliefs that are likely different from the experiences of Latine students and their teachers in other Jewish schools. For example, we should be cautious about assuming that the experience of the child of one non-Jewish Mexican-American parent and one white Ashkenazi Jewish parent living in the American Southwest is similar to the experience of a child of two South American Mizrachi immigrant parents living in New York, even though both children speak Spanish and may identify as Latine. Still, given the absence of other empirical work on racially diverse students in Jewish day schools, these findings represent an important step forward.

Latine Students' Perceptions of Caring Teacher-Student Relationships

Latine students at David Ben-Gurion believe that caring teacher-student relationships affirm their cultures. They describe how affective relationships are built through teacher practices that strengthen students' sense of being cared for at school. They talk about the qualities of caring teachers and identified pedagogy that supports students' needs in the classroom, addresses challenges that students confront in their home lives (outside the boundaries of school), and invites students to co-construct culturally responsive curricula. Moreover, the students appreciate that teachers are warm demanders, i.e., that they are strict in a way that promotes academic success.

Latine students regularly identify how caring is situated in the affective relationships between teachers and students. When teachers share aspects of their own life outside of the classroom and want to know about students' lives outside the classroom, the students perceive those teachers as caring. These students identify caring as taking place when teachers reveal their beliefs and values through personal stories or indicate that they trust students. In response, these Latine students shared a conception of teachers as "like friends" or as an extended family member. Additionally, these Latine students perceive teachers as caring when their teachers knew intimate details about their family life, life cycle events, and activities outside of school.

For example, Raquel, a third grader who is the child of divorce, comments on the way that caring and sharing established relatedness support her academic engagement:

> A caring teacher takes you into account. If your parents are divorced and your dad isn't the best at writing a report, your teacher gives you more time and help with reports. A caring teacher helps you. It is interesting when you hear about them [teachers]. It helps us learn in class when they talk about them and their family... It helps us learn and relate. It helps to know about their personal stuff. Like we know that our teacher's dog died and stuff.

Raquel's comment that "it helps to know about their personal stuff" reinforces a common understanding of caring teacher-student relationships as constructed through personal relations and as promoting academic engagement. Further, Raquel identifies her own desire for school to be familial when she states, "A caring teacher takes you into account." Such a statement echoes a common perception among these Latine students that caring consists of being "taken into account" and "held accountable" even when students identified the teacher's behavior as strict. In Raquel's description of how sharing and caring are connected to academic success, she identifies the teacher's expectations and affective behavior, standing in for a family member and providing academic support, as forms of care. Raquel's comments indicate how a sense of being cared for supports her academic aspirations. She later explains that she feels lucky to be able to talk to her teacher about life. She describes how, when they are not in class, the teacher shares advice that she would "give to her own kids."

Latine students who identify sharing as strengthening caring teacher-student relationships describe how it supports the formation of trust and friendship. When I ask Rubén, a Latino sixth grader, if he thinks caring teachers share details about their personal lives, he responds as follows:

> Rubén: Sometimes, but not to the extent where it would interrupt any normal school activities.
>
> EL: What kinds of things do they share?
>
> Rubén: Well, one example is our language arts teacher this year. When telling us how to make a story more exciting, when writing it, she gave an example of a story when she was a kid. She made it exciting and used that as an example in class.
>
> EL: What was it like to learn a little about her experience as a kid?
>
> Rubén: Well, it was nice and also, if you have a teacher that is okay sharing any information about past events, about their lives, you know they trust you as a student, as a fellow peer, as a friend in a way.

Rubén's comments indicate the way these Latine students experience caring in relational moments with teachers and how the students perceive sharing as developing a friend-like relationship. In his description, Rubén initially conceptualizes the relational moment as limited to teaching as academic instruction, but he then reframes the moment as one of caring when he identifies the teacher's sharing about past events from her childhood as a way of establishing a trusted relationship.

We do not know, of course, how these perceptions and beliefs among the Latine students compare to those of other students. We do not have that comparative data. But the point here is not to argue that Latine students are similar to, or different from, their non-Latine peers in Jewish day schools. Rather, it is significant that Latine students indicate that, when teachers share their own experiences, that sharing reinforces the formation of caring teacher-student relationships. At the same time, it is also important to note that, according to the interview data, when teachers share personal stories, those stories are devoid of Latine cultural knowledge. The stories that teachers tell with the intention of transmitting cultural knowledge are constructed solely on Jewish cultural themes. In other words, every story that a teacher tells may also be another small indication of *difference*, not just of connection. We should be cautious in our interpretation here, because it is unclear whether there is any negative effect on the students generated by the absence of teachers' reinforcing Latine culture through their own stories. Even in the absence of teachers personally identifying with Latine culture, students talk about teachers' care using words that express trust and indicate that schooling feels familial to them. Still, as critical observers, this is one location where we might wonder about the dynamics of race within Jewish day schools that place such a high value on a family-like atmosphere and caring teachers.

Dialogic Interactions in the Classroom

The Latine students in this study are critical consumers of pedagogy and pay attention to how teachers make themselves available as classroom resources. Alejandra, a fifth grader, explains how care is connected to teacher listening and academic expectations. When I ask her, "If you think about teachers who are really caring, what types of behaviors do they have in the classroom?" she responds,

> They'll [the teachers will] listen, definitely, and they'll watch you and they'll make sure that you're okay and what you're doing is good [academic work] ... I'd really want to impress them to make sure that they, yeah... But I think I would do better schoolwork for the person who cared because I wouldn't want to let them down and I'd really want them to know that them being nice is helping me in school.

Alejandra's response reveals the complexity of caring teacher-student relationships. In her comments, she initially identifies care as listening. However, Alejandra expands her initial conception of care and describes teacher listening as an affective behavior that includes knowing the student and ensuring that the student is academically supported by the teacher. Research by Garza and Soto Huerta (2014) has found that Latine students identify teachers as caring when they listen to students, make them comfortable, and provide academic scaffolding. Latine students at David Ben-Gurion also value dialogic interactions and feel that they demonstrate care. Students' narratives describe dialogic interactions as connected to affective behaviors that are described as part of caring teacher-student relationships. This is exemplified in Alejandra's statement that the caring teacher will "make sure you're okay" or that she would work harder at school to "let them know being nice is helping me."

Another aspect of a dialogic relationship is the effective navigation of personal boundaries. Latine students understand that kibitzing requires a level of closeness that is familial. Juan, a fourth grader, explains, "On a test, she'll ask me to 'Come over here.' I'll come over to her desk. She'd be like, 'You did terrible.' And, I'd be like, 'Really?' She'd be like, 'No, you did great.'" A similar understanding of the connection between humor and caring is held by Octavio, a fifth grader. He suggests that if "they're [teachers are] caring" and "have a good sense of humor... they make me feel like I belong here [at school]." Such dialogic moments require that the teacher know the student personally in order to navigate nuanced relationships and ensure that kibitzing is perceived by the student in a manner that affirms the student's self worth and academic capabilities. Latine students at David Ben-Gurion, similarly to Latine students in previous research, perceive teacher listening as connected to developing effective frameworks of care for Latine youth when the interactions validated students' sense of self-worth (Garza & Soto Huerta, 2014).

Latine students at David Ben-Gurion identify dialogic interactions as one way that teachers "know them" and as a form of caring. These dialogic interactions have the potential, then, to serve as a mechanism for including students' cultural heritages in the classroom by supporting their co-authorship of the classroom as a dialogic space. Freire (2016) has suggested that teacher-student relationships that are mutually constructed provide an opportunity for students to be co-authors in their education: "The students—no longer docile listeners—are now critical co-investigators in dialogue with the teacher" (p. 81). The Latine students at David Ben-Gurion confirm that, when they feel listened to by teachers, that experience motivates their academic engagement. We might propose, following Freire and building on the indications in our data, that teachers may be establishing opportunities for students to co-author their experience of schooling. By validating students' cultural frames of reference through dialogic interactions, teachers may construct a liberatory experience of schooling.

Teacher Expectations Support Academic Engagement

Prior research has indicated that teachers' expectations of excellence have historically been lower for racially diverse students (Ladson-Billings, 2009). Thus, the fact that teachers at David Ben-Gurion respond to the individual needs of Latine students could raise a concern that teachers hold lower expectations of them and make exceptions as a way of fulfilling their own perceptions of how students behave in class.

However, the Latine students at David Ben-Gurion perceive teachers who hold high academic expectations and individualize their curricula as warm demanders. Students describe their teachers as warm demanders when they exhibit disappointment and understanding rather than issuing punishments or expressing frustration with students in moments when they underachieve. Teachers frequently work side by side with Latine students to help them navigate mutually acceptable solutions in the form of additional work or in recognizing that family needs might require extended time to complete the work. Teachers who value independent learning outcomes as a form of fairness, rather than seeking a blanket form of equality, are perceived by Latine students as promoting academic achievement and as caring. This description of caring teachers is supported by previous research findings that teachers are perceived as warm demanders when they seek excellence through their behaviors and share responsibility with racially diverse students (Gay, 2010).

Octavio explains the nuanced understanding of teachers' expectations that these Latine students maintain:

> She is strict. And she is really nice still. Like, she cares about us so much. Like, when she scolds us, though, she always has a reason for it. Like, she'll give us an example... So she is like teaching us how to succeed in life.

That teachers' expectations matter even when the teacher is strict or scolds the student confirms that Latine students hold complex understandings of teachers' affective responses and that emotion could be indicative of a caring relationship. As Octavio points out, a teacher may scold a student and still maintain a caring teacher-student relationship. His comments foreground the importance of teachers being in a dialogic relationship with students in which caring can be co-constructed through mutual understandings. In the moment that Octavio talks about, being scolded is a sign of caring because it reinforces his conception of the teacher's responsibility to teach him "how to succeed in life" and furthers a conception of school being familial. This example echoes Howard's (2002) finding that teacher "hollering" could be a form of culturally responsive caring and that teacher-student interactions like these reveal the ability of racially diverse students to decode teacher behaviors accurately and recognize when the teacher is providing a resource for academic success and success in life.

Alejandra also identifies the connection between teacher expectations and caring. When she is asked about caring, she quickly pivots to explain how strictness is a form of academic support:

> I think that sometimes if they're being strict, then maybe it's just to help me more. Yeah, because it will make me think better, because if

> they're being strict, then I have to work harder so that they don't get mad or angry.

Alejandra understands that teacher caring is not always a matter of what teachers say, but sometimes a matter of what they do—"being strict."

Rubén, similarly to Octavio and Alejandra, understands teachers' expectations, or "strictness," as an important element of their support. Rubén shares,

> I like the fact that they focus on everyone and they're caring and they know to a good extent about our personal life and what we do . . . Strictness can be a form of caring depends on how you do it, because in a way, you don't want to give the freedom to do things that could come back and harm the student. So to be too strict and to a certain extent, putting too much regulations, is not a really likable reputation for many teachers. It is sometimes a form of caring when you have agreed with students that it needs, might need, the teacher might need to be a little stricter because it might help the students a little bit more, but to a good extent, it is. It's a good quality for a caring teacher.

When these Latine students describe strictness, they situate the teacher as a resource for academic achievement and indicate that strictness motivated them to work harder in order to satisfy the teachers' expectations of them.

This finding about Latine students in Jewish day schools—namely, that caring teachers are both demanding and empathetic in their teaching practices—echoes previous research by Valenzuela (1999), who found that teacher expectations are perceived by Latine students as caring because they are reciprocal:

> Whereas teachers demand caring about school in the absence of relation, students view caring, or reciprocal relations, as the basis for all learning. Their precondition to caring about school is that they be engaged in a caring relationship with an adult at school. (p. 79)

Once again, we do not have the data to offer a comparison between how the Latine students in Jewish day schools perceive caring teachers and how other students do. But the claim is not that Latine students are somehow unique in this regard. Rather, this finding about how Latine students perceive their teachers is significant because it seems to rule out an alternative possibility, given the racial dynamics of schooling—namely, that when teachers perform as warm demanders, they are perceived as asking or demanding that Latine students should "act white." The data from these Latine students suggest, in contrast, that they internalized caring as establishing a sense of belonging and motivating academic achievement, and, beyond providing merely academic help, perceived teachers as fostering their growth as people.

Latine Students' Perceptions of Belonging

The Latine students at David Ben-Gurion do not perceive themselves as the same as white students. They are aware of ethnic difference and embrace it. Thus, one of the obstacles that Latine students face in belonging at Jewish schools is the result of a cultural divide between their own experience as Latine and their teachers' experiences of whiteness, a cultural divide that has the potential to disrupt their ability to form personal relationships with teachers. When Latine students talk about their perceptions of belonging at school, they confirm the importance of teacher relationships that they perceive as familial, but also, of having their own culture represented at school. The students' narratives provide insight into a complex dynamic of belonging and identity.

The first prominent finding, in this context, is that the Latine students do not feel that they have to "act white." They do not describe the concept of "acting white" or of a burden to "fit in" as a challenge in their experiences of studenthood. Students identify their use of Spanish and the implementation of culturally responsive pedagogies by teachers, which they describe as multiculturalism, as strengthening the feeling of school being familial and their own sense of belonging. Further, they talk about their cultural identities as flexible and express the desire for teachers to understand how they navigate across intersectional identities.

Rubén, for example, shares that his mother had converted to Judaism but that his family celebrates their Mexican heritage through food, language, and holiday activities, such as making *cascarones*:

> Well, my dad is Jewish and my mom converted to Judaism when they got married, but we do, a lot of times, cook foods that are Mexican foods, and also, we sometimes, when we go [out], sometimes, we go [to] places that have the Mexican sense of culture. Sometimes, [we] have some Mexican traditions that we do, like Mexican tradition when... pretty sure, there's a Mexican tradition when you have eggs and you fill them with confetti and then during springtime, we crack them on people's heads. It's kind of a fun thing.

While Rubén does not describe bringing these aspects of his home culture into school, his pride in and comfort with his Latino identity is evident.

Octavio speaks Spanish fluently. When I ask him whether his teachers know this, he states, "Definitely. All [teachers], everybody here knows that. It's not a private detail." He then goes on to explain how he navigates between his Spanish and American identities:

> Because I'm kind of surrounded with a Spanish background at home like half of the week, I'm eating Spanish food, talking and the conversation in my house, unless it's when my dad... isn't Spanish. So it's like I'm always talking in Spanish. I'm always doing stuff that in Spain they do. So I kind of considered myself... most of the time, I consider myself more American than Spanish, but I've had phases in my life when I've considered myself more Spanish than American.

These Latine students seem to move fluidly between school and home identities, even describing school as home-like. Octavio shares, "There's really never been a moment when I feel this shouldn't be where I go [to school], this shouldn't be my home basically."

Lenore, a fourth grader, explains that language operates as a cultural identifier at school. She understands her use of Spanish as way of locating her cultural identity:

> My second language is Spanish, but not the Spanish version, the Mexico version... My father is a lawyer, Mexican... I like to talk about my culture with my teachers. I am really proud to be Mexican.

Lenore thus reports a high level of comfort with and openness about her Latina (in this case Mexican) identity.

Alejandra similarly explains how she views language as a representation of her cultural identity:

> Yeah, I speak Spanish a lot... And Hebrew, I speak that here. I don't speak it that much at home, but sometimes I will talk to my brother in Hebrew if it's like a secret conversation because no one else speaks Hebrew in my house, so it works. But mostly Spanish and English. My grandmother is from Mexico. She was born in Mexico and so my mom grew up speaking Spanish. I see my grandmother a lot, and we speak Spanish because that's the language that she speaks. She knows English, but she prefers to speak Spanish because that's her first language.

Alejandra thus gives us a small window into the multilingual experience of Latine students who learn Hebrew at school. While there is surely much more to be explored about the meaning of the various languages and the cultural identities that they symbolize, these data indicate that, for these students, navigating the complexity of these identities does not entail having to "act white" in school.

Beyond this point, however, these Latine students also particularly welcome opportunities for cultural expression at school, which strengthen their sense of belonging. They acknowledge the racial differences between themselves and the teachers or the majority white student body, but they feel that the school has a multicultural diversity that they like and that is similar to their experiences of home. For example, when I ask Rubén if teachers know he speaks Spanish and is Latino, he confirms that they do and identifies the presence of culturally responsive pedagogy in teachers' use of a multicultural curriculum. Rubén explains:

> There has also actually been days or projects where it is... the main premise is what is your heritage and explain it. We do a lot of projects where we either pick a country to study and study their heritage and their foods and their culture or do the country we're from. We did this

> last year. We did a day where everybody did a lot [of] project[s] and brought some food from a country that they were from. So, I think it's nice that they do multicultural... have a good sense of being multicultural and every descent, ethnic roots in the school.

In this case and others, Latine students perceive school as a place where they belong when it affirms their home culture and when diversity is reflected in the school culture.

Peoplehood as a Culturally Responsive Pedagogy

In the preceding section on students' experience of belonging, we noted that these Latine students do not feel that they have to "act white," and on the contrary, that they appreciate moments when they are encouraged to bring their own cultures into the academic environment as a resource—as an asset, rather than a potential deficit. But there is another very important dynamic that is present in the experience of these racially diverse students in Jewish day schools, specifically regarding how teachers talk about the diversity of the Jewish people. In this context, the pedagogy of Jewish peoplehood should be understood as a culturally responsive pedagogy.

Culturally responsive pedagogies, while called by many different names, may be understood as student-centered frameworks for teaching that take into account the racial and cultural experiences of students in making schooling relevant to them. For racially diverse students, such pedagogies are foundational in the formation of caring teacher-student relationships and in establishing belonging at school. The availability of culturally responsive pedagogies validates students' lived experiences, reduces the likelihood that their heritage is constructed as a deficit in the classroom, and has the potential to promote the activation of their cultural identity at school (Gay, 2010). Further, culturally responsive pedagogies extend beyond the implementation of multicultural curricula and establish the teacher as a resource for racially diverse students. By affirming students' authentic identities, teachers are able to establish caring relationships with racially diverse students that have the potential to counter systemic racism in education and, in doing so, improve academic engagement.

Jewish peoplehood is diverse in its ethnic, racial, and religious construction. The historic and more contemporary themes of slavery, Diaspora, and immigration are ever present in the cultural narratives of Jewish peoplehood and permeate Jewish schooling in a way that is absent in nonreligious and non-Jewish religious schools. The histories connected to Jewish peoplehood may serve as a unique mechanism for teachers in activating culturally responsive pedagogies in Jewish schools. While Jewish students are typically portrayed in educational research as the same as other white Europeans, Jewish identity includes peoples whose identities span across a spectrum of racial and ethnic cultures as well as varied religious practices (Fine et al., 2004; Fordham & Ogbu, 1996; Tosolt, 2009). In its diversity and multivocal expressions of Jewish life, Jewish peoplehood complicates whiteness because, while it may be argued that white, European Jews in North America benefit from white privilege (Goldberg, 1997), these claims fail to encompass the experience and possible marginalization of racially diverse American Jewry. Further, in examining the cultural positionality of the American Jewish population, it is essential to recognize the intersectionality of Jewish racial, cultural, and religious identification that educational research fails to do when it simplistically positions Jewish students as having the same experience of schooling as their white peers.

Thus, a pedagogic focus on the ethnic and racial diversity of the Jewish people has enormous potential to reinforce racially diverse Jewish students' perception of their teachers as caring and to strengthen the students' sense of belonging. As we saw earlier, Rubén responds very positively to the celebration of "every descent . . . in the school." This potential is most obviously the case when teachers emphasize contemporary diversity in a way that allows students to see themselves represented in the constructed image of the Jewish people, or at the very least, to see the subversion of assumptions about the correspondence of Jewishness and whiteness. But it may also be the case when teachers emphasize the historical diversity of the Jewish people as well. Teachers who activate culturally responsive pedagogies help make racially diverse students visible by affirming their authentic identities. Thus, they take strides toward disrupting colorblind notions of education and constructing a liberatory experience of Jewish schooling.

Toward a Liberatory Experience of Jewish Schooling

The insights of Latine students in this study can help us identify characteristics of culturally responsive pedagogies in Jewish schools—pedagogies that, to paraphrase Solórzano and Yosso in the epigraph to this chapter, avoid marginalizing racially diverse students and instead empower them.

First, teachers who share about their personal lives and listen to students are perceived as providing authentic care. More specifically, teachers should seek moments in which they can share in response to Latine students' life experiences and expand students' understanding of the teacher as a person. The desired outcome is to become "a friend in a way" as the students in this research suggested. Such friendships recognize the power relations between teachers and Latine students and still provide the mutuality needed for the carer and the cared for to trust in the relationship.

Second, teachers who listen exhibit practices such as academic flexibility (moving a due date of an assignment in response to a student request) and the use of dialogic encounters (problem posing) that support Latine students' perceptions of being accounted for or that "I matter." Teachers who listen to Latine students are perceived by the students as respecting them and as individualizing their curricula in ways that account for student-centered frameworks.

Third, these Latine students emphasize the importance of teachers' engagement with questions of race and culture in ways that affirm racially diverse students' heritages and understand that they are not the same as white students. Teachers implementing culturally responsive pedagogies will want to interrogate their own understandings of race and culture and implement assignments that provide opportunities for Latine students to co-construct the curricula.

Finally, pluralistic Jewish day schools are organized around shared religious and cultural values that provide a resource for teachers in establishing and sustaining caring relationships with Latine students. But rather than only emphasizing what Jews share, teachers ought to explore concepts of Jewish peoplehood that are inclusive of racial and cultural diversity in order to disrupt the normative notions of the Jewish people as only white and Ashkenazi. In this way, teachers at Jewish schools can reconceptualize practices that research has suggested are effective in Catholic schools

(Benveniste et al., 2003; Jeynes, 2010) through Jewish religious and cultural values in a manner that Latine students have identified as making school feel familial.

The voices of Latine students at David Ben-Gurion challenge educators to understand caring differently and to use students' experiences to problematize and guide the further development of culturally responsive pedagogies and their use in Jewish schools. Doing so can support the activation of Latine students' racial and cultural identities in the classroom and reinforce a dialogic co-construction of knowledge. Implementing culturally responsive pedagogies encourages all students to make the connection between assignments and students' cultures or how race and culture can be experienced differently, affirming the cultural identities of racially diverse students and making it possible for Latine students to experience Jewish schooling as liberatory. The Latine students in this study are, as the title of this chapter indicates, sometimes seen for who they are and who they understand themselves to be. That's the good news. But Jewish day schools can surely do better. Attending to the voices of Latine students is a healthy place to start.

NOTES

1. Solórzano & Yosso, 2002, p. 26.
2. The name of the school and participants' names used in this chapter are pseudonyms.

REFERENCES

Benveniste, L., Carnoy, M., & Rothstein, R. (2003). *All else equal: Are public and private schools different?* Routledge.

Bryk, A., Lee, E., & Holland, B. (1993). *Catholic schools and the common good.* Harvard University Press.

Ferguson, A. (2000). *Bad boys: Public schools in the making of Black masculinity.* University of Michigan Press.

Fine, M., Weiss, L., Pruitt, L. P., & Burns, A. (2004). *Off white: Readings on power, privilege, and resistance* (2nd ed.). Routledge.

Fordham, S., & Ogbu, J. (1986). Black students' school success: Coping with the "burden of 'acting white.'" *Urban Review, 18,* 176–206.

Freire, P. (2016). *Pedagogy of the oppressed* (30th anniversary ed.). Bloomsbury.

Garza, R., & Soto Huerta, M. E. (2014). Latino high school students' perceptions of caring: Keys to success. *Journal of Latinos and Education, 13,* 134–151.

Gay, G. (2010). *Culturally responsive teaching: Theory, research, and practice* (2nd ed.). Teachers College Press.

Goldberg, J. (1997). *Jewish power: Inside the American Jewish establishment*. Basic Books.

Gregory, A., Nygreen, K., & Moran, D. (2006). The discipline gap and the normalization of failure. In P. A. Noguera & J. Y. Wing (eds.), *Unfinished business: Closing the racial achievement gap in our schools* (pp. 121–150). Jossey-Bass.

Howard, T. (2002). Hearing footsteps in the dark: African American students' description of effective teachers. *Journal of Education for Students Placed at Risk*, *7*(4), 425–444.

Jeynes, W. (2002). Educational policy and the effects of attending a religious school on the academic achievement of children. *Educational Policy*, *16*(3), 406–424.

Jeynes, W. (2005). The impact of religious schools on the academic achievement of low-SES students. *Journal of Empirical Theology*, *18*(1), 22–40.

Jeynes, W. (2010). Religiosity, religious schools, and their relationship with the achievement gap: A research synthesis and meta-analysis. *The Journal of Negro Education*, *79*(3), 263–279.

Kelman, A., Tapper, A., Fonseca, I., & Saperstein, A. (2019). Counting inconsistencies: An analysis of American Jewish population studies with a focus on Jews of color. https://jewsofcolorfieldbuilding.org/wp-content/uploads/2019/05/Counting-Inconsistencies-052119.pdf/.

Ladson-Billings, G. (2009). *The dreamkeepers: Successful teachers of African American children* (2nd ed.). Jossey-Bass.

Morris, E. (2007). Ladies or loudies? Perceptions and experiences of Black girls in classrooms. *Youth & Society*, *38*, 490–515.

Neal, D. (1998, March). What have we learned about the benefits of private schooling? *Federal Reserve Bank of New York Economic Policy Review*, 79–86.

Noguera, P. (2003). The trouble with Black boys: The role and influence of environmental and cultural factors on the academic performance of African American males. *Urban Education*, *38*(4), 431–459.

Noguera, P., & Wing, J. (2006) *Unfinished business: Closing the racial achievement gap in our schools*. Jossey-Bass.

Ogbu, J. (2003). *Black American students in an affluent suburb: A study of academic disengagement*. Lawrence Erlbaum Associates.

Pew Research. (2014). *U.S. high school dropout rates reaches record low, driven by improvements among Hispanics, Blacks*. www.pewresearch.org/fact-tank/2014/10/02/u-s-high-school-dropout-rate-reaches-record-low-driven-by-improvements-among-hispanics-blacks/.

Pew Research Center. (2021). *Jewish Americans in 2020*. www.pewresearch.org/religion/2021/05/11/race-ethnicity-heritage-and-immigration-among-u-s-jews/.

Roorda, D., Kooman, H., Split, J., & Oort, F. (2011). The influence of affective teacher-student relationships on students' school engagement and achievement: A meta-analytic approach. *Review of Educational Research*, *81*(4), 493–529.

Rothstein, R., Carnoy, M., & Benveniste, L. (1999). *Can public schools learn from private schools? Case studies in the public and private nonprofit sectors*. Economic Policy Institute.

Sander, W. (2001). *The effect of Catholic schools on religiosity, achievement, and competition*. National Center for the Study of Privatization of Education, Teachers College, Columbia University, Occasional Paper No. 32.

Solórzano, D., & Yosso, T. (2002). Critical race methodology: Counter-storytelling as an analytical framework for education research. *Qualitative Research*, *8*(1), 23–44.

Tatum, B. (1997). *Why are all the Black kids sitting together in the cafeteria?: A psychologist explains the development of racial identity*. Basic Books.

Tobin, D., Tobin, G., & Rubin, S. (2005). *In every tongue: The racial and ethnic diversity of the Jewish people.* Institute for Jewish & Community Research.

Tosolt, B. (2009). Middle school students' perceptions of caring teacher behaviors: Differences by minority status. *The Journal of Negro Education*, *78*(4), 405–416.

Valenzuela, A. (1999). *Subtractive schooling: U.S.-Mexican youth and the politics of caring.* State University of New York Press.

Valenzuela, A. (2008). Ogbu's voluntary and involuntary minority hypothesis and the politics of caring. In J. U. Ogbu (ed.), *Minority status, oppositional culture, & schooling* (pp. 496–530). Routledge.

CONCLUSION

What We've Learned about Teaching and Learning in Jewish Day Schools, and What We Still Need to Learn

JON A. LEVISOHN

As historians of education such as Larry Cuban have taught, it is notoriously difficult to open up the "black box" of education (see Cuban, 2013, and for the origin of the metaphor, see Black & Wiliam, 1998). The intended curriculum may be available in the files of a school. But it is more difficult to understand the enacted curriculum, which is a function of the myriad educators who make choices about what to include and what to exclude, what to emphasize and what to marginalize, every day. The pedagogic vision may be articulated in internal professional development documents. But it is more difficult to gather information about pedagogic practices. School policies may be communicated to teachers, families, and children and thus available to scholars who have access to those communications. But it is more difficult to know how those policies are carried out. Demographic data on students is sometimes available. But it is more difficult to learn about their actual experiences.

The authors of the chapters in this book have each cracked open the black box of the institution of the Jewish day school in the twenty-first century—not entirely, not wide open, but just a little bit. Each chapter, in different ways, provides a window into a particular aspect of teaching and learning, based on specific empirical data drawn from real schools, real students, and real teachers. Collectively, then, we come away with a set of insights that challenge preconceptions, that illuminate and illustrate, and that offer new ways of thinking about familiar phenomena.

What We've Learned

So what have we learned about teaching and learning in Jewish day schools?

The opening chapter of our volume, Sivan Zakai's chapter on how the thinking of a group of Jewish day school children about Zionism evolves over time, offers a kind of basic research on a central topic in Jewish day school education—"basic" in the sense of studying what kids know and how they think, rather than focusing more narrowly on what knowledge or ideas are generated by particular interventions. But this particular aspect of her research is "basic" in another sense as well, because she begins by asking what we might think of as the most basic question: Do these kids know what Zionism is? The answer is unequivocal: They do not. That, however, is the beginning of the story, not the end. It turns out that, while they lack any familiarity with the term Zionism, and hence might fail on a multiple-choice exam question about the term, they actually do articulate a number of sophisticated conceptual understandings of the *ideas* of Zionism as early as ages five and six. What we learn from this chapter, then, is that we need to be much more nuanced than we usually are when talking about children's understanding of one of the core subject areas of Jewish day schools, and much more curious about those understandings. More generally, we ought to take seriously Zakai's suggestion that our children are learning to speak languages—in this case, the language of Zionism, internalizing conceptual frameworks that then emerge in their descriptions and their aspirations—even before they know all the words. Taking her suggestion seriously would entail listening much more closely to what children are saying, rather than only attending to what they are failing to say.

From the chapter by Jonah Hassenfeld about the outcomes of Israel education, we learn about students a bit later in their learning trajectories than the elementary-age students whom Zakai has studied. Hassenfeld's questions are also different than Zakai's. For him, his interviews with tenth graders were an opportunity to investigate, and eventually critique, the familiar idea that Israel education should foster knowledge about and connection to Israel. Both of these concepts, it turns out, do not adequately capture the complexity demonstrated by the students in the study—and it turns out that they are not easily disentangled. This is not a mandate for a relentlessly cognitive mode of instruction, neither about Israel nor about anything else. It does suggest, however, that trying to influence affect in the absence of deep inquiry may not lead to outcomes that meet our aspirations.

The third chapter, by Ziva Hassenfeld, takes us deep into particular interpretive conversations about Tanakh. But her focus is primarily on what the students do rather than on what the teacher does, and not what they do as individuals but rather what they do collectively, or what theorists have recently called "intercomprehending." What is particularly important, here, is that textual conversation is now understood not merely as an outgrowth of learning, and not even as a mechanism through which (individual) learning happens. Rather, textual conversation is the location of learning itself.

Notice that this is different from how we usually think about the unit of analysis in discussing education, and especially, in assessing educational efforts. We are conditioned, especially under the pressure of assessment practices, to assign ownership over ideas to a particular individual student. We imagine a mental model of ideas residing in minds, and minds of course are located in individual human heads. There is certainly value in this model, especially when it leads us to pay attention to and respect the individual child standing in front of us. But Ziva Hassenfeld's analysis of textual discussion, like some other areas of intellectual and creative activity, may serve us well as a reminder of the limitations of that model of learning.

From Ilana Horwitz's chapter on the "gender confidence gap," we learn that girls in American Jewish day schools seem to feel differently than boys do—not that they feel differently about Israel (in the sense of their concern for or sense of attachment to Israel) but that they feel differently about their own *knowledge about* Israel. The former is about the object of study. The latter is about the school subject itself. This distinction is itself significant. Some might casually respond that this latter kind of attitude is not relevant; what we ought to care about is actual knowledge, not attitudes toward that knowledge. But how a student feels about the subject that they are studying, and how they feel about themselves as students of that subject, is enormously important for their motivation to continue to pursue that subject, and how to do so. Moreover, it is precisely those attitudes that govern how individuals navigate through the relevant epistemic environments, that is, the Jewish communal spaces in which knowledge of Israel carries weight, or the non-Jewish, public spaces in which Israel is discussed.

Horwitz's analysis also indicates that the gender confidence gap with regard to Israel is not explained away as a general gender issue. What this suggests, for the purposes of the teaching and learning of Israel, is that instructors might need to be particularly attuned to the ways in which conversations about Israeli history and politics become dominated by more confident boys rather than less confident girls, even when those same girls exhibit greater confidence in other domains. Finally, Horwitz's analysis points to broader questions about and the need for further research into domain-specific confidence as a desired outcome in Jewish day schools and elsewhere.

From the chapter by Janet Krasner Aronson and Raquel Magidin de Kramer about the "engagement styles" of Jewish day school students, we learn that these students tend to fall into one of six different categories. These are "styles" or "types," of course. Not every student can be neatly categorized in this way. But the data do suggest that there is a meaningful way of thinking about the diversity of different kinds of engagement, or what they also call "orientations toward Jewish life." That diversity is related to denomination, but is distinct from it. Likewise, that diversity is related to parental marriage and other variables, but is distinct from them.

Aronson and Magidin de Kramer suggest, reasonably, that understanding this diversity will help educators adjust their curricular content or pedagogic approaches. And to be sure, it is always better to know more about the students sitting in front of you, even if that means simply being attuned to the possible range of stances or ideas. At the same time, this chapter also raises the intriguing idea that schools might undertake a deliberative process about what kinds of engagement they *want* to emphasize, what styles or approaches to Jewish life represent their particular vision, and thus how they might want to tailor their curricula or pedagogies in those directions—not within any particular subject but rather across all subjects, and indeed, in their co-curricular and extracurricular programming as well.

From the study of the impact of the DeLeT program by Sharon Feiman-Nemser and Shira Horowitz, we learn about a particular Jewish pedagogic practice, the creation of classroom communities rooted in Jewish values and experiences. The idea of classroom community is not unique to Jewish day schools, of course. But neither is it the case that a day school classroom community is the same as the classroom community in a non-Jewish school, with a few Hebrew words slapped on top. And there's no better way to understand this pedagogic practice—not just the phenomenon of day school classroom community but the pedagogy of creating it—than by tracing how novices learn to enact the practice.

In other words, this chapter tells a story about learning—teachers' learning. In this way, too, we have a lot to learn from the work of the authors, because investigating and understanding learning is very difficult to do well (although it's easy to do badly). Feiman-Nemser and Horowitz compose their narrative by informing their readers about how this pedagogic practice found a place in the conceptualization of good teaching that guided the teacher education program, and when and where it was given time and attention in the enactment of that program, i.e., when it was actually taught. That's essential background—but it doesn't answer the question of whether and how it was learned. That story is told, initially, via the evidence gleaned from teachers' work as teacher education students. That data is rich, nuanced, and informative—but even that doesn't tell us whether the teachers actually learned the pedagogic practice. For that, Feiman-Nemser and Horowitz turn to two focal teachers, both telling and showing how they enact the practice within their teaching, many years later, not because they simply affirm its importance but because the examples, and the challenges, are specific and detailed, shedding light on the complexity of the practice even as they affirm its importance.

Next, from the study of parental attitudes toward Hebrew by Sharon Avni, we learn about a significant tension between the disembodied or idealized conception of linguistic fluency as a desired outcome, on the one hand, and the individualized hopes and dreams for parents' children, on the other. We are considering, here, an area (Hebrew language ideologies among parents) about which we know very little, and on which Avni's study sheds some light. That's helpful. But the study also begins to open up deeper and more interesting questions about the broader phenomenon of parental involvement in Jewish day schools, beyond the typical threshold question of what brings them into the day school ecosystem or what keeps them out. That threshold question is important for the purposes of enrollment and the financial sustainability of the system. But once they are in, their beliefs and aspirations play an important role within the pedagogic environment. Avni's inquiry and others like it help us understand the complicated dynamics among stakeholders that influence pedagogic and curricular decision-making every day.

From Joshua Ladon's chapter about conceptions of the subject matter known as "rabbinics" or "Toshba" or sometimes just "Talmud," we learn that teachers—at least the sample of teachers he interviewed—seem to operate with one or more of three distinct conceptions. Given the typical lack of centralized coordination of instruction in this field, these conceptions then presumably shape or at least influence any number of curricular and pedagogic decisions. The point is that the very definition of the subject (whatever name we use for it) is ambiguous and contested. We should therefore not be surprised that there is so much variation in what happens in the classroom on, say, Mondays between 10:20 and 11:05 in a time slot dedicated to "Toshba." But neither should we conclude, from Ladon's argument, that the proper response to this state of affairs is the enforcement of a standard conception. To a certain extent, the kind of intradisciplinary diversity that Ladon uncovered may well be present in any field or "discipline." But rabbinics is not just any field. Unlike Jewish history or Jewish philosophy, unlike Hebrew, unlike even Hebrew Bible, this subject that we call "rabbinics" is a metonym for the entire enterprise of the facilitated encounter with the textual products of the Jewish tradition in any of its religious, cultural, legal, philosophical, and mystical modes. That makes it even more important to attend to and think through what we imagine the subject to be about.

Yaakov Jaffe's exploration of the approaches to the instruction of halakha, like Ladon's, uncovers greater complexity and diversity within a particular subject. In this case, however, we have a school subject—halakha, or Jewish law—that, more explicitly than any other, addresses normative Jewish practice and, perhaps, in some settings, is oriented toward the goal of the enactment of Jewish practice on the part of the student. Most of the subject areas under the umbrella of Jewish studies (or *Limudei Kodesh*, or *Mada'ei ha-Yahadut*) have limited practical or prescriptive implications. But the study of halakha in a Jewish day school seems to be different—and, in fact, this may be why the study of halakha as a distinct subject is typically found only in Orthodox schools. To put the point most sharply, while students of Toshba ought to learn to "do" Toshba, students of halakha ought to learn not just to do the intellectual discipline of the study of halakha, but also, apparently, to do the *mitzvot*, i.e., to enact halakhic practice.

But Jaffe's study is significant for us for an entirely different reason as well, namely, his failure to find any indication that the espoused "vision of halakha instruction" (among the forty-four schools from which he gathered his data) correlates with any particular set of classroom or curricular choices. There are a number of possible explanations. It could be that there are some hidden correlations, i.e., some practices about which Jaffe did not ask and therefore did not find any correlation. It could be that the administrator in each school who responded to Jaffe's survey holds one conception of the subject, but that the instructors of the subject in the school hold another conception. But it also may be the case that curricular and pedagogic decision-making is driven by an entirely different set of considerations—teacher preparation and prior experiences, parental expectations, demands of postsecondary instruction (e.g., in *yeshivot*) or perceptions of those demands, and so on. And if so, then the conception of the subject, which one might think would be the most important driver of decision-making, is actually the least influential. In other words, perhaps Jewish day schools have their own distinctive "grammar of schooling."

Next, Moshe Krakowski's chapter about pedagogic practices in some American haredi boys' schools challenges assumptions, especially within the literature of progressive education, about what constitutes an "authentic" activity in school. The central issue is whether a particular activity that teachers ask students to carry out is the kind of activity that happens only in school, in which case it has a kind of artificiality and inauthenticity about it, or whether it is linked in certain ways to the real world, to other human beings and communities outside of the four walls of the classroom. These are loaded characterizations, of course. Authentic and inauthentic are not neutral terms. But Krakowski wants us to think expansively about them, and pluralistically, in order to see that school can be a place for the enactment of cultural practices that are quite authentic even if they are also, at the same time, quite scholastic. This is particularly pressing when we are thinking about a field that resists instrumentalization, as Jewish studies does.

Susan Shevitz's analysis of the orientation activities at a pluralistic Jewish community high school offers an ethnographic window into those activities, in order to answer (or begin to answer) a simple question: How do students learn to be pluralistic? In general, some aspects of schooling are continuous with real life outside of schools; we can assume that teachers' efforts to help students learn to be respectful of others are more or less aligned with what students have heard at home. But other aspects of schooling are discontinuous with life outside of schools, such that schools may have to socialize students into a new set of norms. Whether pluralism is in the first category or the second is an empirical question, and may vary from place to place. But in Shevitz's analysis, at the school she studied at the time that she first conducted her research (almost two decades ago now), the teaching of pluralism was very much part of the orientation process. Things may well have changed at this particular school since then; indeed, they almost certainly have. But it really does not matter, because the fundamental question remains as centrally important to the educational process within Jewish day schools as ever. We might consider it to be an enduring question for Jewish day schools: When a school wants to inculcate a set of norms that are, in some sense, in tension with the norms that students bring with them to that educational environment, how does it do so?

From the exploration of five dimensions of community by Shira Hammerman, we learn how this concept—centrally important to Jewish day schools—is operationalized and even more importantly how it is experienced by one important constituency, namely, teachers. The dimensions are not exclusive to Jewish day schools; surely other schools have versions of each of them, to varying degrees. Yet the internal connections are a central feature of Jewish day schools, for better or worse—because they can contribute to a sense of inclusion as well as exclusion. When we envision the population of potential or actual day school teachers, and the kinds of preparation or support that they may need or from which they might benefit in order to flourish, the dynamics of community seem centrally important and deserve attention from policymakers at the local level (the level of the individual school) as well as across the Jewish day school landscape more generally.

Finally, from the chapter by Erik Ludwig about Latine students, we gain a better understanding of some of the dynamics around race in Jewish day schools. Not surprisingly, the story is complicated. Jewish day schools, like the Jewish community more generally, and like lots of other institutions, normalize whiteness in a way that can be challenging for non-white students. Yet Jewish day schools, like other kinds of religious schools, seem to have the potential to build strong communities and foster meaningful affective relationships on the basis of shared values across ethnic boundaries, precisely because of the religious context. Thus, students in the study reported feeling cared for in general. However, some teachers (all the teachers studied in this chapter are white) adopt the language and stance of "colorblindness" in a well-meaning effort to strengthen intra-communal bonds and treat all students equally, but that stance does not align with the students' own experience and self-understanding. The Latine students reported feeling different than white students. Instead of welcoming colorblindness, they felt most included when teachers acknowledged their ethnic backgrounds, or when school activities emphasized intra-communal diversity or Jewish multiculturalism.

What We Still Need to Learn

As we wrote previously, these studies crack open the black box of teaching and learning in Jewish day schools, in specific and inevitably fragmentary ways. It hardly needs be said that these new insights are a drop in the bucket, in terms of what we would like to know. It hardly needs to be said—but it's still worth saying, and it's worth articulating exactly what we mean by that. We can do so by focusing on five limits to our knowledge, five ways in which what we have learned points forward to what we still need to learn.

First, almost all of these studies focus on very particular locations. They zoom in. They make no claims to generalizability. What Shira Hammerman found, in her study of how ten teachers at "Tehila Yeshiva" think and talk about community, may or may not appear in a similar study among different teachers in a different school in a different city. What Sivan Zakai found, among the thirty-five children she interviewed numerous times in her longitudinal study, may or may not be replicated by thirty-five other children with some other set of backgrounds in some other city. What Moshe Krakowski found, in his study of how American haredi elementary schools' pedagogic practices rely on and build upon "real-world engagement," may or may not emerge from a comparable study of other similar schools. What Sharon Feiman-Nemser and Shira Horowitz found, in the pedagogic practice of two focal alumni of the DeLeT teacher education program, may or may not be present in the practice of other alumni of the program, much less in alumni of other teacher education programs.

So, in most of these studies, it is perfectly reasonable for the reader to ask: If what the researcher has found is true in this case, is it true someplace else? Is it true *everywhere* else? Nor are those questions limited to geographic location or setting. They could also be framed in chronological terms. If this finding was true at the time that the investigation was undertaken, is it still true a few years later? Was it always true? When might it have started to become true?

Similarly, we could extend the lines of questioning to other dimensions beyond the geographic and the chronological. In other words, we can ask: If this finding is true about these particular kids or these particular teachers, is it true about some other population that is different in some relevant respect? If this finding is true about these particular schools, is it true about schools that are different in some specific way?

These are all good questions; these are questions that the critical reader certainly *ought* to ask. But the reason to ask these questions is not because the questions somehow undermine what we can learn from the chapter in question. These are not "gotcha" questions. On the contrary, the reason to ask these critical questions is precisely in order to think about the significance of what we have read and exactly what we should learn from it. Sometimes, as practitioners, what we learn from a work of scholarship about a particular setting or population other than our own helps us think more clearly and wonder more deeply about our own setting and our own practice. Moreover, the critical researcher ought to ask questions such as these, in order to generate new scholarship that builds on, extends, refines, sharpens, narrows, expands, or perhaps refutes what prior scholarship has found. That's how scholarship works. None of this diminishes the value of these particular explorations. On the contrary, it accentuates that value.

A second way that these studies are limited—and thus a second way in which they leave us wanting more—is that, in the end, alas, they do not tell us much about the learning that does or does not happen in Jewish day schools. In her study of Hebrew language instruction, Sharon Avni turns away from classroom practice to *parents' perceptions* of classroom practice as well as their thinking about the goals of Hebrew in a Jewish day school. In his study of Israel education, Jonah Hassenfeld undertakes what one might imagine would be the *sine qua non* for assessing learning, namely, finding out what students know prior to a particular intervention. But his in-depth interviews of the students in his study reveal degrees of complexity that undermine the casual, and too simple, construct of knowledge and connection. Even a study such as Ziva Hassenfeld's, which takes us inside a particular classroom and lets us hear the voices of students as they engage in the *process* of learning, does not purport to assess learning as an *outcome*. Janet Krasner Aronson and Raquel Magidin de Kramer tackle a large dataset of Jewish day school student attitudes—but the data does not help us say anything about whether those attitudes emerge from the students' experience in those schools (as opposed to attitudes that they brought with them, for example), much less about anything else the students might have learned but about which the survey did not ask.

But we should not be surprised by this, because the truth is that assessing learning in rigorous and systematic ways—and in ways that support learning goals rather than subverting them—is extremely difficult. Some years ago, a well-meaning colleague new to the field of Jewish education wondered why, after all this time, there do not seem to be agreed-upon and broadly assessed measures of learning. At the risk of overinterpreting the tone of her email, she seemed to be suggesting that Jewish education is behind the curve. How can anyone expect to take this field seriously if they have not developed standardized metrics? What other industry could possibly persist with no evidence of the effectiveness of its practices and policies? How does anyone ever make any decisions about what to do or what not to do, in the absence of relevant data?

There is certainly a grain of truth to these questions. Indeed, Jeff Kress and I argued a few years ago in *Advancing the Learning Agenda in Jewish Education* (Levisohn & Kress, 2018) that the field needs more consistent and more robust attention to learning—both learning processes and learning outcomes. What are the most creative assessments of learning in Jewish day schools, and what do they tell us about what students can do? What does learning *look like*? How might creative assessments, and the data that we might generate from their experimental use, help us conceptualize ambitious learning outcomes, either within subjects or across subjects? How might we develop a better understanding of learning trajectories, within particular subjects or across subjects, in the way that second language acquisition has so successfully done? And how might practices of consistent and regular data collection inform teaching that is tailored to the needs of students—to their questions and challenges within the subject?

At the same time, it is not at all surprising that the field of Jewish day school education does not have widely accepted measures of learning. The acceptance of those measures would require consensus about what the desired learning outcomes should be, but so many of the studies in this volume identify and explore dissensus about learning outcomes. Moreover, we do not have consensus about what good evidence looks like, nor do we have the power to implement a particular set of assessment instruments across a diverse population. In other words, the use and consequences of testing and assessment are always wrapped up in the politics of the priorities, values, and concerns of the school and the community it serves. That is why a one-size-fits-all declaration of the desired outcomes of Jewish day school education is both impossible and impractical. And to make matters even more complicated, day schools operate within the cultural context of American education in general, which has always (until relatively recently) emphasized local control over state or national standards.

We might also consider the deeply problematic history of the standardized testing industry in general education. Hardly a testing season goes by, it seems, without a new revelation about the corruption of testing protocols, inconclusive or biased test items, the influence of test prep programs, teaching-to-the-test pedagogic practices that undermine learning goals, and more. Interestingly, the Covid pandemic surfaced these questions with new urgency, with the results that many K–12 districts canceled their assessments, and many colleges abandoned standardized tests as a requirement of application. Logically, there would seem to be no reason to do so. To focus on the latter phenomenon for a moment, if we actually believe that standardized tests tell us what they are supposed to tell us (and what the companies that design and sell them claim that they do) about the aptitude of particular students to do academic work in college, then the extreme conditions of the pandemic—as challenging as they may be—should have had no bearing on the use of the tests. But by the third decade of the twenty-first century, everyone knows how problematic these tests are and how inequitable the system of testing is. What Covid provided was the extreme cultural context to overcome the inertia.

Now, it is also important to note that a number of colleges have recently concluded that standardized tests do a better job of finding the "diamonds in the rough" than the rest of the hopelessly broken application system, and therefore decided to reinstate standardized tests as requirements. But part of the reason they have done so is that they observed that, when tests are optional, students from more privileged backgrounds have tended to submit scores at higher rates than students from less privileged backgrounds, regardless of the actual scores. Moreover, they have realized that, without these exams, they do not have the resources to assess the applications from the potential proverbial "diamonds." Pragmatically, these policy decisions may be justifiable—but they hardly represent a robust defense of the conceptual coherence or empirical validity of the exams themselves.

Given this rather more sober understanding of the condition of assessment in other educational environments, the condition of assessment in Jewish day schools doesn't look quite so bad. And for some, the fact that Jewish day school education is liberated from contemporary testing regimes is a great benefit. No one should be naive about the infiltration of high-stakes academic pressures into the environment of the contemporary Jewish day schools, pressures that are driven by middle-class anxiety around academic achievement and economic insecurity. Day schools are, alas, no refuge from those pressures. In fact, in certain respects, they may well accelerate those pressures due to the relative homogeneity of social class within the Jewish day school population. But at least Jewish day schools do not have to comply with the accountability mandates that public schools do; in this small way, perhaps, they can preserve the possibility of more creative pedagogy in the service of more aspirational outcomes.

Some readers might go further and argue that we need to know a lot more than what students are or are not learning, in general; we also need to know "what works." This is the third way in which we want to know more. Which approaches to the teaching of Tanakh or rabbinics or Hebrew language are most effective? What works to produce the kinds of students or alumni that we want to see in the world? Given a set of possible pedagogic options, how might research inform that choice? Surely we want and need to rely on more than the idiosyncratic predilections of individual faculty members to "do their own thing." For many community decision-makers, including in the philanthropic sector, "what works" is the primary question that research ought to answer.

Some of the chapters in this volume do provide us with critical insight into pedagogy. Notably, however, they do so while also avoiding the reductive question of "what works." For example, Yaakov Jaffe develops a taxonomy of four approaches to the teaching of halakha and explores how those approaches may be manifest in various schools—but he avoids endorsing any of them. And rightfully so. Let's imagine that Jaffe could be confident about "fidelity of implementation," i.e., that schools were actually and consistently teaching in accordance with one particular approach. This is always a challenge in educational scholarship, and on the basis of the data that Jaffe has gathered, he does not and cannot actually make this claim. But let's imagine that he could. Even if he knew that, on the basis of what evidence could he possibly defend one approach as more effective than others? To be sure, he could defend one approach as more coherent, or more exciting and creative. He could argue that one approach is more traditional than others, or that one is more subversive than others, or that one has more of some other quality that we might come up with. Any of those may be relevant criteria, if combined with an argument about the goals of the teaching of halakha within a particular cultural context. But none of them can serve as a straightforward proxy for "what works."

Let's consider another example: Sharon Avni's careful description of the internal tensions within parents' language ideologies. One might have thought that the desired outcome of Hebrew language instruction is obvious, and that that domain is more susceptible to inquiry into "what works" than any other. Can the students speak and understand Hebrew? Yes or no? How much? But her chapter disrupts those casual assumptions, helping us see that the stakeholders themselves are not clear on what the deceptively simple term "works" should mean, never mind how to achieve that. A panel of experts might lament the confused parental language ideology that muddies the waters around what ought to be clear, namely, that the goal of second language acquisition is proficiency in (the four skills of) the language. Perhaps the parents ought to listen to the experts. But unless and until they do, we as scholars can only notice the persistence of deep dissensus around desired outcomes.

Joshua Ladon's inquiry is another case that helps us see the challenge of "what works," in his taxonomy for the teaching of rabbinic literature. He wants his reader to think more critically about the internal diversity within the subject, which inevitably complicates any effort to pursue "what works." On the contrary, his inquiry is generated by the diversity of responses by a group of Jewish day school teachers to the question of what constitutes expertise in the domain of rabbinics, and who the respondents would nominate as experts. We should make the link between the concepts of "what works" and "expertise" explicit: experts are those who have succeeded in the domain, for whom particular educational experiences have "worked" to bring them to their level of expertise. And yet, even setting aside the question of whether what "works" for prominent individuals at the top of their field can reasonably be expected to "work" for everyone else, the resulting diversity of models derails any effort to answer the question with confidence.

One chapter seems to come very close to making an argument for "what works," namely, Erik Ludwig's study of the experience of Latine students in Jewish day schools. We seem to find, here, a claim that "culturally responsive pedagogy" will validate Latine students' experiences, and more specifically that a focus on the diversity of historical Jewish communities will increase their sense of belonging in the Jewish day school community. Indeed, in one sense, Ludwig does make these claims, and reasonably so. But a closer reading reveals a hidden complexity to the argument. First, the metric that we used previously for the desired outcomes—validation and an increase in a sense of belonging—may well be important, but they are surely not the only important desired outcomes. In other words, the argument is properly understood as a conditional statement: *If* we desire outcome *a*, *then* we ought to employ strategy *b*. The argument on behalf of the desired outcome itself is implicit. Second, since we have no comparison of Latine kids studying under one set of conditions to Latine kids studying under another set of conditions, we cannot really say how the preferred pedagogies affect them. And third, Ludwig's study undertook an enormously valuable step, namely, he asked questions of the students themselves. At the same time, their perceptions and impressions are only that—perceptions and impressions. The students are telling us what they think about their educational environments. We have no access to actual learning outcomes. Thus, this chapter, too, while it may appear to endorse a particular pedagogy for its effectiveness, actually does so only in very circumscribed ways.

The fourth way in which we want to know more than we currently do is that we want to ask deeper and more critical questions, to develop the critical study of Jewish day school education—not in the sense of critiquing current practice but rather in the academic sense of asking deeper and more critical questions about the assumptions that we bring to bear. Horwitz's chapter on the gender confidence gap that she discovered in one particular area is important as a contribution to the gender analysis of Jewish day school education, but it only begins to explore the ways that gender shapes the educational experience of students, as well as how gender-related concepts themselves are taught and learned. In what ways do the educational trajectories of girls and boys differ, if they do, among various kinds of schools? What is the nature of educational gender differentiation or segregation, formal or informal, explicit or implicit? How do the gender dynamics in Jewish day schools parallel or differ from those of independent schools, or of schools embedded within other religious traditions? How is Judaism, Jewish culture, and Jewish studies itself gendered within the school setting? Unfortunately, we have precious little contemporary scholarship that pursues these questions about gender in Jewish day schools.

Likewise, Ludwig's exploration of the experience of Latine students is an important contribution, but it unfortunately highlights the almost complete absence of literature on race and ethnicity in Jewish day schools. Where and how do American Jewish day schools construct a norm of whiteness among (Ashkenazi) Jews? How do Sephardic, Mizrachi, Syrian, Persian, and other non-Ashkenazi (and sometimes, although not always, non-white) Jewish communities experience Jewish day schools, either embedded within the larger Ashkenazi majority or in separate, ethnically homogenous schools?

Perhaps most importantly, in the American context, we have, to our knowledge, no rigorous scholarship that explores the role of class in the Jewish day school classroom. This is surely related to questions of race and ethnicity, but it is also distinct. There are, of course, many professional and lay leaders who are concerned about and working on questions of financial access to Jewish day schools, on the issues of affordability and sustainability, but those are different questions. We are focusing here not on who gets to be in the school or how to expand that pool, but on the more analytical questions about how class functions within the teaching and learning environment. What assumptions are made about the resources that are available to students (material or intellectual)? How are students treated, on the basis of class markers? What class ideals or norms are promoted or assumed, and in what ways? How do class anxieties and pressures intrude upon and perhaps even subvert educational ideals? In what ways do schools function—and communicate their function—to reinforce upper-middle-class social norms, and how are those norms experienced by students?

Finally, the fifth way in which we want to know more is that we ought to be able to think about the purposes of Jewish day schools, and the kinds of growth and learning that may happen within them, above and beyond the specific subjects of Jewish studies. Those subjects, together with general school subjects (sometimes called "secular studies"), are the organizational framework for Jewish day school education. Several of the studies in this volume focus on these familiar subjects—Tanakh, Talmud or rabbinics, halakha, Israel, Hebrew. (One subject that is notably missing: Jewish history.) This makes sense. Jewish day schools are still organized around these subjects. There is variation, to be sure—classes on halakha are unlikely to be found outside of Orthodox schools, and many schools have a class labeled "Jewish studies" that addresses different subjects (or, to be more precise, different textual corpora) serially. But fundamentally, these subjects form the basic building blocks of the curriculum. And given that this is the case, subject specificity is important for scholarship that hopes to make a difference for practice. Moreover, as we have argued elsewhere (Kress & Levisohn, 2018), the students' experience of learning is subject or domain specific, and we ought to be especially concerned about creating environments where students can make progress *within* a domain.

This state of affairs is historically contingent, however. It wasn't always so. And once we think about that, we might wonder whether there are other ways of organizing the curriculum, or at least, other ways of thinking about desired outcomes. Susan Shevitz's chapter on how the students at a pluralistic high school were socialized and enculturated into the school's pluralistic ethos might be a model for us here. There is no pluralism class, of course—but that's not the point. Pluralism is in the air and on the agenda. Pluralism is taught, and pluralism is learned. The questions of pluralism (including critical questions) are central to the discourse of the institution.

Following this model, what if we stopped thinking primarily about particular textual corpora (or, alternatively, "disciplines," with all the problematic conceptual baggage of that term) and started thinking instead about certain fundamental questions—especially fundamental questions that have a particular contemporary urgency? We have in mind questions such as these:

- How can Jewish day school education develop citizenship and civic responsibility, including both American civic responsibility and its Jewish equivalent (sometimes called "peoplehood")?
- How can Jewish day school education cultivate consciousness of class, including both its privileges and its particular pressures, and commitments to equity and justice?
- How can Jewish day school education prepare students for an unstable and uncertain world, rapid change, and unpredictable social structures?
- How can Jewish day school education cultivate greater resilience in learners, teachers, and communities, especially in the face of grief and loss?

These questions—and there are surely others like them, about love and learning and compassion and critical inquiry—are generated by asking ourselves about our highest aspirations, our vision of the good life for individuals, communities, and society.

We are not proposing that Jewish day schools ought to create an entire curriculum around these questions, so that Period 1 of the day would be "Citizenship" (rather than "Talmud"), Period 2 would be "Justice" (rather than "Mathematics"), Period 3 "Instability" (rather than "English"), Period 4 "Resilience" (rather than "Hebrew"), and so on. There are any number of reasons why that's a bad idea. Still, for the most part, we are blind to the effects of the choices that we have made or that have been made for us—historically contingent choices, not necessary ones—about what constitutes a school subject and how to organize and think about students' learning. When we liberate ourselves from the constraints of the traditional school subjects, and instead think about the milieu—which is to say, when we think about the particular students in particular communities located within particular social, cultural, economic, and political contexts at a particular moment in time—we may start to ask entirely new questions about teaching and learning.

The preceding paragraphs were written in light of developments in American culture in the last decades—developments including the rise of antisemitism on both the political right and the political left, the hyperpolarization of political discourse and the corollary decline of an older vision of civic engagement that assumed the need to work across political lines to accomplish shared goals, the acceleration of technological change and the emergence of profound shifts in how people relate to each other and what those changes do to their sense of well-being and social integration (Haidt, 2024), and looming behind everything else, the profound climate crisis that is no longer a far-off and abstract issue but a very concrete one.

But from our perspective now, writing these words six months after October 7, 2023, the milieu within which the American Jewish day school is situated calls for yet another important question specific to this moment about which we do not know enough—namely, how can Jewish day schools respond to, and prepare students and communities to live within, this post–October 7 world?

Here it may be helpful to call attention to two comparisons. The first comparison, perhaps somewhat ironically, is to contemporary American

Islamic education, an education that occurs within a context of cultural hostility to Islam. Randa Elbih, for example, writes as follows:

> The distorted Islamic identity presented by the media and the educational curriculum has more than just an external effect; it also affects the construction of Muslim Americans' self-identification . . . This, coupled with peer pressure and wanting to fit in, result in negative self-identification, rejection to [*sic*] their Muslim identity, assimilation to mainstream society, or developing an identity split. (Elbih, 2012, pp. 160–161)

What Elbih is pointing to here, and what other thoughtful Islamic educators also document, is that Islamic education in America—they are talking in particular about the post-9/11 period, which was a profoundly important turning point for the Muslim American community, although of course Islamophobia was present beforehand—cannot be satisfied with just teaching Islam (whatever exactly that would mean) and hoping that students will navigate their way as Muslim Americans successfully on their own. As Habiba Farh writes,

> Islamic school teachers . . . have to teach students how to cope with the hostile Islamophobic environment students are living in. Teachers express having difficulty explaining away the frustration and confusion Muslim students have about US portrayals of Muslims and US foreign policy in Muslim-majority countries. Furthermore, teachers attempt to find ways to explain Islamophobia and other forms of discrimination their students experience as a result of their skin color, country of origin, or gender. (Farh, 2018)

Contemporary Islamic education has to acknowledge the challenging cultural environment in which the students live and within which Muslim communities are embedded, and has to do what it can to help both individuals and communities thrive within that environment. American Jewish education may now need to do likewise.

The second comparison to the present moment is from an earlier moment in American Jewish education, a moment that many of us thought we had left behind for good, the interwar and postwar period in which, as Krasner (2019) documents, a concern for the negative impact of antisemitism on "Jewish identity" was a prominent theme. For Krasner, the work of the psychologist Kurt Lewin is central to the story. "What distinguished Lewin's voice... and made him a darling of Jewish educators," Krasner writes, "was the combination of his scientific pedigree and reputation, and his conviction about the centrality of Jewish education in promoting Jewish psychological wellbeing" (p. 41). Krasner's broader argument is that this focus—the psychological concern for being "well-adjusted" in the face of hostile or assimilatory pressures—was eventually replaced by a very different kind of focus and a very different concept of Jewish identity, one that was measured with social scientific metrics of Jewish behavior rather than indicators of psychological well-being. But for our purposes, what is significant is how we seem to be revisiting those earlier concerns, in a way that has not seemed particularly salient for generations. To be clear, Levin did not argue for direct psychological treatment; his point was that a robust education in one's own culture is the mechanism for arriving at the goal of "adjustment." But it has been a long time since we talked and thought about Jewish education in these terms. We have not been exercising those muscles.

This is not the place for a comprehensive analysis of the present moment for American Jews, and it is probably too soon to make conclusive judgments about the long-term effects of an acute crisis. Still, when we think about what we have learned and what we have not yet learned about American Jewish day schools, we ought to consider the ways in which these schools may or may not be responding to these new or more intense challenges for our students and our communities generated by the social, political, and cultural milieu. We do not yet know whether Jewish day schools are up to the challenge of educating students to cope with antisemitic environments, which means pulling off what seems to be a trifecta of tasks—first, teaching students to recognize the tropes and themes of antisemitism even in the face of gaslighting to the contrary; second, on the other hand, teaching students not to internalize those tropes and themes, and also, third, teaching students to be resilient rather than traumatized by the hostility that we are teaching them to recognize. Enormous resources have been mobilized to "fight" antisemitism, understandably so. But we would also be well served by allocating time and resources toward a deeper conceptual and empirical understanding of how our educational institutions, including day schools, are helping students deal with this new environment, and how they might.

To conclude, we have sought to articulate five ways in which the studies in this volume leave us wanting more—or to put the matter in the appropriately charitable terms of standard scholarly discourse, five ways in which these studies generate new and better questions that deserve more and deeper scholarly attention. First, almost all of these studies focus on very particular locations; they make no claims to generalizability, and instead invite further inquiry to explore how their findings do or do not apply elsewhere. Second, they do not tell us conclusively about the learning that does or does not happen in Jewish day schools, but they do point to some of the ways that serious and sophisticated studies of learning might be pursued. Third, they avoid asking the reductive question "what works," but they do succeed in providing us with critical insight into pedagogy. Fourth, they begin to develop the critical study of Jewish day school education, especially around questions of race, class, and gender, yet they only scratch the surface. Finally, in their general focus on the school subject as the relevant domain within the Jewish day school, they invite not-yet-asked questions about how Jewish day schools pursue, or might pursue, desirable outcomes for individuals and communities that transcend particular subjects but that are responsive to the particular social and cultural milieu in which those individuals and communities find themselves—including, not least, the potentially profound challenges of the post–October 7 moment.

References

Black, P., & Wiliam, D. (1998, October). Inside the black box: Raising standards through classroom assessment. *Phi Delta Kappan*, 139–148.

Cuban, L. (2013). *Inside the black box of classroom practice: Change without reform in American education*. Harvard Education Press.

Elbih, R. (2012). Debates in the literature on Islamic schools. *Educational Studies*, *48*(2), 156–173.

Fahr, H. (2018). Research memo (unpublished).

Haidt, J. (2024). *The anxious generation: How the great rewiring of childhood is causing an epidemic of mental illness*. Penguin Press.

Krasner, J. B. (2019). On the origins and persistence of the Jewish identity industry in Jewish education. In J. A. Levisohn & A. Y. Kelman (eds.), *Beyond Jewish identity: Rethinking concepts and imagining alternatives* (pp. 36–64). Academic Studies Press.

Kress, J. S., & Levisohn, J. A. (2018). Subject-specific learning versus Jewish developmental outcomes in Jewish education: What should we aim for? In J. A. Levisohn & A. Y. Kelman (eds.), *Advancing the learning agenda in Jewish education* (pp. 205–219). Academic Studies Press.

Levisohn, J. A., & Kress, J. S. (eds.). (2018). *Advancing the learning agenda in Jewish education*. Academic Studies Press.

Acknowledgments

A volume like this can only appear thanks to the care and support of many individuals. The genesis of the book was a conference on teaching and learning in Jewish day schools, which was organized by the Jack, Joseph and Morton Mandel Center for Studies in Jewish Education and held at Brandeis University. Arrangements for that event were coordinated by senior department coordinator and events and communications manager Elizabeth DiNolfo with the assistance of Sarah Flatley and Hannah Baker-Lerner. Early assistance in developing and editing the chapters was provided by former Mandel Center associate director Susanne Shavelson and subsequently by Mandel Center associate director Shani Winton. The more recent management of the editorial process was expertly and patiently handled by the Center's current associate director, Jenny Small. We also extend our gratitude to the other members of the Center team who contributed to the development and publication process, including Candice Kiss and Masha Lokshin.

Series co-editor Sharon Feiman-Nemser navigated relations with the press and read the entire manuscript, offering helpful advice and suggestions. A special thank you to the anonymous peer reviewers and to Brandeis University Press editorial director Sylvia Fuks Fried and director Sue Berger Ramin for their assistance and collegiality.

Finally, we appreciate the patience and support of the contributors to this volume who have waited a long time to see this project come to fruition.

Contributors

Co-editors

JONATHAN B. KRASNER is the Jack, Joseph and Morton Mandel Associate Professor of Jewish Education Research at Brandeis University. His 2020 book *Hebrew Infusion: Language and Community at American Jewish Summer Camps* (Rutgers University Press), co-authored with Sarah Bunin Benor and Sharon Avni, was the recipient of the 2020 National Jewish Book Award in Education and Jewish Identity. Krasner is co-editor of the Mandel-Brandeis Series in Jewish Education at Brandeis University Press.

JON A. LEVISOHN is the Jack, Joseph and Morton Mandel Associate Professor of Jewish Educational Thought and director of the Jack, Joseph and Morton Mandel Center for Studies in Jewish Education at Brandeis University. He is the author or editor of four books and dozens of articles on topics in philosophy of Jewish and general education, including most recently *Teaching Historical Narratives: A Philosophical Inquiry into the Virtues of Historical Interpretation* (Bloomsbury, 2024). He is co-editor of the Mandel-Brandeis Series in Jewish Education at Brandeis University Press.

SHARON AVNI is a professor of academic literacy and linguistics at Borough of Manhattan Community College (BMCC) at the City University of New York (CUNY). She is co-leader of the Jewish Learning Through the Cultural Arts project at the Jack, Joseph and Morton Mandel Center for Studies in Jewish Education at Brandeis University. Her 2020 book *Hebrew Infusion: Language and Community at American Jewish Summer Camps* (Rutgers University Press), co-authored with Sarah Bunin Benor and Jonathan B. Krasner, was the recipient of the 2020 National Jewish Book Award in Education and Jewish Identity.

Chapter Authors

JANET KRASNER ARONSON is the associate director of the Cohen Center for Modern Jewish Studies and Steinhardt Social Research Institute at Brandeis University.

SHARON FEIMAN-NEMSER is the Jack, Joseph and Morton Mandel Professor Emerita of Jewish Education and founding director of the Jack, Joseph and Morton Mandel Center for Studies in Jewish Education at Brandeis University.

SHIRA HAMMERMAN is director of faculty learning and professional development at the Jewish Educational Center in Elizabeth, New Jersey.

JONAH HASSENFELD is director of learning and teaching at Solomon Schechter Day School of Greater Boston.

ZIVA R. HASSENFELD is the Jack, Joseph and Morton Mandel Assistant Professor in Jewish Education and assistant director of research for the Jack, Joseph and Morton Mandel Center for Studies in Jewish Education at Brandeis University.

SHIRA HOROWITZ is an instructor and coach in the Graduate Teacher Leadership Program at Brandeis University.

ILANA M. HORWITZ is an assistant professor of Jewish studies and sociology and the Fields-Rayant Chair of Contemporary Jewish Life at the Stuart and Suzanne Grant Center for the American Jewish Experience at Tulane University. She is the director of the Doctoral Fellows program at the Jack, Joseph and Morton Mandel Center for Studies in Jewish Education at Brandeis University.

YAAKOV JAFFE is dean of Judaic studies at the Maimonides School and rabbi of the Maimonides Kehillah in Brookline, Massachusetts.

MOSHE KRAKOWSKI is a professor and director of Fanya Gottesfeld-Heller Doctoral Studies in the Azrieli Graduate School at Yeshiva University.

JOSHUA S. LADON is the vice president for the West Coast and senior faculty for the Shalom Hartman Institute of North America.

ERIK LUDWIG is president and CEO of Jewish Federation of Orange County.

RAQUEL MAGIDIN DE KRAMER is an associate research scientist at the Cohen Center for Modern Jewish Studies and the Steinhardt Social Research Institute at Brandeis University.

SUSAN L. SHEVITZ is associate professor emerita at Brandeis University, where she taught in the Hornstein Program for Jewish Communal Service for over twenty years and served as director for eight.

SIVAN ZAKAI is the Sara S. Lee Associate Professor of Jewish Education at the Hebrew Union College-Jewish Institute of Religion and an affiliated scholar at the Jack, Joseph and Morton Mandel Center for Studies in Jewish Education at Brandeis University. She is the co-editor of *Teaching Israel: Studies of Pedagogy from the Field* (Brandeis University Press).

Index